DRUG ABUSE
Current Concepts and Research

Drug Abuse

Current Concepts and Research

Compiled and Edited by

WOLFRAM KEUP, M.D.

Director
K. Bonhoeffer-Nervenklinik
Berlin, Germany
Clinical Associate Professor of Psychiatry
State University of New York
Downstate Medical Center
Brooklyn, New York

CHARLES C THOMAS · PUBLISHER
Springfield · Illinois · U.S.A.

Published and Distributed Throughout the World by
CHARLES C THOMAS • PUBLISHER
BANNERSTONE HOUSE
301-327 East Lawrence Avenue, Springfield, Illinois, U.S.A.

© *1972, by* CHARLES C THOMAS • PUBLISHER
ISBN 0-398-02331-X
Library of Congress Catalog Card Number: 70-172459

With THOMAS BOOKS *careful attention is given to all details of manufacturing and design. It is the Publisher's desire to present books that are satisfactory as to their physical qualities and artistic possibilities and appropriate for their particular use.* THOMAS BOOKS *will be true to those laws of quality that assure a good name and good will.*

Printed in the United States of America
N-1

Contributors

K. AKAI, M.D.,
New York State Exchange Visitor, New York State Psychiatric Institute, New York, New York

G. ALEXANDER, M.D.,
Neurotoxicologic Research Unit (Bronx State Hospital), New York State Psychiatric Institute, New York, New York

JEFFREY L. ANKER, M.D.,
Department of Psychiatry, Yale University School of Medicine; The Connecticut Mental Health Center, New Haven, Connecticut

MICHAEL M. BADEN, M.D.,
Deputy Chief Medical Examiner, Office of the Chief Medical Examiner, City of New York, and Associate Professor of Forensic Medicine, New York University, School of Medicine

WALTER C. BAILEY, Ph.D.,
Assistant Professor, City College of the University of New York; New York State Narcotic Addiction Control Commission, New York, New York

HERBERT BERGER, M.D.,
Staten Island, New York, Associate Professor of Medicine, New York Medical College

D. VINCENT BIASE, Ph.D.,
Research Consultant, Phoenix House Research Unit, New York, New York

HENRY BRILL, M.D.,
Director of Pilgrim State Hospital, West Brentwood, New York

LEON BRILL, M.S.S.,
Program Director, Regional Training and Support Center, Division of Addiction Sciences, Department of Psychiatry, University of Miami School of Medicine, Miami, Florida

DAVID BROWN, M.D.,
New York Hospital, Cornell Medical Center, White Plains, New York

A.N. BROWNE-MAYERS, M.D.,
New York Hospital, Cornell Medical Center, White Plains, New York

LOUIS A. CANCELLARO, M.D., Ph.D.,
Chief Education and Training Sections, National Institutes of Mental Health, Clinical Research Center, Lexington, Kentucky

CARL D. CHAMBERS, Ph.D.,
Director of Research, New York State Narcotic Addiction Control Commission, New York, New York

MURRAY A. COWEN, M.D.,
Clinical Investigator VA Hospital, Assistant Professor, State University of New York, Upstate Medical Center, Syracuse, New York; Psychophysiologist in Attendance, Marcy State Hospital, Marcy, New York

RICHARD DEMBO, Ph.D.,
Research Officer, Centre for Mass Communication Research, University of LEICESTER, Leicester, England

GERALD A. DENEAU, Ph.D.,
Head Drug Abuse Division, Southern Research Institute, Birmingham, Alabama

HELMUT E. EHRHARDT, M.D., Ph.D.,
Professor and Director, Institute of Forensic and Social Psychiatry, University Marburg/Lahn, Ortenbergstrasse 8, West Germany

STANLEY EINSTEIN, Ph.D.,
Associate Director, Division of Drug Abuse, College of Medicine & Dentistry of New Jersey, Newark, New Jersey; Martland Hospital Unit; Executive Director, Institute for the Study of Drug Addiction and Editor of the International Journal of Addictions

EVERETT H. ELLINWOOD, JR., M.D.,
Associate Professor of Psychiatry, Duke University Medical Center, Durham, North Carolina

MORTIMER R. FEINBERG, Ph.D.,
Professor of Psychology, Baruch College, City University of New York; President of BFS Psychological Associates, Inc., New York, New York

MARCUS A. FEINSTEIN, M.D.,
Attending Physician, Beth Israel Medical Center; Senior Physician, Morris J. Bernstein Institute, New York, New York

DIANNE FEJER,
Addiction Research Foundation, Toronto, Canada

MARIA FLEETWOOD, M.D.,
New York Hospital, Cornell Medical Center, White Plains, New York

WILLIAM F. GEBER, Ph.D.,
Associate Professor, Department of Pharmacology, Medical College of Georgia, Augusta, Georgia

VICTOR GIOSCIA, Ph.D.,
Associate Professor of Sociology and Philosophy, Adelphi University, Executive Director, Center for the Study of Social Change, Department of Psychiatry, The Roosevelt Hospital, New York, New York

G. GOLD, M.D.,
Bronx State Hospital and New York State Psychiatric Institute, New York, New York

EDWARD GORDON, M.D.,
Director, Methadone Treatment Program, Westchester Community Mental Health Board, White Plains, New York

EDWIN H. HASTINGS, LLB,
Attorney at Law, partner, Hastings, Tillinghast, Collins & Graham, Providence, Rhode Island

MILTON HELPERN, M.D.,
Chief Medical Examiner, Office of the Chief Medical Examiner, City of New York and Professor and Chairman, Department of Forensic Medicine, New York University, School of Medicine

RICHARD E. HICKS, M.D.,
Assistant Professor, Assistant Director, Psychiatric Education, Department of Mental Health Sciences, Hahnemann Medical College and Hospital, Philadelphia, Pennsylvania

JAMES A. INCIARDI, M.A.,
Deputy Director of Research, New York State Narcotic Addiction Control Commission, New York, New York

ARTHUR E. JACOBSON, Ph.D.,
Laboratory of Chemistry, National Institute of Arthritis and Metabolic Diseases, National Institutes of Health, Bethesda, Maryland

DONALD R. JASINSKI, M.D.,
Chief, Clinical Pharmacology Section, National Institutes of Mental Health, Addiction Research Center, Lexington, Kentucky

S. SEYMOUR JOSEPH, M.D.,
Deputy Commissioner, Program Planning & Research, New York State Narcotic Addiction Control Commission, New York, New York

C.R.B. JOYCE, Ph.D.,
Medical Department CIBA-GEIGY Ltd., CH-4002, Basel, Switzerland; Charing Cross Hospital Medical School, Department of Pharmacology, London, England

EDWARD KAUFMAN, M.D.,
Associate Attending Psychiatrist, St. Luke's Hospital, Instructor in Psychiatry, Columbia University, Staff Psychiatrist in Realty House, New York, New York

M. KAUFMAN, M.D.,
Neuropathology New York State Psychiatric Institute, Department of Pathology, Columbia University, New York, New York

WOLFRAM KEUP, M.D.,
Director, K. Bonhoeffer-Nervenklinik, Berlin, Germany and Associate Clinical Professor of Psychiatry, State University of New York, Downstate Medical Center, Brooklyn, New York

BENJAMIN KISSIN, M.D.,
Director, Division of Alcoholism and Drug Dependence, Professor of Psychiatry, State University of New York, Downstate Medical Center, Brooklyn, New York

JAMES H. KNEPSHIELD, MAJ, MC, USA,
Chief, Renal Dialysis Service, Walter Reed Army Institute of Research, Walter Reed Army Medical Center, Washington, D.C.

MARY KOVAL,
Chief, Epidemiological and Narcotic Education Research, New York State Narcotic Addiction Control Commission, New York, New York

DAVID LASKOWITZ, Ph.D.,
Director of Research, Drug Abuse Program, Lincoln Hospital, New York, New York

MARVIN A. LAVENHAR, Ph.D.,

Director Biostatistics, Department of Public Health and Preventive Medicine, College of Medicine and Dentistry of New Jersey, Newark, New Jersey

C. LAWLER, Ph.D.,

Neurotoxicologic Research Unit (Bronx State Hospital) and New York State Psychiatric Institute, New York, New York

FREDERICK J. LUDWIG, M.Sc., Jur.D.,

Chief Assistant District Attorney Queens, New York

ANDREW I. MALCOLM, M.D.,

Staff Psychiatrist, Addiction Research Foundation of Ontario, Toronto, Canada

WILLIAM R. MARTIN, M.D.,

Chief, National Institute of Mental Health, Addiction Research Center, Lexington, Kentucky

B. MILES, M.D.,

Neurotoxicologic Research Unit (Bronx State Hospital) and New York State Psychiatric Institute, New York, New York

DORIS H. MILMAN, M.D.,

Associate Professor of Pediatrics, State University of New York, Downstate Medical Center, Brooklyn, New York

JOHN S. O'BRIEN,

Behavior Therapy Consultant, Drug Rehabilitation Unit, Boston City Hospital, Department of Psychiatry, Harvard Medical School, Mattapan, Massachusetts

MARVIN E. PERKINS, M.D.,

Professor of Psychiatry, Mount Sinai School of Medicine of the City University of New York; Director of Psychiatry at Morris J. Bernstein Institute, Beth Israel Medical Center, New York, New York

ESRA S. PETURSSON, M.D.,

Principal Research Scientist, Drug Addiction Research Unit, Manhattan State Hospital, Ward's Island, New York

MARK A. QUINONES,

Director of Administration, Department of Public Health and Preventive Medicine, College of Medicine and Dentistry of New Jersey, Newark, New Jersey

A.E. RAYNES, B.Sc., M.B., B.S.,

Director, Drug Rehabilitation Unit of Boston City Hospital; Clin. Instructor in Psychiatry, Harvard Medical School

ALEX RICHMAN, M.D.,

Associate Director, Department of Psychiatry, Beth Israel Medical Center and Professor of Psychiatry, Mount Sinai School of Medicine, City University of New York, New York, New York

LEON ROIZIN, M.D.,

Chief of Psychiatric Research, Neuropathology, New York State Psychiatric Institute, Department of Pathology, Columbia University, New York, New York

RALPH S. RYBACK, M.D.,

Harvard Medical School and McLean Hospital Belmont, Massachusetts

RICHARD EVANS SCHULTES, Ph.D.,
Professor of Biology and Director, Botanical Museum of Harvard University, Cambridge, Massachusetts

BARBARA K. SHERIDAN, B.A.,
Assistant Research Scientist, New York State Narcotic Addiction Control Commission, New York, New York

EDWARD E. SEELYE, M.D.
New York Hospital, Cornell Medical Center, White Plains, New York

REGINALD G. SMART, Ph.D.,
Associate Research Director, Addiction Research Foundation, Toronto, Canada

BARRY STIMMEL, M.D.,
Co-Director, Methadone Maintenance Treatment Program, Associate in Medicine, Assistant Dean Student Affairs; Mount Sinai School of Medicine of the City University of New York, New York, New York

ROBERT E. STOESSEL,
School Psychologist, New Hyde Park High School, New Hyde Park, New York; Department of Clinical Psychology, Columbus Hospital, New York, New York

WILLIAM J. STONE, M.D.,
Assistant Professor of Medicine, Department of Nephrology, Vanderbilt University School of Medicine, Nashville, Tennessee

W.J. RUSSELL TAYLOR, M.D., Ph.D.,
Director, Clinical Pharmacology and Toxicology Center, Philadelphia General Hospital Philadelphia, Pennsylvania

HAROLD L. TRIGG, M.D.,
Director, Drug Addiction Service, Unit Director Methadone Maintenance Treatment Program, Morris J. Bernstein Institute, Beth Israel Medical Center; Associate Clinical Professor of Psychiatry, Mount Sinai School of Medicine, City University of New York, New York, New York

TORRINGTON D. WATKINS, M.A., Senior Research Scientist
Senior Research Scientist, New York State Narcotic Addiction Control Commission, New York, New York

A.G. WHITE, M.D.,
Beth Israel Medical Center, Chief of Medicine, Morris J. Bernstein Institute, New York, New York

THOMAS WILLIS,
Special Research Scientist, New York State Narcotic Addiction Control Commission, New York, New York

MARVIN ZUCKERMAN, Ph.D.,
Department of Psychology, University of Delaware, Newark, Delaware

* * *

The following participants have substantially contributed to the success of the meeting by acting as organizers, as session chairmen or officers of the Eastern Psychiatric Research Association:

LARRY A. BEAR—*Session Chairman*

HENRY BRILL, M.D.—*Speaker, Citation and Presentation of the Gold Medal Award 1970 for Special Scientific Achievement to Dr. Nathan B. Eddy*

CHARLES BRIGHT, M.D.—*Session Co-chairman and EPRA Councilor*

A.N. BROWNE-MAYERS, M.D.—*Speaker and Session Co-chairman*

EMERICK FRIEDMAN, M.D.—*Session Co-chairman*

WILLIAM A. FROSCH, M.D.—*Session Chairman*

WILLIAM FURST, M.D.—*Session Co-chairman and EPRA Councilor*

WILLIAM HOLT, M.D.—*Session Co-chairman*

DAVID IMPASTATO, M.D.—*Session Chairman and EPRA Councilor*

WOLFRAM KEUP, M.D.—*Speaker, Program Chairman, EPRA President*

BENJAMIN, KISSIN, M.D.—*Speaker and Session Chairman*

JOACHIM LUWISCH, M.D.—*Session Co-chairman, Meeting Secretary, EPRA Councilor*

MARVIN PERKINS, MD.—*Speaker and Session Chairman*

JOHN D. RAINER, M.D.—*Session Chairman and President Elect of EPRA*

JAMES RAPPA, M.D.—*Session Chairman and EPRA Vice President*

ALEX RICHMAN, M.D.—*Speaker and Session Chairman*

THEODORE, ROBIE, M.D.—*Session Co-chairman and EPRA Councilor*

ARCHER TONGUE—*Session Chairman*

A Citation—To Dr. Nathan B. Eddy

TODAY WE ARE HONORING Dr. Nathan B. Eddy, a scientist of international stature in the field of drug dependence. He is listed formally as a pharmacologist in the 1970-1971 *Who's Who in America,* but in actuality his work has cut across many disciplines, since his interests have been centered not on any one discipline but on the one topic of drug dependence. As a result Dr. Eddy has become a truly multidisciplinary scientist, and it may be that this has contributed to his success, because it has been said that multidisciplinary science is most effective when the various disciplines are all within one head. Dr. Eddy's knowledge of drug dependence extends from the basic chemistry at one extreme to its sociology and epidemiology at the other. In addition he knows and is known by virtually everyone of significance whose work relates to drug dependence, and it may be that this has helped make him the effective research administrator that he has been for decades.

As we review his life story it can be seen as a series of logical steps leading to his present position as an internationally recognized leader in this field. He was born in Glen Falls, New York, on August 4, 1890, graduated from the Cornell Medical School in 1911 and practiced medicine until 1916 in New York State. He then moved to McGill University where he was instructor in physiology from 1916 to 1920, and from there he went to Alberta, where he first was assistant professor and later associate professor of physiology during the years from 1920 to 1930. The next decade he spent as research professor of pharmacology at the University of Michigan, a period which closed with the 1939 publication

Note: This speech was delivered to Dr. Eddy on November 5, 1970, when he was presented with the Gold Medal Award of the Eastern Psychiatric Research Association at their 15th Annual Meeting.

of *Pharmacology of Opium Alkaloids,* which he wrote in collaboration with Kreuger and Sumwald.

In 1939 he became principal pharmacologist at the National Institute of Health in Bethesda, Maryland, and consulting biologist in alkaloids for the United States Public Health Service. In succeeding years he has worked in various capacities with agencies of the U.S. Government and with many other organizations to promote the study of drug dependence and its prevention and treatment. During this time Dr. Eddy has been one of a small group of men working cooperatively in various locations, particularly Washington, Ann Arbor and Lexington, and the contributions of this group have constituted a major part of our entire national activity in this field. An important vehicle for this co-operative enterprise has been the Committee on Drug Dependence of the National Academy of Sciences, National Research Council (NAS-NRC), and Dr. Eddy was its executive secretary from 1947 to 1967. In this capacity he exercised unusual administrative skill in coordinating the efforts of the pharmaceutical companies, university centers and large public health hospitals as well as scientific and governmental units here and abroad, all with an incredibly low special financial support and in accordance with the strictest ethical standards. Under the auspices of this Committee some 1600 compounds were screened between 1947 and 1970, 560 of them were tested in monkeys, 80 were tried in man, and 35 were marketed. The official budget for 1970 is given as $184,000, obviously far below the real cost of the operations.* In addition the methodology for identification and evaluation of dependence liability of several types of dependence-producing drugs has been much advanced.

Out of this work has come a vastly increased understanding of the agonist-antagonist relationships, an understanding which has already enabled scientists to find drugs which dissociate the morphine-type analgesic effect almost totally from dependence liability, a development of great practical and theoretical signifi-

---

Heroin and Heroin Paraphernalia, Second Report by the Select Committee on Crime, 91 Cong. 2d Session Union Calendar No. 869, House Report No. 91-1808.

cance. Dr. Eddy* has also made important contributions on the conceptual level, and he is one of the authors of a series of publications which draw together the complex and conflicting semantics which had grown up around the terms "addiction," "habituation," "abuse," "misuse," and so forth, and replaced them all with the single unifying concept of "drug dependence."†

It was in his capacity as executive secretary of the above-named prestigious Committee on Drug Dependence of the NRC that I first met Dr. Eddy in 1958, and I shall never forget nor shall I cease to be grateful for his courtesy and his help when I appeared in his office in Washington. At that time, New York State was beginning to be worried by an increase in its heroin problem. Having made the "mistake" of showing an interest in the subject, I had been commissioned to explore the situation with a view to developing a pilot program within the Department of Mental Hygiene. Dr. Eddy then, as now, was a prime source of information on all aspects of drug dependence and his assistance proved invaluable. Since that time, I have had the opportunity of seeing him at work in Tokyo, Geneva, Honolulu, Washington and in many other locations and in many contexts, and I can attest to the universal respect which he commands everywhere for his vast and diversified knowledge and equally for his scrupulous regard for facts. Needless to say my own personal regard for him has grown with each experience.

Finally, I would like to say a few words about Dr. Eddy's attitude about the development of methadone maintenance. From the very beginning he has been among the most open-minded of all authoritative figures in the field, a leader in the direction of a full and objective evaluation of a method that was contrary to tradition and previously established beliefs on the subject. This type of achievement is very reassuring to those of us who are over thirty—it shows that what they say these days about people over thirty is not necessarily so. We have in Dr. Eddy an out-

*Eddy, N.B., Halbach, H., Isbell, H., and Seevers, M.H.: Drug dependence: Its significance and characteristics. *Bull WHO, 32*:721-733, 1965.

†Thirteenth Report of WHO Expert Committee on Addiction Producing Drugs, 1964.

standing example of flexibility combined with significant maturity of experience.

It is an honor to join the many other scientific bodies which have formally acknowledged their debt to Dr. Eddy as a scientist, administrator and humanitarian.

HENRY BRILL

Introduction

DURING THE PAST DECENNIUM, the patterns and concepts of drug abuse have taken so many turns and undergone so many changes that a review of present knowledge seemed almost mandatory. The Meeting of the Eastern Psychiatric Research Association (EPRA) on November 7/8, 1970, the proceedings of which are presented in this volume, was called for this purpose: to give an overview on where we stand and, at the same time, to lead the participant right to the frontier of present-day knowledge, to learn about the latest concepts and scientific findings as well as treatment attempts. Thus, summary papers stand side by side with original contributions.

Books on "the drug scene" for the layman, even for the user, are plentiful—almost a part of the "drug explosion"—whereas books for the specialist and the worker in the field are rare.

The material presented here is structured by chapters so as to view the topic from all possible angles.

Causes for the present wave of abuse are multiple; there are roots and rootlets anchored in the development of social concepts, the family, current ways of advertising and of handling young people, the many biological imbalances and the feeling of helplessness before a highly automated and overpowering societal machinery. These are coupled with a relaxation of controls throughout all layers of the old pyramidal structure and with an emphasis on the young. There are still more roots. But, looking into the future, it would indeed be important to know what part fad and fashion play in the current situation and what part social evolution might play. Lately, there seem to be signs of leveling off, but we do not know whether we simply have reached the ceiling of those potentially affected or whether we see the ebbing of a fad wave that is becoming impotent to promise any novelty. This book will give glimpses into these questions.

Alcoholism, so much a part of the syndrome of toxicomania, is not dealt with here in detail; room simply does not allow. However it is used as a background when viewing modern trends of toxicomania.

All research and all endeavors to find mechanisms ultimately aim at an improvement of our therapeutic abilities. Undoubtedly, this is the realm where solutions are most urgently needed, but still the problem is spreading faster than it can be remedied. This book tries to help narrow that serious gap.

It would not have been possible to bring together so many specialists without their willingness to give freely of their experiences and their time. Our heartfelt gratitude goes to them and to all those who have helped organize the Meeting. Our sincere thanks also are due to the publisher for his support and collaboration in making this book available in so short a time.

WOLFRAM KEUP

Acknowledgments

THE EASTERN Psychiatric Research Association acknowledges with gratitude donations received in support of its 15th Annual Meeting from

Eli Lilly and Company, Indianapolis, Indiana

Merck Sharp & Dohme, Division of Merck & Co., Inc., West Point, Pennsylvania

Pfizer Pharmaceuticals, Pfizer Laboratories Division, J. B. Roerig Division, New York, New York

Roche Laboratories, Division of Hoffmann-La Roche Inc., Nutley, New Jersey

Sandoz Pharmaceuticals, Division of Sandoz Inc., Hanover, New Jersey

Schering Corporation, Bloomfield, New Jersey

Smith Kline & French Laboratories, Research & Development Division, Philadelphia, Pennsylvania

Winthrop Laboratories, New York, New York

Contents

SECTION I
INTRODUCTORY PAPERS

SECTION II
PHYSICAL AND MEDICAL ASPECTS

SECTION III
PSYCHOLOGICAL AND SOCIOLOGICAL ASPECTS

SECTION IV

PSYCHOPHARMACOLOGICAL ASPECTS

DRUG ABUSE
Current Concepts and Research

SECTION I

INTRODUCTORY PAPERS

Chapter 1

Comparative Addiction

Esra S. Petursson

COMPARATIVE STUDIES LEAD to a more comprehensive understanding of widely distributed phenomena. Living in several
cultures and studying them broadens the outlook and reveals associations otherwise unavailable. Psychotherapy and psychoanalysis similarly increase awareness in the superconscious, subcon-
scious, preconscious and conscious spheres, by providing, in a
manner of speaking, a better opportunity to live in and study
those spheres. Without such opportunities people have great difficulty learning from their own mistakes and mostly find it impossible to learn from other people's mistakes.

The concept of mankind, viewed as a whole brotherhood and
a part of the biosphere, is, of course, strictly scientific and can provide us with a convenient tool, capable of overcoming nationalis-
tic and individualistic biases. In practice we already have several
institutions operating with these central spherical concepts, namely the United Nations and the World Health Organization
(WHO), to mention only two of the most outstanding international groups.

Perhaps, as this kind of mentality grows it can provide mankind the opportunity to learn itself, as a whole, from its mistakes,
regardless of in which country the mistake was localized. In the
individual sphere each human body has to learn from the pathology of each individuated organ for the benefit of the whole
human being, in order to be made whole, by the proper healer,
and then to remain healed.

DEFINITION

In 1964 the WHO decided to adopt the diagnostic categories of "drug dependence," specifying the addicting drug, instead of the older terms of "addiction" and "habituation." This has many advantages including preciseness and specificity. However, it does not cover the full range of the concept of the addictions to even abused substances, such as food. Drugs are only a part of the conditions to which people can be addicted. It is possible, according to dictionary definitions[1] to be addicted to gambling, to the rites of pagan ancestors, to severe studies and to work. These addictions are quite prevalent and are to be found in varying degrees in most groups, present company of course excluded. In order to compare the factors that can be allowed to gain "a strong, habitual, and enduring hold upon action, inclination, or involuntary tendency, as to habit or indulgence," I find it preferable to retain the word "addiction."

PATHOLOGY AND TOXICITY OF THE ADDICTIONS

A linear and two-dimensional toxic rating is relatively meaningless when applied to the addictions, and few attempts have been made to do so. In order to evaluate, in a meaningful way, their harmfulness, we must use more parameters for a multi-dimensional approach. The following are some of the more useful parameters:

1. Direct toxicity and its quality.
2. Reversible and irreversible destructiveness to self.
3. Reversible and irreversible destructiveness to others.
4. Process and rates of flow with incidence, prevalence and other epidemic and endemic characteristics. Quantity measurements.
5. Contamination, deterioration and sludging of body structure, body fluids and mental and emotional atmospheres. The effects of such internal environmental pollution and the effect and interaction with external environmental pollutants.
6. The articulations and other connections of the addictions with warfare and other chronic behavioral aberrations of mankind. Antisocial effects.

7. Thresholds. Metrazol® and tetrahydrocannabinol produce seizures and psychosis respectively, in all subjects, above a certain level, with some individual variations in the level of the threshold.

I shall now discuss the harmfulness of the addictions in terms of these parameters.

Direct toxicity with immediate death from an overdose is found in the opiates, barbiturates and alcohol. Death from food abuse, formerly called gluttony, is rarely, if ever, recorded now. The incidence of such immediate deaths is not very high, being highest in the opiates and barbiturates, numbering in the hundreds or at most thousands. Generally the cause of death is some form of asphyxiation or anoxia.

Reversible and irreversible destructiveness to self, primarily, with less measurable effects on others, is found in food and tobacco abuse and in addiction to work and study. They, with perhaps the exception of tobacco, are as all other addictions essentially disinhibiting and disintegrating. They are distancing mechanisms, placing walls of fat and in other ways separating the individual, at least partially, from his environment.

Foodoholism is a misnomer. There is nothing holistic about it. Quite the contrary it disintegrates rather than integrates. Seventy-nine million Americans suffer to some degree from this affliction. Of course it would be excessive to regard all of them as being food addicts. Nevertheless their rate of cancer, diabetes and cardiovascular illness is much higher than in the rest of the population, and their life expectancy is shortened on the average by ten years. It takes about fifty to sixty years to commit this form of slow chronic suicide by food abuse.

Tobacco kills probably comparably as slowly as food abuse, shortening the life expectancy by five to ten years. Cardiovascular and respiratory illnesses burden and restrict these people's lives, at times severely. According to the AMA figures the end result is that there are 300,000 excess deaths a year in the United States alone, attributable to the delayed effects of tobacco smoke inhalation, many more than are caused at any time by all warfare, including the two world wars, by this one addiction alone.

Reversible and irreversible destructiveness to others, as well as to self, occurs with alcohol, marijuana and in all the other drug dependencies, excepting the barbiturates. When I was a psychiatric consultant to the Manhattan House of Detention for Men in 1965-1966, we saw about ten newly arrested murderers each week. Because of the rapid rise in the crime rate this has almost doubled now. About three of them were alcoholics, three were drug dependent and the rest had lesser involvement with intoxicating substances. Probably about one third of murders are committed by alcoholics, another third by drug-dependent persons, and the remaining third has less involvement with such substances. A few do not use them. Manslaughter on the highways amounts to over 50,000 deaths annually. Alcohol intoxication is found in over half of them, and an undisclosed number of the rest has some intoxication from marijuana, heroin, amphetamine and the barbiturates. The New York State Addiction Control Commission is conducting a preliminary investigation into that serious matter.

Marijuana is undoubtedly, no less than alcohol, proportional to consumption, connected with violent crime, in spite of contrary propaganda by its apologists and condoners. People who murder for a reward or for fanaticism are called assassins. Originally they were called hashshishim or hashish eaters, and they were a fanatic Moslem sect. Butchers in India eat it before they ply their trade. A greater effort must be made to document and collect more evidence of this connection of marijuana to crime.

It becomes increasingly the responsibility of the medical profession to *study and chart the evidence, prevalence and other epidemic and endemic characteristics of the addictions* in each community, city and nation as a whole. The rise and fall of the addictions is probably the best barometer available in charting the misbehavioral fluctuations in people. Possibly it accounts for over half of the total psychopathological manifestations of mankind and organized crime as well as the collective crime of warfare. Gross national consumption of addicting substances should be measured and/or evaluated and publicized. Such an evaluation provides an essential base and a guideline for therapeutic measures particularly with regard to primary prevention, which is so important in all epidemics.

The internal environment of mankind is adversely affected by many drugs and other abused substances. *Deterioration, contamination and pollution* may occur in all areas of the body structure, body fluids and in the mental and emotional atmospheres. The brain structures are severely eroded in Wernicke-Korsakoff's disease caused by alcohol addiction. Even in food abuse sludging of the bloodstream occurs from excessive free fatty acids and cholesterol. Sludging of the bloodstream appears in the blood vessels of the eye after only one or two cocktails. A similar effect is seen in the marijuana smokers, probably more related to the irritative effects. Heroin abusers suffer from frequent serum hepatitis, bacterial endocarditis and anoxic areas with brain softening and cyst formation are found at autopsy. Milton Helpern[2] has described such areas, possibly related to one or several larger doses of heroin, more or less long before the final fatal overdose. Some of this may be due to the indirect effect of the asphyxiation occurring when the tongue falls back in the larynx of the drug-dependent person thus choking him while he is unconscious.

Tobacco smoke inhalation is potentiated by all the other air-pollutants. Together they lead to a much increased prevalence of respiratory and cardiovascular disorders. The carelessness and apathy engendered by the manifold addictions increase, directly and indirectly, the filth, squalor, garbage, water and air pollution of the inner cities producing necrotic slum areas, akin to areas of cavitation and caseation in tuberculosis. A rise in the internal environmental contamination level may be reflected in a concomitant rise in the external environment of the noxious substances and vice versa. Normally rats do not become alcoholic even with a readily available and liberal supply of alcohol. If they are placed in a polluted atmosphere, they do become alcoholic given the opportunity. In the human and mental and emotional atmosphere there is a great increase in anxiety, rage, and depression, produced by all the addictions in varying ways, both during the use and especially during the withdrawal of the substances. Some of them temporarily ameliorate these emergency emotions, only to be followed by increasingly severe rebound phenomena in many cases. All addictions are regressive, at least stalling and frequently actually retarding the process of maturation.

Antisocial effects, often of a very severe nature, are the inevitable fellow travellers of the addiction. Soldiers and murderers for hire have at all times tended to use as great amounts of intoxicants as have been available to them. Many armed forces have, therefore, set limits for their use by prohibiting or rationing their use. Many massacres have been fueled by addicting substances. Their relationship to crime was studied and described in a classical paper by Lawrence Kolb in 1925.[3] The heroin addict, in fact, has two addictions—the dependency on the drug and the addiction to the way of life of a drug addict, which is criminal—both nurturing and feeding on each other. I interviewed a patient with brain dysfunction, last summer. By his own estimate he had manufactured and supplied half of the illegal Dexedrine® needs of Manhattanites, including the leaders of the SDS movement. Amphetamines increase paranoid manifestations greatly and at least some of the rioting, bombing and violence of the extremists is related to its use. The rapid rise in crime and the sudden flood of marijuana abuse is possibly not only coincidental but, to some degree, causative of this crime increase, or at least related to it. This requires immediate research instead of having to wait for centuries to realize the noxious effects of marijuana, as we had to do with reference to both alcohol and tobacco. The apathy about the destructiveness of tobacco seems to be lessening, but there are practically no indications in this country that familiar apathy about the effects of alcohol is lessening. This amounts to almost criminal neglect, since, to name but one example, child abuse is related to it, and it is also rising.

Addictive habits and substances potentiate and are synergistic with each other. The heroin addict's way of life is dependent on his heroin habit to a large degree. The fatal synergism of barbiturates and alcohol is well known. Less well recognized is the probable potentiation of these substances in the so-called drug reaction deaths, that may, at least in some cases, be caused by the lethal effect of combining several drugs. The use of "uppers" and "downers"—that is, barbiturates and amphetamines—is another example. The noxious substances in air pollution are strengthened by the interaction between solid particles with water vapor, sulfur doxide, carbon monoxide and other gases. This occurs in a similar way in the rivers and oceans, as well as in the internal environs of mankind. Illegal gambling is another relevant and seriously impoverishing and addiction-promoting factor. It is also one of the most intractable and difficult of all the addictions. It may be said that organized crime as a way of life is an addiction, and it may be the most important factor of all in fleshing out and articulating the addictions one with the other. Symbolizing all the addictions as superwoman may be helpful in realizing more fully the interdependence and interaction of the addictions altogether as one more or less well-organized body.

Many substances and drugs have distinct *threshold effects*. Metrazol and tetrahydrocannabinol were previously mentioned, causing seizures and psychosis respectively. The minimum lethal dosages of alcohol, barbiturates and heroin are fairly well established. Practically unknown are threshold effects in large populations, but it seems probable that changes, possibly irreversible changes, may occur in certain communities or countries if the gross national consumption or the national incidence and prevalence rises above some unknown threshold level.

PSYCHODYNAMICS

The addiction-prone individual may come from all classes and psychiatric classifications. In widespread addictions such as tobacco, food and alcohol, the sufferers, many of whom are pain-dependent people, tend to have the same characteristics as the general population. About half of mankind has not attained more than a 14- to 16-year-old emotional and mental level. Such early teenagers, regardless of their actual chronological age, are inconsistent and impulsive and have poorly developed limit setting, even without drugs dissolving the limits they can set for themselves. Actually the 15- to 16-year-olds commit more crimes than any other age group. Alcohol and other antisocializing, maturity preventing and retarding drugs increase these tendencies tenfold.

A teenager, or adult with a teenager mentality, is ten times more likely to commit a crime or to get into other kinds of trouble if addicted to an intoxicating substance. People with teenage mentalities are usually keyed up and restless, with varying degrees of motor overactivity, in contrast with the schizophrenic where the muscular tension is more tonic, manifesting as rigidity. The fidgety motor overactivity in the personality and behavior disorders is related to attempts to cue off the anxiety, resentment and depression that underlie all these disorders. Joking around, horseplay, the gay life of the homosexual, promiscuity and prostitution are related defensive maneuvers or collateral manifestations and resultants of the addictions. Typically the Minnesota Multiphasic Personality Inventory (MMPI) profiles of alcoholics, heroin addicts and criminals are very similar. The highest scores in the alcoholic are the psychopathic deviate, the depression, mania and psychasthenic scales.[4] Common to all of them are fathering, grandfathering and great-grandfathering deficiencies. The men in these families are weak, harsh and usually absent either physically or psychologically, and frequently both. Probably the degree of the personality disorder is proportionate to these kinds of absenteeism of the fathering principles. If schizophrenogenic mothers affect schizophrenic disorders, it seems still more likely that psychopathogenic fathers have even a greater influence miscreating characters into character disorders.

TREATMENT

Primary, secondary and tertiary prevention has been and still is being used against the addictions in various parts of the world. In such epidemic and endemic diseases the results are increasingly limited unless emphasis is on primary prevention and then fatherly, rigorously and consistently stressed. In the old Norse literature, primary prevention is rather graphically described in the story about Thor, the god of masculine principles. On his travels he came to a river flooding the country. It was so wide, deep and fast flowing that he could not cross it. Looking upstream he saw a gigantic female troll, sitting on her haunches making the river. Heaving a huge rock at her he hit her centrally in the spot he aimed for saying: "Á skal ad ósi stemma," which freely associated means: Block a river at its source. The river dried up at once and he continued his progress.

Prohibition is being used against heroin addiction, and nobody in his right mind advocates its repeal. Doing so would probably be a major calamity, possibly even precipitating total dissolution of the country. A sizable proportion of the population with teenage mentalities might increasingly and rapidly become addicted, dissolving the last shreds of the tattered remains of a conscience that they still have, that helps them set some reasonable limits for their behavior. Alcohol prohibition in the United States and in Denmark and Iceland led to a two to three fold decrease in the gross national consumption of alcohol. Even after repeal, this consumption has never gotten anywhere near its previous sickening high levels. In the United States, prohibition was not fully effective because it was inadequately enforced, due to the complicity and corruption of the enforcers. In Iceland it was so effectively enforced, resulting in the disappearance of crime, that they had to rent out the jail as an apartment house, because it stood empty. Comparable results were achieved in Prince Edward Island, which is surrounded by "wet" counties, as well as the St. Lawrence River. Recently when its prohibition was repealed the crime rate soared. Primary preventive measures are rigorously applied in all other epidemic and endemic diseases, reliably reducing the incidence and prevalence. Primary prevention is said to have been used by the Communists in China to eradicate opium addiction. Opium-dependent persons there at that time may have numbered up to one hundred million. They simply cut a few heads off. They never smoked opium again and that almost ended the opium endemic in China. Following World War II, amphetamine addiction suddenly became epidemic in Japan, reaching millions of abusers. Passing a law against it with considerable jail terms as penalities, they cleaned up the epidemic in a few months. Their police force was free from corruption and they rigorously enforced the law. Henry Brill,[5] in his article, "Rise and Fall of a Methampetamine Epidemic," says that "When supplies of a suitable drug are free and drug control is absent, drug dependence can assume epidemic proportions within a relatively short time."

Historians, sociologists, epidemiologists and transcultural psychiatrists have more than enough material already to teach us how various parts of the world have at times astoundingly successfully dealt with their addiction problems. We should listen more to them and apply those measures that have proven effective, using the minimum amount of severity that produces reliable results. Most effective of all are probably religious tenets "For of the Most High cometh healing." Among, for instance, really faithful Jews, alcoholism does not exist.

Secondary prevention to shorten the duration of the addictions are such temporizing measures as repeated hospitalizations and short jail sentences. Revolving doors may, if anything, lead to an increase both in incidence and prevalence of the condition for the same reason as does tertiary prevention; namely the fear of the destructive effects of the dependency is lessened, no longer deterring as many from indulging in them as before such half measures were introduced. Tertiary prevention reduces the disability from the addiction. If we as doctors were able to prescribe substituting snuff and chewing tobacco for cigarettes, we could make a valuable contribution to saving most of the 300,000 lives a year now dying from the delayed effects of tobacco smoke inhalation. Likewise, were we able to change all alcoholics to beer drinkers and wines we might possibly reduce their disability somewhat, though that is much more debatable. If we can convert many or most heroin addicts to methadone, we will reduce their disability considerably and also their addiction to a criminal way of life. Perhaps we should also try it out for the alcoholics?

CONCLUSION

Failing to recognize the importance of primary prevention in the addictions is mankind's greatest mistake. It inevitably leads to a rise in both their incidence and prevalence. First things first. Emphazising tertiary and secondary prevention to almost the exclusion of primary prevention is putting the cart before the horse. The rapid increase of the addictions is a phenomenon that is rapidly spreading throughout the world, threatening to inundate its internal environment with flood-like quantities of drugs and other abused substances. Religion, or rather its perversion, which is religiosity, no longer is the opiate of the masses. Religiosity was, still is, and always will be a very dangerous opiate, but some of these substances are still more dangerous.

Secretary General U Thant recently stated that drug addiction is a universal menace. He is in one of the best positions to make such a statement on the solid basis of factual information available to him. However, the drug addictions are only the tip of the huge submerged iceberg of the addictions altogether.

In the brotherhood of mankind, the majority with a 17-year-old or better maturity are responsible for the fate of their irresponsible younger brethren, who are in the minority. The older members have to stop sending the younger ones out to kill themselves and each other with drug, alcohol and mankind's old addictions to crime and warfare. To this end, age and maturity appropriate legal curbs and controls have to be optimally utilized. Proper timing of such restrictive frustration for the adolescent mentalities is essential. Even more important is the better utilization of ethical considerations in forming constructive groups, so necessary for the adolescent mentality. The great efficacy of truly religious precepts and tenets is amply demonstrated in those cultures that apply them constructively and in the work of Alcoholics Anonymous. We have to devise more avenues to utilize such creative forces more abundantly.

Stated in truly religious terms, mankind must lose faith in its guns, drugs and money, and instead gain faith in its Creator and in its own creative human resources and energies, thus divorcing itself from its alienation and idolatry of the addictions.

REFERENCES

1. Funk and Wagnals: *New Standard Dictionary of the English Language.* New York, Funk & Wagnals, 1963.
2. Strassman, G., Baden, M., Helpern, M., and Sturner, W.: Hypoxämische Gehirnschäden bei Heroinsüchtigen, bei Schlafmittelvergiftung, Erhängungsversuch und nach Herzstillstand in der Narkose. *Beitr Gerichtl Med,* XXVI, 1969.

3. Kolb, L.: Drug addiction and its relation to crime. *Ment Hygiene, 9:*74, 1925.
4. Catanzaro, R.J.: *Alcoholism.* Springfield, Charles C Thomas, 1968.
5. Brill, H., and Hirose, T.: Rise and fall of a methamphetamine epidemic. *Seminars in Psychiatry, 1(2):*179-194.

Chapter 2

The Utilization of Hallucinogens in Primitive Societies—Use, Misuse or Abuse?

Richard Evans Schultes

This association of hallucinogens with religious ideas may be accounted for by the fact that the sense-illusions evoked by the drug are taken for actual occurrences by the intoxicated subject. It is a state of the soul which tears him away from the realities of everyday life and makes him acquainted with new, incomprehensible and agreeable things. This spiritual state has become indispensable to the drug-taker and will always remain so.

LOUIS LEWIN

I.

THERE is a vast difference between the utilization of natural hallucinogens in primitive cultures and the recent escalating large-scale employment of these narcotics in Western societies. Does the aborigine use, misuse or abuse his hallucinogens? Underlying any answer is a consideration of the purposes of aboriginal utilization of these drugs and the many and varied reasons behind their vital place in the scheme of things.

Notwithstanding the fact that some psychologists have considered it to be an oversimplification, the truth is that taking hallucinogens—in every culture—is always related to release from bonds of what we normally consider reality. In primitive cultures the world around, man lives intimately with his ambient vegetation. He has always experimented with the hundreds of thousands of species—putting most of them into his stomach. Some nourished him. Some relieved him of pain or cured his ills. Some made him sick. Some killed him outright. A very few had unearthly, startling effects, transporting him to other worlds, to realms of ethereal wonder, to abodes of the spirits. This effect explains the reason

17

why all of these hallucinogens have become integral parts of aboriginal religious practices and beliefs.[10,16]

To the aboriginal mind everywhere, sickness and death result from the workings of spirit forces through hexing. Consequently, plants with psychic effects are frequently more highly valued as "medicines" than those with merely physical properties. In the narcotic complex of the New World aborigine, for example, the doctor usually takes the "medicine," not the patient. This is logical, since "it is the shaman who needs the supernatural 'power' to effect a cure . . . to contest a rival's malevolent magic causing the illness, to prognosticate, for clairvoyance, to control the weather, etc . . . the shaman-visionary has power over an illness, manifestly, because with supernatural power he has recovered from it."[9]

Yet the hallucinogens themselves may be even more significant than as mere "medicines." They permeate nearly all aspects of living in primitive societies. They reach into prenatal life, influence life after death, operate during earthly existence. They play roles not only in health and sickness but in relations between individuals, villages and tribes, in peace and war, at home and in travel, in hunting and agriculture—in fact, one can name hardly any aspect of living or dying where hallucinations do not play a part.

II.

Some of the motives underlying aboriginal esteem of specific hallucinogens may help clarify employment of these agents in primitive societies.

Perhaps *soma* might be taken as the most outstanding example. All other hallucinogens have been regarded as holy mediators between man and the pantheon. Soma, the ancient narcotic of India, was actually deified, becoming a real god. It has long since died out of use but is known from the rich *Vedic* literature. Recently identified as the *fly agaric* mushroom *(Amanita muscaria)*, soma was so holy that it has been suggested that perhaps even the idea of deity may primitively have arisen from experiences with its weird effects.[24]

This mushroom is valued in modern times amongst isolated Finno-Ugrian tribesmen in eastern and western Siberia. The Chuckchis, for example, believe that it possesses powerful spirits that delight in visiting the places where the dead dwell. While it often plays practical jokes on a person under its influence, it may also guide him to other realms or guard him from harm in this world. The Koryaks hold that the god Vahiynin (Existence) left the fungus on earth to instruct man in the mysteries of Nature.[10,21]

In Mexico, the fungal world plays perhaps its greatest hallucinogenic role, with at least twenty-four species of mushrooms and several puffballs as protagonists. The mushrooms (species of *Conocybe, Panaeolus, Psilocybe, Stropharia*) have a long history in magic and religion. Elaborate mushroom stones from highland Maya cultures in Guatemala tell us that at least three thousand years ago these plants were central to sophisticated religious rites. Highly valued by the Aztecs who called them *teonanacatl* ("flesh of the gods"), they were ingested sacramentally for communion with the spirit forces—for divination, prophecy and witchcraft, uses persisting amongst contemporary tribes in Mexico.[21] The Mixtecs of southern Mexico employ as auditory hallucinogens several puffballs (*Lycoperdon* spp.) to hear voices and receive answers to questions put to the spirits who own these voices.[20]

The seeds of two species of morning glories were revered as sacred in ancient Mexico: *ololiuqui (Rivea corymbosa)* and *tlitliltzin (Ipomoea violacea)*. One early chronicler wrote that "it is remarkable how much faith the natives have in the seed . . . which they consult as an oracle to learn many things . . . especially those beyond the power of the human mind to penetrate . . . ." So holy were these morning glories that the Aztecs tried to protect them from molestation by Spanish ecclesiastical authorities, doing "all in their power so that the use of the plants does not come to the attention of the authorities . . . ." Still another chronicle reports that the "seeds are held in great veneration . . . . The Indians place offerings to the seeds in secret places . . . and put the seeds amongst the idols of their ancestors . . . ." Morning glories are still widely used for divination and prophecy in modern Mexico, where one native name for the seeds means "the god."[13,20,21]

Mexico is likewise the home of an hallucinogenic mint *(Salvia divinorum)*, the leaf of which is still employed in divination, especially for diagnosing disease and solving thefts. There is another leaf *(Calea zacatechichi)* which the Chontal Indians call *thle-pela-kano* ("leaf of god") and take to "clarify the senses" and see visions in a dreamlike state.[20,21]

Probably the most famous and important Mexican hallucinogen, however, is the *peyote* cactus *(Lophophora Williamsii)*, the sacramental use of which has, in the last eighty years, swept through many Indian tribes in the United States and Canada.[8] Peyote helps the Huichols of Mexico "find their life." It is identical with the deer, their sacred animal, and with maize, their sacred plant and staff of life: deer, maize and peyote are fused into a single symbol complex. These natives ceremonially "hunt" peyote. The first peyote-collecting expedition was led by Tatewari ("Our Grandfather")—equivalent to Fire and the Original Shaman—and the leader of modern peyote quests becomes the embodiment of Tatewari and is addressed as such by the pilgrims.[4]

Attitudes about the peyote plant are most sharply accentuated probably amongst the Tarahumares, who claim that peyote sings happily in the field when approached by the pilgrims and continues singing in the bags once it has been collected. Peyote prolongs life, they say. It protects hunters from wild animals. At death festivals, it guards mourners from ghosts. People who have never eaten peyote must not touch the plant lest they become demented.[4,11]

When peyote came north to tribes of the United States, it "did not have to win its way into a system of religion . . . without visions. Rather it facilitated obtaining visions already sought,"[22] for, while visions were important to all North American Indians, usually in puberty rites when a boy gained his guardian spirit, the Plains Indians considered the puberty vision only the first of many visions.[8] "Periods of mourning, desire for revenge, initiation into certain societies, the organization of a war party"—all of these called for visions of mature men.[8] But peyote's phenomenally rapid spread is due as much, if not more, to its reputation as a supernatural "medicine" as to its strong hallucinogenic properties, if indeed the two can be separated.

Ayahuasca, caapi or *yajé* (*Banisteriopsis* spp.) is a narcotic drink employed throughout the western Amazon and elsewhere in tropical South America for its extraordinary hallucinogenic powers.[3,7,12,14] An early report stated that Ecuadorian Indians take it "to foresee and to answer accurately in difficult cases, be it to reply opportunely to ambassadors from other tribes in a question of war, to decipher plans of the enemy . . . and take proper steps for attack and defense, to ascertain, when a relative is sick, what sorcerer has put on a curse, to carry out a friendly visit to other tribes, to welcome foreign travellers, or, at last, to make sure of the love of their womenfolk."[23] It is still widely used for these same purposes. Many natives talk with the *oprito* or heavenly folk through yajé.[2] The Kofans of the westernmost Amazon believe that yajé reveals the *real* world to them, that daily living is, in fact, a fantasy.[17] The Kechwa term *ayahuasca* means "vine of the soul" and stems from the frequent experience that the soul separates from the body and wanders free during the intoxication. In fact, many Indians insist that they even come to know death under the influence of the drug. Psychological experiments with sophisticated subjects under harmaline, one of the alkaloids of ayahuasca, indicate that the visual hallucinations often have the theme of serpents, felines and birds as well as experiences of flight, of death and "an acute awareness of a human soul separated from its body."[14,15]

It is a recognized fact that hallucinogens in general are very frequently associated with birds or flying.[24] One of the characteristics most often attributed to ayahuasca intoxication is sensation of flight or floating in air. Amongst the Kubeos of Colombia, who call the drug *mihi*, this hallucinogen is associated with *miwá* (birds), patrons of ecstatic drunkenness. This association is expressed visually by the hanging from the house beams during the mihi dance of the figure of a vulture. "The body is an ear of corn, the head is carved of wood, and the spreading wings and tail feathers are made of old basket fragments. The bird hangs like a mobile. It is said to be 'drunk' on mihi, and it presides over the . . . ceremony to give the proper spirit of intoxication. The vulture of intoxication is the patron, so to speak, of the . . . ceremony. Mobiles of other birds are also hung about the house . . ."[5] One

of the important symbols in the peyote ceremony is the Thunder
Bird. The ashes of the peyote altar fire are shaped into a figure,
usually that of a bird: the Comanches call it a "sun eagle"; the
Kiowas, a humming bird; the Shawnees and Kickapoos, a "water
bird."[8] The fruits of the toxic *shanshi (Coriaria thymifolia)* of the
Andes are ingested in Ecuador to induce the sensation of flight.[20]
The miraculous drink basic to the Jurema Ceremony of Indians
of eastern Brazil (prepared from the root of *Mimosa hostilis*) was
taken to "pass the night navigating through the depths of slum-
ber." A bowlful enabled participants to see glorious visions of the
spirit lands with flowers and birds, with clashing rocks that destroy the souls of the dead journeying to their destination or the
Thunder Bird shooting lightning from a tuft on his head and
producing thunder by the flap of his wings.[21] In our Southwest, it
is *toloache* or *Datura* that is associated with birds. The Zuni, for
example, permit only the rain priests to gather the plant. The root
is powdered and put into the eyes, and a tea is drunk to enable
them to commune at night with the feathered kingdom and contact the spirits of the dead who will intercede for rain.[21]

Many hallucinogens apparently are deeply engrained in tribal
thought and philosophy.[1] Studies of symbolism amongst the
Tukano of Amazonian Colombia, for example, indicate that drinking caapi ". . . represents a return to the maternal womb, to the
source and origin of all things. The partaker 'sees' all the tribal
divinities; the creation of the universe, of the first human beings
and of the animals; and the establishment of the social order,
especially regarding the law of exogamy. The Indians claim to see
not only abstract designs but also figures of people and animals
. . . in complex mythological scenes. Having had this experience,
the individual is firmly convinced of the verity of his religious
beliefs. But the return to the womb is also an acceleration of time
and is equivalent to death . . . the individual 'dies' but later re-
vives in a state of great wisdom. At the same time, the hallucina-
tory experience is symbolically a sexual act, essentially incestuous,
in which he returns momentarily to the mythical stage of Creation."[15]

Another basically significant use of hallucinogens is their role in adolescent initiatory rites. This role is very widespread. In the Tukano Yuruparí Ceremony, for example, caapi has an almost sacramental part.[7] In Gabon, African tribesmen take *iboga* root (*Tabernanthe iboga*) in initiation rituals for entering secret societies into which an adolescent may be admitted only after seeing the cultural hero Bwiti.[21] Algonkian Indians of eastern North America administered *wysoccan,* an intoxicating medicine containing *jimson weed (Datura stramonium),* to youths about to undergo initiation rituals. The initiants went raving mad for twenty days, losing all memory, unliving their former lives and starting manhood by forgetting that they had ever been boys. The Indians of the Southwest similarly valued toloache *(Datura inoxia).* The Luiseño give it to youths who dance, screaming wildly like animals and finally falling into a stupor to find their adult life. The Yumas take it to gain occult power during the adolescent rites. The Yokuts value it in a spring ceremony to ensure future good health and long life to adolescent initiants.[21] Hallucinogens are especially noteworthy in adolescent rites throughout New World cultures where, in a "male-centered hunting society . . . a boy's manhood and manly prowess in hunting and war and sexuality all come as gifts from the outside, from the stronger ones—that is, as 'medicine' power from the outer generalized supernatural . . . At adolescence, this power was acquired or struck in like lightning or imbibed by the individual, whether in the individual vision quest, the shamanistic spirit-possessed ecstasy or in the . . . sacred eating, drinking or smoking of psychotropic plants."[9]

Then, there are the many unusual and occasional uses to which aboriginal peoples put their hallucinogens—unusual to us, but probably very logical in the context of their cultural philosophy. Highland Indians of Peru take the mescaline-containing columnar San Pedro cactus *Trichocereus* to make themselves owners of others' identities.[21] In Mexico, the leaves of *sinichichi (Heimia salicifolia)* are made into a slightly fermented drink which acts as an auditory hallucinogen.[20] The natives hold that it helps them recall events which took place many years earlier or that they can remember even prenatal happenings. African tribesmen administer *Datura metel* as an ordeal poison. The Jivaro of Ecuador give a preparation of tree daturas to refractory children so that the spirits of the ancestors may speak to and admonish them in the intoxication-dream and hallucinations. The Chibchas of pre-Conquest Bogotá gave a drink of datura seeds to wives and slaves of dead warriors or chieftains to induce a state of stupor before burying them alive with their departed husbands or masters. The highly toxic *latué* or *arbol de los brujos (Latua pubiflora)* was employed by medicine men of central Chile malevolently to produce delirium and hallucinations that often led to permanent insanity.[21]

III.

It is obvious that aboriginal employment of hallucinogens must, from the aboriginal point of view, be understood as *use,* not as misuse or abuse. Aboriginal utilization of hallucinations has a discrete, constructive, necessary purpose. It is religious. It is not frivolous nor casual. Hallucinogens are not taken for the pleasure that they afford—in fact, some afford no pleasurable sensations but are most definitely a trial to take. Misuse and abuse seldom—and then more or less abnormally—enter the picture. All the examples cited above, and many more which could be noted, indicate the vital, pervasive importance of hallucinogens to all aspects of primitive cultures. They are simply one of the integral parts of primitive societies. It is quite distinct from what obtains in contemporary sophisticated Western cultures, where the taking of hallucinogens on any significant scale is a newly imported and superimposed trait wholly without natural roots in cultural history. This, precisely, is why in primitive cultures the taking of hallucinogens has a built-in control not present under most circumstances in more advanced societies, where hallucinogens are essentially meaningless in any profound sense of the term; this is why the taking of hallucinogens amongst primitives constitutes effectively a use, whereas in more complex populations on a more sophisticated level of advancement the tendency towards misuse and abuse may be not only easier and natural but is certainly far more common and widespread.

As an anthropologist has recently written: "The use of hallucinogenic plants poses, for the anthropologist, a most interesting series of problems, but it is also quite evident that only interdisciplinary collaboration will provide the answers to these problems."[15] This interdisciplinary collaboration, now gaining in favor, has begun to yield results. Botanists, anthropologists, archaeologists, geographers, chemists, physiologists, psychiatrists and others each have their contribution to the whole. An understanding of the true *use* of hallucinogens in primitive societies requires such a broad outlook.[9,10,18,19]

REFERENCES

1. Cooper, John M.: Stimulants and narcotics. In *Handbook of South American Indians,* edited by J. H. Steward. *Bur Amer Ethnol Bull, 5 (No. 143):*525-558, 1949. Washington, D.C., U.S. Government Printing Office.
2. der Marderosian, Ara, Pinkley, Homer V., and Dobbins, M. Murrell F.: Native use and occurrence of N,N-dimethyltryptamine in the leaves of *Banisteriopsis rusbyana. Amer J Pharm, 140:*137-147, 1968.
3. Friedberg, Claudine: Des Banisteriopsis utilisés comme drogue en Amerique du Sud. *J Agr Trop Bot Appl, 12:*403-437; 550-594; 729-780, 1965.
4. Furst, Peter T.: *Ariocarpus retusus,* the 'false peyote' of Huichol tradition. *Econ Bot,* in press.
5. Goldman, Irving: *The Cubeo-Indians of the Northwest Amazon.* Urbana, University of Illinois Press, 1963.
6. Harner, Michael J.: The sound of rushing water. *Nat Hist, 77:*28-33; 60-61, 1968.
7. Koch-Grünberg, Theodor: *Zwei Jahre unter den Indianern.* Berlin, Germany, Verlag Ernst Wasmuth, I (1909) 298.
8. LaBarre, Weston: *The Peyote Cult* (enlarged ed.). Hamden (Conn.), Shoe String Press, 1964.
9. LaBarre, Weston: Old and New World narcotics: A statistical question and an ethnological reply. *Econ Bot, 24:*73-80, 1970.
10. Lewin, Louis: *Phantastica—Narcotic and Stimulating Drugs.* London, Routledge & Kegan Paul, 1964.
11. Lumholtz, Carl: *Unknown Mexico.* New York, Scribner & Sons, 1902, vol. 1, p. 356-379.
12. Naranjo, Plutarco: *Ayahuasca, religión y medicina.* Quito (Ecuador), Editorial Universitaria, 1970.
13. Osmond, Humphrey: Ololiuqui: The ancient Aztec narcotic. *J Mental Sci, 101:*526-537, 1955.

14. Reichel-Dolmatoff, Gerardo El contexto cultural de un alucinógeno aborigen: *Banisteriopsis caapi. Rev Acad Col Cienc Exact Fis Nat, 13:* 327-345, 1969.

15. ————— Notes on the cultural extent of the use of yajé *(Banisteriopsis caapi)* among the Indians of the Vaupés, Colombia. *Econ Bot, 24:*32-33, 1970.

16. Söderblom, Nathan: *Rus och religion.* Uppsala (Sweden), Bokfenix, 1968.

17. Sakara (Dr.) [Robinson, Scott S.]: Yagé y la religión de los indios cofanes. *El Ecuador 2 (no. 3):*11-17, 1969.

18. Schultes, Richard Evans: The role of the ethnobotanist in the search for new medicinal plants. *Lloydia, 25:*257-266, 1962.

19. Schultes, Richard Evans: The place of ethnobotany in the ethnopharmacologic search for psychotromimetic drugs. In Ethnopharmacologic Search for Psycho-active Drugs, edited by D. Efron. Public Health Service Publication No 1645. Washington, D.C., U.S. Government Printing Office, 1967, pp. 33-57.

20. Schultes, Richard Evans: The botanical and chemical distribution of hallucinogens. *Ann Rev Physiol, 21:*571-598, 1970.

21. Schultes, Richard Evans: The plant kingdom and hallucinogens. *Bull Narcotics, 21 (No. 3):*3-16, 1969; *(No. 4):*15-27; *22 (No. 1):*25-53, 1970.

22. Shonle, Ruth: Peyote, the giver of visions. *Amer Anthrop, 27:*53-75, 1925.

23. Villavicencio, Manuel: *Geografía de la República del Ecuador* New York, R. Craighead, 1858, p. 371.

24. Wassén, S. Henry: Some general viewpoints in the study of native drugs especially from the West Indies and South America. *Ethnos, 1-2:*97-120, 1964.

25. Wasson, R. Gordon: *Soma, Divine Mushroom of Immortality.* New York, Harcourt, Brace & World, Inc., 1969.

Chapter 3

Drug Abuse in Europe: Medical and Legal Aspects

Helmut E. Ehrhardt

FOR ABOUT five years, many European countries have had a rapidly increasing and surprisingly fast expanding problem of drug abuse which focuses on the young and the adolescent. The "drug wave" shows a peculiar north-south progression. In Sweden and Great Britain it started earlier than elsewhere; the transition to more dangerous types of abuse, to the use of hard drugs, was a quicker one. In France, the problem plays—*still* plays—a minor role compared to its neighboring West Germany, and in Italy or Spain, drug abuse is, up to now, no significant public health problem at all.

This phenomenon cannot easily be explained, since there are not yet sufficient epidemiological investigations at hand. Apparently, it is not a coincidence that the traditional wine countries seem to be less vulnerable to drug abuse. West Germany too, however, is a wine-growing country. Yet, in this respect, one can hardly compare it to the European South. The social use of alcohol, particularly of wine and beer, in all these countries is based on tradition and is culturally fully integrated, which is different from the use of old and new hallucinogens and, of course, also opiates. Alcohol use, and abuse, has maintained its predominant role also in those European countries which were stricken by the new drug abuse wave. The number of alcoholics is still on the increase.

Parallel to the progress of Western civilization is the advancing use and abuse of alcohol in the Oriental and Eastern countries, where hashish has its home and traditional consumption. If there exist any cultural barriers at all, concerning the use of drugs, they seem to be more or less loosely knit and subject to change, depending on political and social conditions or changes. Since the European South seems to be less vulnerable to drug abuse than the North, we have to consider also religious ties, the economic and social structures, as well as the type of government and political influences, if we want to better understand the situation. Altogether, it is an interesting task for transcultural-psychiatric studies.

An empirically founded overview of the drug scene of 1970 in Europe is not yet possible. In most countries we fail to have the necessary epidemiological investigations. Let us not forget either that the problem hit us, so to say, within a very short span of time and that the scenery changes quickly. Just during the last few months, larger quantities of heroin made their appearance on the German illegal market and lately also cocaine which, for the past forty years, hardly existed in Germany. From Sweden and Great Britain come broad spectrum investigations with correspondingly useful statistical values. I refer to the Cannabis Report by the Advisory Committee on Drug Dependence (London 1968) ; the substantial Swedish Commission Report on drug abuse and the fight against it (Stockholm, 1969) ; and also, to the two reports of L. Goldberg, "Drug Abuse in Sweden."[12]

In Austria, the first warning signals for an increased drug abuse came in 1966. Police arrests for violations of the Drug Law numbered 63 in 1966, 363 in 1969 and 312 during the first half of 1970. The percentage of youngsters under 21 increased during the same period from 3 percent in 1966 to 53 percent in 1969 and 70 percent during the first six months of 1970. Correspondingly, the admissions of drug addicts to the Psychiatric University Clinic of Vienna increased from 5 in 1966, to 54 in 1969, and 64 up to July 1970. As to frequency of used substances, hashish and opium are followed by stimulants, sleeping drugs, sedatives and cough medicines. The transition from cannabis to opium was often observed. According to police reports, 35 percent of the drug abusers used a combination of hashish and opium. Measured by the quantities of raw opium confiscated by the police, the smuggling of the drug from Turkey into Austria is, for the last two years, steadily increasing. Based on the number of clinically observed cases, Sluga estimates the unrevealed current number of drug addicts in need of treatment to be 1 to 10 or 12. The therapeutic results in the Vienna Clinic to date are very modest.[22,33] Of 32 patients treated in 1969 only 2 were off drugs after 12 to 18 months.

At the Psychiatric University Clinic in Basel, Switzerland, Kielholz and Ladewig[15,17] examined since 1967 some 120, mostly young, patients constituting a selection of 550 known hashish smokers. Age distribution was 14 to 30 years with a peak in age groups 14 to 18 and 18 to 22 towards the 22 year mark. Sex distribution showed 62 percent male and 38 percent female patients. A simple grouping of professions revealed 42 percent apprentices and school pupils, as against 26 percent blue-collar workers, 16 percent college students and 16 percent white-collar workers. The continuity record of work performance was poor; 76 percent were found not working. The psychiatric history showed no abnormal development in 26 percent of the youths investigated; in 56 percent of them maturation and belated puberty crises were found; broken homes were a factor in 52 percent. All patients had experiences with cannabis, 72 percent of them with so-called substitute drugs such as isoaminile or dextromethorphan and 68 percent with amphetamines. Of these 46 percent had smoked hashish regularly over a longer period of time. On the other hand, LSD and opium were used by only 10 and 12 percent respectively. Another 38 percent of the patients had used sedatives or sleeping tablets; however rather seldom and intermittently.

In West Germany, the published observations and studies are few: they come from Berlin,[5,6,7] Frankfurt,[31,32] Hamburg,[5a] and Marburg.[8,24] All these studies are yet to be completed and their results are preliminary. In Frankfurt, three hundred drug users were subjected to a very differentiated investigation. Dr. Wanke reported the preliminary results in form of an analysis of 165 drug users before the Congress of the German Psychiatric Association. About one half of these drug users were hospital patients, the other half were ambulatory cases. They were 80 percent male and 20 percent female patients, with 80 percent of the group being between 16 and 24 years old. In a third of the sample, age groups 13 to 18, the sex proportion was 50:50. The average age was 21. Early child-hood behavioral defects were traced in 52 percent. Of the youths 48 percent came from disrupted families. In 24 percent, the father was a blue-collar worker, in 20 percent he had an academic back-ground. More than 25 percent of the parents had a monthly in-come of over 2000 D-Mark, an equivalent of perhaps $800 to $1000. Of the drug users 98 percent used cannabis; 82 percent, LSD or DOM; 68 percent, amphetamines; 61 percent, opiates (heroin excluded) ; 50 percent, sedatives; 42 percent, mescaline; 36 percent, analgesics; 34 percent, other drugs; and 27 percent, heroin. A distinct psychological dependence was found in 45 per-cent of the sample while there was reason to believe that an addi-tional 20 percent was equally dependent. Of the youths 41 percent had their first drug experience prior to the age of 16; 11 percent of the subjects had gone from cannabis to more potent hallucino-gens; 15 percent further added amphetamines and 62 percent opiates. Investigations in other big cities revealed similar results.

The Psychiatric University Youth-Clinic of Marburg, an old university city with 65,000 inhabitants, admitted over the past one and a half years thirty young addicts (14 to 18 years old) . If this special clinic with sixty beds could satisfy the requests coming from all parts of the country for admission of such youngsters, it would be filled and blocked for a long time to come. I mention the case of Marburg only to illustrate the fact that the growing drug problem afflicting the young in Europe is no longer limited to large cities. We find it in rural areas where the people other-wise are still tradition-bound. Universities and high schools are the real trading posts for drugs of all kinds. Reliable statistics regarding the frequency of drug abuse among high school and university students are not available at this time. According to a recent poll in Denmark, 25 percent of its registered students had at least once smoked hashish. This corresponds to earlier studies made in the United States according to which 20 to 30 percent of college and university students have had experiences with mari-juana. The investigation of Manheimer *et al.,* published last year, which was a representative screening of the population of San

Francisco, reports considerably higher figures. I believe that the value of such statistics is relatively small. However, these studies may serve a purpose in making us realize the perturbing extent of the problem.

In order to depict the situation in West Germany further, let me give you a few data of the Federal Criminal Bureau. One clear fact is the rapid increase of confiscated illegal cannabis (hashish, marijuana) which was 2.6 kilos (one kilo equals 2.2 pounds) in 1961 as against 381 kilos in 1968 and approximately 2278 kilos in 1969. The illegal import and smuggling of raw opium from Turkey via Austria into Germany increases. Police secured about 48 kilos in 1969 but this quantity has been stepped up considerably during the past months. It was only during the past year that larger quantities of LSD and heroin, and lately also cocaine, were confiscated. Pharmacy robberies with the only goal of procuring opiates also increased during the past few months. Furthermore, the growing portion made up of young people in the overall number of drug criminals is alarming. That portion rose from 1.4 percent in 1955 to 8.6 percent in 1966 and 35.5 percent in 1968; in 1969 it had reached 47.8 percent. The offenses involved were illegal trade or smuggling, acquisition or possession or distribution of narcotic drugs as well as violations of the Narcotic-Prescription Regulation. An investigation on "the public health implications of recent developments of drug addiction," made in 1969 as requested by the "Europarat"—Council of Europe—confirmed what official statistics and various European authors had already indicated, namely that drug abuse in Europe is undoubtedly on the increase. In this connection, the four following trends merit our attention: (a) the shift towards a younger age; in other words, the earlier start of drug abuse and the spreading of the evil to more and more youngsters; (b) an increase of female drug users; (c) a considerable accumulation of polytropic forms of drug dependence; and finally (d) the frequent and rapid change from the oral application or inhaling to the intravenous injection of narcotic agents.

In all European countries swept by the drug wave the questions of treatment, rehabilitation and prevention are, of course, in the foreground—questions that are, in turn, connected with the difficult questions of national and international control of production of and trade with dependence producing substances. The complex system of international agreements, starting with the first agreement of 1909 in Shanghai, was, after long-term efforts in the United Nations, summarized into the Single Convention in 1961 and was ratified in 1964. Joining the International Convention automatically obligates the individual nation to enact corresponding laws on a national level. In Germany, this legislation was the so-called Opium-Law of December 12, 1929, which, in the following years and up to present times, was again and again amended and updated. For instance, two years ago, LSD was added to the list of narcotic substances controlled according to the Opium Law. The other European countries have similar laws; their limited effectiveness in the light of today's phenomena of drug abuse is commonly known. The biggest portion of the drugs we are currently concerned about, still reaches the consumer through illegal channels.

The necessity of including various drugs in the pertinent control regulations is repeatedly contested, particularly because of the penalty imposed for the violation of the law. In Germany, for instance, a wave of protest is being launched against the penalization of the acquisition of hashish and its inclusion in the list of controlled narcotics. The ban on hashish allegedly is contrary to the Constitution or contradicts the principle of equality before the law; if the prohibition of hashish is maintained, one should equally outlaw alcohol and nicotine, so they argue. The Supreme Court of Bavaria, in its decision of August 27, 1969, stipulated clearly that the penalization of the acquisition of cannabis under the Opium Law is totally in accord with our constitution. The Supreme Constitutional Court of the FRG confirmed that point of view in its decision of December 17, 1969. With this, the debate will, however, not have come to an end. Some people in Germany do not like anything better than to quote the constitutionally guaranteed right of free development of one's personality. This is a pseudo-argument and one forgets that the Federal Republic of Germany, according to its Constitution, is not only a liberal state under the rule of law but a social welfare state as well. Such a social state cannot simply leave it to the citizen to destroy himself "his way." The social state has the duty to help the addicted patient and such help always goes at the expense of the other citizens.

As the observations in Europe have shown, the use of hashish, particularly by our youths, cannot be ridiculed as harmless. This is also the predominant view of the European psychiatrists. According to our investigations to date, which in size are of course not comparable to studies in this country, there can be no doubt that, with too many youngsters, hashish stands at the threshold of their career as hard-drug users and is the stepping stone on the way to opiate addiction with its serious and often irreparable damages. With this in mind, the European League of Mental Health, at its Annual Meeting in Istanbul, has gone on record on September 20, 1969, explicitly warning not to liberalize in any way the production of, the trade with and the use of cannabis, LSD and of other hallucinogenic substances. The Board of the German Psychiatric Association, in December 1969, officially approved and supported that motion.

Our experience has further shown that the center of gravity of an effective treatment and control of today's drug abuse lies at the edge of the realm of our penal laws. It does not make sense to simply put into prison the high school boy apprehended with a hashish cigarette in his pocket, because no one would be served. The persecution of those who are "in the business"—the merchants, smugglers, pushers, etcetera, remains *the* important task of the police. The solution of this problem, however, becomes more and more difficult and requires, therefore, greater efforts and funds.

The trade with narcotics is not a "gentlemen offense," and the stand of police and courts towards these criminals must be firm and consequent. Sweden has already stiffened sentences for illegal trade and smuggling of narcotics; West Germany will soon follow suit. I regard such procedures as essential and right although they are of limited effectiveness. Within a state constitution under the rule of law, it is rather difficult to distinguish the "small retailer," the one who acts illegally only *ad usum proprium* from those who —consumers themselves or driven by ideological factors—supply a small or larger group with narcotics and those belonging to the class of cool, calculating crooks of grand style.

Addiction control and prophylaxis are primarily psychohygienic tasks. The individual help and therapy must begin as early and as thoroughly as possible and must be concentrated upon prophylaxis. In the case of adolescents, in particular, an early and thorough clarification of the motivation and of the background of the dependence behavior will be of utmost importance for therapeutic success. A broad, intensive as well as factual information and education of youth itself, of parents and teachers may well be indispensable. This, however, will be achieved only, if all organizations concerned with our youth will actively participate in the efforts to solve this serious and urgent problem.

REFERENCES

1. Angst, J.: Halluzinogen-Abusus. *Schweiz Med Wschr, 100:*710, 1970.
2. Beringer, K.: *Der Meskalinrausch.* Berlin, Springer, 1927.
3. Beringer, K.: Zur Klinik des Haschischrausches. *Nervenarzt, 5:*337, 1932.
4. Biener, K.: *Genussmittel und Suchtproblem im Jugendalter.* Basel 1969.
5. Bschor, F.: Jugend und Drogenkonsum. *Soz Arb, 19:*525, 1970.
5a. Burchard, J.M. *et al.:* Ergebnisse von standartisierten BeFragungen unter Hamburger Oberschülern und unter Langjährigen konsumenten über Drogengebrauch und -missbrauch. *Zbl Neur, 201:*247, 1971.
6. Coper, H., and Hippius, H.: Missbrauch von Haschisch. *Deutsch Ärztebl, 67:*1618, 1970.
7. Coper, H., and Hippius, H.: Haschisch, eine Analyse und Wertung. *Kosmos, 66:*521, 1970.
8. Dauner, I., and Remschmidt, H.: Polyvalente Sucht bei Jugendlichen. *Med Welt, 21:*1490, 1970.
9. Ehrhardt, H.: *Rauschgiftsucht.* Hamm, Hoheneck, 1967.
10. Ehrhardt, H.: Drug Dependence. *Universitas* (English ed.), *10:*157, 1968.
11. Ehrhardt, H.: Rauschgiftsucht, aktuelle Probleme und Aufgaben. *Deutsch Ärztebl, 67:*1151, 1970.
12. Goldberg, L.: Drug Abuse in Sweden. *Bull Narc, XX:*1,2, 1968.
13. Haenel, T.A.: Kulturgeschichte und heutige Problematik des Haschisch. *Pharmakopsychiat, 3:*89, 1970.
14. Hofmann, G. *et al.:* Moderne Erscheinungsformen der Medikamentenabhängigkeit bzw. -sucht. *Wien Klin Wschr, 81:*605, 1969.

15. Kielholz, P., and Ladewig, D.: Über Drogenabhängigkeit bei Jugendlichen. *Deutsch Med Wschr, 95*:101, 1970.

16. Kleiner, D.: Aktuelle Rauschgiftprobleme bei Jugendlichen. *Unsere Jugend, 21*:1, 1969.

17. Ladewig, D.: Neuere Suchttrends bei Jugendlichen. *Schweiz Med Wschr, 99*:781, 1969.

18. Langen, D.: Rauschmittelgefährdung und Jugend. Ärztebl Rheinland-Pfalz, Sept. 1, 1970.

19. Laubenthal, F.: *Sucht und Missbrauch.* Stuttgart, 1964.

20. Leuner, H.C.: *Die experimentelle Psychose.* Berlin, 1962.

21. Luban-Plozza, B.: Suchtprobleme im Jugendalter. *Österr Ärzte Ztg, 9*:1100, 1969.

22. Mader, R., and Sluga, W.: Soziale Verläufe und Katamnesen rauschgift- und drogen-abhängiger Jugendlicher. *Wien Med Wschr, 119*:604, 1969.

23. Mader, R., and Sluga, W.: Veränderungen im Erscheinungsbild sucht-kranker Jugendlicher. *Wien Med Wschr, 120*:330, 1970.

24. Remschmidt, H., and Dauner, I.: Klinische und soziale Aspekte der Drogenabhängigkeit bei Jugenlichen. *Med Klinik, 65*:1993, 2041, 2078, 1970.

25. Schrappe, O.: Gewöhnung und Süchte. *Nervenarzt, 39*:337, 1968.

26. Stringaris, M.G.: *Die Haschischsucht.* Berlin, 1939.

27. Strunk, P.: Psychische Gesundheit von Jugendlichen und Jungerwach-senen. *Deutsch Ärztebl, 66*:2919, 1969.

28. Stutte, H.: Suchtgewohnheiten und Suchtgefährdung aus der Sicht des Kinde und Jugendalters. *In Flucht in die Sucht.* Wuppertal, 1969.

29. Sutter, J.M. *et al.:* Les substances hallucinogènes. *Encyclop Med Chir,* 37630 F 10, Paris 1970.

30. Vierth, G.: Psychopathologische Syndrome nach Haschischgenuss. *Münch Med Wschr, 109*:522, 1967.

31. Wanke, K. *et al.:* Jugend und Rauschmittel. *Rehabilitation, 23*:H.2, 1970.

32. Wanke, K.: Neue Aspekte zum Suchtproblem, maltifaktorielle Analysen klinischer Erfahrungen mit jungen Drogenkonsumenten. Habil. Schrift, Med. Fakultat, Univ. Frankfurt/M. 1971.

Chapter 4

What Psychiatry Can Do for Law in the Prevention of Drug Abuse

Frederick J. Ludwig

OR ME, A LAWYER, to suggest policies to you, men trained in medicine and psychiatry, on the treatment and prevention of the abuse of dangerous drugs currently in vogue would be like some fellow whose voyages in life have been limited to a trip from home to his office each day. Imagine this chap getting up to give a travelogue on Outer Mongolia with the full realization that almost everyone in the audience is Marco Polo. I feel that way with respect to you in the area of treatment and prevention of drug abuse. It is so much within your expertise and so little within mine. Nevertheless, I have come to ask you questions to help us solve a problem of social control by legislation and law enforcement.

There is an opinion that people drink because they want to drink and indulge in the abuse of drugs because they want to do so. The criminal law, despite its centuries of experience, is a feeble influencer of human behavior. Primarily its effect is negative in nature: it cannot compete successfully in making people want to do the right thing with positive programs offered by home, church, synagogue or school. The criminal law has never been able to build character or develop desirable habits, attitudes, interests and ideals. Whatever influence it has, makes itself felt by (a) subjecting actual offenders to unpleasant treatment in the hope (often in vain) that its memory will intimidate them from offending again; (b) treating actual offenders so that potential ones will be dissuaded by that example [this we call deterrence of potential offenders—a big class that includes you and me.]; (c) restraining or incapacitating those more likely to commit crime than the generality of persons [the best way to prevent a dangerous criminal from committing another crime is to put him behind bars]; and (d) rehabilitating, reforming and reeducating corrigible offenders. Transforming a law breaking defendant into a law observing member of the community is obviously the optimum method of preventing crime.

There is a great deal of confusion surrounding laws that regulate drugs. The whole criminal law is concerned with two things:

1. Drawing a line between lawful and unlawful behavior. What sort of conduct ought to be made criminal?

2. What happens to a person who has overstepped that line? What sort of treatment should be prescribed once it has been determined beyond a reasonable doubt that someone has committed a crime?

Under the first inquiry—drawing a line between permitted and unpermitted use of drugs—four major questions must be answered if we are to enact a sound body of law:

1. Is it desirable to deter by threat of punishment use of a given drug?

The ultimate answer depends on findings with respect to several subquestions: (a) What is the probability that physical, mental, social or other harm will result from use? (b) What is the probability that such use will also have desirable results, and what is the degree of their desirability? (c) If such use has desirable results (e.g. relief of anxiety), are there less dangerous and equally efficacious means of serving the same desirable end?

There is quite a bit of controversy in this area. For example, in New York we allow you to have certain kinds of drugs and purchase them in the drugstore. You may lawfully buy an ounce of a medicinal preparation that contains 2 grains of papaverine, 2 grains of noscapine (narcotine), 1 grain of codeine or $\frac{1}{4}$ grain of ethylmorphine. These may be purchased without prescription, provided you are over 21, willing to give your name and address, and provided the substances contain something beside the narcotic ingredient. These are narcotic (i.e. stupefying) drugs capable of leading to habituation and addiction. Should we prohibit their use entirely or require use only by prescription? Where should we draw the line?

The major controversy is whether or not use and possession of marijuana should be made lawful. One drug of great and widespread use in this country is alcohol. We have found that in the last twenty-five years the nationwide increase in production of alcohol has been 113 percent while the population has increased only 49 percent. Our national consumption of alcohol has more than doubled. If we permit widespread use of alcohol, concededly an addictive drug, why not allow smoking of marijuana, concededly nonaddictive? My reaction to this argument (I'll give you several other reactions) is that any attempt to justify adoption of a new evil by asserting that it is no worse or even slightly better than a different prevailing vice is inane. In terms of extent of use, there is no question that alcohol is easily first among the psychoactive drugs in the United States. But only about 4 percent of the estimated 125 to 150 million users abuse alcohol and become alcoholics. Nobody ever became an alcoholic on two martinis a day. Nor has anybody become addicted to barbiturates on one sleeping pill a night, nor to heroin or morphine on a single therapeutic dose. Nobody becomes a significant social hazard on an occasional marijuana cigarette. The American experience that led to repeal of the Eighteenth Amendment was that the interest of the 96 percent of the nonabusers of alcohol are paramount to those of the 4 percent who abuse it. For that reason we allow alcohol to be sold throughout the United States today under those circumstances.

As to the general opinion on whether possession, sale or distribution of marijuana should or should not be made criminal, reaction of the people varies. Several polls have been taken within the last two years. Gallup, from October 3 to October 6, 1969, had 15,039 adults in three hundred localities interviewed. They were asked if they had ever used marijuana. Six percent of the men and 2 percent of the women said they had. In the age group 21 to 29, 12 percent of the people interviewed admitted use. But in the age group 50 and over, 99 percent denied use. In the same poll, with regard to the question on whether they would ever use marijuana if it was offered to them, 6 percent of the men again (the same 6 percent possibly who said they had used it before) and 3 percent of the women said they would use it. Should marijuana be legalized? 84 percent, no; 16 percent, yes. Another survey made by *Life* magazine asked people of all ages whether they *ever* used marijuana and came up with a 1.5 percent admission of use. In my own alma mater, Columbia Law School, students surveyed themselves on November 11, 1969. Of 800 law students on Morningside Heights, 491 responded. Sixty-nine percent said, "Yes, we use marijuana." So "grass" seems to be very popular among would-be lawyers. In answer to a second question, Do you find conflict between this unlawful use (possession of marijuana is criminal) and being a lawyer? 55 percent of the 491 found there was no conflict. In other words, they believed that they could violate the law by using marijuana and yet become lawyers, officers of the court and ministers of justice. Forty-five percent said, in effect: "Even though some of us might use it, we find a little conflict between being a minister of justice and being a violator of the law."

Remember our second subquestion—the probability that use of drugs will have desirable results and the degree of desirability. Many argue that marijuana leads possibly to the use of other addictive drugs like barbiturates, LSD and heroin. There has been no such significant correlation demonstrated in any large-scale study that I know of. The study ordered by Mayor LaGuardia in 1944 was unable to make that correlation. Many feel that users of heroin began by using marijuana, but usually you will find at least 50 percent of the people who use heroin are regular users of other drugs. They use barbiturates, an addiction in my opinion, much more serious than heroin. It is more difficult to detoxify a barbituric addict than a heroin user. About three thousand persons are estimated to die annually from barbituric overdose taken either intentionally, recklessly or negligently in the United States. Fourteen billion pills of barbiturates originate in the United States, about half of them finding their way into unlawful channels and accounting for a thriving business of about one-half billion dollars annually. The statistics on the production of barbituric acid in the United States are interesting. In 1936, there were 252,000 pounds of barbituric acid manufactured in the United States. In 1967, this increased by 250 percent to 852,000 pounds.

Assuming it is desirable to deter use of a given drug by threat of punishment, the second hurdle to making such conduct criminal is posed by the next question.

2. *Is it possible to deter by threat of punishment use of the drug?*

More sorts of behavior are socially undesirable but not made criminal. Somnambulists, epileptics and persons lacking substantial capacity to understand what they are doing or that it is wrong may kill another without any justification whatsoever and not be subject to prosecution. While it is desirable to deter such homicidal behavior, it is not *possible* to deter such obviously non-deterrable persons by threat of punishment. The question in connection with users of certain drugs is whether or not the threat posed by a criminal penalty is capable of deterring some well-defined classes of drug users.

The fact that certain persons use proscribed drugs in spite of the threat of punishment does not automatically make them non-deterrable. As with most violations of the criminal law, they may belong in the broad category of "undeterred but deterrable." This is the class of responsible criminal defendants.

3. *Is such use indicative of a dangerous person?*

Even though drug use may be desirable and possible to deter by threat of punishment, before making such conduct criminal, we must be satisfied that this behavior is indicative of a dangerous person—that is, a person more dangerously likely to engage in socially harmful conduct than the generality of men.

Penal drug statutes are in the nature of sumptuary laws—that is, ancient and medieval regulations designed to prevent extravagance and overindulgence.

In determining whether conduct with respect to drugs is indicative of dangerousness it is important to ascertain whether the harm is directed only against the user himself or against third persons. In New York, for example, suicide—the greatest harm that may be directed against one's self—is not made criminal, and unsuccessful attempts to take one's own life are not punishable.

4. *Assuming a given use is both desirable and possible to deter, and indicative of a dangerous person, would the bad consequences of making this conduct criminal outweigh the good ones?*

Excessive imbibation of alcohol—concededly a social evil of considerable magnitude—led once upon a time to the nationwide noble experiment of prohibition. After a dozen years, it was clear that the consequences of attempting to make alcohol unavailable to 96 percent of the population who do not abuse it were clearly outweighed by the evil results of official corruption and crime that attended the noble experiment.

You cannot legislate morality.

A fifth question remains, one of treatment, assuming *all* four questions on drawing the line between permitted and unpermitted use of drugs are answered affirmatively.

5. *Assuming a given use is both desirable and possible to deter and indicative of a dangerous person and that the good consequences of making it criminal are not outweighed by bad ones, should the threat of punishment be severe or lenient?*

Recently, the New York Legislature prescribed the most severe penality—reserved theretofore for murder and kidnapping —for selling a pound of heroin, cocaine or opium. The wisdom of preventing undesirable behavior by drastic penalties has been questioned for two hundred years. When penalties are too severe, witnesses refuse to testify, grand jurors refuse to indict and petit jurors will not convict. This is the phenomenon of nullification. Whatever conduct is made criminal with respect to drugs, it must avoid penalties that nullify the prohibition of the law. Nullification may well be worse than no criminal statute: in nonenforcement of statutes prescribing severe penalties, general disrespect for all statutes may easily follow.

If you men and women trained in medicine and psychiatry are able to supply solid answers to these questions on the basis of empirical knowledge, then lawmakers will be able to deliver appropriate criminal codes with suitable sanctions and programs of treatment.

Chapter 5

Limitations of Law in Drug Control

Edwin H. Hastings

I WANT TO share with you my own very deep concern for the gap which has been growing between the young on the one hand and the middle-aged and the elderly on the other. Do any of you not believe that there is such a gap? Do any of you not believe it is growing? How many of you react negatively to long hair on boys? How many of you react negatively to headbands, beads or fringed jackets? How many of you think our young people entertain a deep and abiding respect for the Pentagon? For the Vietnam war? For the Air Force and its daily tonnages of bombs dropped in Cambodia, Laos and Vietnam? How many of you have boys or girls of college age? Do their views on hair length and Vietnam agree with yours? Do their views on drugs agree with yours?

I wonder how many of you realize the great influence of the Vietnam war on marijuana usage. Most of us are aware that troop usage in Vietnam has been rapidly increasing. Returned enlisted men tell me that around 75 percent of the enlisted personnel are using it—some experimentally. The figure may be high, but usage is far from minimal. They tell me that there is little or no penalty risk in enlisted units—marijuana is readily available. I suggest that the Vietnam experience is so frustrating, so demoralizing, that it cannot help leading to the use of drugs, where available, including alcohol.

The usage of marijuana by soldiers in Vietnam is part of what I regard as the many-sided problems of law enforcement with drugs. Here we have the government, inadvertently perhaps, making it possible to enjoy drugs in Vietnam and at the same time attempting to prohibit the use of drugs in the United States by threat of fine and imprisonment—a major inconsistency in the minds of young people.

The second major inconsistency in the minds of young people stems from the bitter comparison of the success of our generation and the failure of theirs. Does anyone not know what success I refer to? We were prohibited the use of a major drug in the 1920's. We were successful in having the prohibition repealed in 1933. Not so the young people of today. They have succeeded in persuading the Federal Government and some state governments to moderate the penalties regarding marijuana, but in most states, possession and/or sale of marijuana remains a high crime.

Here is the real offense for most young people. They have seen skid row alcoholics; all of us have seen them. They know the tremendous cost to society of alcoholics and of problem drinkers, and so do all of you. Yet, they know that you and I are free to sell a bottle of liquor to an alcoholic without risking penalty, while if they were to sell a marijuana cigarette to a friend, who turns out to be an informer or police agent, they run immense risks—up to forty years in Rhode Island or up to life if they sell marijuana to a minor. The young people know these maximum sentences; they know they are rarely given, but the threat is there, and their disrespect for the Establishment which made these laws is immense.

My thesis, as you can see, is that the laws relating to drugs, particularly as applied to marijuana, are counterproductive, especially at this stage of the deepening chasm separating the young from the middle-aged and elderly. I regard the laws not only as useless but as more harmful than the offense they seek to punish.

Let me outline a few cases. Jack, age 18, dropped out from high school. He had wealthy parents who drank heavily and gambled heavily. Jack had only one talent—guitar music. In March 1967, one of his guitar-playing friends had his apartment raided one night. The next day he came to Jack and asked him to keep a pound of grass for him which the officers had "missed" in their search. A few days later he came to Jack's house along with Pat Johnson, who he introduced as a pimp, who wanted to get some grass for his girls. If Jack would provide the grass, Pat would arrange a party with some of his girls. Jack was tempted; he had no girl friend, but he refused. His friend, however, persuaded him to come back to his apartment with him, and there gave Jack a small quantity of hash—about dime size—and told him that Pat Johnson was a real sucker and would pay them $20 for what would normally have brought $4 or $5. Jack was short of money, went out and sold it to Pat, kept $10 for himself and went home. As it happened, Pat Johnson was a C-squad (drugs) officer, and Jack's friend had been caught in the earlier raid and was now "cooperating" in order to stay out of jail. So the police came for Jack at his home about 11:30 one night. He was out, so they waited for him, picked him up and then asked him to open the house so they could search.

He asked if they had a search warrant. They said no, but if he didn't let them in they would be back at noon the next day in three squad cars with sirens full on, with a search warrant. He let them in.

When he was arraigned, the judge fixed bail at $20,000—so his parents had to pay $2000 for a bail bondsman (10 %). In a pretrial conference, the judge indicated that he felt marijuana and heroin were equivalent and told the defense counsel that, if Jack were convicted, he would be given two years in our state prison. So we had to bring in expert witnesses, Dr. Schultes among others and the state brought in experts (Dr. Brill among others) and at the conclusion, the judge changed his mind and said Jack was a good candidate for probation on a deferred sentence.

There is a sequel. Some months later, Jack's father got a phone call threatening to work Jack over unless $1000 was paid. Jack was slightly built (130 lbs.) and passive—no fighter. The father called me. I told him to call the police; he refused at first because he had no respect for them, having seen them searching his house. I told him that the detective division was quite different from the C-squad. He finally called, and the detectives arranged for a supervised payoff. They caught a man trying to retrieve the $1000 from the payoff location and arraigned him in court. The arraigning judge fixed bail for the extortioner at $1000, and Jack and his parents and friends were outraged.

Let me give another example—a story from last Christmas which O. Henry would have liked. Ronald was 21, career Air Force man. His father was a career petty officer in the Navy. He had a sister, 20, going to Roger Williams College in Rhode Island.

Just a year ago (around November 15, 1969), Ronald was stationed in South Vietnam and he had a Christmas leave coming up—30 days' leave starting December 23. On November 15, he mailed a Christmas package home—a cashmere sweater for his sister, some ivory-carved bookends for his parents, a jade necklace and earring set for his mother, some clothing for his thirty-day leave, and 4 ounces of marijuana to help him while away on the leave. He was a helicopter repair mechanic; he had repaired them for twelve months in Vietnam; and he was scheduled to report back to Vietnam after his leave for another six months. He occasionally smoked marijuana in the evening just as some of you occasionally drink alcoholic beverages. His commander considered him an excellent helicopter mechanic.

Marijuana dogs at the San Francisco post office sniffed his package. It was sent to Boston, where it was opened; the marijuana was weighed, repacked and resealed and delivered to his home in Rhode Island on January 10, two or three weeks after Christmas. It was followed about half an hour later by five federal customs officers who arrested him and brought him into Providence to be arraigned. He was released on bail but charged with importing marijuana and possession of marijuana.

The charge of importing carries a minimum penalty of five years—with no probation. The charge of possession—a federal charge—carries a minimum penalty of two years, but a court had power to suspend the sentence. (This was January, 1970; the penalty for possession has now been reduced to misdemeanor status under the recent Federal Act.)

In Ronald's case, they had to drop the charge of possession because of *Leary v. U.S.,* a Supreme Court decision in 1968 which held the statute unconstitutional, so they only had the importing statute left. That statute made no distinction as to quantity. Four ounces or a ton—the minimum was five years and no probation.

I spoke to the Federal District Judge and told him he wasn't going to like having to send Ronald up for five years while this boy had performed so well in Vietnam and was scheduled to return—who was going to fix the helicopters? The federal judge said, "Go see the district attorney; he is a reasonable person." I did, and he said, in effect, I hate to prosecute but my hands are tied—the customs officers want him prosecuted and there is no out.

As it turned out, the search warrant was defective—no affidavit was attached, and the Federal Commissioner who had issued the search warrant was immensely pleased to quash it.

In the meantime, the boy and his parents had been thoroughly distressed and had had to pay what was to them a substantial legal fee and had had the specter of an entirely unrealistic federal criminal law hovering over them.

In all of the drug cases which I have come in contact with, the defendants have developed an intense disrespect for the legislators who have passed the laws and for the police enforcing the laws; and in my opinion, in almost every case, that disrespect has been well founded and has spread to the parents, relatives and friends of the defendants.

The elements inviting disrespect are clear and troublesome.

1. We begin with laws that the defendants view as unreasonable, particularly for the complete lack of correlation with alcohol. What legislator will sponsor prohibition legislation for alcohol with the fervor he sponsors such legislation for marijuana?

2. We have the tremendous political bandwagon overflowing with politicians declaiming against drugs and youth. From the White House down to the lowest municipal office—all promise to deal with the "drug threat," none promise to deal with the existing alcohol problem.

3. We have, what is worse, a widespread use of campus and peer informers—informing in exchange for leniency, assisting in setting up what are virtual entrapment situations for their fellows.

4. Finally, we have two problems with the police themselves: (a) the overreacting to the hair and the clothes in the direction they seek to enforce the drug laws, and (b) the frequent practice of "planting" by the police on a defendant during a "search." There are frequent reports of such action, a number of which have been corroborated and many of them I believe to be true. Would you believe your son or daughter if they tell you that the police planted a drug on them—the boys and girls reporting this are college students, like your sons and daughters and they are deeply bitter.

CONCLUSION

There is a trend in the legislation—national and state—toward moderating the penalties. I suggest this will do more harm than good. It means, I think, that there will now be more arrests an a tendency to give at least short sentences, ninety days to six months, in many drug cases which would have gone free when a judge could only give a minimum of five years.

Jail terms, I suggest, will more often than not turn a college or high school student "drug criminal" into a potential thief, breaking and entering specialist, and other postgraduate trades one learns in most prisons.

I foresee a continuation of the immense geometric progression of drug arrests of the last few years. I foresee it adding its own explosive quality to an already explosive, divisive national situation.

I foresee increasing disrespect for the police and the Establishment.

I would advocate legalization as a means of defusing the hates that are building up for the police in an influential group—the college students. But I realize as a practical matter that legalization will not come in the near future, and before it does, things will be worse than they are now.

Please bear in mind what I do not say. I do not say that marijuana should be used. Nor do I say that alcohol should be used. I have tried both, but I use neither. I do say, however, that if some person wishes to take the risk that goes with a relaxing drink of whiskey or a relaxing smoke of marijuana, he should be able to do either without the imposition upon him of the Puritan Ethic of someone else, which makes him a criminal when he harms no one but himself.

I close with what seems to me an obvious observation. It seems wasteful to devote police efforts and budgets to the enforcing of sumptuary laws—the laws which relate only to the conduct of a person affecting that person—when there is so much serious crime committed against the persons and properties of others, such as larceny, murder, assault, robbery and so forth, to which these efforts might better be directed.

SECTION II

PHYSICAL AND MEDICAL ASPECTS

Chapter 6

Deaths Resulting from Narcotic Addiction—
A Major Health Problem

Milton Helpern

BEFORE BEGINNING my own chapter, I should like the privilege of commenting on the previous one dealing with the subject of marijuana. Much of the discussion was bogged down with the questions of legality and enforcement of the law without too much regard as to whether marijuana and its derivatives are useful or wholesome substances or harmful to the individual, especially the student, when it is being used. All of the comments seem to skirt the fact that when students are smoking pot, they are not doing their homework. Aside from its other specific detrimental pharmacologic effects, pot is a relaxant substance and diminishes the power of concentration and intellectual effectiveness in contrast to the immediate effect of tobacco smoking. Granted that the use of tobacco over a long period of time is harmful in that it may be complicated by the development of lung cancer or pulmonary emphysema, but when it is being used it does not interfere with performance and for some may improve it. I cannot see anything good that can be said for marijuana. It has provoked much discussion about miscarriages of justice arising out of the attempt of the authorities to handle the problem. The fact that the problem of control is a difficult one does not warrant the legalization of marijuana or establish that it is a harmless substance no worse than tobacco not to be denied our youth in school or out.

The increase in incidence of addiction to narcotic drugs, especially heroin, particularly in the younger groups of the population of large urban centers such as New York City is of great concern to the community and has been the subject of many surveys and reports. It has become a major public health problem which in this country is not new. During the period between the end of World War I and the beginning of World War II, the mode of utilization of drugs by narcotic addicts underwent a significant change. The subcutaneous injection of solutions of morphine or heroin, which as you know is made from morphine, and the inhalation or sniffing of dry mixtures of heroin or cocaine were replaced by intravenous injection of crudely prepared solutions of drug mixtures of heroin diluted with other substances. The powdered drug, formerly mixed with large quantities of lactose and more recently with mannitol and quinine, is dissolved in a small amount of water heated to a boil by match flame in a crude receptacle such as a teaspoon or bottle cap.

The injection apparatus is usually improvised from an easily obtainable medicine dropper, its tip fitted tightly with a paper flange into the hub of a hypodermic needle, the latter usually obtained either by theft or illegal purchase. More recently, addicts have come into possession of discarded disposable plastic syringes, preferring to use only the needle in combination with a medicine dropper, the rubber bulb of which is easier to manipulate than the rigid plunger of a syringe for self-injection into a vein. The apparatus used by addicts is called "the works" and the intravenous addict a "mainline shooter." The injections are most often made into the superficial veins of the elbow fold and adjacent part of the forearm.

The solution of heroin is drawn up into the improvised syringe through a small wad of cotton which filters out solid particles of undissolved material. In recent years the powdered diluents with which the heroin is mixed have varied, and other bitter-tasting substances like quinine are added to disguise the strength of the sample and fraudulent substitutes. Quinine seems to have been first added as a diluent during the 1930's, a period when malaria was rampant among intravenous heroin addicts who had become infected directly as the result of the common use of unsterilized, unwashed syringes. The addicts and those who prepared the drug mixtures soon learned that quinine was a cure and preventive of malaria and began adding it as a diluent of the heroin mixtures. The remarkable fact remains that despite the marked increase in addiction, there have been no cases of artificially transmitted malaria in intravenous addictis in New York City since 1943. Recently some tertian malaria cases have been reported in California among addicted members of the military forces returned from Vietnam, who transmitted the diseases to other addicts. Quinine is not used as a diluent of heroin in California.

The possible admixture of poisonous substances like nicotine and cyanide also must be kept in mind and considered another reason for careful, complete toxicologic analysis in fatal cases. Diluted heroin mixtures sold to addicts by "pushers" are dispensed in glassine envelopes. These packets contain from 3 to 5 grains (0.2 to 0.3 gm) of diluted drug of which about 18 percent is heroin. There is considerable variation in total weight and strength of samples. The result of recent extensive detailed analysis of so-called "street" samples sold to addicts in New York City and confiscated by the police before or after sale are contained in the report by Fulton.

The practice of taking heroin intravenously is believed to have begun in Cairo, Egypt, in the 1920's and the method was copied by addicted seamen and in turn by other addicts in maritime cities. It soon became the method of choice almost everywhere for the utilization of narcotic drugs. The use in common of narcotics and the indiscriminate sharing of unsterilized improvised syringes for intravenous injection of drugs were the basis for a substantial epidemic of estivo-autumnal malaria among the addict population of New York and other urban centers in the 1930's.

Prior to 1943, there were relatively few deaths of addicts from overdosage. In addition to fatalities from malaria, there were occasional deaths caused by sepsis from large subcutaneous abscesses or by bacterial endocarditis secondary to infected needle punctures in the skin, septic thrombophlebitis in injected veins and tetanus in subcutaneous addicts.

During the period of World War II, heroin was practically unobtainable in the United States. Some addicts continued their addiction with the use of substitutes, such as the amphetamines and various barbiturates, and there were some fatalities among these from septic infection originating in the injection sites; but the number of deaths from this type of addiction was relatively small.

After the end of the war in 1945, with the resumption of unrestricted international travel and commerce, the very lucrative organized illegal traffic in heroin was resumed, and the drug was again smuggled into the United States from other countries in ever-increasing quantities. With this renewed supply there has been an alarming increase, especially in the larger urban centers like New York, in the incidence of intravenous narcotic addiction, an extremely expensive habit for the addict who, to satisfy the intense craving for heroin, becomes involved in other criminal activities ranging from theft to selling of drugs, robbery, assault, homicides and prostitution.

There are no precise figures on the incidence of narcotic addiction today. The estimates vary, but there is ample evidence from law enforcement, social welfare, health, hospital and voluntary agencies that it has been steadily increasing despite the concern and the diligent efforts of these groups to combat it.

An important indicator of the extent and distribution of narcotic addiction among the population is provided by the official investigation and determination of fatalities directly caused by such addiction and by evidence of addiction in persons dying of other causes, in which cases the addiction can reasonably be considered an important circumstance. There has been a steady increase in such fatalities during the last twenty years, especially in acute deaths directly caused by narcotism. The incidence has been greatest during the last three years.

The diagnosis of acute narcotism or of direct complications of narcotic addiction as a cause of death is based on an investigation of the circumstances of the death, the gross and microscopic pathologic findings of a complete autopsy, and toxicologic study, the last not productive of results in all cases.

There has been an increase in the total number as well as percentage of deaths from narcotic addiction, the increase becoming abrupt in 1959 and continuing in the years thereafter. The incidence of deaths in 1960 was 215. This first striking increase was noted in 1961, with an incidence of 311 deaths. The incidence for 1962, 1963 and 1964 remained high—roughly 300 per year.

The total number of deaths from narcotism from 1950 through 1959 was 1076. Approximately 1,400 additional fatalities were encountered in the next five-year period, making a total of about 2,500 deaths during the fifteen-year period from 1950 through 1964; approximately 1,400 or three fifths of all the deaths occurred during the last five years of the fifteen-year period studied. Of the 1,076 deaths during the first ten years through 1959, there were 823 males and 253 females; a sex ratio of approximately 4 to 1 that still continues. Deaths from narcotism occur with considerable, although uneven, frequency throughout the year.

During the next nine-year period from 1960 through 1968, there were 3,354 deaths. In 1969 there were more than 900 additional deaths making the total for the last decade about 4,300 or more than four times the incidence of the decade of 1950–1959.

The ratio of deaths from narcotism in blacks as compared with white persons is about 12 to 1. The ratio of deaths in male blacks compared with white males is 10 to 1; the female ratio, black to white, is greater, almost 15 to 1. The figures for white persons include approximately 34 percent males and 20 percent females of Puerto Rican extraction.

During the first ten years (1950–1959) about 10 percent of all deaths caused by narcotism occurred in adolescents or so-called teenagers. Approximately 25 percent of the deaths were in individuals under 25 years of age. About 60 percent of the deaths occurred below the age of 30 years, about 75 percent before the age of 35 years, and more than 90 percent of all narcotic deaths before the age of 50 years. It should be pointed out that in the beginning of the study from 1950 to 1959 some of those in the older age group who died had become addicted incident to medical administration of narcotics during palliative treatment of painful diseases or self-administration for mood elevation. Narcotic addiction encountered at the present time and the fatalities arising therefrom are predominantly among the younger age groups who comprise the bulk of so-called street addicts and who use heroin, in contrast to the older "medical" addicts who had become addicted to morphine.

The average mean age at death from narcotic addiction for

Drug Abuse

both sexes over the twelve-year span from 1950 through 1961 was twenty-nine years. There was a definite decrease in the average mean age of persons whose deaths resulted from narcotics over the twenty-year period studied.

Narcotic addiction and the fatalities arising therefrom are encountered predominantly in the younger age groups (from 15 to 39) who comprise the bulk of so-called street addicts who use heroin. During the decade 1950–1959, 110 of the 1,076 (about 10%) deaths occurred in adolescents or teenagers from 15 to 19 years of age. In the past decade from 1960–1969, 536 of the approximately 4,300 fatalities from addiction occurred in this adolescent group, an incidence of 12 percent.

For the first six months (through June 26) of 1970 there have been 389 deaths from narcotic (heroin) addiction. Of these 89 occurred in adolescents (14 to 19 years) and 300 between the ages of 20 and 40. During this six months period there were 120 addicts who died of other causes not directly related to the addiction. Many of these deaths were homicidal. This information is contained in Tables 6-I and 6-II.

TABLE 6-I

FATALITIES FROM NARCOTISM, FIRST 6 MONTHS OF 1970

Deaths Directly Due to Narcotism (acute reactions or direct complications; sepsis, tetanus, hepatitis, endocarditis, etc.)		Deaths Suspicious of Narcotism Pending Further Confirmation		
Age	*Incidence*	*Age*	*Incidence*	
14–19	81	14–19	8	
20–24	98	20–24	2	
25–29	78	25–29	5	
30–34	44	30–34	7	
35–39	29	35–39	2	
40 & up	32	40 & up	3	
	—		—	
	281		19	
Total	362		27	389

The highest percentage of addiction deaths and presumably of total addiction occurs in the unskilled worker or laborer group, with a lower incidence in the semiskilled and skilled worker

TABLE 6-II
ADDICTS DYING OF OTHER CAUSES, NOT DIRECT COMPLICATIONS
FIRST 6 MONTHS OF 1970

Age	Incidence
14–19	13
20–24	26
25–29	25
30–34	23
35–29	13
40 & up	20
Total	120

groups. Unskilled workers provide the highest percentage of addicts and deaths from addiction and skilled workers the lowest percentage.

Geographic Distribution

In New York City the greatest number of narcotic deaths occurred in the Borough of Manhattan. Approximately 75 percent of all such deaths in New York City formerly took place in this borough. A comparison of the total number of deaths in each borough indicates that the Manhattan incidence was more than twice that of the Bronx, which had the second highest percentage of narcotic addiction fatalities. In recent years, the incidence of fatalities has increased in all the boroughs.

The relatively lower incidence of narcotic deaths in jurisdictions outside of New York City is subject to question and in part may be explained by a reluctance of the local medical examiner or coroner to attribute a death to narcotism in the absence of confirmation by chemical analysis. This reluctance may also account for the lack of positive reports of such deaths from other jurisdictions. It is the opinion of the writer and that of his associates that a diagnosis of acute death from narcotic addiction is more reliably arrived at from the investigation of the circumstances under which the body is found and the findings of the complete postmortem examination than from the toxicologic analysis, which has proved revealing in less than half the cases. The discovery rate of these deaths would have been considerably

lower if one had insisted on chemical verification. It is also probable that many deaths from acute narcotism have gone unrecognized because of failure to study the scene of death and recognize
the subtle findings which are easily overlooked or misinterpreted
by the inexperienced observer.

Place of Death

The character of the premises in which the narcotic addict is
found dead is very significant and a useful circumstance for
arousing suspicion on the part of the medical investigator or
examiner that he is being confronted with a narcotic death even
in the absence of more positive evidence. As a rule, the addict
selects a place for self-administration of heroin where there is
some assurance of privacy, or he may indulge himself with one
or more addicts in surroundings where it would be likely that the
activity would not be discovered. The location of the dead body
of an addict on a roof, in a hallway, an elevator, on a stairway or
in a vacant lot does not establish that death occurred in such
location, and the possibility must always be kept in mind that
the body was removed, either before or after death, from the
actual place where the fatal injection was administered. Cases have
been encountered in which the bodies of dead addicts had been
transported to distant places in other jurisdictions to conceal the
original circumstances. Bodies of deceased addicts have also been
discovered in lavatories, bathrooms, seated on chairs or lying in
bed. In some instances, the body is not discovered until putrefac-
tion has set in and directed attention to its presence. Not infrequently the apparatus or "works," consisting of improvised
syringes, needles, empty and full packets of heroin mixtures,
spoons or bottle caps with holders devised from bobby pins,
matches, absorbent cotton and crudely fashioned tourniquets are
found alongside the body of the deceased; in some cases death or
loss of consciousness has occurred so rapidly that the tourniquet is
still in place on the arm and the needle of the syringe stuck in the
skin, with the syringe partly filled with blood mixed with residual
heroin solution, the blood indicative of penetration of the needle
into the vein. Just as there are scenes to which the body of a

victim has been transported without any of the telltale injection equipment any longer in evidence, so there are others where the death has actually taken place but from which the injection materials have been surreptitiously removed by interested parties for the purpose of disguising the true nature of death. Many cases initially are unlabeled or incorrectly labeled, and it is easy for an inexperienced pathologist to fail to recognize the cause of death at autopsy.

The subcutaneous rather than intravenous injection of narcotics is more prevalent among women addicts and more apt to be complicated by relatively less rapid sepsis and abscess formation and other complications. Thus more women addicts are likely to get to the hospital while still alive. Tetanus is also more likely to occur in such addicts, and the manifestation of this complication usually leads to hospitalization.

Pathologic Findings and Causes of Death

The largest number of deaths result from "acute reactions," and in the compilation for the twelve-year period from 1950 through 1961 the percentage of these cases was 48. Although this constituted about half of the total, it is important to point out that in the recent years of the study, with a considerably higher death rate from addiction, the "acute reaction" deaths have greatly exceeded the incidence of such acute deaths in the earlier years and of other less rapid fatal complications of narcotic addiction.

Unexpected acute deaths may occur in addicts who inject themselves with heroin mixtures even though other addicts who take the same usual aliquot dose from the same sample at the same time suffer nothing other than the usual effect. The same dose taken in the same way may be unpredictably fatal. In some fatal acute cases, the rapidity and type of reaction do not suggest simple overdosage but rather an overwhelming shock-like reaction due to sensitivity to the injected material. The toxicologic examination of the tissues in such fatalities, in which the reaction was so rapid that the syringe and needle were still in the vein of the victim when the body was found, demonstrated only the presence of the alkaloid and not overdosage. In other acute deaths, in which the circumstances and autopsy findings were positive, the toxicologist could not detect any evidence of alkaloid in the tissues or body fluids. Thus, there does not appear to be a quantitative correlation between the acute fulminating lethal effect and the amount of heroin taken, as there is with overdosage of morphine and other alkaloids.

External Findings

In the acute fatal reactions to the intravenous injection of crude mixtures of heroin and other substances, in addition to those not infrequent instances in which collapse and death were so rapid that the syringe was found in the vein of the victim or on the floor after having dropped out of the vein, and the tourniquet was still in place on the arm, examination of the body in most cases also revealed very suggestive, almost characteristic, appearances.

It is not uncommon to find an abundance of partly dried frothy white edema fluid oozing from the nostrils or mouth indicative of severe pulmonary edema. The skin over the superficial veins of the elbow folds (antecubital fossae) and adjacent portion of the forearms may reveal one or two fresh needle punctures which are not always conspicuous and can be confirmed by incision through the immediately adjacent skin to demonstrate the subcutaneous hemorrhage emanating from the punctured vein. The injection sites are usually not difficult to discern and are readily confirmed by incision of the skin. Careful scrutiny is sometimes needed because the needle puncture may be located in other areas and be difficult to find, especially in addicts who do not have the usual characteristic row of closely placed pigmented needle-puncture scars in the skin overlying the veins used for intravenous injection of heroin.

It is remarkable how many pigmented needle-puncture scars may be found in the skin delineating the superficial veins, usually in the elbow fossa but sometimes throughout their continuity from shoulder to wrist. Despite the numerous punctures and nonsterile technic of injection, there may be no more effect on the involved vein than a chronic fibrous thickening of its wall and induration of the overlying skin, indicative of a low-grade inflammatory and reparative reaction incident to the needle punctures and repeated injection of irritating material.

The involved veins occasionally become thrombosed and grossly infected, with the development of purulent thrombophlebitis. Intravenous addicts are likely to penetrate the skin and underlying vein perpendicularly. It is curious that despite the lack of surgical cleanliness, the veins that are used repeatedly by intravenous addicts show less incidence of closure by thrombosis than the veins of patients subjected to repeated punctures by physicians for medical purposes. The pigmentation of the skin over the injected veins is the result of the introduction of insoluble foreign material contained in the crude solution of the heroin mixture.

The presence of old pigmented scars in the skin overlying the superficial veins is diagnostic of chronic intravenous narcotic addiction. Fresh needle punctures may be easy or difficult to find and can only be confirmed by incision of the skin to reveal the fresh hemorrhage extravasated into the subcutaneous tissue from the punctured veins. Chemical analysis of tissue from such fresh puncture sites may or may not reveal evidence of the narcotic drug. In recently addicted persons or in more fastidious individuals, the skin over the veins may not be conspicuously scarred, and careful scrutiny including incision is required to detect the fresh injection sites.

The subcutaneous injection of narcotics, a method encountered more often in women and in older addicts, is usually indulged in without any pretense of sterilization, and crude unsterilized solutions of the drug may be injected through the clothing into the skin of the shoulders, thighs, arms, abdomen and sides of the chest. At these sites, severe inflammation and subcutaneous abscesses frequently develop, and the latter may discharge through the skin with the formation of numerous conspicuous, characteristic, round and oval or irregularly shaped, unevenly pigmented depressed skin scars. Fatal sepsis may complicate the abscesses. In some cases repeated subcutaneous injections merely produce a diffuse uneven induration of the skin and subcutaneous tissue, especially in the thighs or arms, without abscess formation or skin scars and only evident on palpation.

As already mentioned, the subcutaneous injections may also introduce tetanus organisms and give rise to fatal tetanus infection with characteristic symptoms. Such cases are more frequently encountered in women than in men addicts, and death is more likely to occur after hospitalization for convulsive seizures and trismus. A possible reason why tetanus is less frequent in addicted men is that working men, especially in the laborer class, are more likely to be immunized with tetanus toxoid as part of a prophylactic program designed to combat this disease. It is interesting to note that in New York City in recent years, fatalities from tetanus are observed almost exclusively in the narcotic addict population.

A method formerly used by addicts who were unable to obtain hypodermic needles with which to inject themselves was to jab large safety pins into the skin to produce a channel into which the tip of the medicine dropper could be forced and the solution squeezed directly into the tissues. This technic resulted in considerably more septic infection and scarring. In addition, most of the injected solution ran out of the puncture and was wasted from the addict's point of view. This crude method is now rarely used.

SUMMARY

This report includes introductory background information describing the evolution of narcotic addiction as it is encountered today in the large metropolis of New York City. It is based on thirty-seven years of experience in officially investigating the circumstances and determining the cause of all deaths of addicts occurring during that period of time.

The increasing incidence and total number of deaths due to addiction are of great significance and provide an important indicator of the extent of the problem. At present narcotic addiction is the greatest single cause of death of adolescents and young adults from 15 to 35—exceeding deaths from any other single cause: accident, suicide, homicide or natural disease.

REFERENCES

1. Helpern, M., and Rho, Yong-Myun: Deaths from Narcotism in New York City: Incidence, Circumstances, and Postmortem Findings.

2. White House Conference on Narcotic and Drug Abuse, Proceedings, September 27 and 28, 1962, Washington, D.C., U.S. Government Printing Office, 1963.

3. President's Advisory Commission on Narcotic and Drug Abuse, Final Report, Washington, D.C., U.S. Government Printing Office, November, 1963.

4. Report on Drug Addiction II, New York Academy of Medicine, Committee on Public Health, New York City, 1963.

5. Helpern, M.: Epidemic of fatal estivo-autumnal malaria among drug addicts in New York City, *Am. J. Surg., 26*:111 (1934) .

6. Fulton, C.C.: An analytical study of confiscated samples of narcotic drugs, *Int. Microfilm J. Legal Med.,* (Fall) 1965, vol. 1.

7. Siegel, H., Helpern, M., and Ehrenreich, T.: The rapidity of death in acute fatal intravenous narcotism, presented at International Congress of Legal Medicine, Paris, September, 1964.

8. *Idem:* The diagnosis of death from intravenous narcotism, with emphasis on the pathologic aspects, presented in part at the seventeenth annual meeting, American Academy of Forensic Sciences, Chicago, Illinois, February 25, 1965; *J. Forensic Sci., 11*:1 (Jan.) 1966.

9. Huntington, R.: Reappearance of tertian malaria in intravenous narcotic addicts in California, verbal communication, 1971.

Chapter 7

Alcoholism As Related to Drug Addiction—A Medical Examiner's View

Michael M. Baden

PRESENT PROBLEMS of heroin addiction and drug abuse are the result of past unwillingness and inability of society, the medical profession and psychiatry to deal with other mental health problems similarly manifest by self-destructive behavior: in particular, alcoholism and suicide. It may appear presumptuous for a pathologist to stress to psychiatrists the mental health aspects of substance abuse, but it is the medical examiner who investigates the ultimate failure—the unnatural death that is potentially preventable—and perhaps this experience with the dead may help to identify questions for which you who treat the living will provide answers.

The majority of heroin addicts whose deaths we investigate have had histories of antisocial activity such as truancy, juvenile delinquency or arrests, or diagnosed psychiatric illness prior to use of narcotics. Similarly, interviews with families and friends of deceased alcoholics often reveal social maladjusments prior to onset of alcoholism. Twenty percent of the addicts we autopsy are also alcoholics.

The psychiatrist much prefers to treat the grateful normal neurotic who is appreciative, accepts the physician's status and expertise, and pays his bills rather than the addict—or alcoholic—who is dishonest, manipulative, not appreciative, does not accept the doctor's status, steals and does not pay his bills. However, if psychiatrists do not contribute their unique expertise to providing solutions to these problems, no one else may be able to; good intentions, logic, concern and hard work are not, in themselves, sufficient to treat mental illness. Prerequisite for the treatment of any symptom or disease is an accurate initial diagnosis: Is the addict or alcoholic schizophrenic, neurotic, sociopathic? Is he responding to peer pressure or socioeconomic conditions? Is he 11 years old, 21, 61? All substance abusers are not alike and proper diagnosis is mandatory to begin to determine appropriate treatment. Are we to abdicate the taking and interpretation of a mental status to the bright ex-addict or well-meaning community worker?

Traditionally, society's concern for the alcoholic, the addict and the suicidal person has not been directed toward identifying, understanding and treating the individual's underlying emotional disturbances or even to determine if such disturbance is present, but rather toward preventing inconvenience to others. Last year more than 1200 persons died by suicide in New York City (probably half of whom had seen physicians within two weeks of death), but as long as the person jumping from a window does not land on someone, nobody cares—we do not have a single official suicide prevention program in this city. Alcoholism directly caused or contributed to more than 6000 deaths in New York City last year with little public concern and less than $1,000,000 allocated for alcoholism programs. There has been great concern, however, about the heroin addict, 1000 of whom died last year, because he steals from others so $40,000,000 has been allocated by New York City for narcotic programs.

Unfortunately, in our concreteness we still attempt to treat the suicidal patient by removing the razor used to cut the wrists; we attempt to treat the alcoholic by removing the bottle; and we treat the addict by removing the heroin or by giving maintenance narcotics. We will do anything, no matter how irrelevant and how previously unsuccessful, except deal with the more abstract, more difficult to define and measure, but more pertinent issues of mental health. We suture the wrist, control the delirium tremens or hepatic failure, painlessly detoxify the addict in withdrawal and with the satisfaction of accomplishment assume that we have done something while giving no consideration to the long-term management necessary to prevent reoccurrences.

Unfortunately, as Dr. Helpern has indicated, there has been a marked increase in teenaged addict deaths in the past two years: in 1966, 33 narcotic users died who were 19 years old or younger; in 1969 there were 248 such deaths and this rate has continued in 1970. Some of these young people do not have antisocial histories; it appears that the continued existence in the community of so many addicts who derive from the emotionally ill or marginal groups has created, perhaps even encouraged, a peer group attractive to their normal and mentally healthier colleagues.

Current heroin use has been referred to by some as an epidemic and I have no quarrel with such use of the term; instead of a bacterium, the infective agent is the addicted peer role model. The Board of Education has stated that there are at least 35,000 heroin users of school age in New York City; yet we do nothing to identify, isolate and treat these students. We isolate the person with smallpox or tuberculosis so that proper treatment can be provided and others do not become infected. The same must be done for the addict so that he does not die from the next injection and the students sitting next to him do not become infected.

It is apparent to me as a medical examiner that one reason for relative complacency about alcoholism is the lack of appreciation of the true extent of alcoholism as a cause of death. Of 88,-000 deaths in New York City last year 6000 were related to alcoholism but in only 1716 instances was alcoholism stated on the death certificate. Two factors contribute greatly to this widespread underreporting: fears of stigmatization by the certifying physician and the nature of the death certificate itself. When the older alcoholic dies, his physician often feels more comfortable in listing another cause of death such as heart disease, which is usually more acceptable to the family. Should the diagnosis of alcohol-induced liver failure be unavoidable, the doctor may list cirrhosis as the cause of death without including alcoholism, perhaps with the rationalization that alcoholism is implicit in such diagnosis; but this is not understood by the statisticians, epidemiologists and program planners who interpret these data. Certainly in New York City much more than 90 percent of cirrhosis of the liver is due to alcoholism. However, last year in this city there were 1383 deaths recorded as due to cirrhosis associated with alcoholism and 1746 as due to cirrhosis not associated with alcoholism—patently misleading data. Further, if the alcoholic dies of a natural disease due to alcoholism such as pancreatitis, lobar pneumonia, carcinoma of the liver or various nervous system disorders, the alcoholism is often improperly not indicated. Thus, these data reflect more the individual biases of physicians rather than true differences in cause of death.

Further, the death certificate requires that when a chronic alcoholic while drunk drives his car into a tree, the cause of death include the traumatic injuries incurred and there is no provision for indicating the predisposing alcoholism. Last year alcoholism was a significant factor and was found at autopsy to be present in approximately 50 percent of all persons dying violently in New York City, which included automobile fatalities (1000), homicides (1050), narcotism (1000), accidental falls (850), fires (325) and drownings (50). It was also significant in a large percentage of the 1200 suicides. In none of these deaths was alcoholism indicated on the death certificate. If a person who has been a chronic alcoholic for thirty years, a severe problem to his family and friends, and a drain on the community's resources dies because he falls to the ground and injures his brain or is stabbed by his wife, there is no way to presently indicate alcoholism for purposes of vital statistics so that the truer data can be used in effective alcohol prevention program planning. More difficult to approximate are the numbers of persons who die because of the actions of drunken people, such as the many persons who die in fires that are the result of the carelessness of someone who is drunk or pedestrians struck by drunken drivers.

The Latin motto on the wall at the Office of the Chief Medical Examiner indicates that "this is the place where death delights to help the living." There is much to be learned from the dead alcoholics and addicts—not only relative to the true incidences of these diseases but also toward their identification, not only by postmortem findings but also by premortem histories; these histories indicate that it is naive to consider each type of drug abuse as unique and requiring a single specific solution: one antidote for the heroin addict, another for the alcoholic, another for abusers of barbiturates or amphetamines or LSD or catnip or mace, et cetera. We must begin to deal with the broad and common reasons, many of these psychiatric, for substance abuse, for self-destructive behavior, for inability to function productively in an increasingly complex society. The medical profession in general and psychiatry in particular can no longer abdicate their responsibilities in these areas to those who do not possess their uniquely pertinent training and expertise.

Chapter 8

The Assessment of the Abuse Potentiality of Narcotic Analgesics

William R. Martin

~~~~~~~~~~~~~~~~~~~~~~~~~~~~~~~~~~

THE ROLE OF THE ADDICTION Research Center in this effort has been to asses the abuse potentiality of newly developed narcotic analgesics in man. These efforts have transcended this initial purpose, because in assessing the abuse potentiality of new analgesics, methods and criteria have been developed that can aid in the detection of the abuse potentiality of other types of drugs. One of the most effective ways of limiting drug abuse at the present time is through prevention. It is obvious that the number and types of psychoactive drugs that will be available will increase and some of these new drugs will be quite addictive. If their abuse potentiality can be identified early and their use limited, the size of the addiction problem will be minimized. Further, through these efforts new therapeutic modalities of low toxicity and abuse potentiality that may be effective in the treatment of psychopathy and neurotic conditions may be developed.

The effort to assess the abuse potentiality of the narcotics was started over thirty-five years ago by Dr. C. K. Himmelsbach. One of the important contributions of Himmelsbach was the characterization of the morphine or heroin abstinence syndrome in man. He also clearly demonstrated the phenomena of cross-tolerance and cross-substitution of morphine-like drugs in man. This was one of the very early methods that was used in identifying morphine-like properties of new drugs. Patients who were dependent on morphine or heroin were given experimental drugs,

Note: A complete discussion of the problem herein discussed with pertinent references can be found in references cited at the end of this chapter.

and the ability of these drugs to suppress abstinence was assessed. Both Dr. Himmelsbach and his successor, Dr. Harris Isbell, were clearly cognizant that the ability of a drug to produce physical dependence was only one factor that determined its abuse potentiality and that changes in subjective state were also important. Initially, subjective changes were assessed by asking post-addict patients whether the experimental drug was "dope" or not. Subsequently, Fraser and Isbell developed the single dose questionnaire. When given doses of narcotics, patients are asked if they "feel" the drug and to identify it. They are then asked to complete a checklist of symptoms which includes such items as "turning of the stomach," which may be related to the emetic actions of morphine; "itchy skin"; "relaxation"; "coasting," a type of apathetic sedation; "soap-boxing" or becoming talkative and loquacious; a "pleasant sick"; "driving" or feelings of energy; "sleepiness"; "nervousness"; or "drunkenness." Finally, they are asked whether they like the medication and to indicate on an ordinal scale how much they like it. Subsequently, pupils are photographed and measured. This measure helps validate subjective responses. I will not go into the technical details of analyzing the data that are thus acquired, but will suffice to say that dose response relationships are obtained for pupils as well as opiate signs and symptoms and observers' and patients' "liking" scores. The relative potency of the experimental drug in relationship to a standard drug (usually morphine) is then calculated.

An analysis of the signs and symptoms produced by heroin and morphine revealed that the frequency of certain signs and symptoms such as drive, coasting, itching and being relaxed were dose related; whereas, others were not. Subsequently, it was learned that frequency of the signs and symptoms of drunkenness and sleepiness was dose related for barbiturates and the narcotic antagonists cyclazocine and nalorphine, but not for morphine or heroin. The analysis of signs and symptoms has thus provided another means of distinguishing morphine-like drugs from other types of drugs.

More recently, drug scales developed by Drs. Haertzen and Hill have been used in classifying the subjective effects of drugs.

These drug scales have been derived from a 550-item questionnaire called the Addiction Research Center Inventory that contains many drug-sensitive items. A variety of scales have been developed using different criteria groups. An LSD scale was developed which contains items that are frequently endorsed by patients while under the effects of LSD but not under a no-drug or placebo condition. Similarly, a pentobarbital-chlorpromazine-alcohol group scale (PCAG) was developed which consists of those items which differentiate these three drugs from the response to all other drugs studied. A final scale that will be of immediate interest is the morphine-Benzedrine® group scale (MBG) which differentiates morphine and amphetamine from other drugs studied. The LSD scale has items which reflect feelings such as nervousness, anxiety and sensory distortions. The PCAG scale has items that are related to lack of motivation, apathy and sluggishness. The MBG scale contains items which reflect feelings of well-being, efficiency and competence. The narcotic antagonists increase the scores on the LSD scale and the PCAG scale in a dose-related fashion, but do not increase the MBG scale scores. In contrast, narcotic analgesics such as morphine increase MBG scale scores in a dose-related fashion, but not PCAG and LSD scale scores. Thus, antagonists such as nalorphine and cyclazocine produce one kind of subjective effects; morphine another.

I would like to return to the problem of physical dependence. Himmelsbach showed that patients dependent on morphine exhibited an abstinence syndrome when withdrawn which had specific symptoms and signs. Himmelsbach weighted each sign and used the sum of these weighted signs as an indication of the severity of abstinence. A subsequent analysis of data acquired at the Addiction Research Center by Drs. Himmelsbach, Williams and Fraser indicated that the relative contribution of each sign to the total score remained the same regardless of the dose upon which subjects were dependent and the intensity of the abstinence syndrome. Subsequently, while studying the dependence-producing properties of cyclazocine and nalorphine, it was found that the abstinence syndrome observed following withdrawal of patients receiving large doses of these drugs had quite a different distribution of points. Thus, the two largest sources of points for the morphine abstinence syndrome were due to an increase in blood pressure and increase in respiratory rate; whereas, an increase in body temperature was the largest source of points for the nalorphine and cyclazocine abstinence syndromes. Using a correlation analysis, it was found that there was a significant correlation between the sources of abstinence points for cyclazocine and nalorphine, but there was no significant correlation between these drugs and morphine. These data concerning differences in subjective effects and the abstinence syndromes, as well as kinetic arguments, have led to the conclusion that two distinct types of receptors, a morphine type of receptor and a nalorphine type of receptor, are responsible for the dependence-producing properties of these types of drugs and for their analgesic properties. Although I do not have time to provide detailed information, we have accumulated evidence that drugs that interact with both the morphine-type receptor and the nalorphine-type receptor can differ in their intrinsic activities. Further findings suggest that there are drugs that occupy both the morphine and the nalorphine-type receptors.

I would like to conclude with two points: (a) the clinical tools herein described can be used as bases for formulating and testing hypotheses concerning the mode of action of centrally acting drugs, and (b) these same tools can be used in the development and testing of new therapeutic agents.

REFERENCES

1. Martin, W.R.: Assessment of the dependence producing potentialities of narcotic analgesics. In *International Encyclopedia of Pharmacology and Therapeutics,* edited by C. Radouco-Thomas and L. Lasagna. Glasgow, Pergamon, 1966, Sec. 6, Vol. I, pp. 155-180.
2. Martin, W.R.: Opioid antagonists. *Pharmacol Rev, 19:*463-521, 1967.

Chapter 9

The Measurement of Addiction Potential by Self-Injection Experiments in Monkeys

Gerald A. Deneau

~~~~~~~~~~~~~~~~~~~~~~~~~~~~~~

S EVERAL CLASSES OF DRUGS are abused by man. The abuse of each class of drugs can be characteristically defined as consisting of a predictable set of phenomena. With the narcotic analgesics, abuse begins when an individual experiences pleasureable or euphoric effects from the drug. The individual then injects the drug repeatedly in order to maintain or to reexperience this state of well-being. At this stage, the individual may be said to have developed psychological dependence on the drug. As drug use continues, tolerance develops which necessitates an increase in dosage in order to regain the desired degree of euphoria. Continued use of the drug also leads to the development of physiological dependence. When this occurs the patient becomes ill and exhibits a characteristic abstinence syndrome unless minimum tissue levels of the drug are maintained continuously. Meanwhile the patient's interests have narrowed down to the point where his only interest is in maintaining an adequate supply of the drug and he has thus become a nonproductive member of society. Additionally, the patient nearly always resorts to crime in order to obtain the money to support his habit. The nonproductive life and the crime are forms of antisocial behavior which burden society and cause us to be concerned with the patient's abuse of drugs.

A somewhat similar progression of events occurs with the sedative-hypnotic class of drugs. Pharmacologically speaking, the

Note: This research was supported by USPHS Grants MH 2814, MH 5320 and MH 12277.

This paper won the 1970 Best-Paper-Award donated by the Gralnick Foundation, Port Chester, New York.

abuse of these drugs is essentially the same as the abuse of alcohol although the predisposing factors which lead to abuse may be quite different in the two cases. Individuals may find that they cannot sleep without a sedative. This situation may then progress so that sedatives are taken during the day for the relief of anxiety and tension, thus psychological dependence is established. Continued use of sedatives leads to slight tolerance development, but there is always a tendency for the patient to overdose himself and to show the signs of incoordination and impaired mental function typical of alcoholic intoxication. Under these conditions the patient is not only in a state of diminished productivity but is also a menace to himself and society whenever he drives a car or makes critical decisions involving others. Thus these agents produce a more or less continuous form of psychotoxicity as a direct result of their pharmacological action.

Prolonged use of sedatives also results in the development of physiological dependence. This is a different and medically a more serious type of physiological dependence than that which develops to the narcotic analgesics. The abstinence syndrome which results upon decreased ingestion of sedatives is characterized by psychosis and grand mal convulsions—in other words, the DTs. Thus, a second form of psychotoxity is associated with the sedatives—in this case it is caused by under ingestion.

The stimulants, such as cocaine and amphetamine, produce an exhilarating euphoria. There is a strong tendency on the part of users to take repeated injections of the drug in sprees which last for several days. During this time there is a continual narrowing of the subject's attention to some trivial matter such as the reflection of light off a doorknob. The fascination is so intense that the patient cannot be detracted for any significant period of time. This same tendency to narrow the focus of thought may also lead to the development of drug-induced psychoses. The resulting antisocial behavior is unpredictable but potentially very dangerous.[1]

Adventurism or cultism may contribute more to the formation of psychological dependence on the so-called hallucinogenic drugs than do their euphoric or anxiety-relieving properties. There is no need to document here the well-known and diverse forms of psychotoxicity and antisocial behavior which result from the use of this class of drugs.

The pharmacological effects and the biological phenomena such as tolerance and physiological dependence vary widely from class to class of drugs as well as within classes. There are, however, two aspects which are constant features of all forms of drug abuse. These are (a) the development, by some individuals, of a psychological dependence on a drug and (b) the misuse of the drug to the extent that the effects of the drug produce psychotoxicity which results in antisocial behavior.

If a laboratory procedure would accurately predict addiction potential of drugs, it would have to somehow measure psychological dependence and psychotoxicity. The subject would have to somehow tell the observer whether he enjoyed the effects of a drug sufficiently to want to repeat the experience and the observer would have to determine whether and to what extent the subject's behavior was impaired as a result of the drug effects.

We had been using the rhesus monkey for a number of years to evaluate the physiological dependence capacity of narcotic analgesics. We had also been attempting, with rather disappointing results, to get monkeys to self-administer narcotic analgesics by means of drinking solutions of the drug in preference to water. While some monkeys voluntarily drank enough morphine solution to become physiologically dependent, they refused to drink solutions of synthetic narcotics when these were substituted for morphine even though the synthetic narcotics (levorphanol, methadone) were essentially equivalent to morphine by most pharmacological tests. Weeks[2] then developed a procedure in the rat, using an indwelling intravenous catheter, whereby drug solutions could be automatically infused or the animal could press a lever to activate the injector. Using this principle, we developed a procedure whereby the rhesus monkey could, if he wished, voluntarily initiate and maintain intravenous self-administration of drugs.

Monkeys are semirestrained by means of a light tubular stainless steel harness and flexible arm. A catheter, implanted in the jugular vein, passes through the flexible arm to the exterior of the

cage where it is connected to an injector. The monkey can activate the injector by pressing a switch which is located on the wall
of the cage or the injector can be activated with an automatic
timer. A naive monkey is placed in the equipment for a few days
during which it becomes accustomed to the conditions of semi-
restraint. The catheter is then implanted and a saline solution is
automatically infused during the course of recovery from the
minor surgery. Two switches are then mounted on the wall of the
cage. The monkey can activate the injector by pressing either
switch but activation through only one of the switches actually
delivers a solution to the monkey. Pressing the other switch
causes the drug solution to be returned to the reservoir. The
monkey's baseline operant behavior is determined with saline in
the system. The saline is then replaced with a solution of a test
drug. The individual dose of the test drug is usually that which
produces barely detectable overt effects.

It is assumed that a monkey has developed psychological dependence on a drug if he voluntarily initiates and maintains a
pattern of self-administration of the drug. Psychotoxicity can
manifest itself in a variety of ways—by the appearance of motor
incoordination, by the loss of ability to perform tasks involving
short-term memory, by the loss of natural curiosity, by the appearance of bizarre behavior and by the development of physiological dependence.

Because of our long-standing interest in the narcotic analgesics,
morphine was the first drug we tested. Seven of eleven monkeys
spontaneously initiated self-administration of morphine—all in a
similar manner. All of the monkeys gradually increased their dose
over a period of five or six weeks and then maintained a stable
daily intake. During the period of escalating dosage they were
drowsy and apathetic; thereafter, they were less active than control monkeys but appeared normal to casual observation. The
monkeys took little or no drug throughout the night. No monkey
voluntarily discontinued the self-administration of morphine.

The four monkeys which did not spontaneously initiate self-
administration of morphine were given programmed injections
at four-hour intervals. Within three weeks all of these monkeys
established a typical pattern of self-administration.

Whenever saline was substituted for morphine solution or whenever a mechanical failure occurred, the monkeys displayed typical, severe abstinence signs. With morphine, at least, this procedure permitted the demonstration of psychological dependence and psychotoxicity in laboratory subjects. It remained to be determined whether the procedure was suitable for all classes of drugs which man abuses.

Pentobarbital and ethanol were studied as representative of the sedative hypnotics. In both cases, some, but not all, monkeys voluntarily initiated self-administration of the drug. With both drugs the monkeys maintained themselves in a state of extreme intoxication. As soon as they recovered sufficiently from the last dose to stagger or stumble back to the switch, they took another dose of the drug. Physiological dependence developed to both drugs. The abstinence syndromes were indistinguishable and included grand mal convulsions and bizarre behavior which indicated the monkeys were probably experiencing hallucinations.

One aspect of marked contrast between the pentobarbital and ethanol monkeys was their nutritional status. The monkeys receiving pentobarbital ate more than normal amounts of food and grew fat. Those on ethanol ate very little food and became emaciated. In addition, some of these monkeys developed peripheral neuritis and dermatitis. It is presumed that the caloric content of the ethanol suppressed the monkeys' appetites to the point that they developed frank signs of vitamin deficiencies. Another difference between the two groups was that the pentobarbital monkeys never voluntarily abstained whereas the alcohol monkeys did occasionally abstain voluntarily—even though they experienced serious abstinence syndromes.

Cocaine and d-amphetamine were studied as representative of the CNS stimulants. The monkeys on cocaine self-administered the drug continuously in sprees which lasted several days. During the periods of self-administration they displayed increasingly severe signs of psychotoxicity. These signs included tremors, loss of control of fine motor movements and postural control, repetitive stereotyped behavior and apparent paresthesia as evidenced by chewing of the forearms, fingers and toes. The monkeys also frequently behaved in ways suggesting that they were experiencing visual and auditory hallucinations. Finally, grand mal convulsions occurred as a result of cumulative toxicity. Upon discontinuance of self-administration, either voluntary or imposed, the monkeys slept, regained their appetite and responded normally to environmental stimuli.

Similar psychological dependence and psychotoxicity was demonstrated by monkeys which self-administered d-amphetamine although the signs were less severe than with cocaine. Convulsions and self-mutilation were not observed in the amphetamine monkeys.

Of the hallucinogens, mescaline and LSD-25 were studied. None of four monkeys initiated self-administration of mescaline either spontaneously or after one month of programmed administration at doses of 1 to 10 mg/kg every two hours. Severe signs of autonomic stimulation were observed after each injection but no abstinence signs were observed upon discontinuance of programmed administration.

With LSD-25, four of six monkeys took occasional doses (0 to 4 per day) of 10μg/kg. These monkeys showed no overt signs of disrupted behavior although we have no way of determining whether they experienced distortions in sensory perception. In one instance a mechanical failure caused one monkey to receive twelve injections in immediate succession. This monkey became semicatatonic and refused to respond to any stimulus for forty-eight hours.

Among the many centrally acting drugs which are not abused by man, several have been studied in the monkey. These include nalorphine, chlorpromazine and imipramine. In no instance has a monkey voluntarily initiated self-administration of any of these drugs.

Ideally, for the laboratory evaluations of addiction potential it would be necessary to (a) have an experimental subject whose behavior towards drugs closely resembles that of man; (b) determine whether the drug will be self-administered by at least some of the animals (i.e. demonstrate psychological dependence); (c) determine what form of psychotoxicity results from self-administration of the drug; and (d) compare the psychotoxicity of the test drug with that of known drugs.

To what extent does the present procedure approach the ideal?

The monkey's behavioral repertoire more closely resembles man's than that of any other experimental animal in common laboratory use. The monkey's response to centrally acting drugs in most cases is qualitatively similar to that of man. In the studies described here, the hallucinogens represent an exception. One would predict from our results that the narcotic analgesics, the short-acting sedatives and the stimulants would all have high abuse liability. One would also predict that mescaline and LSD would not present serious abuse problems. We conclude from this that the demonstration of psychological dependence and psychotoxicity in the monkey has high predictive validity but that negative findings, especially with the hallucinogens, are not as meaningful. Another limitation of this procedure is that only those drugs which are soluble in water can be evaluated.

In summary, the measurement of addiction potential by self-administration experiments in monkeys is, at present, the best laboratory procedure available. The procedure is not ideal, however, and should not be used as the one and only basis for predicting abuse liability. All available pharmacological information should always be considered in making such predictions.

REFERENCES

1. Deneau, G., Yanagita, T., and Seevers, M.H.: Self-administration of psychoactive substances by the monkey; A measure of psychological dependence. *Psychopharmacologia, 16:*30-48, 1969.
2. Weeks, J.R.: Experimental morphine addiction: Method for automatic intravenous injections in unrestrained rats. *Science, 138:*143-144, 1962.

Chapter 10

Clinical Diagnosis of Heroin Addiction

Barry Stimmel

~~~~~~

To state that the prevalence of drug abuse and dependency is increasing is to belabor the obvious. The medical examiner's office in New York City has reported heroin addiction to be the leading cause of death in men from 13 to 35 years of age.[1] The rise in mortality among teenage addicts is also startling, many youths are being found with signs of minimal heroin addiction, some with only one needle puncture site noted. It is therefore important for the physician to be able to identify the heroin-dependent person as early as possible in an effort to prevent the major complications of heroin addiction.

At the present time many methods exist for the diagnosis of the heroin addict. They range from a complete history and physical examination to more specific measures such as the Nalline® test and actual laboratory analysis for heroin utilizing ultraspectrophotometry, chromatography or spectrophotoflurometry. However, in order to utilize these aids, one must first think of the possibility of the patient being dependent on heroin. This, unfortunately, may not be apparent from the history. Many individuals are quite hesitant to admit heroin abuse in fear of the social stigma attached at the peer and family level in addition to the legal implications of their disclosure. Others may prefer to manufacture physical complaints in an attempt to obtain medications through legal channels. Finally, a person who admits to heroin dependency may be reluctant to talk about his abuse of other drugs in fear of its prejudicing his chances of being accepted into a specific therapeutic program.

It is therefore important for the physician to be able to identify, in the absence of a positive history, those individuals who are dependent on heroin either alone or in combination with other medications. This chapter will describe a method of careful physical examination, with emphasis on inspection of the patient, that will enable the identification of the heroin-dependent person.

The physical findings in heroin addiction can be divided into two major categories (Table 10-I) : the definitive signs which are almost always indicators of heroin abuse and the associative signs which are not diagnostic but are found in a considerable number of dependent individuals.

TABLE 10-I

PHYSICAL EXAMINATION OF THE HEROIN-DEPENDENT PATIENT

Definitive Signs

1.	Opthalmologic:	Miotic pupils
2.	Nasal Septum:	Excoriation or hyperemia
3.	Venous System:	Jugular scar
		Hyperpigmentation over veins
		Track marks
		"Silver streaking"
4.	Dermatologic:	Acute ulcerating nodules
		Round hyperpigmented lesions
		Punched out lesions with atrophic changes
		"Puffy hand" sign

Associative Signs

1.	Lymphatic:	Adenopathy in epitrochlear or axillary areas
		May be unilateral
2.	Hepatic:	Hepatomegaly
		Icterus
3.	Dermatologic:	Urticarial reactions
		Tattoos
		Rosette sign
		Subcutaneous abscesses
		"Decubitus" changes

Pupillary constriction is perhaps the most consistent finding. Miosis starts to occur within twenty minutes after heroin injection. In some individuals pupillary response to Nalline testing can be noted in up to seventy-two hours following the last heroin dose.[2] Characteristically, the pupils are nonreactive to light or accommodation.

Hyperemia, excoriation and perforation of the nasal septum

have been previously described only in cocaine abuse. However, in recent years, the prominence of heroin use by sniffing has been recognized. Since, in many cases, the heroin is mixed with a small amount of cocaine by the addict, speculum examinations of the nasal mucosa becomes an important part of the physical examination in an individual suspected of heroin addiction who has no other external stigma.

The peripheral venous system can offer some of the most useful information in diagnosing the mainliner. Scarring over the cervical and external jugular veins, a phenomenon noted during the period of paregoric abuse[3] several years ago, is no longer prominent today. The earliest venous sign is a hyperpigmentation over the injected area. This usually progresses to formation of track marks most frequently located over the antecubital fossa (Fig. 10-1). These marks are secondary to repeated injections of contaminated material into the vein starting at a distal site and moving proximally with a corresponding venous thrombosis usually occurring. After the vein has become totally thrombosed, silver streaking may occur (Fig. 10-2). This may be the only sign of heroin abuse in an individual who is now drug-free.

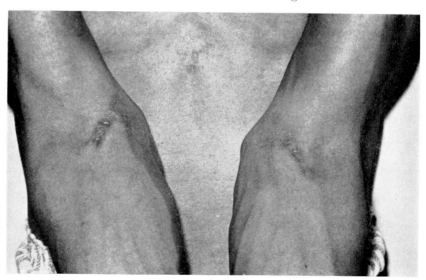

Figure 10-1. Track marks over the antecubital fossa.

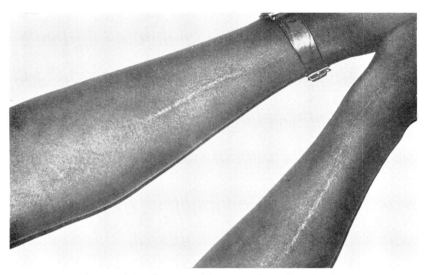

Figure 10-2. Silver streaking over thrombosed veins.

Dermatological findings in heroin addicts can be divided into two groups. The first group consists of signs of the direct effects of subcutaneous injections of heroin (termed "skin popping" by the addict). Acute ulcerating nodules have been reported.[4] However, in the personal experience of the author, this has been an infrequent finding. The most common lesions consist of round, hyperpigmented areas with healed abscesses frequently located below the skin and punched out lesions with atrophic changes. Repeated subcutaneous injections of this material lead to a broadening type of edema with subsequent distortion of muscular landmarks (Fig. 10-3). This is responsible for the "puffy hand" sign of heroin addiction which is a loss of the normal curve of the dorsum of the hand (Fig. 10-4).

The associated dermatological findings in heroin addiction are quite important to stress since it may be the first clue provided to the physician as to the presence of heroin abuse. Urticarial reactions, either generalized or locally confined to the extremity where injection has occurred, are not infrequent. The rosette sign can be seen in the examination of the chest. Areas of hyperpigmenta-

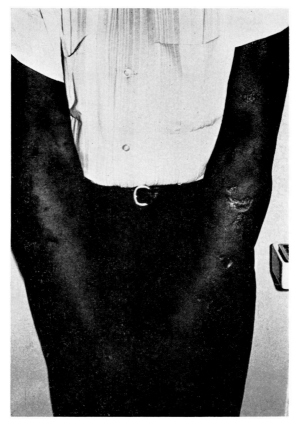

Figure 10-3. Edema with distorted muscular landmarks after repeated subcutaneous injections.

tion are noted in a rough, semicircular pattern over the upper
third of the sternum. These lesions are produced by repeated
cigarette burns suffered by the addict shortly after the injection of
heroin when he "goes on the nod" while smoking. It should be
noted that alcohol-dependent persons may also frequently exhibit
this sign.

Tattoos are quite important in alerting the physician to the
presence of heroin use. In general, they can be classified as either
professional or amateur. The professional tattoos are familiar to

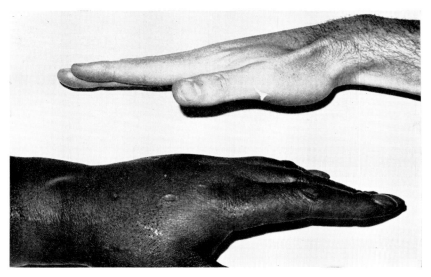

Figure 10-4. "Puffy hand," a typical sign of heroin addiction.

most people and consist of impressive drawings of hearts, ships, etcetera, that are put on with a degree of expertise. These are seen in a variety of people, most frequently in members of the armed services, and are usually not associated with significant personality disorders or criminal activity (Fig. 10-5).[5] This is in contrast to the amateur or what may be termed the "sociopathic" tattoo which is usually multiple, more often visible when normal clothing is worn, and associated with significant personality disturbances and even psychoses.[6,7] Some characteristic examples are the words "mother," "love," "hate," "shit" or the person's initials scrolled hastily on the skin overlying the extremities, usually the hands or forearms. It is the personal experience of this author that these tattoos are almost consistently associated with drug abuse. A special tattoo of this kind is the "pacheco" mark (Fig. 10-6). This sign was originally popular among addicts of Puerto Rican extraction as a means of rapid peer identification. Unfortunately, it also led to rapid police identification with a resulting decrease in frequency of the pacheco now being seen.

Subcutaneous abscesses among skin poppers and discoloration

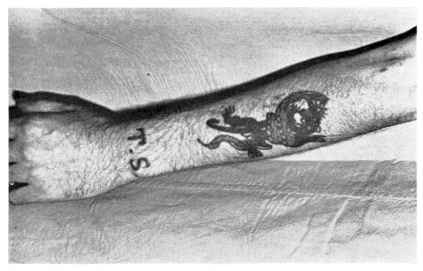

Figure 10-5. Professional tattoo, usually not associated with significant personality disorders or criminal activity.

with swelling and blister formation in dependent parts of the body in individuals unconscious from an overdose have also been described. These findings can be seen with parenteral abuse of drugs other than heroin.

Other associated signs of drug addiction such as axillary or epitrochlear lymphadenopathy, especially unilateral, can often be found. Hepatomegaly or icterus in an otherwise asymptomatic person should make the physician consider the possibility of parenteral drug abuse existing.

Having made a diagnosis of heroin addiction in an individual, the question of multiple drug abuse arises. Although this can be quite difficult to detect, in the absence of actual laboratory analysis, certain helpful criteria exist (Table 10-II) .

The presence of extreme lability of affect, acute psychotic reaction, with or without paranoid ideation, in a known heroin-addicted individual tends to incriminate the stimulant or psychomimetic agents. A marked slurring of speech is frequently found in sedative and alcohol abuse.

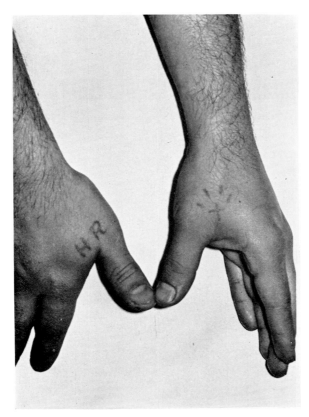

Figure 10-6. "Pacheco" mark, originally popular among Puerto Rican addicts used as peer identification.

Ocular signs are quite important in evaluating the heroin addict. An individual who is maintained on a large habit with normal reactive pupils may be abusing sedatives or alcohol. Dilated pupils, if reactive, incriminate psychomimetic agents; if slowly reactive, amphetamine compounds, and if not reactive, anticholinergic agents. Nystagmus is frequently seen in barbiturate intoxication.

Finally, examination of the cardiovascular system revealing arrythmias or hypertension in a young individual may indicate

TABLE 10-II
SIGNS OF MIXED HEROIN ADDICTION

1.	*Mental Status*	
	A. Extreme lability of affect	Alcohol, psychomimetic agents, inhalants
	B. Acute psychotic reactions	Psychomimetic agents, anticholinergic agents, inhalants
	C. Paranoid ideation prominent	Cocaine, amphetamines, psychomimetics
	D. Marked slurring of speech	Barbiturates, nonbarbiturate sedatives, alcohol
2.	*Ocular Signs*	
	A. Pupils	
	1. Normal size	Alcohol, barbiturates, minor tranquilizers
	2. Dilated	
	a. Reactive	Psychomimetic agents,
	b. React slowly	Amphetamines, Doriden
	c. Nonreactive	Anticholinergic agents
	B. Nystagums	Barbiturates
3.	*Cardiovascular*	
	A. Arrythmias	
	1. Tachycardias	Cocaine, amphetamines, anticholinergics
	2. Premature ventricular contractions	Amphetamines, nutmeg
	3. Bigeminal rhythms	d-Propoxyphene
	B. Hypertension	Amphetamines
4.	*Diabetes Insipidus*	d-Propoxyphene

existing stimulant abuse. It should be noted that rapid heart rates have also been reported following mainlining of heroin.

All of these signs are important to record during the routine evaluation of a patient by the physician regardless of his specialty. It should be stressed that most of the signs described can be noted merely by careful inspection of the patient in the office setting.

I would like to close by mentioning the case of a 28-year-old man with a six-year history of heroin addiction. This gentleman used sterile "works" for injections and had been employed by various agencies without his habit ever being noted. This was the only sign of his addiction: a beetle tatoo with its head over an antecubital vein through which the heroin was injected daily (Fig. 10-7).

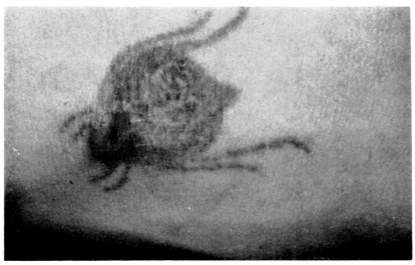

Figure 10-7. Beetle tattoo with beetle head over antecubital vein, used as disguise by a heroin addict.

There is no socioeconomic group today that is immune from heroin usage. Only by thinking of this diagnosis can the physician identify the heroin-dependent individual in an attempt to prevent the tragedies associated with this disease.

REFERENCES

1. Baden, M.M.: Methadone related deaths in New York City. *Int. J. of Addict., 5:*489-498, 1970.
2. Way, E.L., Mo, B.P.N. and Quack, C.P.: Evaluation of the nalorphine pupil diagnostic test for narcotic usage in long term heroin and opium addicts. *Clin. Pharmcol. and Ther., 7:*300-311, 1966.
3. Lerner, A.M. and Oerther, F.J.: Characteristics and sequelae of paregoric abuse. *Ann Intern. Med., 65:*1019-1030, 1966.
4. Minkin, W. and Cohen, H.J.: Dermatologic complications of heroin addiction. *N. Engl. J. Med., 277:*473-475, 1967.
5. Earls, J.H.: Tattooed sailors: some sociopsychological correlates. *Milit. Med., 132:*48-53, 1967.

6. Gittleson, N.L., Wallen, G.D.P. and Dawson-Butterworth, K.: The tattooed psychiatric patient. *Br. J. Psychiatry, 115*:1249-1253, 1969.
7. Taylor, A.J.W.: Tattooing among male and female offenders of different ages in different types of institutions. *Genet. Psychol. Monogr., 81*:81-119, 1970.

Chapter 11

Medical Complications of Heroin Addiction

Marcus A. Feinstein, Alex Richman and A. G. White

WITHIN RECENT years many papers dealing with medical aspects of drug addiction have been published. These papers deal with literature reviews, statistical data and detailed description of some particular medical complication of addiction. This chapter describes the kinds of medical complications seen in a large group of addicted inpatients.

At the Morris J. Bernstein Institute, a division of the Beth Israel Medical Center, New York City, between 8000 and 9000 patients, predominantly heroin addicts under 25 years of age, are voluntarily admitted each year for inpatient treatment. Addiction to opiates is a prerequisite for admission. Some applicants come in with a medical complaint but the majority come in for detoxification from their addictive drug. Every patient is assessed by a physician and gets a medical screening. If a medical condition is found, the patient is housed in a special unit. Here all necessary diagnostic and therapeutic facilities, backed by the resources of the Beth Israel Medical Center, are available. It is on the basis of our observations of these patients that this report is submitted. It is not only a description of medical problems seen by us, but also a medical survey of a large cross-section of the drug-addicted population.

The very first intravenous injection of heroin by an addict creates a potential medical complication. The syringes (an eye dropper is frequently used as a substitute) and needles are used and reused without sterilization, and they frequently are shared with other addicts; skin cleansing is most unusual; heroin is adulterated with unsterile and chemically irritant powders; the mixture is dissolved in unsterile and contaminated water, and occasionally saliva is used instead of water. These primitive conditions of self-administered injections are necessitated not only by ignorance and a lack of equipment but also because possession of "tools" (needle, syringe) is evidence upon which arrest by the police and conviction is made.

Locally, besides the hyperpigmentation, there are "railroad tracks" or cutaneous scars of needling pathognomonic of heroin addicts. There is also thrombophlebitis, periphlebitis and cellulitis causing abscesses and ulcers. When the superficial veins become destroyed, subcutaneous injection (skin popping) is practiced, causing ulcers and later a characteristic punched-out scar. Scars are also seen in various degrees of severity and healing. Deep thrombophlebitis, especially in the lower extremities, is, fortunately, seen much less frequently. With repeated destruction of veins, however, a stage of obstruction of venous return is reached when the limb has become swollen, firm, indurated, nonpitting on pressure, and covered with ulcers; the hand looks as though it is wearing a boxer's glove. Prolonged hospitalization is required to reach a partial improvement in the healing of ulcers. Cultures of the purulent material from the ulcers usually produce a mixed flora, predominantly staphylococci; fungi are not seen. It is of interest to note that the regional lymph nodes are not enlarged as frequently as one would expect.

The destructive infection does not always remain local. The course of the venous blood flow makes it inevitable that bacteria and the infected particles in the veins break off and travel to the lungs which act as a filter for the material that reaches them. Embolic pneumonias, lung abscesses, and even, on one occasion, gangrene of the lung are seen. These are in addition to the lung abscesses seen with tricuspid valve endocarditis to be described later in this chapter. On the chest x-ray the most common finding is fibrosis (scarring) of the lungs caused by minute emboli of material detached from thrombophlebitis, as well as from inert material (starch, talc, cotton fibers) present in the infected mixture—all this resulting in very many angiothromboses, small areas of atelectasis and granulomatous lesions. Asthma and emphysema are frequent, probably further enhanced by heavy tobacco smoking. Healed tuberculous lesions in the lungs are very common and active open lesions were seen in eight patients in 1969 and seven patients in 1970.

Pulmonary hypertension, right ventricular enlargement, dyspnea and a pulmonic ejection murmur are the end result of this diffuse pulmonary fibrosis. Impaired normal pulmonary function is seen very frequently. Fortunately, we have not seen the fatal so-called overdose syndrome among our patients, but it is reasonable to postulate that the lung changes described above strongly contribute to a combination of factors leading to this dramatic cardiopulmonary death, whether it is triggered off by an anaphylactic or a hypersensitivity reaction.

When the bacteria are not completely filtered out by the lungs, sepsis and endocarditis follow. Blood cultures are repeatedly taken on all patients who have either an elevated temperature for which there is no definite explanation or when a clinical finding makes us suspicious of the possibility of endocarditis. We must say that our index of suspicion in this respect is high. Within the past year we treated eight patients with endocarditis—six men and two women. The women had a preexisting rheumatic heart disease and were the only ones in our group whose blood cultures grew *Streptomyces viridans;* one of these women died from a recurrent gastric hemorrhage, not from the endocarditis. Five men had *Staph aureus* sepsis with endocarditis of the tricuspid valve without any evidence of a preexisting valvular disease and very minimal and transient signs on auscultation. Septic pulmonary emboli were seen in three of these patients. All recovered. The choice of antibiotics was guided by the sensitivity tests on the isolated bacteria. The eighth patient in this group (still living and improving at the time of writing of this chapter) has fungal endocarditis caused by *Candida* on a preexisting rheumatic heart disease, mitral insufficiency and mitral stenosis. Beside the cardiac findings at the time of admission he was extremely weak and had a cachectic appearance.

Our experience with sepsis and endocarditis is similar to that of others, but we wish to point out that the isolated *Staph aureus* in the cultures was resistant to penicillin and ampicillin. We have not observed either renal, cerebral or spleenic embolization. Not all bacteremias lead to endocarditis.

Serum hepatitis is the foremost cause of admission to the medical service of our Institute. The disease is transmitted by way of the needle used by another addict whose blood carries the hepatitis virus, possibly for many months, and who may not have been aware of the infectivity of his blood to those with whom he shared a needle.

While our patients with serum hepatitis generally have a benign course of about four to six weeks, some remain with a very high bilirubin for a longer period of time, have more severe symptoms and require steroids in their course of treatment. A few patients have had a previous attack of hepatitis and their biopsies show extensive liver tissue necrosis. Their recovery is slow and they remain chronically ill, debilitated persons. Within the past year three patients were admitted with deep icterus, confused, uncooperative and agitated. Within twelve to twenty-four hours they lapsed into hepatic coma. All three died.

Besides the icteric form of serum hepatitis, we also see an anicteric, clinically mild, active hepatitis manifested by elevated SGOT, SGPT and alkaline phosphatase, and a palpable tender liver, all of which recede during hospitalization.

It may be of interest to note at this point that only about 10 percent of our patients with serum hepatitis had a positive Australian Antigen test. Also, a sampling of about one hundred consecutive patients admitted to a general ward were tested by the immunoelectrophoresis technique for Australian Antigen. All were negative.

Tetanus is another disease more common among addicts than nonaddicts and is also transmitted by a contaminated needle into a very fertile soil of infected skin. We treated four female patients with tetanus, of whom two died. We routinely give tetanus toxoid intramuscularly to all admitted patients unless we know they have received it within the previous three months, as tetanus can recur. No immunization is perfect. Tetanus may be difficult to diagnose when first seen because dysphagia ("hysterical"), painful muscle spasms, backache and fever may all resemble anxiety of withdrawal from heroin, before the onset of the diagnostic trismus.

Neurological conditions seen by us are predominantly due to direct peripheral nerve injuries, particularly of the radial and ulnar nerves, usually from stab wounds, and less frequently caused by the needle used by the addict. We have seen only one patient with transverse myelitis involving thoracic segments described by Dr. R. Richter (*JAMA*, Nov. 4, 1968.) Our patient had paraplegia with thoracic sensory levels. His illness had had an acute onset a few weeks after release from prison where he had received no opiates. He had resumed his heroin habit shortly before the onset of transverse myelitis. This is not an embolic disease but is probably an allergic or hypersensitivity reaction. Other neurologic conditions were due to trauma to the head in the frequent confrontations with police as well as other addicts assaulting for possession of either heroin or money. In this respect there is no code of loyalty among addicts.

Epileptic seizures, some very severe, are very frequent at our hospital. These seizures are due to either previous head injuries, or idiopathic, but most commonly are caused by barbiturate or Doriden® addiction in addicts using these drugs in addition to heroin. The neurologic manifestations of chronic barbiturate use (ataxia, eye muscle incoordination, peripheral nerve palsies, memory deterioration) can resemble many clinical entities taxing the diagnostic skills of the examiner.

Besides the conditions described above which are direct medical complications of the heroin addict's practice of self-administered injections of adulterated heroin purchased by him, there are medical problems to which this habit contributes both in frequency of occurrence and in severity of illness as compared with the general population. It is felt that active pulmonary tuberculosis, chronic bronchitis, malnutrition from poor eating habits, secondary anemia due to iron deficiency, a high incidence of gastrointestinal disorders, chronic pelvic infections in women, and venereal disease in both sexes occur more frequently and are of greater severity than in nonaddicts of a similar socioeconomic

strata. Some of these common conditions assume unusual forms
(active tuberculosis of the liver) .

Psychiatric, behavioral and drug withdrawal problems are not
part of this chapter and were not discussed. Neither did we describe the experience gathered and documented by our Department of Pediatrics in treating the newborn of addicted mothers.

Chapter 12

Toxosynpathies (A Multifactor Pathogenic Concept)

Leon Roizin, Milton Helpern, Michael M. Baden,
M. Kaufman and K. Akai

W E USED TO think of diseases produced by germs, metabolic disorders (inborn or acquired), neoplastic processes, environmental (physical and chemical agents) and stressor reactions (functional wear and tear, social-economical and meteoropathic), and so forth; but now we should think also in terms of *drug-induced diseases* and *toxo-synpathies*. The latter have developed, on the one hand, as a result of the overall technicological development, industrialization (including agriculture) and proliferating commercial improvements which have contaminated the atmosphere with threatening pollutants; have fed the waters with poisonous chemicals, insecticides, pesticides, detergents, radioisotope discards, etcetera; and have despoiled the earth with all kinds of fertilizers, weed controls, et cetera; while most of our canned foods are being mixed with preservatives and additives of all kinds. On the other hand, the current "drug culture" of our times and its by-product, "the pill" myth,* is prophesying the chemical cure of all human ills from pinprick to cancer and prevention of diseases, contraception and population control. Furthermore, additional psychological and biochemical pathogenicity is caused through the use of narcotics, hallucinogens and energizers by a large number of people who are seeking the fulfillment of imaginary pleasures or gratifications in a dreamland of artificial securities or retreat from increased demands of life responsibilities and hardships.

As if all this "toxic cocktail" of ills was not enough, malnutri-

---

*Multiple "pill" intake with tendency to "more" rather than careful evaluation and selective prescription.

tion burns up the available nutrient storage of the individual, and alcohol joins the decaying company with its own damaging self-indulgence. The present report is concerned principally with a study on possible pathogenic mechanisms in the CNS of man and experimental animals following the intake of neuropsychotropic agents. In this framework, we would like to emphasize, in particular, the significance of various facilitating, precipitating and potentiating factors of adverse toxicologic tissue reaction patterns.

Because of space limitation, only some basic principles of the multifactor pathogenic concept will be briefly discussed.

MATERIALS AND METHODOLOGIES

Human Material

Central nervous system tissue and viscera from humans was limited principally to that from patients who have received neuro-psychopharmacologic agents and who have developed adverse neurologic symptoms (extrapyramidal, dystonic, convulsive, etc.), liver disorders (jaundice, hepatitis, hepatorenal insufficiency) and/or agranulocytosis, organic brain syndrome, and semicoma or coma (caused by accidental overdosage or suicide). Also included was material from patients who have had prolonged therapy (i.e. for a minimum of four months) as narcotics and hallucinogen dependents. The investigative and control material was obtained from various hospitals and institutions of the New York State Department of Mental Hygiene, through the Neuropathologic Registry at the New York State Psychiatric Institute, and from Chief Medical Examiner's office of the Forensic Institute, New York City. This material combined with reviewed cases from the literature, amounted to date to a total of 1711 cases with adverse drug reactions.

Animal Experiments

Up to present a total of 750 animals was used for neurotoxi-cologic studies. This included mice, rats and monkeys of both sexes and of variable strains and ages (from embryos to adults). The methodologies consisted of (a) quantitative estimation of the chemical agents in 8 to 12 regions of the CNS (according to the species of the animals) and fourteen CNS specimens in humans, as well as viscera, blood, urine and when possible, gastro-intestinal contents; (b) histochemical technics for oxidoreduction and hydrolytic enzyme systems; (c) electron microscopy and (d) neuropathologic technics on fresh and variously fixed material.

RESULTS

The clinicopathologic features of some adverse effects and causes of death in humans are summarized in Tables 12-I, II and III.

TABLE 12-I
ADVERSE EFFECTS (HUMANS)

Cardiovascular:	Variations in blood pressure, tachycardia vasomotor disorders.
Endocrinological and neurohumoral:	Galactorrhea, hypertrophy of breasts, amenorrhea, diabetes mellitus, obesity, changes in sexual desire; variable effects on the storage, receptor and transfer of biogenic amines and neuromediators or neurotransmittors and related mechanisms (principally in experimental animals).
Secretory:	Dysfunction of secretion of lacrimal, salivary and sebaceous glands, altered secretion of nasal mucosa, effects on neurosecretory mechanisms (rats and humans) hypothalamus-hypophysial-adrenal axis.
Dermatologic:	Dermatitis and/or erythema, photosensitization, edema.
Liver:	Dysfunctions with or without jaundice.
Renal:	Oliguria, polyuria.
Articular:	Rheumatoid symptoms, activation or aggravtion of pre-existing rheumatoid state.
Gastrointestinal:	Diarrhea or constipation, anorexia or bulimia, vomiting and pyrosis
Hematologic:	Blood dyscreasias (3 cases of leukemia), altered coagulation, agranulocytosis.
Myoneural:	Muscues twitches, tremors, effects on myoneural syn-synapses and intramural vegetative plexi.
Central Nervous System:	a. *Neurological:* extrapyramidal, dystonic, motor, epileptogenic, thermoregulatory, diabetes insipidus, cerebellar, sphincter control,
	b. *Psychiatric and behavioral:* restlessness, emotional oversensitiveness, mental impairment, overestimation of capabilities, tendency to withdraw from social contacts, paranoid states with delusions of persecution, visual, auditory and tactile hallucinations, 'depraved dope fiend' (chronic cocaine), dependence syndrome and withdrawal reactions (including newborns).

TABLE 12-II
LIVER BIOPSIES AND AUTOPSY MATERIAL EXCLUSIVE OF NEUROPATHOLOGIC FINDINGS

Case No.	Diagnosis	Age, Sex	Drug Dosage Daily	Duration of Rx	Clinical Findings	Outcome	Pathological Findings
PI 2907	Psychosis with cerebral arteriosclerosis.	58, M	Chlpr. 50 mg IM.	120 days	Jaundice, obstructive type.	Death 13 months after the onset, due to hepatorenal disease.	*Gross:* Generalized jaundice of tissues. *Microscopic:* Biliary stasis central portion of lobules, with biliary thrombi; mild fatty degeneration of hepatic cells, central zone.
PI 2908	D.P. paranoid type.	38, M	Chlpr. dosage unknown.	Unknown	Jaundice.	Recovery 180+ days later.	Biliary stasis with biliary thrombi, central portions of lobules. Biliary pigments in hepatic cells of central zone. Periportal mononuclear infiltrations.
PI 2909	D.P. paranoid type.	26, F	Chlpr. 300 mg.	31 days	Bile in urine, bilirubinogen in serum 14.5. Laparotomy; bile tract negative.	Recovery in 180 days.	Biliary stasis with biliary thrombi and biliary pigments, central portions of lobules.
PI 2873	D.P. catatonic type.	27, F	Chlpr., 1. 150–300 mg 2. 300-mg.	1.129 days 2. 47 days	Fever 106–104. Combiotic Rx. Jaundice. BUN 96 mg%; WBC 20,000.	Death due to bronchopneumonia, 15 days after 1st symptom.	Jaundice of viscera. Bronchopneumonia, pulmonary congestion and edema, fatty infiltration of liver. Fibrosis around central veins with biliary stasis. Biliary casts in renal tubules.
PI 2725	Mental deficiency.	14, M	Serpasil 1–2.5 mg. Chlpr. 200–150 mg. with electrostim. (10)	102 days	Epileptic seizures.	Death due to cardiac arrest with acute dilatation of heart.	*Gross:* Acute dilatation of heart, right ventricle; apneumatosis of lungs, acute congestion of kidneys, liver, and spleen. *Microscopic:* Periportal and mild peribiliary fibrosis with slight lymphocytic infiltration.
PI 2755	Manic depressive psychosis, manic ..... alcoholism.	52, F	Serpasil 12 mg, Chlpr. 100 mg plus Serpasil 4 mg.	97 days	Discoloration of body, unsteady gait, sialorrhea, difficulty in swallowing.	Death due to pulmonary zedema and congestion from aspiration of feeding tube 32 days after first symptom.	*Gross:* Acute pulmonary edema and congestion, hydrothorax, pachymeningitis hemorrhagica with contusion of skull, chronic cholelithiasis and cholecystitis. *Microscopic:* Peribiliary and periportal fibrosis, biliary pigments in renal ......

PI 2735	D.P. paranoid type.	49, F	Chlpr. 68 mg Cogentin 3 mg.	21 days	Agranulocytosis.	Death due to bronchopneumonia? and agranulocytosis.	*Gross:* Bronchopneumonia, petechial hemorrhages lungs, liver, myocardium, kidneys, spleen. Generalized adenitis. *Microscopic:* Petechial hemorrhages on surface and around hepatic lobules.
PI 2821	Huntingtons chorea with psychosis.	58, M	Chlpr. 150–300 plus Serpasil 1–3 mg.	112 days	PEG cortical atrophy. Internal hydrocephalus. Temperature 103.	Death due to bronchopneumonia? aspiration pneumonia? 14 days after first fever.	*Gross:* Congestion of liver and kidneys, edema of brain.
PI 2840	D.P. paranoid type.	51, F	Chlpr. 75 mg.	127 days	Temperature 101. Loose stools. Vomiting. Acutely ill.	Death due to acute hemorrhagic pancreatitis due to stenosis of papilla Vateri.	*Gross:* Pulmonary congestion and edema, hemorrhagic pancreatitis, fatty infiltration of liver. *Microscopic:* Fatty infiltration of liver.
PI 2872	D.P. paranoid type. Epileptic seizures?	43, M	Chlpr. 100–1200, Equanil 100 mg, ECT 6.	158 days	Epileptic seizures?	Death due to pulmonary edema.	*Gross:* Chronic interstitial pneumonia, bilateral, severe. Acute congestion of viscera. Arteriosclerosis, coronary arteries.
PI 2895	D.P. catatonic type.	55, F	Chlpr. 300 mg.	14 days	Liver dysfunction. Laparotomy, external drainage of common bile duct.	Death due to postcholedochostomy with secondary infection, pulmonary congestion and edema.	*Gross:* Icterus of tissue and viscera, absces of drainage tract, serofibrinous peritonitis, acute enlargement of spleen, fibrosis of ovaries, obesity, Laennec's cirrhosis.
PI 2861	D.P. hebephrenic type.	53, F	Chlpr. 150–250 mg, Dilantin 1½ gr., Phenobarbital 1 gr., Phenergan unknown, Cogentin 2 mg.	142 days	Postlobotomy epileptiform seizures.	Death due to bronchopneumonia, bilateral, severe.	*Gross:* Bronchopneumonia, coronary artery disease, chronic congestion of abdominal viscera.

Legend: Chlpr. = Chlorpromazine; M = male; F = female; 1 and 2: Rx at different periods of time.

TABLE 12-III
NEUROPATHOLOGICAL FINDINGS

Case No.	Brain Wt. (gm)	Cerebral Cortex	Basal Ganglia	Thalamus	Hypothalamus
PI 2725	1200	Cytoarchitecture irregular 1–2+. Lipid degeneration of neurons 1+. Neuronophagia 1–2+. Perivascular enlargement with glia reaction & gitter cells.	Neuronal satellitosis & neuronophagia 1+. Occipital grouping of glia nuclei. Neuronal degeneration +, 1+.	Chromatolysis+ 1+.	Cytoarchitecture irregular 1–2+. Satellitosis & neuronophagia 1–2+. Irregular distribution Nissl substance. Chromatolysis 1–2+ with nuclear eccentricity.
PI 2733	1300	Cytoarchitecture irregular 2+. Chromatolysis 1–2+. Satellitosis & neuronophagia 2–3+. Fatty degeneration 1+. Rarefaction nerve cells in Sommer's sector.	Chromatolysis 2+. Neuronophagia, fatty degeneration 1+. Amyloid bodies.	Chromatolysis 1–2+. Lipid degeneration 1–2+.	Disorganization of paraventric nuclei. Irregular distribution. Nissl substance.
PI 2735	1030	Neuronal rarefaction with acellular areas. Satellitosis & neuronophagia 1–2+. Astroglial proliferation. Deep layers subcortical region. Neuronal lipid degeneration 1–2+.	Chromatolysis 2+. Satellitosis & neuronophagia 1–2+. Pigments in neurons. Lipid degeneration neurons 3+.	Neuronal degeneration with lipid deposits 1–2+.	Disorganized neuronal arrangement paraventricular nuclei 1–2+. Variable size & distribution. Nissl substance. Intraneuronal & extraneuronal granular material.
PI 2872	—	Chromatolysis 1+. Satellitosis & neuronophagia. Grouping of glia nuclei, especially perivascular spaces white matter.	Satellitosis neuronophagia 1+. Enlarged perivascular spaces with glial reaction.	Chromatolysis in some neurons 1+.	Being cut serially sections not available at present.
PI 2821	1208	Cytoarchitecture irregular 2–4+. Neuronal alteration 2–4+. Lipid material nerve cells, endothelial cells, vascular walls & perivascular spaces.	Satellitosis, neuronophagia 2–4+. Neuronal alteration with lipid degeneration 1–4+. Amyloid bodies.	Neuronal degeneration with lipid deposits 1–2+.	Neuronal irregular. Satellitosis & neuronophagia. Neuronal lipid degeneration 1–2+.
PI 2873	—	Cytoarchitecture irregular. Dropping of neurons in Sommer's sector. Lipid degeneration 1–2+. Perivascular astrocytic proliferation.	Neuronal alterations & neuronophagia 1+. Circumscribed groupings of glia.	Lipid degeneration 1+. Scattered neuronophagia.	Some irregular neuronal distribution. Variable distribution & staining Nissl substance.

Key: 1+ to 4+ = Various degrees of intensity of the pathological process.
+ = Doubtful changes; 1+ = mild alterations; 2+ = marked alterations; 3+ = severe alterations.
4+ = complete disorganization of structure.

Mesencephalon	Pons, Medulla	Cerebellum	Spinal Cord	Remarks
Vascular congestion. Enlargement of perivascular spaces.	Vascular congestion. Pallor & chromatolysis neurons, especially inferior olives.	Diminution of Purkinje cells with chromatolysis, including neurons dentate nuclei.	Chromatolysis motor neurons with occipital satellitosis 1+.	Congestion of blood vessels. Endothelial cells with lipid material.
Neuronal rarefaction & neuronal alterations substantia nigra 1–2+, more pronounced one side.	Neuronal pallor throughout. Chromatolysis 1–2+.	Reduction of Purkinje cells & chromatolysis, including neurons, dentate nuclei. Neuronal lipid degeneration 1+.	Not available.	Capillaries throughout cortex and basal ganglia present enlarged perivascular spaces containing macrophages & lipid material. Perivascular astrocytic proliferation.
Chromatolysis & lipid neuronal degeneration 1+.	Same as mesencephalon. Chromatolysis & lipid degeneration inferior olives 2+.	Irregular arrangement Purkinje cells. Chromatolysis & lipid degeneration 1–2+.	Not available.	Enlarged perivascular spaces containing macrophages with lipid material especially white matter.
Vascular congestion, neuronal lipid degeneration periaqued. gray matter 2+.	Neuronal lipid degenration 2+, especially inferior olives.	Dropping Purkinje cells 2+. Neuronal lipid degeneration 2+.	Chromotolysis & neuronal lipid degeneration. Cervical & lumbar enlargements.	Disorganized Sommers sector & neuronal lipid degeneration 2+.
Irregular, in cellular organization substantia nigra. Neuronal lipid degeneration throughout 1–2+.	Neuronal lipid degeneration 1–2+.	Loss Purkinje cells. Remaining ones and dentate nuclei lipid degeneration 2+.	Not available.	Lipid degeneration of endothelial cells, vascular walls & presence of lipid material in macrophages perivascular spaces.
Vascular congestion. Neuronal alterations substantia nigra — 1+.	Vascular congestion. Lipid degeneration neurons inferior olives 1+.	Dropping of Purkinje cells in some folia 3+.	No remark. alteration.	Lipid material in endothelial cells in some regions of cerebral cortex, white matter & basal ganglia.

The distribution of drug estimations in the CNS and viscera in experimental animals[1-4] and humans[5] disclose marked variations in different anatomotopographic regions.[1-5] Histologic and particularly histochemical (oxidoreduction and hydrolytic enzyme systems),[6-9] and electron microscope findings of the CNS showed diversified reactions.[2-10] The neuron and the glial cells both of the gray matter (especially glial satellites) and those of the white matter showed anatomotopographic heterogeneity. These in turn showed also variations in relation to the drugs under study.[5-6]

DISCUSSION

Working Hypothesis: Simultaneous occurrence of multiple variable interreactions intensify the toxopathogenesis of the independent drug potentialities.

Estimating Parameters

Biological Cofactors[16-30]

Anatomofunctional and metabolic characteristics of the CNS are represented by: differential embryological metamorphosis and evolution of the morphological and histochemical constituents; functional and metabolic plurality; and the pathological diversified and selective tissue reaction patterns. In this light the variable qualitative and quantitative reaction products of the oxidoreduction and hydrolytic enzyme systems may be attributed to some of the following conditions[6-9]: (a) structural characteristics of the correlated anatomotopographic regions of the CNS (from cellular to the ultrastructural level of organization) ; (b) heterogeneous metabolism (structurally dependent), (c) correlated physiological activities and (d) pharmacodynamic properties of the chemical agents. The wide range of their effects such as modification of the rate of enzyme activity, transfer or conduction mechanisms, stimulation or inhibition of synthetic processes, and so forth, suggests that each drug may have several sites of actions which may or may not coincide with other drugs or factors. Thus two or more drugs, as encountered in chemotherapy, frequently induce unexpected reactions, because of synergistic or antagonistic effects of key tissue processes that is, ATP synthesis, oxidation reduction mechanisms, biogenic amine metabolism (inhibition of storage or liberation and depletion, etc.) causing variations in the concentration of neurochemical mediators at receptor site or along the neuronal transmission pathways (presynaptic or at the synaptic levels), protein synthesis, lipid membrane integrity, neural barrier permeability, and so forth.

In addition, these conditions may display some diversification of tissue reactivity in accordance with the following cofactors.

1. *Ontogenetic variants:* from conception, DNA and the fine pleomorphic metamorphosis, chemical evolution and physiological maturation of the neural structures show differential susceptibility or vulnerability as demonstrated by the effects of various biophysical (x-ray and ultraviolet irradiation)[31] and chemical agents (including phenothiazines, thalidomide, hallucinogens, etc.)

2. *Phylogenic variants* with regard to drug idiosyncrasies or drug resistance, in some ethnical groups of people, have been attributed to inborn enzyme defects.[18,23,33-40] For instance, primaquine, sulfonamides and phenacetin, causing hemolytic anemia in 10 to 15 percent of Negro males and various ethnical groups in the Middle East, is due to the absence of the sex-linked glucose-6-phosphate dehydrogenase which protects RBS from hemolysis. Prolonged apnoea following normal dose of suxamethonium was noted in patients with genetic defect causing low plasma pseudocholinesterase level. A defective conjugation of chloramphenicol in the liver (especially in premature children) is due to lack of glucuron transferase which leads to high chloramphenicol level inducing dangerous circulatory collapse known as the "grey syndrome." Barbiturates and other drugs may cause hepatic porphyria in individuals with abnormal inducibility of d-aminolevulinic acid synthetase (autosomal dominant inheritance).* Analogous individual and strain variations with respect to drugs were also observed in experimental animals. For instance, rabbits are resistant to atropine, due to the presence of atropine esterase;

---

*In addition genetic and environmental factors may play a role in immune mechanisms of drug allergy.[41]

mice are resistant to insulin due to the presence of insulinase but display remarkable variability to histamine.

3. *Age variant:* the deficient capacity for metabolizing sulfonamides due to lack of glucuron transpherase may cause kernicterus in the newborn after administration of sulfonamides to the mother during the last period of pregnancy or to the newborn itself. Adaptive enzyme activity (cortical cholinesterase) variations according to age have been demonstrated in three strains of rats.[42] The well-known tragic teratogenic effects of thalidomide in human embryos was apparently harmless to the mother. Drugs may act very selectively, but still affect a specific biochemical reaction in a number of different tissues.[38] Adverse side effects of drugs must be also considered in the latter light.

4. *Sex variants:*[10,43,44] Agranulocytosis in humans due to amidopyrine, phenylbutazone and phenothiazines (particularly chlorpromazine) occurs more frequently in females than in males (ration approximately 3 to 1). Pancytopenia, due to chloramphenicol, was noted more frequently in young females than in males. In these instances the bone marrow damage, especially early erythroblasts (vacuoles) is possibly related to a disorder of RNA synthesis caused by the bacteriostatic effect of the antibiotic.[23] Male heroin addicts outnumber females 3 or 4 to 1.

As far as laboratory animals are concerned male mice suffer massive cortical necrosis of the kidneys when exposed to low concentration of chloroform. Castration of the male abolishes the susceptibility; whereas ovariectomy induces a partial susceptibility in the kidneys of female mice. Female mice become fully susceptible to renal damage by chloroform after treatment with androgens and male mice are rendered partially resistant by the administration of estrogens.[45] Female rats sleep a shorter time than male rats when the same milligrams per kilogram dosage of hexobarbital (Evipal®) is administered i.v. The difference disappears when the females are castrated or the males are treated with estrogens.[46]

Drug Cofactors[17,23,27,37,38]

The basic features are represented by pharmacodynamic properties of the drug, the therapeutic index,* dosage, mode of administration, frequency and duration of treatment. In relation with our topic under discussion the tendency of the current poly-pharmacology or the multiple drug intake and the toxicity due to the interaction between drugs is of particular interest. Tranquilizers and hypnotics potentiate the cerebral depressant effect of each other and alcohol. The combination may cause fatal alcohol intoxication in cases where both the amount of alcohol and the amount of barbiturates were moderate. In patients treated with MAO inhibitors, a fatal hypertensive crisis may be induced by sympathomimetic agents, such as adrenaline, ephedrine and amphetamine, and also after eating cheese rich in tyramine. Misuse of morphine, phenothiazines and imipramine may cause excitement, hyperthermia and coma. In anesthesia, when the patient has used hypotensives,[23] dangerous shock may develop as a result of exhaustion of catecholamines. The concomitant administration of salicylates, phenylbutazone derivatives, broad spectrum antibiotics and alcohol may increase and prolong the effect of anticoagulants so as to cause severe hemorrhages because of reduced prothrombin. Conversely, a drug may reduce the pharmacologic activity of another by stimulating its metabolic inactivation. Barbiturates stimulate the metabolism of anticoagulants, thereby lowering the anticoagulant activity. When the administration of the barbiturate is stopped, severe bleeding may occur. Severe and protracted hypoglycemia in diabetes are treated with sulfonylurea agents (tolbutamide, tolazamide) and especially chlorpropamide. This potentiation may occur in elderly patients and in patients with impaired renal function. The interaction may occur when not only long-acting but also short-acting sulfonamides are administered.[23]

$$*\text{T.I.} = \frac{\text{toxic d.}}{\text{pharmacol. d,}}$$ if the value of the ratio is large, the drug is relatively safe to use. If it is small (close to unity), then the dosage must be controlled with utmost precaution.

Environmental Factors[24]

In addition to those *metereopathic variants* mentioned in the introductory remarks, death records during the "London fog" (Dec. 5-9, 1952) show that about four thousand more deaths occurred than would have been expected on the basis of the data from previous years. During another similar episode many patients presented symptoms of acute bronchiolitis without the evidence of infection.[38] Respiratory insufficiency due to hypoxaemia associated with hypercapnia (as in cases of bronchial asthma, kyphoscoliosis, severe anemia) may cause alarming dangerous or comatose states when narcotics or sedatives, in otherwise normal doses, are administered.[23]

Nutritional variants[48,49] are related not only to insufficient quantity but also to deficient quality (poor in proteins and vitamins, rich in carbohydrates). Many of the drug addicts have also poor appetites, erratic eating habits and suffer from digestive disorders as well as develop a malabsorption syndrome. It has been also demonstrated that laboratory animals subjected to partial starvation[48] and nutritional stress are more susceptible to toxic adverse reactions as compared with controls.[14,17]

Geographical Differences

Recently it has been reported that nephrotoxicity has been increased in Switzerland following the use of analagesics with phenacetin.[50]

Stressor Cofactors[51-57]

Many investigators have compared the initial symptoms of adverse reactions to the peak of an "iceberg"[58-60]—that is, the most extensive and most damaging part is beneath the surface. The stressor effects of a physical and chemical character upon the CNS, neurohormonal and psychogenic mechanisms have been extensively reviewed, in particular, by several investigators[51-57] and for this reason they are not reviewed here, except to mention that they are also acting as potentiating mechanisms through neurogenic and neurohumoral (including the electrolytes) homeokinetic mechanisms. Accordingly, histometabolic dysergia may cause reversible or irreversible changes through pathergia and pathocli-sis.[25]

Miscellaneous Medicobiological Factors*

Patients with hyperthyroidism may develop toxic conditions, even coma, after small doses of morphine. The opiate addict is often amenorrhoic but may become pregnant and there is a high incidence of obstetrical complications, including stillbirths.[66,67] Infant withdrawal symptoms shortly after birth[68] are expressed by restlessness, crying, irritability, poor feeding, vomiting, yawning (a great deal), corrhyza, gooseflesh, et cetera.

Recent socioepidemiologic studies[64,76,77] have disclosed that the abuse of marijuana, amphetamines, barbiturates, hallucino-gens and other psychotropic substances have spread to all levels of society and from schoolchildren to young adults.

Some difficulties in the evaluation of "drug reactions" in human pathologic material exist, since correlations are not syn-onymous with explanations. Although several validation criteria for drug reactions have been devised, in accordance with several investigators,[69] still some difficulties are encountered in evaluating retrospective drug reactions in human cases such as (a) inadequate information about the dosage of the drug and the overall medico-biological conditions of the patient; (b) multiple drug intake; (c) uncertainties of the chemical identification and its temporal relationship to the adverse reaction; (d) existence of inborn or acquired "predisposing" or facilitating factors, (e) inadequate surveillance or follow-up of outclinic patients and (f) the body's limited means of reaction.

Significance of Animal Experimentation

To facilitate or recognize, at least, some fundamental "drug reaction profiles," animal experimentation[26,63,72,73] may help to establish (a) the pharmacodynamics of drug administration, (b) the sites of drug distribution (body fluids and anatomical loca-tion), (c) the sequence of the physiological and toxic reactions, (d) short and prolonged (chronic) effect of medications, (e)

*See the following references: 18, 23, 24, 27, 38, 61-65, 70, 71.

temporal relationship between drug administration and chemical, histometabolic and structural examinations, (f) monitoring system, close surveillance and direct observations of reaction patterns of the organism, (g) the role of age, sex and race or strain variables, and (h) correlation of *in vivo* with *in vitro* experimentation; as well as controlled studies. However, although the animal model experiments may be informative, delayed effects are very little known and casual associations which, as an integral part of human life, are artificially excluded. Furthermore, no single animal may be adequate for all studies at all times and for all diseases.[73] A few human cases, at times, are more crucial than hundreds and thousands of experiments.[74] For instance, the analogy between the syphilitic shanker and the aortic aneurysms was observed long before the spirochette and the Wasserman reaction were discovered. There are many similar observations which lead to the conclusion that the animal is no substitute for human. In summing up, it appears, that the human findings may serve a useful purpose for "hypothesis generating," while the preclinical animal experimentation for hypothesis testing[75] and a wise research investigator must use both.

CONCLUDING REMARKS

The simultaneous occurrence of multiple variable interreactions intensify the toxogenetic or pathogenetic potentialities of the independent pharmacodynamic agent.

Comparative studies of human and experimental drug toxicology suggest that the tissue reaction patterns (relative tissue reaction scale, Table 12-IV) is the result of the interplay between the overall biological cofactors of the reacting organism (inherited and acquired) and the pharmacodynamic properties of the chemical agents with the co-participation of accessory or secondary cofactors (environmental, nutritional, socioecological, stressors, etc.)

Correlated chemical, histometabolic, histologic and electron microscope methodologies are able to investigate the pathogenic mechanisms up to the molecular level of the structural organization of the chemically induced pathologic processes.

TABLE 12-IV

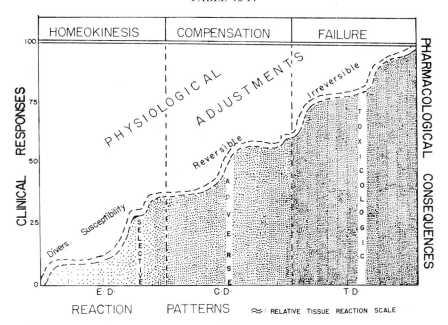

Finally adverse reactions to drugs are not always of a negative significance. In some instances they may lead to important discoveries: polyuria was recognized as a toxic reaction of mercury treatment; this in turn suggested to use mercury salts as a diuretic. Some patients affected by T.B., while being treated with iproniazid, demonstrated euphoria and these observations initiated the new MAO antidepressant therapy. The initial use of "neuroleptic agents" for hypotension resulted in a much wider application of the "tranquilizers" for psychiatric and behavioral disorders treatment.

REFERENCES

1. Wechsler-Berger, M., and Roizin, L.:: Tissue levels of chlorpromazine in experimental animals. *J Ment Sci, 106*:1501, 1960.
2. Roizin, L., Kaufman, M., and Casselman, B.: Structural changes induced by neuroleptics. Extrapyramidal system and neuroleptic. *Rev Canad Biol, 20*:221, 1961.
3. Bollard, B. M., Roizin, L., Sabbia, R., and Horwitz, W.: Distribution of

free and S[35] labelled prochlorperazine (compazine) in mammalian tissues. *Fed Proc, 22:*317, 1963 (Abstract).

4. Cuatico, W., Roizin, L., Sabbia, R., Wodraska, G., and Delli Bovi, B.: S[35] prochlorperazine autoradiography of the central nervous system. *Fed Proc, 23:*129, 1964.

5. Forrest, F., Forrest, I., and Roizin. L.: Clinical, biochemical and postmortem studies on a patient treated with chlorpromazine. *Agressologie, 4:*259, 1963.

6. Iyengar, V.K.S., DiVirgilio, G., Robinson, E.H., Wodraska, G., and Roizin, L.: Some histochemical-cytochemical patterns of ATPase in CNS of rat. *J Cell Biol, 23: (pt. 2):*45A, 1964.

7. Roizin, L., Iyengar, V.K.S., DiVirgilio, G., Wodraska, G., and Liu, J.C.: Effects of prochlorperazine on the rat C.N.S. succinic dehydrogenase and diphosphopyridine nucleotide diaphorase. (Lactic linked). *J Cell Biol, 27:*88A, 1965 (Abstract).

8. Roizin, L., Iyengar, V.K.S., Marquez-Alba, E., and Yahr, M.D.: Correlated neuropathologic and cyto-enzymatic studies following atropine administration. *Trans Amer Neurol Ass, 90:*281, 1965.

9. Roizin, L., Iyengar, V.K.S., Di Virgilio, G., and Robinson, E.: Cytochemical patterns of ATP-ase (mitochondrial) in the C.N.S. 2. Diversified neuronal reaction in normal rats and after prochlorperazine administration. *Fed Proc, 24:*493, 1965.

10. Roizin, L., True, C., and Knight, M.: Structural effects of tranquilizers. The effect of pharmacologic agents. *Proc Ass Res Nerv Ment Dis, 37:* 285, 1959.

11. Roizin, L., Wechsler-Berger, M., and Brock, D.: Ultracellular functional and pathogenic mechanisms. V. *In vivo* and *in vitro* C.N.S. and liver mitochondrial following administration of phenothiazines. *Trans Amer Neurol Ass, 89:*247, 1964.

12. Roizin, L., and Nishikawa, K.: The Golgi complex of the C.N.S. Anatomotopographic studies following administration of prochlorperazine (Compazine, S.K.F.). *J Neuropath Exp Neurol, 24:*165, 1965.

13. Nishikawa, K., and Roizin, L.: The fine structures of synapses of the C.N.S. and their content following administration of phenothiazines. *6th Int'l. Cong. Electron Microscopists.* Proc. 441, Kyoto, Japan, 1966.

14. Roizin, L., Gold, G., Kaufman, M.A., Fieve, R., Alexander, G., and Ueno, Y.: Experimental potentiation of phenothiazine toxicology. 1. Effects of liver disorders. 2. Inter'l. symposium on Action Mechanisms and Metabolism of Psychoactive Drugs. *Agressologie, 9:*379, 1968.

15. Roizin, L., Nishikawa, K., Cuatico, W., Iyengar, V.K.S., and LiVolsi, V.: Golgi complex and correlated intracellular organelles of the C.N.S. following administration of neurotropic agents. *Fed Proc, 26:*793, 1967.

16. Giese, A.C.: *Cell Physiology.* Philadelphia, W. B. Saunders Co., 1962.

17. de Reuck, A.V.S., and Knit, J. (Eds.) . *Animal Behavior and Drug Action*. Ciba Foundation Symposium. Boston, Little, Brown & Co., 1964.

18. Meyler, L.: *Side Effects of Drugs*. Amsterdam and New York, Excerpta Medica Foundation, 1969.

19. Ebert, J. D.: *Interacting Systems in Development*. New York, Holt, Rinehart & Winston, 1965.

20. Woolam, D.H.M. (Ed.) : *Advances in Teratology*. New York and London, A Logos Press Book, Academic Press, 1966.

21. Farber, E., and Magee, P.N.: *Biochemical pathology*. Baltimore, Williams & Wilkins, Co., 1966.

22. Kment, A.: In *Cell Research and Cellular Therapy,* edited by F. Schmid and J. Stein. Switzerland, Ott Publishers Thoune, 1967, p. 29.

23. Meyler, L., and Peck, H. M. (Eds.) : *Drug Induced Diseases* (Vol. 3) . Amsterdam, New York, Excerpta Medica Foundation, 1968.

24. Handler, Ph. (Ed.) : *Biology and the Future of Man*. New York, London, Toronto, Oxford University Press, 1970.

25. Roizin, L.: Evolution of CNS pathogenic mechanisms. In *The World Biennial of Psychiatry & Psychotherapy* edited by S. Arieti. New York, London, Basic, 1971, vol. 1, p. 560.

26. Miller, Clem. O (Ed.) : *Proceedings Conference on Nonhuman Primate Toxicology*. Warrenton, Virginia, Airlie House, June 12-14, 1966.

27. Lennard, H. L., Epstein, L. J., Bernstein, A., and Ranson, D. C.: Hazards implicit to prescribing psychoactive drugs. *Science, 169:*438, 1970.

28. Roizin, L., Lazar, M., and Gold, G.: Prenatal effects of phenothiazine. *Fed Proc, 25:*353, 1966.

29. Roizin, L., Gold, G., Alexander, G., Miles, B., Kaufman, M. A., and Lawler, C.: Prenatal effects of hallucinogens. *Amer J Psychiat, 124:* 185, 1968.

30. Alexander, G. J., Gold, G. M., Miles, B. E., and Alexander, R. B.: Lysergic acid diethylamide intake in pregnancy: Fetal damage in rats. *J Pharmacol Exp Ther, 173:*48, 1970.

31. Roizin, L., and Schade, J. P.: V. Ultrastructural findings. In Pathogenesis of x-irradiation effects in the monkey cerebral cortex. *Brain Research, 7:*87, 1968.

32. Wikler, A.: *Opiate Addiction*. Springfield, Charles C Thomas, 1953.

33. Hurst, W. E.: Sexual differences in toxicity and therapeutic action of chemical substances. In *Evaluation of Drug Toxicity,* edited by R. L. Walpole and J. Spinks. London, Churchill, Ltd., 1958, p. 12.

34. Barnes, J. M.: Testing of drugs for toxicity. In *Evaluation of Drug Toxicity,* edited by A. L. Walpole and J. Spinks. Boston, Little, Brown & Co., 1958, p. 48.

35. Albert, A.: *Selective Toxicity*. London, Methuen & Co., Ltd.; New York, John Wiley & Sons, Inc., 1960.

36. Litchfield, J. T.: Symposium on clinical drug evaluation and human

pharmacology. XVI Evaluation of the safety of new drugs by means of tests in animals. *Clin Pharmacol Ther, 3:*665, 1962.

37. Meier, H.: *Experimental Pharmacogenetics.* New York and London, Academic Press, 1963.

38. Goldstein, A., Aronow, L., and Kalman, S. M.: Principles of drug action (The basis of pharmacology). New York, Evanston and London, Harper & Row, 1969.

39. Walpole, A. L., and Spinks, J. (Eds.) : *The Evaluation of Drug Toxicity.* Boston, Little, Brown & Co., 1958.

40. Albert, A.: *Selective Toxicity.* London, Methuen & Co., Ltd.: New York, John Wiley & Sons, Inc., 1960.

41. Levine, B. B.: Immune mechanisms of drug allergy. *Inter'l. Conf. on Adverse Reaction Reporting Systems.* Washington, D. C., Oct. 22-23, 1970.

42. Rosenzwerg, M. R., Krech, D., and Bennett, E. L.: Brain enzyme and adaptive behavior. In *Neurological Basis of Behavior.* (Ciba Foundation Symposium) edited by G. E. W. Wolstenholme and C. M. O'Connor. Boston, Little, Brown, & Co., 1958.

43. Chance, M. R. A.: Discussion in Hurst (33, pg. 23) .

44. Paget, G. E., and Barness, J.: Toxicity test. In *Evaluation of Drug Activities: Pharmacometrics,* edited by D. R. Lawrence and A. L. Bacharach. London and New York, Academic Press, 1968, vol. 1, p. 135.

45. Hewitt, H. B.: Discussion. In *The Evaluation of Drug Toxicity,* edited by A. L. Walpole, and J. Spinks. London, A Churchill, Ltd. 1958, p. 22.

46. Brodie, B. B.: Pathways of drug metabolism. *J Pharm Pharmacol, 8:*1, 1958.

47. Ferraro, A., and Roizin, L.: Cerebral histologic changes in acute experimental inanitation in cats. *J Neuropath Exp Neurol, 1:*81, 1942.

48. Dixon, R. L., Shultice, R. W., and Fouts, J. R.: Factors affecting drug metabolism by liver microsomes. IV. Starvations. *Proc Soc Exp Biol Med, 103:*333, 1960.

49. Roizin, L.: Tissue reaction patterns of the white matter of the CNS. In *Cytology and Cellular Pathology of the Nervous System,* edited by W. Haymaker, and R. Adams. 1971, in press.

50. Dubach, U. C.: Studies of nephrotoxicity in relation to regular intake of analgesics. In *Inter'l. Conference on Adverse Reaction Reporting systems.* Washington, D. C., Oct. 22-23, 1970.

51. Kenedy, F.: Interrelationship of mind and body. *Proc Ass Res Nerv Ment Dis, 19:*1, 1938.

52. Cannon, W. B.: *The Way of an Investigator* (A Scientist's *Experience in Medical Research)* . New York, W. W. Norton, & Co., 1945.

53. Weiss, E., and English, O.S.: *Psychosomatic medicine (The Clinical*

Application of Psychopathology to General Medical Problems). Philadelphia and London, W. B. Saunders, 1949.

54. Cobb, S.: *Emotions and Clinical Medicine.* New York, W. W. Norton, & Co., 1950.

55. Selye, H., and Fortier, C.: Adaptive reactions to stress. In *Proc Ass Res Nerv Ment Dis, 29:*3, 1950.

56. Engel, G. L.: Selection of clinical material. In *Psychosom Med, 16:*369, 1954.

57. Richter, C. P.: Neurological basis of responses to stress. In *Neurological Basis of Behaviour* (Ciba Foundation Symposium), edited by G.E.W. Walstenholme and C. M. O'Connor. Boston, Little, Brown & Co., 1958, p. 204.

58. Dunlop, D.: Definition of the adverse reaction reporting problem. In *International Conference on Adverse Reaction Reporting Systems.* Washington, D.C., Oct. 22-23, 1970.

59. Oates, J. A.: Metabolic data in drug interactions. In *International Conference on Adverse Reaction Reporting Systems.* Washington, D.C., Oct. 22-23, 1970.

60. Lasagna, L.: The diseases drug cause. *Perspect Biol Med, 7:*457, 1964.

61. Peters, R. A.: Biochemical lesions. *Lancet, 1:*1161, 1936.

62. Kalow, W.: *Pharmacogenetics, Hereditary and Response to Drugs.* W. B. Saunders, Philadelphia, 1962.

63. Seidel, L. G., Thornton, G. F., Smith, J. W., and Cluff, L. E.: Studies on the epidemiology of adverse drug reactions. III. Reactions in patients on a general medical service. *Bull Johns Hopkins Hosp, 119:*299, 1966.

64. Walpole, A. L., and Spinks, J. (Eds.) : *The Evaluation of Drug Toxicity.* Boston, Little, Brown & Co., 1958.

65. Sussman, S.: Narcotic and amphetamine use during pregnancy. *Amer J Dis Child, 106:*325, 1963.

66. Stern, R.: The pregnant addict. *Amer J Obstet Gynec, 94:*253, 1966.

67. van Leeuven, G., Guthrie, R., and Stange, F.: Narcotic withdrawal reaction in newborn infant due to cocaine. *Pediatrics, 36:*635, 1965.

68. Irey, N. S.: Registry of tissue reactions to drugs. In *International Conference on Adverse Reaction Reporting Systems* Washington, D. C., Oct. 22-23, 1970.

69. Ray, A. K., and Ghosh, J. J.: Changes in the hypothalamo-neurohypophyseal neuro-secretory materials of rats during different phases of morphine administration. *J Neurochem, 16:*1, 1969.

70. Cushman, P., Jr., Bordier, B., and Hilton, J. G.: Hypothalamic-pituitary-adrenal axis in methadone treated heroin addicts. *J Clin Endocr, 30:*24, 1970.

71. Brown, A. M.: *Evaluation of Drug Activities: Pharmacometrics,* edited by Dr. R. Lawrence and A. L. Bacharach. 1964, vol. 1, p. 11.

72. Rünke, Chr. L.: Some limitation of animal tests. In *Evaluation of Drug Activities: Pharmacometrics,* edited by D. R. Lawrence and A. L. Bacharach, Academic Press, London and New York, 1964, vol. 1, p. 125.

73. Inman, W. H. W.: British experience with voluntary reporting. In *International Conference Adverse Reaction Reporting Systems.* Washington, D. C., Oct. 22-23, 1970.

74. Long, J. W.: Problems related to the dissemination of drug adverse reaction information. In *International Conference on Adverse Reaction Reporting Systems.* Washington, D. C., Oct. 22-23, 1970.

75. Jick, H.: Intensive surveillance systems. In *International Conference on Adverse Reaction Reporting Systems.* Washington, D. C., Oct. 22-23, 1970.

76. Rado, S.: Narcotic bondage. *Amer J Psychol, 114:*165, 1957.

77. Eddy, N. B., Halbach, H., Isbell, H., and Seevers, M. H.: Drug dependence: Its significance and characteristics. *Bull WHO, 32:*721, 1965.

Chapter 13

Blockade of Teratogenic Effect of Morphine, Dihydromorphinone and Methadone by Nalorphine, Cyclazocine, and Naloxone in the Fetal Hamster

William F. Geber

T HE PRESENT INVESTIGATION is part of a long-term research project designed to develop a new, unified concept of the mech-
anism(s) involved in the production of congenital abnormalities.
One of the primary objectives within the parameters of this major
goal is the formulation of a method of production of a model of
abnormal central nervous system development and function.

Since the theme of this book is drug abuse, a correlation should
be established between the theme and the contents of this chapter. The correlation lies in the inherent capability of the drugs
to be discussed to produce both a state of dependence in the adult
animal and human and fetal congenital abnormalities in animals.
Hopefully, it can be established that both phenomena utilize common mechanism pathways if a blocking compound or antagonist
to one phenomenon will effectively block or antagonize the second
phenomenon. Thus, additional information may be developed
about the concept of drug dependence by a detailed study of the
pharmacodynamics of the induction of congenital abnormalities
by drugs capable of producing both reactions.

METHODS

Pregnant hamsters (Lakeview Colony) were used throughout
the study. All females were caged individually in a room with
controlled temperature, lighting and noise level. Each drug,
agonist as well as antagonist, was given as a single, subcutaneous
injection on the eighth day of gestation. The eighth day is utilized

117

since this period in the hamster is the time of greatest susceptibility to the induction of many types of congenital abnormalities, including central nervous system lesions.[1] Following the injection(s), each female was returned to her cage until sacrificed four days later on day 12 of gestation. Each antagonist was injected twenty minutes before the agonist was administered. Each fetus was removed from the uterus of the sacrificed females and examined for various gross anatomical lesions.

The pregnant female hamsters were divided into sixteen groups of twenty animals each and given the following sequences of drug injections: (a) morphine alone, 300 mg/kg; (b) dihydromorphinone alone, 150 mg/kg; (c) methadone alone, 80 mg/kg; (d) nalorphine alone, 100 to 300 mg/kg; (e) cyclazocine alone, 50 to 100 mg/kg; (f) naloxone alone, 100 to 300 mg/kg; (g) morphine preceded by nalorphine; (h) morphine preceded by cyclazocine; (i) morphine preceded by naloxone; (j) dihydromorphinone preceded by nalorphine; (k) dihydromorphinone preceded by cyclazocine; (l) dihydromorphinone preceded by naloxone; (m) methadone preceded by nalorphine; (n) methadone preceded by cyclazocine; (o) methadone preceded by naloxone; and (p) saline control.

RESULTS

Morphine, dihydromorphinone and methadone administered alone produced an average of 33 percent, 45 percent and 55 percent abnormal fetuses per litter. Minimal fetal abnormalities were observed with the narcotic antagonists and saline injections. Exencephaly and cranioschisis were the most dominant anomalies observed although a wide range of anatomical lesions was produced. The narcotic antagonists produced a dose-dependent blockade of the teratogenic action of the narcotic agents. Table 13-I lists the various combinations of drugs studied. The data presented represent that obtained at one dose level of each of the compounds. The percentage of abnormal fetuses produced by each of the narcotic agents is dose related.[2] Since the degree of blockade by each of the narcotic antagonists is dose dependent also, a wide range of interrelationships is possible by varying the

TABLE 13-I

AGONIST-ANTAGONIST RELATIONSHIP IN BLOCKADE OF
TERATOGENIC ACTIVITY OF OPIATES/OPIOIDS

Drug	% Abnormal Fetuses		
	(A) Agonist	(B) Antagonist	B + A
Morphine—Nalorphine	33.2	0.7	0.0
Morphine—Cyclazocine	33.2	0.5	5.2
Morphine—Naloxone	33.2	0.2	0.9
Dihydromorphinone—Nalorphine	45.1	0.7	10.1
Dihydromorphinone—Cyclazocine	45.1	0.5	19.4
Dihydromorphinone—Naloxone	45.1	0.2	0.0
Methadone—Nalorphine	38.6	0.7	6.4
Methadone—Cyclazocine	38.6	0.5	1.5
Methadone—Naloxone	38.6	0.2	3.1
Control (Saline)	0.0	—	—

concentrations of either or both types of compound singly or together. For the purposes of this report morphine was administered at 300 mg/kg, dihydromorphinone 150 mg/kg, methadone 80 mg/kg, nalorphine 300 mg/kg, naloxone 300 mg/kg, and cyclazocine 100 mg/kg.

In column A (agonist) the percentage of abnormal fetuses produced by the narcotics alone is shown. In column B (antagonists) the percentage of fetal abnormalities produced by the blocking compounds is listed. In the third column (B & A) the fetal protection afforded by injection of the antagonists twenty minutes before the administration of the narcotics is shown.

TABLE 13-II

INDUCTION AND BLOCKADE OF SUMMATION OF TERATOGENICITY

Drug	% Abnormal Fetuses
Dihydromorphinone	9.3
Morphine	5.1
Methadone	15.2
DMM	32.5
Nalorphine—DMM	8.1
Naloxone—DMM	0.5
Control (Saline)	0.0

Table 13-II represents a variation on some of the interrelationships established above. Dihydromorphinone, morphine and methadone were each administered at a 55 mg/kg level to three groups of pregnant females. A fourth group received a combination solution of the three compounds amounting to 165 mg/kg. A fifth group received 300 mg/kg nalorphine before being injected with the combination. A sixth group received 300 mg/kg naloxone before the combination was administered. It will be noted that the combination (DMM) produced approximately the degree (percentage abnormal fetuses) of teratogenic activity as would be expected from simple additive action of each of the compounds alone. Both nalorphine and naloxone were effective antagonists to the combination effect as would be predicted from results in Table 13-I.

TABLE 13-III
INDUCTION AND BLOCKADE OF POTENTIATION OF TERATOGENICITY

Drug	% Abnormal Fetuses
Dihydromorphinone	2.6
Isoproterenol	15.3
Trypan blue	8.1
DIT	60.8
Nalorphine—DIT	35.2
Control (Saline)	0.0

Table 13-III indicates the possibility of potentiation occurring when a number of teratogenic compounds of different chemical structure, class, and physiologic and pharmacologic action and function are administered as a combination solution to the pregnant animal. Dihydromorphinone 18 mg/kg, isoproterenol 50 mg/kg, and trypan blue 9 mg/kg were injected as a single solution (DIT). Note that the total effect of the combination is significantly larger than simple addition of the effectiveness of each of the compounds alone. Nalorphine 300 mg/kg administered twenty minutes prior to injection of the combination was partially effective as an antagonist to the teratogenicity of the combination of the three compounds. Both isoproterenol and trypan blue have been shown to be teratogenic in the fetal hamster in previous studies.[3]

DISCUSSION

The present study is part of a long-term investigation into the various phenomena capable of producing a deviant pattern of fetal development.[4-6] Many types of factors are capable of inducing congenital abnormalities in the animal.[7-9] As is well known, the same type of anatomical (and functional) lesion can be produced by a wide range of factors. The major thesis of the author's investigations has been that a common biochemical pathway must be involved at some level of action of each one of the diverse factors activity spectrum. Therefore, if this common pathway can be delineated or described either directly or indirectly, a certain measure of control (both induction and blockade) of the phenomenon of development of abnormal fetal differentiation can be exercised.

With the establishment of the teratogenicity of the various opiates/opioids,[2] the opportunity to integrate another phenomenon into the general scheme presented itself. The possibility exists that all or some part of the common pathway utilized by a diverse spectrum of teratogenic agents may be involved in the induction of the state of dependence/tolerance to compounds being considered in the present investigation.

The primary correlative finding that emerges from the present study is the ability of the established narcotic antagonists (or blockers) to be equally effective as agents capable of blocking or antagonizing the teratogenic activity of the narcotic analgesics. A possible common background upon which both actions of the narcotic compounds could work may be their relation to protein synthesis or the disruption thereof. Recent evidence indicates the development of both tolerance and physical dependence is prevented by the administration of cycloheximide,[10] a compound capable of inhibition of protein synthesis. Therefore, it may be postulated that tolerance, physical dependence and abnormal fetal embryological development occur in response to the presence of the narcotic agent by the production of newly synthesized, abnormal protein protoplasmic constituents that become incorporat-

122 Drug Abuse

ed into the total body organization. The narcotic antagonists may be effective due to their ability to occupy activity sites on enzyme systems responsible for controlling various aspects of protein synthesis necessary for initiating either the development of physical dependence or abnormal fetal growth patterns.

REFERENCES

1. Ferm, V.H.: The use of the golden hamster in experimental teratology. *Lab Animal Care, 17:*452-462, 1967.
2. Geber, W.F., and Schramm, L.C.: Teratogenic potential of various narcotic and non-narcotic analgesic agents. *Proceedings of the Committee on Problems of Drug Dependence.* Published by National Academy of Sciences, National Research Council 1970, pp 6571-6577.
3. Geber, W.F.: Isoproterenol induced congenital malformations in the fetal hamster. *Proc Soc Exp Biol Med, 130:*1168-1170, 1969.
4. Geber, W.F.: Maternal influences on the fetal cardiovascular system in the sheep, dog, and rabbit. *Am J Physiol, 202:*653-660, 1962.
5. Geber, W.F.: Developmental effects of chronic maternal audiovisual stress on the rat fetus. *J Embryol Exp Morph, 16:*1-16, 1966.
6. Geber, W.F.: Congenital malformations induced by mescaline, lysergic acid diethylamide, and brom-lysergic acid in the hamster. *Science, 157:* 265-267, 1967.
7. Ingalls, T.H., Curley, F.J. and Prindle, R.A.: Experimental production of congenital abnormalities: timing and degree of anoxia as factors causing fetal deaths and congenital abnormalities in mouse. *New Eng J Med, 247:*758-768, 1952.
8. Kalter, H., and Warkany, J.: Experimental production of congenital malformations in mammals by metabolic procedure. *Physiol Rev, 39:* 69-115, 1959.
9. Wilson, J.G.: Teratogenic interaction of chemical agents in the rat. *J Pharmacol Exp Ther, 144:*429-436, 1964.
10. Way, E.L., Loh, H.H. and Shen, F.: Inhibition of morphine tolerance, physical dependence, and brain 5-hydroxytryptamine synthesis. *Proceedings of the Committee on Problems of Drug Dependence.* Published by National Academy of Sciences, National Research Council 1969, pp 5991-6001.

Chapter 14

Prenatal Effects of Hallucinogens

Leon Roizin, G. Gold, G. Alexander, B. Miles,
M. Kaufman, C. Lawler and K. Akai

~~~~~~

W E ARE, AT PRESENT, faced with an exuberant and kaleido-
scopic literature on the behavioral, psychiatric, neurophysiological, biochemical, clinicopathological and other effects of hallucinogens, particularly LSD-25. This is the result of the involvement of the most diversified professions such as the medical, biological, social, religious, legislative and creative and performing
arts. Furthermore, because of the sensational publicity through
newspapers, radio and television, frequently misunderstanding or
misconceptions have contaminated and confused the proper evaluation of objective facts. Fortunately, several excellent scientific
symposia, as well as several critical reviews of the medical and
psychiatric literature have been published.* However, the mechanisms of action of LSD-25 and analogous hallucinogens are still
much debated and poorly understood. Moreover, the prenatal
effects of these hallucinogens have become one of the most
pressing concerns of the last two years. Concomitantly, teratogenic effects in humans[12,28,32] and experimental conditions* as
well as chromosomal abnormalities have been reported by several
investigators.[8,12]

None the less, for a more comprehensive exploration of the
possible pathogenic mechanisms of the teratogenous effects of
LSD-25 and analogous hallucinogens, additional investigations

Note: This chapter, in its unabbreviated form, was presented at the First Multi-
state Interhospital Conference, New York City, April 17-18, 1970, which was sponsored by the Eastern Psychiatric Research Association. It was supported, in part,
by General Research Grant FR-05650-04 (157-1) .

*See the following references: 1, 9-11, 13, 15, 17, 25, 26, 29.
*See the following references: 2-4, 6, 16, 19-24, 27, 30, 31.

are needed, since the reported human material is still limited or rather inadequately studied, whereas the experimental material consists of relatively limited short-term experiments and reports of a preliminary character.

On the basis of these criteria and our previous studies on prenatal effects of x-irradiation[22] and phenothiazines[23,24] we planned to study the prenatal effects of hallucinogens with three different experimental procedures.

MATERIAL AND EXPERIMENTAL PROCEDURES

The first group consisted of selected young rats (Wistar-O'Grady strain) which served as self-controls in the sense that they were allowed to have two successive normal deliveries. The mating animals which showed any abnormalities were eliminated. The second experimental group consisted of randomly selected mice (FCI-S, Swiss-O'Grady strains) and rats (Wistar-O'Grady) and seven macacus rhesus monkeys (India strain) which were used after a preliminary two week quarantine. The third group consisted of CH3 (HeJ) strain of mice which spontaneously shows a higher incidence of anomalies as compared with the FCI-S strain (the latter being less prone to teratogenesis).

RESULTS

To date, observations of 6,684 mice and rat embryos have revealed interference of pregnancy or induced resorptions, stillborn, early and late embryonal or fetal deaths, stunted and small offspring and occasionally exencephaly, defective development of one extremity or tail were observed in randomly selected mice (CFI-S and Swiss-O'Grady) and rats (Wistar-O'Grady) following administration of effective and high dosages of LSD-25 (2.5 to 40 mg/kg), mescaline (2.5 to 5 mg/kg) and DOM (4-methyl-2,5-dimethoxy-amphetamine hydrochloride, 15 mg/kg), administered by i.v., i.m., s.c., and i.p. injections. Some control animals (CFI-S) also showed a certain amount of failures in pregnancy, variations in size of the offspring (particularly in larger litters) some stunted, one exencephaly, a defective extremity and a maldeveloped tail. Two of the six LSD-25 treated macacus rhesus monkeys delivered stillborn offsprings with malformed faces; one of which had two premature upper incisor teeth. The offsprings showed marked variations in size and weight.

CONCLUSIVE REMARKS

It seems to us that the type, severity and frequency of the chemically induced teratogenic effects by LSD-25, mescaline and DOM depend, at least in part, and to a certain degree upon the interaction of several factors as summarized in Table 14-I. Some of these observations appear analogous to the experimental findings of the tissue distribution and the rate of biotransformation or metabolitization of LSD-25 (Axelrod *et al.* 1956; Boyd *et al.* 1955; Evarts, 1957) in experimental animals. It is also of interest to note that some of the qualitative and quantitative teratogenic features of the experimental animals also seem to be similar to the incidence and character of certain clinical side effects in humans, particularly in relation to predisposing factors.*

TABLE 14-I
SOME FUNDAMENTAL BIOLOGICAL CRITERIA

Drug pharmocodynamies:	Biochemical properties, dosage and mode of administration, duration of action, differential tissue distribution.
Animal model:	Species (strain) and or individual (age, sex, constitution) predisposition or susceptibility.
Structural character:	Histometabolic and pathologic selectivity (at cellular and ultrastructural levels) .
Functional State:	Physiological and metabolic homeokinesis, stressor and pathergic effects.
Environmental conditions:	Internal and external (including seasonal variants) .

REFERENCES

1. Abramson, H.A. (Ed.) : *The Use of LSD in Psychotherapy and Alco-holism XI-697*. New York, Bobbs-Mervill Co., Inc., 1967.
2. Alexander, G.J., Machiz, S., and Alexander, R.B.: Inherited abnormalities in three generations of offspring of LSD treated rats. *Fed. Proc. (Abstr.), 27:*220, 1968.

*Pre–LSD-25 psychosis are much higher than in general population, prolonged psychotic reactions, recurrent LSD-25 experiences, release of psychopathic personality trends, etc.

3. Alexander, G.J., Miles, B.E., Gold, G.M., and Alexander, R.B.: LSD: Injected early in pregnancy produces abnormalities in offspring of rats. *Science, 157:*459, 1967.
4. Auerbach, R., and Rugowski, J.A.: Lysergic acid diethylamide: Effect on embryos. *Science, 157:*1325, 1967.
5. Axelrod, J., Brady, R.O., Witkob, B., and Evarts, E.V.: Metabolism of LSD. *Nature, 178:*143, 1956.
6. Bignami, G., Bovet, D., Bovet-Nitti, F., and Rosnati, V.: Drugs and congenital abnormalities. *Lancet, 2:*1333, 1962.
7. Boyd, E.S., Rothlin, E., Bonner, J.F., Slater, I.H., and Hodge, H.C.: Preliminary studies of the metabolism of LSD using radio-active carbon-marked molecules. *J. Nerv Ment Dis, 122:*470, 1955.
8. Cohen, M.M., Marinello, M.J., and Back, N.: Chromosomal damage in human leukocytes induced by lysergic acid diethylamide. *Science, 155:*1417, 1967.
9. Cohen, S., and Ditman, K.: Prolonged adverse reactions to lysergic acid diethylamide. *Arch Gen Psychiat (Chicago), 8:*475, 1963.
10. Ditman, K.S.: Complications associated with lysergic acid diethylamide (LSD-25). *JAMA, 181:*161, 1962.
11. Ditman, K.S., Tietz, W., Prince, B.S., Forgy, E., and Moss, Th.: Harmful aspects of the LSD experiences. *J Nerv Ment Dis, 145:*464, 1968.
12. Egozcue, J., and Irwin, S.: Chromosome aberrations reported in LSD users. *Med. News, 1:*3, 1967.
13. Elkes, J.: The dysleptics: Note on a No Man's Land. *Compr Psychiat., 4:*195, 1963.
14. Evarts, E. V.: A review of the neurophysiological effects of lysergic acid diethylamide and other psychotominetic agents. *Amer. N.Y. Acad. Sci., 66:*479, 1957.
15. Frosch, W., Robbins, E., and Sterim, M.: Untoward reactions to LSD resulting in hospitalization. *New Eng J Med, 273:*1235, 1965.
16. Geber, W.F.: Congenital malformations by mescaline, lysergic acid diethylamide and bromo-lysergic acid in the hamster. *Science, 158:*265, 1967.
17. Hoffer, A.: D-Lysergic acid diethylamide (LSD): A review of its present status. *Clin Pharmacol Ther, 6:*183, 1965.
18. Kleber, H.D.: Prolonged adverse reactions from unsupervised use of hallucinogenic drugs. *J Nerv Ment Dis, 144:*308, 1967.
19. Misiti, D., Rosnati, V., Bignami, G., Bovet-Nitti, F., and Boret, D.: Effects of d,L-3-phthalimidoglutarimide on rat pregnancy. *J Med Chem, 6:*464, 1963.
20. Nora, J.J., Trasler, Daphne, G., and Frasser, F. Clarke: Malformations in mice induced by dexamphetamine sulphate. *Lancet (Letters to the editor), 2(7420):*1021, 1965.
21. Roizin, L., Lazar, M., and Gold, G.: Prenatal effects of phenothiazines. *Fed Proc, 25:*353, 1966.

22. Roizin, L., Rugh, R., and Kaufman, M.A.: Neuropathologic investigations of the x-irradiated embryo rat brain. *J Neuropathol Exp Neurol, 21:* 219, 1962.

23. Roizin, L., True, C., and Knight, N.: Structural effects of tranquilizers in the effect of pharmacologic agents. *Proc Ass Res Nerv Ment Dis, 37:*285, 1959.

24. Sawin, P.B., Crary, D., Fox, R.R., and West, H.M.: Thalidomide malformations and genetic background in the rabbit. *Experientia, 21:*672, 1965.

25. Schwarz, C.J.: The complications of LSD: A review of the literature. *J Nerv Ment Dis, 146:*174, 1968.

26. Smart, R.G., and Bateman, K.: Unfavorable reactions to LSD: A review and analysis of the available case reports. *Canad Med Ass J, 97:*1214, 1967.

27. Somers, G. F.: Thalidomide and congenital abnormalities. *Lancet, 1:*912, 1962.

28. Sotelo-Avila, C., and Shanklin, D.R.: Congenital malformations in an autopsy population. *Arch Path, 84:*272, 1967.

29. Ungerleider, T., Fisher, D., and Fuller, M.: The dangers of LSD. *JAMA, 197:*389, 1966.

30. Warkany, J., and Takacs: Lysergic acid diethylamide (LSD) : No teratogenicity in rats. *Science, 159:*731, 1968.

31. West, H.M., Sigg, E. B., and Fratta, I.: Pharmacological properties and teratogenic action of 2 (hexahydrophthalimido) glutarimide and 2-phthalimido-N-methylglutarimide. *Life Sci, 3:*721, 1964.

32. Zellweger, H., McDonald, J.S., and Abbo, G.: Is lysergic-acid diethylamide a teratogen? *Lancet, 2:*1066, 1967.

SECTION III

PSYCHOLOGICAL AND SOCIOLOGICAL ASPECTS

Chapter 15

The Background of the Affluent
Acting-out Student

Mortimer R. Feinberg

~~~~~~~~~~~~~~~~~~~~~~~~~~~~~~~~~~~~~~~

I RECENTLY was on a plane and the pilot said, "I have good news for you and bad news. I'll give you the bad news first—I don't know where I am, I have lost all radar contact. The good news is we have a marvelous amount of tail wind." We have a marvelous tail wind today coming from our student population, the drugs are merely one symptom. I would like to tell you about my credentials. I am a former acting chairman of the Psychology Department; I teach in an open enrollment institution; and I am also an industrial psychologist—that's like the sex life in elephants, it's practiced at very high levels amongst much noise and confusion. I have two sons, one is a psychologist, one is a surgeon. The surgeon is 17, the psychologist is 19.

I think the college student population is divided into four parts. First there is the "relative conservative." He's the kind of kid that listens to Dr. Helpern, when Helpern says, "Listen kids, you smoke pot, you can't study." All he wants to know is how he can get into medical school and what he's got to do to pass his biochemistry exams. Now he is a *relative* conservative because he is nowhere near as conservative as a conservative would be perceived of about thirty years ago. He represents maybe 30 percent of the population of the students. Then there is the "idealist reformer." These students hate the word "liberal" because they perceive the word "liberal" as associated with the ineffectual people of the past who mouthed certain ideas about society but weren't able to do anything. This group represents almost 50 percent of the present college population. They see pot as alcohol to be enjoyed after, not during, study. I have never seen pot smoking in an examination. (There's some research you will read about in a later chapter regarding the idea that when students obtain responsibility, they stop smoking pot. Mr. Hastings referred earlier to the fact that when people start drinking after they get into the Country Club, they drop the pot bit.) Then you have the third group, which is our black student population, with a specific agenda, with a specific kind of situation which I do not have time to elaborate. Then you have the fourth group, which is a very small percentage of the population of college students—they are the revolutionaries. They want to destroy the order, they want to burn the buildings. They pick on the universities because they are the most vulnerable of all our institutions. They can't burn down Dow Chemical; they can't get involved with burning down the state departments, so they pick on the poor academicians. Presidents of colleges today are the most vulnerable target because they are professors, intellectuals who believe in dialogue, and the radicals know this and know they can take us over. One student said to me once, "You know, Professor Feinberg, you're like a marshmallow—you're sweet and soft and syrupy, and I want to put you in the fire to see what happens." This kind of rhetoric, by the way, is characteristic of this generation of young Americans and why they have to be rude, why they have to use the slang words to get their points of view across, I haven't figured out yet. But there is a rhetoric of rudeness. It is important to understand the nature of society or you can't understand the nature of the problem.

First, this generation of American students has never been more affluent, except for certain areas of poverty. I was with the president of a company recently and he took me to Scarsdale where he pointed out his son's home, with a swimming pool and a tennis court, and I commented that his son must be doing great. He said yes! "He got two A's and a B last term." The avoidance of the adolescent development period because of affluence must be understood; never has a generation been richer, provided with more and expected so much. This is true of the old as well as the young. Next door there is no scientific meeting, it's a bunch of old women dancing. Now where the heck do they get the time or the money to dance with those gigolos. They have the time and the money provided by our affluent culture. When I was a young boy, we only had two kinds of cookies, Fig Newtons and Hydrox; If you were very good, you earned Lorna Doones. You know there are 150 cookies on the cracker counters. Even Captain Kangeroo is a hustler. He's constantly pushing more into the kids' mouths, whether it's cookies or something else. We have become a consuming society. Why? Because we were deprived by two world wars, because we fought a depression and when we got money, we consumed more than any generation in the history of the world. We created grand larceny against the future. So they, the young today, (a) understand the nature of affluence and (b) are terribly afraid of science and where it will lead us if not controled. For example, most of you believe that the best use of a dead body is as spare parts for a live body; give an arm, give a leg, give a piece of your head—you'll do it. Now the next question is how many of you would keep a 10-month-old child alive long enough to get a heart transplant because the baby is going to die anyway; well most people would stop. The next question logically concerns the idea of no more funerals, just one big icebox with all the spare parts. Finally, how many of you know people whose best use of their body would be as spare parts for a live body. (A new market place for the Mafia would be available.) Can 1984 be far behind? I said to my son, the surgeon, the other day, "Why do you criticize the Establishment and yet you want to use the car and you want to have all the luxuries." He said, "If you're on the Titanic, you want to go first-class." The young's fear about the future and about scientific development, plus the factor of affluence, creates great confusion. In addition, there is a cold revolution in our moral values, and this started with us. I don't know how many of you saw the ad: a genital deodorant for men and another one a female counterparted douche, merchandised under four flavors: raspberry, cherry, champagne, orange blossom, and if you don't believe me, here's the ad and it's for today's liberated women. It appeared in a medical journal. Arnold Toynbee said, "Never has the human mind been put under such intense pressure because of change." To summarize, affluence, fear and a desire to change things is shocking our society and placing a stress on current joys. Some of our economists at the college are terribly frightened that we are going into a severe depression unless we solve some of the social problems. Underneath economic order there is a social order.

Finally, one last point relevant to pot, with regard to the exploring of the inner life. That's why the young are for Zen Buddhism and chasing false Gods. Now I say to them, how are you going to study when you're smoking pot and they say, "Well, we stop studying when we smoke and then we go back to work more creatively." The doctors told W. C. Fields if he didn't stop drinking, he was going to start losing his hearing, and he said, "I think I'll continue drinking because the things that I have been hearing are much worse than the things I have been drinking." Perhaps this is part of the reason for the college students' retreat into their inner lives. I want to end with an ancient Chinese curse which is, "You should only live in interesting times."

Chapter 16

Pleasurable and Unpleasurable Feeling States in Hallucinogenic Drug Experience

Richard E. Hicks

THE DEVELOPMENT of affects and corresponding subjective states of feeling during hallucinogenic drug experience encompasses three major parameters: (a) the direct pharmacologic effects of the drug, (b) the psychological state of the subject at the time of the particular drug experience and (c) the external environmental influence on the subject during the drug experience.

The neurophysiological actions of the hallucinogens and the relationship of these actions to affects and states of feeling are by no means clear. At present it is possible to postulate two major effects at these levels: (a) a set of neuropharmacologically induced conditions and phenomena, which are relatively constant from subject to subject and from one equivalent dose experience to another, with which the subject interacts psychologically, and (b) the stimulation and facilitation of responses which are otherwise functions of the remaining two major parameters, the psychological state and the environment.

These general assumptions are supported by data on both the objective physiological responses of subjects[1-8] and by the finding of certain basic subjective responses which seem to serve as a background against which other widely diverse subjective responses occur.[9]

My purpose here is to consider how we may approach an understanding of the part played by the most uncontrollable set of variables that are embodied in the personality of the subject.

Only a limited number of studies of feeling state responses to hallucinogenic drugs have been reported. In those of Kuramochi and Takahashi,[10] Linton and Langs[11,12] and Katz, Waskow and Olsson,[9] groups of responders were identified by their objective and subjective responses. Especially in the studies of Linton and Langs, correlations with predrug personality factors were demonstrated. The study of Katz *et al.* is particularly instructive concerning basic responses shared by most subjects in the early stages of the LSD experience and in describing three general states of feeling in response to LSD, which the authors identify as moderately euphoric, dysphoric and ambivalent.

All of the authors mentioned and many others looking at hallucinogenic drug responses, either as clinicians or formal investigators, have recognized that an alteration of ego functions is an essential factor in the shaping of responses.[9-22] Many authors explicitly or implicitly relate their assessment of drug responses to the conceptual framework of psychoanalytic theory.[16-18,22] Lindemann and Clarke in 1952,[20] and Klee in 1963,[19] specifically called attention to the value of relating psychopharmacological data to psychoanalytic theory. Klee offered tentative theoretical formulations concerning effects of LSD on the stimulus barrier, and autonomous and defensive ego functions, and he saw the possibility of relating the effects on the stimulus barrier and autonomous functions to specific neurophysiological changes.[19]

Now I want to discuss some psychoanalytic concepts which I believe can serve especially well as a conceptual framework within which to organize and interpret psychopharmacological research concerning feeling states.

PRINCIPLE OF MULTIPLE FUNCTION

In consideration of Freud's formulation,[23] that the ego, confronted by the drives, might either accede to the drives or adaptively master them; Robert Waelder[24] in 1930 observed that "the same method might be adopted and fundamentally applied to all psychic phenomena and that a . . . multiple conception of each psychic function would be . . . altogether necessary. . . ." He noted that every psychic action represents an attempt by the ego to solve problems and that the ego is at all times confronted with problems to be solved in relation to the instinctual drives, the outside world, and, following its development, the superego.

These are sources of conflicting demands, and the relative success of the ego in finding solutions will determine whether comfort, pleasure or unpleasure is the result. According to Waelder, the ego also assigns itself problems. It seeks ways to turn the sources of its problems into resources for its problem-solving activities. Waelder postulated, "It appears now as if our psychic life were directed by a general principle, which we may name the principle of multiple function . . . No attempted solution of a problem is possible which is not . . . an attempted solution of other problems." The complete and simultaneous solution of all of these problems is impossible. Each psychic act is therefore, ". . . a compromise. . . . An attempted solution solves one problem with more success than the other." Every psychic act therefore has multiple meanings to the subject: Quoting Waelder again, "Since the organism reacts in its entirety . . . each attempted solution of a problem must be conjointly determined, modified and arranged through the existence and the working of the others, until it can serve, even if imperfectly, as an attempted solution for all these problems and thus necessarily preserve its multiple meaning." Taking more literary license, Waelder commented that ". . . each (psychic) act is a chord . . . in which there is consonance and dissonance."

The principle of multiple function refers to intrapsychic activity without regard for levels of consciousness. From psychoanalytic observations we know that a person may become consciously aware of none, or a number of meanings of the ego's solutions, even contradictory meanings, depending on the screening or censoring functions of the ego. Likewise, he may or may not become consciously aware of feelings, even contradictory feelings, associated with these multiple meanings, with or without becoming aware of any associated thought content.[25,26]

Hallucinogenic drugs produce alterations in ego functions which facilitate subjective awareness of the derivatives of multiple stimuli making demands on the ego, of multiple meanings (or derivatives of them) and of associated multiple feelings. They therefore influence the production, the form and the level of awareness of thoughts and feelings.

PSYCHIC ADAPTATION

Over the past ten years Joseph Sandler and his fellow authors have made significant contributions to the psychoanalytic psychology of adaptation.

I want to first excerpt some remarks by Joseph Sandler and Walter Joffe in their most recent article, *Towards a Basic Psychoanalytic Model:*[26]

(a) "Psychoanalytic psychology can be regarded as a psychology of adaptation."

(b) ". . . this is an 'intrapsychic' view . . . adaptation to the external world is only one aspect of adaptation . . ."

(c) "Other aspects of adaptation have also to be included—to inner drives and wishes, as well as to those internal standards . . . which we normally refer to as 'superego'."

(d) ". . . not only . . . the ego . . . has to 'adapt' but the apparatus as a whole is involved."

(e) ". . . In moment to moment functioning the psychic apparatus can be regarded as adapting in the 'best' possible way to all the demands being made on it."

(f) ". . . The apparatus responds to only one basic regulating principle. This is its own awareness of . . . changes in the conscious or unconscious feeling state."

Subjective states of feeling, according to this point of view, are derivatives of the multiple function and meanings of psychic activity—more specifically, of the ego's efforts to regulate associated conscious and unconscious feeling states to maintain a basic feeling of safety. Adaptation to reality and the gratification of drives are important but secondary considerations.

In their model, Sandler and Joffe postulate an experiential and a nonexperiential realm. The experiential realm of "subjective phenomenal representations" refers to ". . . experiential content of any sort, including feelings . . .," and this experiential content ". . . can be either conscious or unconscious . . . . the individual may 'know' his own experiential content outside consciousness, . . . ideas can be experienced and feelings felt outside conscious awareness; and . . . he does not know that he unconsciously 'knows'."[26] The hallucinogenic drugs appear to facilitate proportionately greater conscious awareness of this experiential realm.

The nonexperiential realm is the realm of ". . . forces and energies, of mechanisms and apparatuses, of organized structures, both biological and psychological, of sense organs and means of discharge. The nonexperiential realm is intrinsically unknowable, except insofar as it can become known through the creation or occurrence of a phenomenal event in the realm of subjective experience."[26] The hallucinogens appear to facilitate a heightened awareness of more such phenomenal events.

Sandler and Joffe further postulate a psychic representational "field" comprised of the subjective phenomenal representations formed when new perceptions are related with past experience (structures). These representations are scanned for their potential as solutions to multiple problems. Perception of new stimuli results in the formation of a succession of representations. This process is progressively regulated by the ego, which also controls their access to conscious awareness and motor activity. The basic regulatory principle in this process, the aim of which is psychic adaptation, is the need to maintain "a basic stability of the central feeling state" of the individual. They define, in this respect, a "safety principle," which operates along with, but is superordinate to, both the pleasure principle and the reality principle.

> As feelings differentiate, one type of feeling . . . becomes the dominate criterion in determining the activity of the psychic apparatus. This is the feeling of safety . . . generated by smooth and integrated functioning of the apparatus as a whole. . . .[26]

The advantages of this conceptual model for the consideration of psychopharmacological data are several: (a) It clearly incorporates the principle of multiple function. (b) It recognizes explicitly the interrelationship between a nonexperiential realm of neurophysiological and psychological structures and processes, and a realm of psychological experience. (c) As I interpret their model, it defines the basic regulatory principle of psychic activity as that of a homeostatic system in which psychic functions are organized to serve, primarily, the maintenance of a relative affective equilibrium, experienced by the individual as "safety." Just as the term "affect" refers to both the physiological and feeling aspects of a psychophysiological event, "affective equilibrium," which I believe must be essential to the basic feeling of safety in the Sandler-Joffe model, refers to homeostasis in both the biological and psychological aspects of life. (d) The model incorporates the genetic, topographic, structural, economic and dynamic aspects of metapsychology, as interrelated aspects of psychic activity.

FORMATION OF FEELING STATES

Internal Environment in Table 16-I represents the instinctual drives and other physiological processes and also the neural and psychological systems which interact with and process perceptions. *a (2)* and *b (1 and 2)* represent the nonexperiential Realm in the Sandler-Joffe model.

TABLE 16-I
PSYCHIC ACTIVITY

1. *External Environment*
   Perceptible Stimuli
2. *Internal Environment*
   a. Stimuli from
      (1) General bodily processes
      (2) Neurophysiological processes
   b. Existing structures and
      apparatuses
      (1) Neurophysiological
      (2) Psychological

It is assumed throughout the steps postulated in the Table 16-II that all psychic activity has neurophysiological correlates and vice versa. The asterisk referring to affect is to indicate that the subjective phenomenal representations are accompanied by an affect state, with or without conscious awareness of feeling, and that these affect states are perceived by the ego as signals in the regulatory process. If the affect state is too intense or if the ego cannot adequately modify the subjective phenomenal representation, then uncontrolled feeling may be experienced consciously.

The formation of subjective phenomenal representations of incoming stimuli and their modification through association with

TABLE 16-II
PSYCHIC ACTIVITY

1. Conscious or unconscious perception of stimuli.
2. Subjective phenomenal (psychic) representation in the representational field.*
3. Association with nonexperiential structures.
4. Formation of a modified representation.*
5. Interaction of phenomenal representations with psychic structures resulting in a succession of new representations.*

*Affect.

previously established psychic structures is monitored and progressively controlled by the ego. This process would be interfered with by impairment of the stimulus barrier, or the ego's autonomous, defensive, synthetic or reality testing functions, and this would secondarily affect the nature of the phenomenal representations and feelings reaching conscious awareness or motoric expression.

TABLE 16-III
MANIFEST EGO RESPONSE

1. Conscious feeling state (and observable signs of affect).
2. Conscious ideation.
3. Motor activity.

The manifest response (Table 16-III) will be more or less reality adaptive, depending on the integrity of ego functions, the nature of external and internal stimuli, and the nature of the previously established psychic representations (such as earlier representations of self, objects [introjects], drive organization and modes of ego functioning) to which the ego must relate new experiential phenomena.

The principle of multiple function and the interpretation I have presented of the Sandler-Joffe model provide a conceptual framework for constructing hypotheses about the determination of feeling state responses during drug experiences. Once LSD, for example, is active in the CNS, changes in neurophysiological activity appear to modify ego functions in such a way that there is greater conscious awareness of the subjective representations of internal and external stimuli, and of a greater number of associations of new representations with structures laid down by earlier experience. That is, there is greater awareness of sensory experiences, fantasies and associated affect states. The ego, in the interest of maintaining psychic adaptation (i.e. affective equilibrium and a subjective feeling of safety), responds to affect signals produced in association with a succession of subjective representations. It attempts to regulate the formation of fantasies and find compromise solutions to the multiple pressures exerted by drives, superego and its precursors, and the external environment. Pleasurable feelings, experienced against a background feeling of safety and even reality-appropriate unpleasant feelings represent relatively successful solutions. Unpleasant or ambivalent feelings and even pleasurable feelings which are not objectively appropriate, and which are not associated with a basic feeling of safety represent less successful solutions. The manifest feeling states are related to the nature and relative strength of the ego, drives, superego and superego precursors in the presence of the neuropharmacologic effect on ego functions. There is no basis at present for postulating any primary effect of the hallucinogens on drives or superego.

PROBLEMS FOR RESEARCH

In hallucinogenic drug experience the neuropharmacological state appears, according to Klee,[19] to directly impair the stimulus barrier and autonomous ego functions. Using the model of Sandler and Joffe, this might be thought of as presenting the ego with an exceptional problem in controlling the formation and admission into consciousness of subjective phenomenal representations. Impairment of the stimulus barrier alone would cause an increase in associations of perceptual representations of new stimuli with existing psychic structures (such as earlier representations of self, objects [introjects], drive organization and modes of ego functioning). The resulting feeling state would depend on the ego's ability to organize, synthesize, employ defenses and test reality in the presence of this overload of demands. The outcome would depend on the nature, strengths and weaknesses of the ego with the stimulus barrier impaired. Direct pharmacologic impairment of autonomous or other ego functions would further modify the ego's adaptive capacity.

These possibilities suggest a number of difficult problems for future research, among them, the following:

1. What ego functions are directly modified by the neuropharmacologically induced state and what ego functions are only secondarily affected?

2. Are perhaps all ego functions both directly and indirectly affected by the action of hallucinogenic drugs in the CNS?

3. Are the subjective feelings common to all subjects on a particular hallucinogen the manifest derivatives of direct pharmacologic modifications of specific ego functions?

4. Conversely, are differing manifest feeling states the result of secondary reactions of otherwise unmodified ego functions to the pharmacologically induced state?

5. To what extent are the stimulus barrier and other ego functions, such as the synthetic, reality testing and autonomous functions, dependent on the same neurophysiological systems, or on different systems, which might be differentially affected by a given drug?

There are obviously many other important questions for research into hallucinogenic drug effects; these are cited only as examples, because they highlight several important considerations. One is the specific need for standardized measures of ego functions in drug subjects before and during the pharmacologically induced experience.* Another is the need for adoption of a conceptual framework which can aid in interrelating the data of neurophysiological and neuropharmacological studies with the psychological findings of psychopharmacological research and with psychoanalytic formulations derived from clinical experience with drug

---

*The current work of L. Bellak, M. Hurvich and their co-workers, on the systematic study of ego functions in schizophrenics and normals may provide some direction in this area, as regards both definitions and techniques for measuring ego functions.[27,28]

users, such as those reported by Fink *et al.*,[16] Frosch,[17] Hartmann[18] and Wieder and Kaplan.[22] Finally, it is apparent that psychopharmacological investigation of hallucinogenic drug effects remains a vital area for continuing multidisciplinary research, with especially significant potential for advancing our comprehension of the interrelationship between neurological and psychological activity.

REFERENCES

1. Abramson, H., Jarvik, M., Kaufman, M., Kornetsky, C., Levine, A., and Wagner, M.: Lysergic Acid Diethylamide (LSD-25) : I. Physiological and perceptual responses. *J Psychol, 39:*3-60, 1955.
2. Chapman, L., and Walter, R.: Actions of lysergic acid diethylamide on averaged human cortical evoked responses to light flash. *Recent Advances Biol Psychiat, 4:*23-35, 1965.
3. Mancall, E., Kates, J., White, J., and Jackson, L.: Dimethylacetamide: A hitherto unrecognized hallucinogenic agent. *Science, 136:*151-152, 1962.
4. Murphree, H.: Psychedelic drugs in psychopharmacology. In *Psychedelic Drugs,* edited by R. Hicks and P. Fink. New York, Grune & Stratton, 1969, p. 12.
5. Rodin, E., and Luby, E.: Effects of LSD-25 on the EEG and photic evoked responses. *Arch Gen Psychiat, 14:*435-441, 1966.
6. Salvatore, S., and Hyde, R.: Progression of effects of lysergic acid diethylamide (LSD) . *Arch Neurol Psychiat, 76:*50-59, 1956.
7. Stern, M., and Robbins, E.: Clinical diagnoses and treatment of psychiatric disorders subsequent to use of psychedelic drugs. In *Psychedelic Drugs,* edited by R. Hicks and P. Fink. New York, Grune & Stratton, 1969, p. 56.
8. Unger, S.: The psychedelic use of LSD. In *Psychedelic Drugs,* edited by R. Hicks and P. Fink. New York, Grune & Stratton, 1969, p. 201.
9. Katz, M., Waskow, I., and Olsson, J.: Characterizing the psychological state produced by LSD. *J Abnorm Psychol, 73(1):*1-14, 1968.
10. Kurmochi, H., and Takahashi, R.: Psychopathology of LSD intoxication. *Arch Gen Psychiat, 11:*151-161, 1964.
11. Linton, H., and Langs, R.: Subjective reactions to lysergic acid diethylamide (LSD-25) . *Arch Gen Psychiat, 6:*352-368, 1962.
12. Linton, H., and Langs, R.: Empirical dimensions of LSD-25 reaction. *Arch Gen Psychiat, 10:*469-485, 1964.
13. Bowers, M.: Dynamics of psychedelic drug abuse: A clinical study. *Arch Gen Psychiat, 16:*560-566, 1967.
14. Buckman, J.: Psychedelic drugs as adjuncts to analytic psychotherapy. In

Psychedelic Drugs, edited by R. Hicks and P. Fink. New York, Grune & Stratton, 1969, pp. 210-216.

15. Freedman, D. X.: On the use and abuse of LSD. *Arch Gen Psychiat, 18:* 330-347, 1968.
16. Fink, P.; Goldman, M., and Lyons, I.: Morning glory seed psychosis. *Arch Gen Psychiat, 15:*209-213, 1966.
17. Frosch, W. A.: Report of panel on psychoanalytic evaluation of addiction and habituation. *Amer J Psychoanal, 18(1):*209-218, 1970.
18. Hartmann, D.: A study of drug taking adolescents, In *The Psychoanalytic Study of the Child (Vol. 24).* New York, International University Press, 1969, pp. 384-398.
19. Klee, G.: Lysergic acid diethylamide (LSD-25) and ego functions. *Arch Gen Psychiat, 8:*461-474, 1963.
20. Lindemann, F., and Clarke, L.D.: Modifications in ego structure and personality reaction under the influence of the effect of drugs. *Amer J Psychiat, 108:*561-567, 1952.
21. Savage, C.: Variations in ego feeling induced by D-lysergic acid diethylamide (LSD-25) . *Psychoanal Rev, 43:*1-6, 1955.
22. Wieder, H., and Kaplan, E.: Drug use in adolescence, In *The Psychoanalytic Study of the Child (Vol. 24).* New York, International University Press, 1969, pp. 399-431.
23. Freud, S.: Inhibitions, symptoms and anxiety (1926) , In *The Complete Psychological Works of Sigmund Freud* (Standard Ed., Vol. 20) . London, Hogarth Press, 1964, pp. 87-175.
24. Waelder, R.: The principle of multiple function. *Psychoanal Quart, 5:* 45-62, 1936.
25. Novey, S.: A clinical view of affect theory in psychoanalysis. *Int J Psychoanal, 40(1):*94-104, 1959.
26. Sandler, J., and Joffe, W.: Towards a basic psychoanalytic model. *Int. J Psychoanal, 50:*79-90, 1969.
27. Bellak, L., and Hurvich, M.: A systematic study of ego functions. *J Nerv Ment Dis, 148:*569-585, 1969.
28. Bellak, L., Hurvich, M., Gediman, H., and Crawford, P.J.: Study of ego functions in the schizophrenic syndrome. *Arch Gen Psychiat, 23:*326-336, 1970.

Chapter 17

Relationships Between Parental and Adolescent Drug Use

Reginald G. Smart and Dianne Fejer

MANY PEOPLE HAVE BECOME conditioned to think that adolescent drug use arises from a generation gap or from alienation of adolescents from parents. Little attention has been paid so far to the parents of drug users, although most high school users live at home with their parents. If adolescent drug use is closely related to parental drug use this suggests a number of implications for the treatment and prevention of drug abuse.

An association between the drug use of parents and the illicit drug use of their children would be predicted from several circumstances. A study of 6,447 high school students in Toronto in 1968[3] demonstrated that more marijuana and LSD users than expected had parents who used both alcohol and tobacco. However, this study did not inquire about parental use of psychoactives such as tranquilizers, barbiturates and stimulants. The present generation of parents is the first to have major problems with adolescent drug use, however, it is also the first generation to have tranquilizers, antidepressants and a wide variety of stimulant drugs, in particular amphetamines, available to them. Parry[1] demonstrated that about 25 percent of the American adult population is currently using a psychoactive drug. Drug taking, as a form of mood modification, then, could be a phenomenon which is learned within the family environment.

It is hypothesized in this investigation that (a) both illicit and licit drug use will be more frequent in families where parents are users of psychoactive drugs, and (b) the heavier the use of psychoactives by the parents, the more likely the adolescent's use of licit and illicit drugs.

METHOD

The data for this study were derived from surveys in two areas of the province of Ontario. Both surveys were conducted in 1970, only three months apart. Both surveys used substantially the same questionnaires and for the drug use questions the surveys were identical. Students were asked about their use of the following drugs during the six months prior to the survey: alcohol, tobacco, marijuana, hashish, solvents, barbiturates, opiates, speed, stimulants, LSD, tranquilizers and other hallucinogens (other than marijuana, hashish and LSD). Questions were asked about their mothers' and fathers' use of alcohol, tobacco, tranquilizers, stimulants and barbiturates (sleeping pills). In addition, certain demographic and social areas were covered by the questionnaire. The drug use questions had been matched against a second method of estimation[3] and hence considerable confidence is held in them.

The survey in Lincoln and Welland Counties included rural and urban students.[2] The survey in these counties involved 5900 students in grades 9 to 13 inclusive. This represented a 25 percent random sample of public high school classes in the counties. The Toronto survey included only urban and suburban schools. It comprised a 20 percent sample of high school districts in Toronto. From each of grades 6, 7, 9, 11 and 13, approximately 120 students were chosen at random. The total sample was 8568 students.

RESULTS

Drug Use of Students

Table 17-I shows the proportions of students using various drugs in both studies. Tobacco and alcohol were the most commonly used drugs among both groups of students. Between 30 and 40 percent of the students had smoked tobacco in the last six months and almost half of these smoked more than twenty cigarettes each week or considered themselves regular users. The majority of students (70.3 and 52.9 percent) drank alcoholic beverages.

TABLE 17-I
STUDENTS' RATES OF DRUG USE

Drug	% Users	
	Lincoln and Welland	Toronto
Alcohol	70.3	52.9
Tobacco	40.6	30.4
Marijuana	12.4	14.5
Hashish	10.8*	—
LSD	8.0	7.2
Glue	7.6	4.1
Opiates	3.6	3.5
Speed	5.6	4.1
Other hallucinogens	5.6	6.4
Tranquilizers	10.1	7.6
Barbiturates	5.8	3.8
Stimulants	9.0	5.8

*A separate question on hashish use was not included in the Toronto questionnaire.

Marijuana was the most prevalent of the illicit drugs used. About 12.4 percent of the students in Lincoln and Welland Counties and 14.5 percent in Toronto had smoked marijuana. Fewer had used LSD; 8 percent in Welland and Lincoln Counties and 7.2 percent in Toronto.

Glue and solvents were the next most commonly used of the illicit drugs: 7.6 and 4.1 percent of the students had used them. Speed and other hallucinogens were taken by between 4 and 6 percent of the students. Opiates were the least popular of the illicit drugs (3.6 and 3.5 percent users). A smaller proportion (about 25 percent) of the users of these last four drugs (solvents, speed, other hallucinogens and opiates) had used them seven or more times.

The psychoactive drugs, tranquilizers, stimulants and barbiturates varied in their popularity. Tranquilizers were the most commonly used (10.1 and 7.6) by the students. Stimulants were taken by 9 and 5.8 percent and barbiturates by 5.8 and 3.8 percent of the students.

Drug Use by Parents in Relation to Student's Drug Use

The questionnaire required students to describe their mother's and father's use as "never," "less than once a month," "every week," or "nearly every day," with "don't know" as a residual category. The answers to these questions, represented the students' report of their parents' drug use rather than an actual account of it. It might be argued that some overreporting or underreporting occurred. The figures reported for both surveys were remarkably close to those reported by Parry[1] for a national sample in the United States. (As shown in Table 17-II). Certainly the reported parental drug use was of the magnitude expected and probably serious overestimates or underestimates did not occur.

TABLE 17-II
REPORTED RATE OF PARENTAL DRUG USE

Drug	% Mothers Using		% Fathers Using		% Both Parents (combined)		% US Adults (age 30–49*)
	Lincoln and Welland	Toronto	Lincoln and Welland	Toronto	Lincoln and Welland	Toronto	
Tranquilizers	20.6	18.1	9.9	9.4	15.3	13.8	16.0
Barbiturates	19.7	15.4	9.9	3.8	14.8	9.6	11.5
Stimulants	10.2	6.7	6.0	7.9	8.1	7.3	8.0
Alcohol	40.6		62.3		51.5		
Tobacco	35.1		58.5		46.8		

*Data from Parry (1968).

For both surveys each of the four reported parental drug questions was cross-tabulated with the twelve student drug use questions for mother and fathers separately. The results were remarkably consistent, in that *for every table* in both surveys there was a statistically significant relationship between parental and student drug use. Also, for every drug examined, where parents were frequent users their children were as well. Where parents were infrequent drug users or nonusers their children were likely to be nonusers. This relationship held for psychoactive drugs and also for illicit drugs, such as marijuana and LSD, but to a lesser extent for alcohol and tobacco. Since the association between parental drug use and student drug use showed identical patterns in the two surveys the data were combined for further analyses.

These relationships may be more clearly presented by considering only parental tranquilizer use and student drug use. Mothers who use tranquilizers at all were more likely to have children who used such drugs as marijuana, opiates, stimulants, speed, tranquilizers, LSD, other hallucinogens, glue and barbiturates. The heavier the mother's use of tranquilizers, the more likely the child was to use the above drugs.

Mothers who were daily tranquilizer users were three times as likely to have children who were marijuana smokers or LSD users than mothers who did not use tranquilizers. Their children were six times as likely to use opiates, five times as likely to use stimulants, other hallucinogens, and speed, seven times as likely to use tranquilizers and barbiturates, three times as likely to use glue. However, their children were only about one and a half times as likely to use tobacco and only 19 percent more likely to drink alcohol. It should be remembered that a similar picture could be drawn for mothers and fathers who were users of stimulants and barbiturates.

The extent of drug use among children of mothers who were daily tranquilizer users was perhaps most striking. As shown in Table 17-III about 31.8 percent of their children used marijuana, 15.4 percent used opiates, 16.4 percent speed, 22.4 percent other stimulants, 34.8 percent tranquilizers, 20.6 percent LSD, 18.2 percent other hallucinogens, 14.9 percent glue and 19.2 percent barbiturates. These relationships were also found for parents who were users of stimulants. Both mother and fathers who were stimulant users were more likely to have children who were users of psychoactive and hallucinogenic drugs. The more frequent the stimulant use of the parents, the more likely was the drug use of their children. Compared to the nonstimulant using mothers, children of mothers who were daily users of stimulants were three times as likely to use marijuana, four times as likely to use LSD, six times for glue, stimulants and other hallucinogens, eight times for barbiturates, speed and tranquilizers, and nine times for opiates. However, the use of alcohol and tobacco did not seem much greater than that for children whose parents did not use stimulants.

TABLE 17-III

FREQUENCY OF MOTHERS' TRANQUILIZER USE AND THE PROPORTION OF THEIR CHILDREN USING DRUGS AT EACH FREQUENCY LEVEL

Mother's tranquilizer use	% of Children Using Drugs										
	Alcohol	Tobacco	Mari- juana	Glue	Barbi- turates	Opiates	Speed	Stimu- lants	Tran- quili- zers	LSD	Other hallu- cinogens
Never	56.8	31.0	11.6	4.1	2.9	2.4	3.3	4.9	4.5	5.8	3.6
Less than 1/month	72.5	41.3	17.7	6.8	6.1	4.1	6.6	10.6	18.3	8.8	6.6
Every week	75.0	49.2	26.3	10.8	12.4	8.5	9.6	17.4	29.6	14.7	12.3
Nearly every day	75.5	54.6	31.8	14.9	19.2	15.4	16.4	22.4	34.8	20.6	18.2

Student Users and Nonusers of Marijuana

It was possible to look at the data in another way: marijuana users and nonusers were compared with regard to the drug use of their parents. The differences in parental use of the three psycho-active drugs between marijuana users and nonusers were all significant. Twenty-nine percent of the marijuana users but only 16.5 percent of the nonmarijuana users had mothers who were barbiturate users. About twice as many users' mothers (15 percent) had taken stimulants compared to nonusers' mothers (7.3 percent) and 31.7 percent of the marijuana users' mothers had taken tranquilizers compared to 17.3 percent of the nonusers mothers.

Fathers of marijuana users were more often users of tranquilizers (18.4 percent) than nonusers' fathers (8.4 percent). They were also often users of barbiturates and stimulants.

Student Users and Nonusers of Psychoactive Drugs

The relationship between students' use of psychoactive drugs, tranquilizers, barbiturates and stimulants and their parents' use of the same drugs was very close. Of those students using tranquilizers, 56 percent had mothers who used tranquilizers. Similarly 34.7 percent of the fathers of students using tranquilizers, used them also; while only 7.5 percent of the fathers of those students who had not used tranquilizers took them. When students used barbiturates, 48.1 percent of their mothers used them and 26 percent of their fathers.

DISCUSSION

Two large-scale surveys have shown an apparent positive association between drug use of parents and their adolescents. This relationship held for parental use of psychoactive drugs, tobacco and alcohol on the one hand and for adolescent use of psycho-actives and illicit hallucinogenics on the other. The relationship was closest where parents and adolescents were using the same drugs. The association between parental and adolescent drug use was closer for mothers than for fathers.

An important question concerns the meaning of the association between parental and adolescent drug use. It might be argued that parents use drugs mainly because their adolescents do. Some parents would become distraught if they found that their children were using drugs and so may take drugs to overcome their anxiety. However, this would argue an association between adolescent drug use and parental tranquilizer use but similar relationships were found for stimulants. Also the parent-adolescent relationship was strongest when both took the *same* drugs and not when adolescents took marijuana (their preferred drug).

At present, the evidence favors the view that parents and adolescents use drugs nonconcomitantly or that parental drug use proceeds adolescent drug use. A likely hypothesis is that students are modeling their drug use after their parents' use. In some cases, this drug use generalized to a broader acceptance of hallucinogenic drugs such as LSD and marijuana. In any case it is clear that much adolescent drug use takes place in families where parental, especially maternal, pill use is common. It is possible that much adolescent drug use or abuse cannot be reduced without parallel reductions in parental drug use. This argues the need to consider family dynamics in the treatment of adolescent drug abusers. Perhaps family therapy rather than individual or group therapy is required. It also seems evident that target populations for drug education should not be students but entire families.

REFERENCES

1. Parry, H.: Use of psychotropic drugs by US adults. *Public Health Reports,* *83:*799-810, 1968.
2. Smart, R. G., Fejer, D., and Alexander, E.: Drug use among high school students and their parents in Lincoln and Welland Counties. Substudy 1 - 7 & Jo & Al - 70, Addiction Research Foundation, Toronto, 1970.
3. Smart, R. G. and Jackson, D.: *A Preliminary Report on the Attitudes and Behaviour of Toronto Students in Relation to Drugs.* Addiction Research Foundation, Toronto, 1969.

Chapter 18

Drug Usage as One Manifestation of a "Sensation-Seeking" Trait

Marvin Zuckerman

Drug usage, particularly of psychedelic and amphetamine drugs, is often part of a "life style" which might be characterized as "sensation seeking" or "arousal seeking." The drug user described his experience as "getting high." A dark, freudian Thanatos instinct may underlie the expressed arousal-seeking motive, but it must be recognized that arousal seeking is itself a fundamental trait of humans. The trait may be expressed in dangerous sports, speeding, drinking, sex, partying, rock and jazz music, and modern art, as well as drug taking. The more orderly, safe and predictable man's environment becomes, the more he seems to crave change, excitement, novelty and adventure. He makes war or gets his arousal vicariously at circuses and football games. He strives to create law and order, stability and security, and then throws himself into carnivals, confrontation groups, adultery and revolution.

The author has developed a questionnaire called the Sensation Seeking Scale (SSS),[5] based on the assumption that individuals differ in a reliable fashion in their optimal levels of stimulation or arousal. Validation studies[5,6,8] have shown that the SSS is significantly related to a variety of relevant personality traits and behavioral tendencies, such as a proneness to volunteer for usual experiments like hypnosis and sensory deprivation.

Recently a factor analysis was done on an expanded version of the SSS. In addition to the general factor (Gen) found in previous analyses four moderately correlated factors were found. They may be described as follows:

1. *Thrill and Adventure Seeking (TAS):* a desire for activities or sports involving speed, moderate danger or adventure—that is, driving fast, parachute jumping.

2. *Experience Seeking (ES):* seeking new experience through music, art, drugs, unconventionality in dress or behavior.

3. *Disinhibition (Dis):* seeking sensations by casting off inhibitions—that is, wild parties, drinking, sexual variety.

4. *Boredom Susceptibility (BS):* a dislike for repetitious experience of any kind and a desire for change and novelty in things and people.

The reliabilities of these factors and scales have been reported in the prior study.[4] With the exception of the BS scale all showed good factor, split-half and retest reliability.

A study by Kish and Donnenwerth* showed that the general SSS was related to permissive attitudes toward sex, and a study by Althoff** indicated that the same was true of attitudes toward drugs. It seemed reasonable to assume that the SSS in a college population might be related to actual experiences in sex and drugs as well as attitudes in this area. We decided to first test this hypothesis in the field. Mrs. Ilda Ficher† has been doing counseling with groups of adolescents and young adults in the Philadelphia area. Through her contacts in these groups we located a recently established commune in a house. Under somewhat less than ideal testing conditions, a group of these young men and women were tested in one afternoon session. All of these persons admitted smoking "grass" and "hash" and about half "admitted" using harder drugs. I put the stress on "admitted" because many persons are somewhat suspicious of psychologists "crashing their pads" armed with questionnaires. But as the youth in the movie *Joe* noted, "They can't be Narcs. Narcs wear long hair and beads." At any rate this was a group dancing to the amplified beat of a

*Kish, G. B., and Donnenwerth, G. V. Stimulus-seeking II: Relationship to Some Capacity and Personality Measures (1970). Unpublished study.

**Althoff, M. E.: Personal communication, 1969.

†Zuckerman, M., Neary, R., Brustman, B., and Ficher, I.: Dimensions of Sensation Seeking. Paper presented at the Eastern Psychological Association, Atlantic City, 1970.

different guitar, all of whom used at least one illegal drug. They will be referred to as the "drug group" for want of a better term than "hippie."

We had already collected normative data from various college groups including a sizeable sample from Temple University. The Temple University group seemed a good comparison group for the "drug group" since they were about the same age and from the same area. Many of the "drug group" were actually Temple University dropouts or were still attending classes there, albeit sporadically. This is not to say that the Temple control group did not contain drug users. In view of our later findings at the University of Delaware, we could certainly not say this. But for the commune group, drugs were a more essential part of their lives; they had mostly "tuned out" to the academic "rat race."

The results of this study were encouraging and we decided to look at the relationship between the sensation-seeking trait and drug usage within the "lock-step" college population. We also decided to examine the relation between the SSS and drinking, sex, smoking (cigarettes) and coffee drinking. Some of these findings have been reported elsewhere.[7] This chapter will focus primarily on the drug findings.

METHOD

Fourteen male and fifteen female subjects were tested in a commune as previously described. This group was compared with 160 males and 170 females from Temple University who were tested in large class sections.

Form IV of the SSS was given to forty-five males and forty-five females in sessions of Introductory Psychology at the University of Delaware. Subjects scoring in the upper and lower deciles of the distributions for males and females were asked to take some further tests in smaller groups. The additional tests consisted of the following.

1. *A Drug Experience Questionnaire.* Fifteen classes of drugs were listed and the subjects were asked to describe their experience with each class of drugs by checking "never," "once or twice" "several times" "more than several, less than 10," or "10 or more."

Since there were so many total zero scores, it seemed appropriate to use a score consisting simply of the number of drug items checked, rather than a weighted score, for the total drug score.

In addition to the drug items there were a few additional scales for nondrug items including cigarettes, pipe, cigars, coffee drinking and alcohol. The results with the alcohol scale are of particular interest in this chapter since so many people consider alcohol the older generation's type of sensation seeking (Disinhibition). This scale read: (1) "never," (2) "few times," (3) "1 to 6 drinks per week," (4) "7-10 drinks per week," (5) "10-20 drinks per week."

2. *A Sex Experience Questionnaire.* This included one item for masturbation; fourteen heterosexual items starting with clenched lip kissing and going through oral-genital activities, the less erotic positions for sexual intercourse (the four basic ones: male top, female top, side and rear). Subjects checked each item frequency of experience on the same 1 to 5 frequency scale used for drugs, ranging from "never" to "10 or more." An additional homosexual scale was included with seven items for males and fifteen for females. The correlational results to be reported deal with the unweighted heterosexual scale totals—that is, the number of heterosexual items checked more than never.

After the results were obtained from these extreme scorers on the SSS, we decided to examine the relation between sensation-seeking and drug and sex experience in the total range of SSS scores. One is always curious about the habits of the "silent majority." Are they really like the fabled "Lucky Pierre," "always in the middle?"

Not daring to give our drug and sex questionnaire to unselected "innocent" freshman at the University of Delaware, we gave the SSS and the drug and sex questionnaire to advanced psychology classes in abnormal and personality psychology, in both the extension and day school. This will be referred to as sample 2 in our tables. It included thirty-eight males and sixty females.

RESULTS AND DISCUSSION

Table 18-I shows the mean scores of the small commune group called "drug users" and the large Temple University normative

TABLE 18-I
DRUG USERS VERSUS TEMPLE UNIVERSITY STUDENTS

Scales		Males			Females		
		Temple	Drug	t	Temple	Drug	t
	Ns	160	14		170	15	
Gen		12.1	14.7	3.3'	10.9	14.5	5.26"
TAS		9.7	10.8	1.4	8.5	11.1	4.92"
ES		8.9	13.2	5.6"	8.2	12.9	6.64"
Dis		6.7	6.6	.2	4.6	5.4	1.31
BS		8.2	8.6	.5			

'sig.<.05, "sig.<.01
Gen = General
TAS = Thrill and Adventure Seeking
ES = Experience Seeking
Dis = Disinhibition
BS = Boredom Susceptibility

group. The data is broken down by sex. The male drug group was significantly higher than the university males on the general and experience Seeking Scales. The female drug group was significantly higher than the university females on the General, Thrill and Adventure Seeking, and Experience Seeking Scales. Dividing the drug group into extensive drug users and those who only admitted smoking "grass" or "hash," no significant differences were found in the intragroup comparisons for men, but females who used a greater variety of drugs were significantly higher ($p < .05$) in the Experience Seeking Scale. Of all the subscales, the Experience Seeking Scale appears to be most related to the drug-using tendency. It should be noted that only two of the eighteen items on this scale do indicate a desire to experiment with drugs.

Table 18-II shows the percentages of drug and alcohol users in the SSS ranges (General Scale) of the two University of Delaware samples. These data are also broken down by sex. On the whole, drug usage is more frequent among males than among females. The more commonly used drugs in these samples were: marijuana, hashish, amphetamines, LSD and tranquilizers. On all of these, except tranquilizers, usage was significantly higher in high sensation seekers than in lows with subjects in the middle range generally falling in between. One exception to this trend

TABLE 18-II

CRCENTAGES OF DRUG AND ALCOHOL USERS IN RANGES OF SENSATION SEEKING

S ranges	Male Sample 1			Male Sample 2				Female Sample 1			Female Sample 2			
	High	Low	p*	High	Med	Low	p	High	Low	p	High	Med	Low	p
Ns	26	19		12	15	11		27	18		21	21	18	
·ugs														
arijuana	62%	21%	.01	83%	60%	55%	NS	56%	0%	.005	52%	14%	17%	.005
ashish	46	11	.025	75	40	45	.10	56	0	.005	38	10	17	.05
nphetamines	38	11	.05	50	40	9	.10	41	6	.05	28	10	6	.05
rbiturates	23	5	NS	8	13	0	NS	11	0	NS	14	5	0	.10
ocaine	8	0	NS	17	0	0	.10	4	0	NS	5	0	0	NS
pium	15	0	NS	33	20	0	.10	4	6	NS	10	5	6	NS
eroin	0	0	NS	8	6	0	NS	4	0	NS	0	0	0	NS
emerol	4	6	NS	0	0	0	NS	7	0	NS	0	5	0	NS
orphine	0	0	NS	0	6	0	NS	4	0	NS	5	0	0	NS
D	35	0	.01	42	33	0	.05	4	0	NS	19	0	6	.05
ilocybin	8	0	NS	17	7	0	NS	4	0	NS	0	0	0	NS
escaline	8	0	NS	33	27	0	.10	7	0	NS	10	0	11	NS
lue	12	0	NS	8	0	0	NS	4	0	NS	5	0	0	NS
asoline	8	5	NS	0	0	0	NS	4	0	NS	0	0	0	NS
ranquilizers	35	10	.10	17	6	18	NS	15	28	NS	19	10	6	NS
ny drugs	81	37	.005	90	60	55	NS	67	28	.01	52	19	17	.025
lcohol (1 to drinks/wk. more)	54	25	.05	58	73	45	NS	52	11	.025	35	24	35	NS

ɔ based on chi-square, one tailed test, 2×2 tables corrected with Yate's correction.

was in the second male sample where the trend on marijuana failed to reach statistical significance because of the high incidence of usage in the low and medium sensation-seeking groups. Marijuana usage may be on its way to becoming as common as cigarette smoking. The increase in incidence between samples 1 and 2 may have something to do with the fact that there was a large proportion of Freshmen in sample 1, while sample 2 consisted of upper-classmen and women. Some longitudinal data is needed to see the effect of exposure to the "drug culture" in colleges. Usage of drugs other than the ones already mentioned was infrequent in high and medium sensation seekers but practically nonexistent in lows.

The one exception to the general trend with drugs is interesting. Tranquilizers (used for "nonmedical" reasons) were used equally by high and low sensation seekers in the second male sample and were used more by low sensation seekers than by highs in the first female sample. A sensation seeker may want to go "up" or "down" but he seldom seeks tranquility. Perhaps the high sensation seekers who do use tranquilizers use them to terminate "bad trips." Their "optimal level of stimulation" may be higher than that of other people, but they do have one somewhere in the sky.

Looking at the overall drug picture we calculated the percentages of subjects using any drug in the two or three SSS ranges. These data are in the row labeled "Any drugs" near the bottom of Table 18-II. All differences are significant except in male sample 2 where the trend does not reach significance because of the high frequency of marijuana users in the low group. If we look at the lowerclassmen and women the results are impressive. In male sample 1, 81 percent of the high sensation seekers have tried drugs and only 37 percent of the lows have experimented. In the female sample 1, 67 percent of the high sensation seekers and only 28 percent of the lows have inhaled these heady fumes.

Turning to alcohol the results are not nearly so clear. Because almost everyone had tried alcohol occasionally, we divided the scale between the occasional (less than once a week) and regular (1 to 6 drinks per week or more) drinkers. In sample 1 about half of the males and female high sensation seekers drank regularly and a much smaller percentage of the lows imbibed. These differences were significant. But a curious thing happens when we turn to the upperclassmen (sample 2). There was little or no difference between low and high sensation seekers, primarily because the low sensation seekers have started drinking, rather than any increase in the highs. In the male sample 2, the biggest drinkers are in the middle range of sensation seeking. Although our data are not conclusive, it looks as if the upperclassmen have found something else besides alcohol, while the lows have started drinking and maybe tried a little "grass" on the side. Taking a closer look at sample 2, we found something interesting. Of the six subjects highest on drinking (10 or more drinks per week) seven hardly touched drugs and only one had experimented with more than "grass." If we extend it to the next category of drinking (7 to 10 drinks per week) including ten males, only two are also strong drug users. If we look at it the other way, among eight highest drug users, six do not drink or are light drinkers, while two are heavy drinkers in addition. There were only two heavy drinkers among the females and both were also wide drug users. Heavy drug users among females mostly fell in the light or moderate drinking ranges. Although the data are scanty, it begins to appear that the male students who may be on their way to alcoholism find little to interest them in drugs.

TABLE 18-III

CORRELATIONS BETWEEN SUM DRUG SCORES AND SUBSCALES OF THE SSS

	Males		Females	
	Sample 1	Sample 2	Sample 1	Sample 2
Ns	45	38	45	58
SSS scale				
TAS	.44"	.42"	.32'	.28'
ES	.60"	.47"	.45"	.55"
Dis	.31"	.08	.28	.43"
BS	.40"	.34'	.44"	.32'
Heterosexual Sum Score	.36"	.41"	.42"	.51"

'p less than .025 one-tailed, "p less than .005 one-tailed.

Table 18-III shows the correlations between a Sum Drug Score (total number of drugs used) and the four subscales of the SSS. These data are relevant to the convergent and discriminant validity of the scales. We predicted that the use of drugs would be most highly related to the Experience Seeking Scale. The drug score did correlate significantly with the ES scale in all samples and correlated more highly with this scale than with the others in all samples. But it is also apparent that the differences between the correlations of the drug score with the various scales are not large. It would appear that drug usage is an aspect of a general sensation-seeking trait rather than a specific type of sensation seeking. Also shown in this table are the correlations of drug experience with sex experience. These correlations were also significant in all of the samples. The person who experiments with drugs also experiments with sex.

TABLE 18-IV

CORRELATIONS BETWEEN THE EXPERIENCE SEEKING (ES) SCALE
AND SEX AND DRUG EXPERIENCE

Males	Sample 1		Sample 2	
	ES	Sex	ES	Sex
	Sex .18		Sex .37'	
	Drugs .60"	.36'	Drug .47"	.41"
Females	Sex. 48"		Sex .32'	
	Drugs .45"	.42"	Drug .55"	.51"

'p less than .025 one-tailed, "p less than .005 one-tailed.

Table 18-IV shows the correlations between the Experience Seeking scale of the SSS and the drug and sex scores in all samples. With the inexplicable exception of the correlation between ES scale and Sex Experience in the first male sample (perhaps experience seeking is still only intention in these younger students) all of these correlations were significant. Sex, drugs and the broad range of experiences contained in the SSS appear to be aspects of a single motive. This motive has been conceived of as the need to maintain an "optimal level of stimulation" in order to maintain an "optimal level of arousal."[3] Although such a motive may have its dangerous aspects, bringing one into conflict with a society determined to maintain the "legitimate" modes of sensation seeking, it also has more positive aspects. High sensation seekers tend to be more creative[1] and somewhat higher on certain types of intellectual ability, particularly those involving visualization.[2] They can separate nonessentials from essentials[6] and we call this trait "field independence." The world has always contained sensation seekers and sensation reducers. If high sensation seekers find little stimulation in academic life, conventional materialistic enjoyments, or in work, we might do well to examine the nature of institutions rather than to isolate and even persecute the potentially most creative segments of our college youth.

REFERENCES

1. Kish, G.B.: Cognitive innovation and stimulus seeking: a study of the correlates of the Obscure Figures Test. *Percept Motor Skills, 30:*95-101, 1970.
2. Kish, G.B., and Busse, W.: Correlates of stimulus seeking: Age, education, intelligence and aptitudes. *J Consult Clin Psychol, 32:*633-637, 1968.
3. Zuckerman, M.: Theories of sensory deprivation I., In *Sensory Deprivation: Fifteen years of Research.* edited by J. P. Zubek. New York, Appleton-Century Crofts, 1969.
4. Zuckerman, M.: Dimensions of sensation seeking. *J Consult Clin Psychol, 36:*45-52, 1971.
5. Zuckerman, M., Kolin, B.A., Price, L., and Zoob, I.: Development of a Sensation-Seeking Scale. *J Consult Clin Psychol, 28:*477-482, 1964.
6. Zuckerman, M., and Link, K.E.: Construct validity for the Sensation Seeking Scale. *J Consult Clin Psychol, 32:*420-426, 1968.
7. Zuckerman, M., Neary, R.S., and Brustman, B.A.: Sensation Seeking Scale correlates in experience (smoking, drugs, alcohol, "hallucinations" and sex) and preference for complexity (designs). *Proc. 78th Ann. Convention,* American Psychological Association, 1970, pp. 317-218.
8. Zuckerman, M., Schultz, D.P., and Hopkins, T.R.: Sensation-seeking and volunteering for sensory deprivation and hypnosis experiments. *J Consult Clin Psychol, 31:*358-363, 1967.

Chapter 19

Drugs as Chronetic Agents

Victor Gioscia

I N PREVIOUS STUDIES we have reported data derived from participant observation of the various scenes in which young people
use the drugs of their choice in the special ways they have chosen.
For the most part, the observations were carried out with one or
another drug, the focus of our investigation. For example, we examined the heroin scene and reported on it to the exclusion of
the other drugs concurrently used by the heroin users. Similarly
our investigation of so-called glue sniffers was conducted and reported separately. The same is true of our reports of the psychedelic scene.

Our reasons for doing so were partly historical, since the hey-
days of various drugs were at different times, and partly practical,
since one cannot discuss everything at once. But the principal
reason for the separateness of our studies was a theoretical one, in
that each drug study was conducted as an empirical test of a set of
hypotheses derived from a larger theoretical interest. We have for
some time now been engaged in the study of time processes—that
is, how time and its mysteries are understood in the various disciplines, ranging from astrophysics to anthropology. Our attempt
has been to derive a set of generalizations descriptive of time processes in *any* discipline, in other words, the study of time itself,
not simply the time of the physicist or of the psychologist. We
call this study "Chronetics" and define its scope as the study of
temporal processes in their own right. We seek, in short, to determine whether there are general laws which all time processes
obey and if so to determine what they are.

The first problem we confront in such an effort is one with
which all investigators are confronted, no matter what their field

—namely, to what extent is our ordinary experience a bias which blinds us. In other fields, say, geology, one may experiment with the elements of one's concern, for example, rocks, rivers, rain, et cetera. But how does one experiment with time? How do we know whether our assumption is correct that time is an invariant, which "flow evenly," to use a popular expression, or whether our assumption of invariance blinds us to possible variations in tempo. It is tempting to regard recent evidence from physics as confirming the view that time varies considerably at subnuclear levels of observation and hence that time may also vary elsewhere. However this courts the danger of going beyond the limits of the data.

Thus we were struck very early in our investigations by the almost total unanimity of our research subjects' reports that their drug experiences altered their experience of time. A similar unanimity is found in pharmacological, psychological and phenomenological reports, further confirming our subjects' views. In the remainder of this chapter we shall attempt to summarize our previous findings, on which drugs change the experience of time in which ways, and to justify our tentative conclusion that drugs are taken by those who take them (indeed, also by those who prescribe them) principally for that reason—namely, to alter the rate of experience. In addition to this psychological effect, however, we shall endeavor to show that the temporal aspects of certain social processes are also involved, so that when we refer to drugs as chronetic agents we are not restricting ourselves to exclusively subjective or psychological parameters but explicity to those aspects of experience with which the sociologist is rightly concerned, which we might call "sociological clocks." In this sense, notwithstanding the summary nature of this chapter, the investigations here reported must be regarded as preliminary, for it is a long way from demonstrating that our experience of time may vary under certain conditions to establishing that there are laws of time variation whose discernment the chroneticist properly pursues across the ranges of many disciplines.

We invoke as our measuring instrument the cybernetic notion that human beings in their subjectivity as well as in their sociation may be regarded as information-processing systems, characterized initially (and minimally) as receivers, programmers and broadcasters. That is, we perceive, think and communicate. And of course, more. Much more. How do drugs alter these processes.

CHRONETIC PHENOMENOLOGY

There are three classes of drugs with which we are concerned, which, in the street language of our subjects, are called "downs," "ups" and "trips," referring in the first case to narcotics, sedatives, barbiturates and alcohol (i.e. CNS depressants). "Uppers" refer to the amphetamines in their various forms (i.e. CNS stimulants). "Trips" include marijuana, LSD, mescaline, psilocybin, psilocin, and other psychedelics, to employ Osmond's term. As every neurologist knows, heroin, morphine, methadone and others have the property of constricting the pupils of the eye, which the street talk calls being "pinned." Of course this means that less light is entering the retinal chamber and indicates that the amount of information the suject tolerates is reduced in proportion to dosage. The "input" function to the higher cortical centers is sharply reduced by narcotics, not only visually but across the entire sensorium.

Subjects report that the heroin high is like the astronauts' perspective in that time changes in the environment are seen as from a great distance, so that the net effect is an experience in which things seem to go very slowly, if at all. At high dosages, "time seems to stand still," so that the euphoric experience of timelessness seems paradoxically to last forever. This helps to understand why the heroin experience is so cherished by those who cherish it. Even though, to the outside observer, it seems to last for such a "short" time, to the serious heroin user, time seems to have stopped, and his joy is eternal. Our subjects report it is exactly this temporary eternity they seek. So do the makers of the 7,000-year-old Sumerian tablets which instruct the religious novice in its preparation.

"Ups," on the other hand, have an entirely different set of subjective reports associated with them. One subject described his experience of "meth" (speed) as follows:

Hay man, dig it, here's how it feels . . . Do you like to drive fast in your car, man. Imagine you have this racing car, see, with no wind-shield, see, and they say you can have NYC all to yourself with all the other cars gone. So you go speeding around corners at 90 and open up to 200 miles an hour along Park Avenue, man, whizzing, and spinning around the whole city all to yourself. You can do anything as you want, an' you can go as fast as you want to go. Dig it man, imagine all that power just *walking* man, or screwing. Wow.

Clinicians will be sensitive to the omnipotent undertones in our subject's report, to the grand ideas of power and exhilaration. They will not be unfamiliar with the fact that "coming down" or "crashing" from "speed" (meth) is severely depressing, often to the point of persecutory ideation and feeling characteristic of the paranoid experience.

Note, however, in our subject's report that it is the *velocity* of his experience he centrally cherishes. So much is this the case that he will often use too much, then resort to barbiturates to slow down, in what soon becomes a cycle of speeding, slowing, then speeding again, for days sometimes for weeks at a time, with little thought of food, sleep or sociation. The fact that speed is alleged to confer long periods of sexual potency bordering on Priapism is considered to far outweigh the fact that it renders the serious user an orgastic. It is as if one were trying to move faster than time itself, squeezing more in than mere clock time permits.

Speed "freaks" are notorious broadcasters, who will talk, with-out interruption for four or five hours, at a very fast clip, usually to the considerable consternation of their "straight" friends. They believe they understand things superbly well and deeply for the first time and are very eager to share this new found wisdom with anyone who will listen for as long as they will listen. This seems to be due to the fact that the CNS is stimulated, not at the perceptual-sensory level, but at the higher cortical levels, so that sensory information is processed faster. It is exactly this rapid il-lumination speed freaks report they want.

"Heads" or adepts of the psychedelic experience well know that trips seem to last for far longer than clock time measures. Even half a marijuana cigarette will permit the smoker to feel that a three-minute musical selection has the temporal characteristics of a symphony and the four-hour high correspondingly feels like eight or ten hours. Acid (LSD), a far more potent drug, is almost impossible to describe to those who have not experienced it. Like sex, talking about it does not quite convey the qualities of the experience. For, in addition to its ability to vastly expand the range of sensory delights, LSD induces the most complex chronetic patterns yet known to man, such that serious users regularly report variations in the variations of the time experience. Moments of eternal stillness alternate with extremely rapid pulsations and rhythms: feelings of rest, velocity, acceleration and changes in acceleration are common, and reports of even more subtle and complex changes in time experience are common. That this experience is deliberately sought is indicated in McCluhan's aphorism that "the computer is the LSD of the business world just as LSD is the computer of the counterculture." What computers and acid have in common is the processing of information at extremely high speeds. Computers operate in nanoseconds. No one knows how low LSD reduces synaptic thresholds, nor, consequently, how much it increases the rate of neural firing. What is well known, by heads at least, is that, in addition to its ability to open wide the "doors of perception," acid is also well named, for in the cybernetic analogy, what seems to happen is that the amount of data is increased while the programs for its conceptual management are simultaneously dissolved. It feels like a fuse has blown, so that too much current is flowing. (Hence, the expression "mind-blowing.") It is exactly this experience of sensory overload, de-programming, and re-programming, that heads seek. Whether the insights and experiences had with this powerful substance are "valid" or "illusory" is a question for more research than present federal laws currently permit. Suffice it to note that the extremely rapid chronetic changes LSD includes are cherished by those who favor LSD, as well as the feeling that a twelve-hour experience of this sort is regularly compared to a week or a month of continuous ecstasy. In this context, one is not surprised to find recent opinion in theological literature holding that the sacred mushroom *(Amanita muscaria)* was the agent inducing the mystical experiences that led directly to the formulation of the major world religions.

CHRONETIC SOCIOLOGY

If we focus now upon the *population* who favor the drugs discussed above, not simply upon the subjective experiences of their individual members, a chronetic pattern of another sort emerges. Brevity prevents an extended discussion of the "measuring instrument" we employ as a sociological tool. Suffice it to say that the *rate of social change* is increasingly adopted as a norm in the social sciences, in our area of rapid social change. If we ask what is the relation between our three classes of drugs and the rates of social change experienced by differing classes in America, a clear pattern becomes visible.

Thus, until very recently, narcotics use was principally the predilection of the lower class, whose rate of change was widely acknowledged to be the slowest, in the fastest emerging society in the world. This experience which we have elsewhere termed "achronistic," is severely "painful" to those who experience it, since it is not only an experience of extreme alienation, but of *increasing* alienation, whose rate of increase is increasing. Under such circumstances, heroin might be said to be the medication of choice, since it is *par excellance* the pain killer. It is a situation in which one might turn around Marx's classic phrase that religion is the opiate of the people. Unfortunately, as the *rate* of alienation increases in the middle class, we must predict an increase in the expected incidence of narcotics there as well. That this has already begun is becoming more widely known every day.

The upper lower and lower middle classes are not, as a group, experiencing a rate of social change identical to the lowest class. In fact, it seems that we have an explanation for the popularity of "ups" in this population when we note that their wish to "catch up" with the bourgeoisie which is "moving up" faster than they do is temporarily granted by a class of drugs whose property is to confer the illusion of acceleration. Note also that the illusions of "progress" and "getting ahead" are beliefs entertained by this group far more actively than the lowest class, who despair, or the upper middle class, who pride themselves on "having arrived." The "violence" often attributed to the "coarse, gruff, working culture" is not untouched by "speed's" illusion of omnipotence, nor by its stimulation and feelings of social persecution. They "go" together, as it were.

The most rapid rate of change in our society is experienced by those who, like the computer, must process vast amounts of information in a very little time—that is, the most highly educated, those whose participation in the cybernetic revolution of our times is deepest. Typically, the children of upper middle class parents are those most barraged with novelty in our society, since they paradoxically have the leisure time in which to suffer from information overload. The Berkeley rebels were born the year mass TV was born, and study after study reveals they spent more time in front of their TV sets than they did before parents and school *combined*. Not to mention books, magazines and films. Or the threat of nuclear holocaust. Or planetwide pollution. Confronted with the massive responsibilities to "solve" these massive crises, knowing that species Man will not long survive unless they quickly derive ways and means to turn away from a chemical which confers the ability to process huge amounts of information in a very short time. For theirs is the first generation for whom the experience of accelerating social change is the *norm,* and they know they are expected to thrive on it. Imagine their dismay when they are simultaneously commanded to thrive on change but do nothing to bring it about. Their patience with the slow moving institutions which thus double bind them is therefore somewhat astonishing

Let us hope it doesn't wear too thin. For they are, literally, our future. It is for them that we must attempt to discern the laws of time and change, for without knowledge of these laws, we seem, as a species, about to perish. With such laws, hopefully, the next generation might have a chance to become chronetic agents of an entirely new kind.

Chapter 20

Compulsory Education—A Cause of Drug Addiction

Herbert Berger

ALMOST THREE centuries ago Alexander Pope wrote that "the proper study of mankind is man." If I may paraphrase these immortal words, the study of drug abuse is not to investigate drugs—but rather drug addicts. In order to learn more about drug addiction, 343 young addicts were interviewed at length.

If we are to understand these patients, then we must recognize that we have become a drug-oriented society. Mother's frustrations with appliances that do not work or recalcitrant children are, she hopes, rapidly solved by the use of either the latest nostrum advertised on radio or television or by a tranquilizer prescribed by her doctor. Father's harassing day at the office demands an ounce or two of alcohol as soon as he arrives home.

Similarly some other drug, we believe will make us alert or even creative. Few of us depend on our own inner strength to conquer adversity. If we have artificially created a stressless society by interposing a wall of drugs between ourselves and reality then we will surely lose the ability to respond to stress. A sedentary man could not rise from his desk and run a four-minute mile.

There has always been a generation gap. It is more difficult to cross now in either direction probably because parental discipline has broken down under the urgings of educators and psychologists. Children are not as likely to blindly obey their parents. This is particularly true when parents worship youth themselves. Mothers wear more youthful clothes than their daughters. Thus the adolescent in his fight for individuality negates practically everything his parents held important. He rarely has any positive approaches to the problems of society but rather is against all existing mores. Should father be clean shaven he sports a beard; similarly father's interest in bettering himself financially is money grubbing; his neat appearance is old fashioned; his likes in politics, art, literature or music must be replaced by so called avant-garde substitutes. Thus modern art looks as though it were painted with one's elbows, new music is a cacaphony of noise, and literature has become nonunderstandable.

Most of us who are parents excuse our own young while being hypercritical of our neighbor's brats. We complacently hope that time will bring some maturity. It will if that child is still alive. The young drug addict observes his parents' use of alcohol to escape every frustration or harassment. This permits a rationalization by which he excuses or justifies his own use of drugs. The hazards of drug addiction, however, are too real to be regarded with equanimity. Even if the youngster survives skin infections, endocarditis, brain and kidney abscesses, arrest and incarceration, he still will have lost a minimum of twelve years of precious time. Our studies indicate that drug habits which started at eighteen are rarely cured spontaneously until thirty. This individual may then be too old to qualify for a useful place in a highly competitive society.

Perhaps you will permit me another generality before settling down to the dry statistics of these interviews. We live in a hedonistic world. Enjoy yourself! Have a good time. I even live in "Fun City"! Work and leisure have never been such poles apart as they are now. The former is something to be endured so that we can pay the price of the latter. Work is done for money alone, never for the satisfaction of a job well done. Enjoying one's work is something we dare not mention for fear of castigation in a pleasure-bent social milieu. Using drugs is pleasurable. They satisfy every need of the user, be he hungry, tired, insecure, afraid or nervous. It takes him on a flight from reality to a utopian dream world. If he can only secure another dose soon enough he need never awake to the grim vicissitudes of his environment.

I will summarize the answers to these extensive interviews so as not to bore you with many numbers.

CAUSE

Interpretation of this data is a philosophical exercise. Any interested student of addictive diseases may quite properly reach vastly different conclusions than my own.

Each of these individuals was under close surveillance for several months. Each treatment included a long period of discussion so that they soon began to ventilate. Several factors appeared repeatedly.

Drug addicts are hostile. They hate authority regardless of its source and look upon the nonaddicted population only as a source of funds for the purchase of drugs. Sometimes addicts are frustrated and disillusioned when they recognize that their parents, too, are trying to escape from reality via the pursuit of youth, their cocktail parties, their dishonesty in reporting income and their bribing of police officers. All this adds to the children's disrespect; they quickly recognize the disparity between what father says and what he does. In addition we have become a drug-oriented society using advertised nostrums for every real or fancied symptom. Therefore it is not strange that junior asks, "Is my 'pot' worse than father's martini or mother's sleeping pill?"

Obviously there is no single easy answer to these behavior patterns, but one factor stands out in almost all these interviews—an *absolute hatred of compulsory education!* This symptom was noted by the patients early in primary school and became full blown by the age of 12.

These are usually uneducatable individuals. They believe that adults arbitrarily deny them their freedom and insist on their attendance in school. Like all who are jailed, they resent both the jailer and the jail. Society has incarcerated them in school—against their will. This is, in their eyes, an unjust punishment therefore they feel within their rights to retaliate by breaking school windows, by criminal activity and by disrupting classes.

Are libraries vandalized and disturbed like schools? Not at all. The library is attended by those who want to read. Should they be noisy or discourteous this privilege would be revoked. The obvious antithetical situation vis-à-vis schools is too apparent to require elaboration.

Like all correctional institutions our educational facilities include keepers (monitors), jails (schools), jailers (teachers) and forced activities (learning). How does compulsory education affect those interested in education, the child, his teacher and our community? Compulsory education was initiated to prevent the exploitation of children by employers and parents in the home piecework shop and on farms. These problems do not exist today. Yet we continue to take the privilege of self-determination from these children, something we would not dare to do to adults. We abrogate their civil rights, because we "know what is best for them" (sic). Education has always been a privilege but we have made it a punishment. When the school with its strict regulations and discipline, its truant officers, monitors and attendance clerks becomes a jail, it loses its stature as a privileged educational institution. It can never be both. These are not exaggerated descriptions. Any school uses prodigious amounts of time, effort and personnel to see that the jailees are present, do not go A.W.O.L. and serve the requisite amount of time. Myriads of special classes must be established for these who rebel against this infringement of their prerogatives.

Were education made voluntary, students would compete to enter school for this is where their friends would be and this is where things would be happening. Others would embrace apprenticeship in trades where they are sorely needed.

What is the effect of compulsory education on the faculty? The teacher starts his career imbued with idealism. He enters class and finds many students like those he envisaged. Others, however, fall into the uneducatable variety who hate their confinement and their teacher-jailers. Thus the teacher must adopt the role of disciplinarian which occupies much of his time and prevents him from training those students who are anxious to learn. Some become so cynical that their teaching suffers. Others resign using the poor salaries, of which they were well aware before they entered this profession, as an excuse.

The community must bear the enormous cost of vandalism. In New York City willful damage to school property costs as much as two new schools each year. To this must be added special schools and special classes, truant officers and the like. When its good students fail to learn because the teacher is preoccupied with disciplinary problems then the entire future of the community is endangered.

How does this relate to drug addiction? The student has learned to rebel against a society that he feels has unjustly jailed him. He responds with the antisocial behavior of vandalism and crime. Finally he seeks to escape from this abhorrent milieu through the media of drugs.

METHODS OF TREATMENT

These methods are mentioned only in the interest of completeness. Their very multiplicity is positive proof that we do not know how to treat this disease adequately. However, there is an obverse side to the coin. Many individuals and groups are actively seeking better therapeutic regimens.

1. Self-help through Daytop Lodge or Synanon, where ex-addicts help to rehabilitate others. This is similar to Alcoholics Anonymous.

2. Methadone replacement: a method of narcotic blockade with oral methadone substituted for heroin in such large doses that the latter produces no euphoria. It treats addiction as a deficiency disease—which cannot be cured but can be controlled just as diabetes is managed with insulin. If our criteria for success is rehabilitation of the addict as a useful, noncriminal member of society, then this is an excellent method. If, however, we establish the more unrealistic and more rigid criterion of freedom from drugs as successful therapy, then it is a failure. My own belief is that the former goal is both accurate and attainable.

3. Cyclazocine is a narcotic antagonist similar to the use of antabuse with alcohol addiction. This program is not in use long enough to permit proper conclusions.

4. The City of New York program through the help of ex-addicts—through the steps of motivation, detoxification and finally rehabilitation.

5. Psychotherapy
   a. By psychiatrists

    (1) Analysis
    (2) Shock
    (3) Ventilation
  b. Religious counseling
  c. Medical therapy with tranquilizers, antidepressants and counseling.

Since there is little interest in cure in this group of young people success is extremely infrequent. Abstinence is realized more often by those with some measure of emotional maturity.

Obviously success depends on the motivation of the addict, the enthusiasm of the therapist and the ability of the latter to withstand frustration.

6. Other treatment facilities are available at federal and state levels, the former is psychiatrically oriented; the latter, possibly because of inadequate personnel, is administered by nonprofessionals. This is not a condemnation of the state program which is too new to be evaluated. They both use techniques described above—where failure is all to frequent.

RESULTS

Parents

Only 210 were still married. The rest were divorced, separated, dead or perhaps had never married. No one admits to illegitimacy. (Birth certificates were not investigated because the young addicts came from various parts of the country and drifted into New York City and because they have a variety of names too, because of their various arrests.) The divorce or separation rate is about ten times the national average. Also 218 of the mothers were working which is $2\frac{1}{2}$ times the national average. So there was little parental supervision.

Father's Income

Fathers' incomes ranged from under $5,000 to over $20,000. Only 69 men were on the dole. Thus at least half have had satisfactory incomes. These figures may be inaccurate because these were all private rather than free clinic patients.

Father's Type of Employment

Two thirds were artesians and only one third were office workers. This may explain the large number of educational casualties. Uneducated parents may not place a high premium on education.

Father's Employment Record

Only one seventh had held the same job for ten years and 135 had had over five jobs in the same period. While this may indicate ambition, it is more likely that the reverse connotation is true.

Mother's Health Status

Of the 316 who could be interviewed, 270 had nervous breakdowns, felt jittery, took nerve medicine or sleeping pills. Some of these may have been addicts. None have admitted to it.

Siblings

There were 128 brothers or sisters who had addictions, had been arrested for causes not related to addiction, or were in mental hospitals. These figures are incomplete because many of these patients had lost touch with their relatives. These figures do tend to substantiate the surmise that the addict suffers from defective genetic material.

Encounters with the Law

Only 47 had never been arrested and 156 had been arrested more than once. Also 171 had been arrested even prior to the use of drugs so these are antisocial individuals to begin with.

Reasons Given by the Patient for the Use of Drugs

There were as many reasons as addicts, but after a while one heard the same phrases frequently: others were doing it; I was nervous; I was curious; it made me feel good; my friend gave me some. This is an important explanation. Further questioning revealed that the "friend" often induced them into addiction as a means of supporting his own habit. The friend was not criticized for this, however, after the novitiate had become seriously addicted. Rather, they were grateful for "being introduced to a good thing." One college student described heroin as "having all the advantages of death with none of its permanence." Unfortunately her description was inaccurate since she was found dead several months later.

Finally, practically all addicts actively hated authority whether it was government, parents or school. The latter is of such importance that we will devote more time to it.

The Relationship of Education to Addiction

Here was an area of intense hostility that recurred over and over again. Addicts resented, even hated, school. They abhorred a society which forced school upon them. How did they face this?

1. *Grades in school*—only 29 had never failed a course.

2. *Academic standing*—only 2% of the 343 were ever placed in the top 10 percent.

Amount of Education

These are not good students. Only 22 of the 343 finished college—all the rest were dropouts.

Drugs Used at the Onset of Addiction

Almost all (308) began by smoking marijuana, an ubiquitous weed which can be grown anywhere.

Drugs Used Presently

Practically all had graduated to much more potent materials: 290 used heroin, others used barbiturates, amphetamines, lysergic acid diethyl amide or LSD, down to 4 who used cocaine. Over 200 continued to hallucinate with hemp. Strangely, none of these became alcoholics although all drink frequently even to excess on occasion.

CONCLUSION

Compulsory education engenders in the uneducable a hatred of society. In the expression of this antipathy, the adolescent repudiates his culture. He attempts to destroy his jail and his neighbor's property. Finally, he attempts a chemical escape from the viscissitudes of his environment. He commits crimes against his enemy—society—to support the cost of his addiction (the drugs are artificially expensive because we have made them illegal) and as a revenge against the older generation who, he rationalizes, is entirely responsible.

Left to their own devices, these adolescents may develop at their own pace: some quicker, some slower than that which an arbitrary society has chosen for them. Their goals may be vastly different from those which we have established. They are not necessarily wrong. Who would dare argue that a good carpenter is not a greater asset than a poor lawyer?

Chapter 21

Drug Use Among White and Nonwhite College Activists: "Heads" or "Seekers"?

Walter C. Bailey and Mary Koval

THROUGHOUT THE PAST TEN YEARS there has been increasing interest and excitement regarding what is thought to be the progressive spread of illicit drug use and drug addiction among college students in America. The result of empirical studies and estimates, regarding the extent of illegal drug use, among college students, varies from as low as 5 percent to as high as 75 percent.[3] At the same time that this apparent increase in drug involvement by college students has been going on, there has been a surge of student activism and militancy among both white and black students of the universities of this country. Buildings have been forcibly occupied. Deans have been captured. Students have marched on campuses with their guns. Recent incidents of firepower repression at Kent and Jackson State Universities aroused much of the nation.

Most studies of drug use among college students tend to dwell mainly on the conduct of white students—those representative of the "drug movement," the hippies and yippies with long hair and beads who go about unkempt and frequently unwashed, espousing sexual and political philosophies disturbing to their elders.[2] Little is known regarding drug use among nonwhite college students and no systematic efforts have been made to compare the nature and extent of illicit drug use between white activists and nonwhite militants.*

---

*The attributes of *activism* and *militancy* were determined by reported membership in student organizations "known" to be activist or militant and/or reported participation in one or more "confrontations."

Our central hypothesis for this study was formulated as follows:

> *When groups of college student-white activists are compared with college student-nonwhite militants in terms of the extent of illicit drug involvement, there would be a marked difference in the direction of a greater drug involvement for white activists than nonwhite militants.*

Keniston has divided college-student drug users into three major categories: (a) *tasters*, (b) *seekers* and (c) *heads.*[3] Within this context, we are asking the following question: How are these three categories of drug users distributed among white activists and nonwhite militants?

METHODOLOGY

In this pilot project, the attempt was made to establish a basic four-cell design comparing white student activists with nonwhite student militants, on the basis of drug use versus nondrug use.

The study was conducted during the 1968-1969 school year on the campus of one of the country's larger universities.

Roughly 90 percent of the sample was obtained by direct contact with students. The remaining 10 percent of the study population was obtained indirectly. Questionnaires were left in the offices of known white, black and Puerto Rican activist organizations with the request that they be completed and returned to the investigators. The number of refusals under the indirect method is unknown. There were no refusals under the direct method of contact. This "chunk" sample is not representative of the college population at large; however, it is believed to be fairly representative of white activists and nonwhite militants on this college campus.

FINDINGS

The salient findings to be presented here include the following: (a) the relative extent of drug involvement of whites and nonwhites, generally; and (b) our tentative answer to the central question posed—namely, a comparison of the differences, if any, in drug involvement between white activists and nonwhite militants.

Drug Involvement: *Whites versus Nonwhites*

When one looks at the total study population of 154 students (including white activists, nonwhite militants and politically inactive students, regardless of race), one finds that the majority of both white and nonwhite students were classified as drug users* with the highest proportion found among the white students. As shown in Table 21-I, 35 (61 percent) of the white students were

TABLE 21-I
DRUG USE AND ETHNICITY OF SUBJECTS

Drug Use	White		Ethnicity Nonwhite		Total	
	N	%	N	%	N	%
Drug Users	35	61	49	51	84	55
Nonusers	22	39	48	49	70	45
Totals	57	100	97	100	154	100

$\chi^2 = 1.71668$ .1 $<$ P $<$.2   not significant at .05 level.

categorized as drug users, while 49 (51 percent) of the nonwhite students were so designated.

Drug Involvement: *White Activists versus Nonwhite Militants*

A partial answer to our central question regarding the differentials in drug involvement between white activists and nonwhite militants is provided in Table 21-II. Of the 20 white activists in

TABLE 21-II
ACTIVISM BY DRUG USE

Drug Use	White Activists		Ethnicity Nonwhite Militants		Total	
	N	%	N	%	N	%
Drug Users	15	75	38	58	53	62
Nonusers	5	25	28	42	33	38
Totals	20	100	66	100	86	100

$\chi^2 = 1.97056$ .1 $<$ P $<$.2   not significant at .05 level.

*For the purpose of this study, drug user was defined as any student reporting the illicit use of any of the "dangerous" or "addicting" drugs, one or more times.

the study population, 15 (75 percent) had illicitly used one of the specified "dangerous" or "addicting" drugs one or more times, whereas of the 66 nonwhite militants only 38 (58 percent) were so classified. At this gross level of differentiation, although over one half of both white activists and nonwhite militants have at least experimented with illicit drug use, white activists appear markedly more drug involved than nonwhite militants.

Drug Involvement: Ethnic Activists versus Ethnic Nonactivists

When the 84 drug users (55 percent of the total study population) are placed in rank order of percentage of drug users for each of the categories covering the ethnic-activist continuum, as shown in Table 21-III, we see a steady progression in the proportion of drug-involved students from a low of 43 percent for black nonmilitants to a high of 75 percent for white activists. The six Puerto Rican nonmilitants did not respond to the question on drugs.

TABLE 21-III
PERCENTAGE OF DRUG USERS BY ETHNIC ACTIVISM

Subjects	Total	Drug Use	
		N	% of Total
White activists	20	15	75
Black militants	53	31	58
Puerto Rican militants	13	7	54
White nonactivists	37	20	54
Black nonmilitants	23	10	43
Puerto Rican nonmilitants	6	—	—
Other and no response	2	1	55
Totals	154	84	55

Inspection of Table 21-III suggests that although the black militants were second to white activists in reported incidence of drug use, they were a very poor second (58 to 75 percent, respectively). Also, black nonmilitants showed the lowest percentage of drug involvement.

Opiates

Table 21-IV suggests that more than twice as many nonwhite militants as white activists (86 to 40 percent, respectively) *never*

TABLE 21-IV
OPIATE USE BY WHITE ACTIVISTS AND NONWHITE MILITANTS

Use of Opiates	White Activists		Nonwhite Militants	
	N	%	N	%
Use opiates currently	8	40	8	12
Used opiates in past but not currently	4	20	1	2
Used drugs but never used opiates	3	15	29	44
Never used any drugs	5	25	28	42
Total Activists	20	100	66	100

used an opiate at all and three times as many white activists as nonwhite militants (40 to 12 percent) reported current opiate use.

Table 21-V shows the rate of opiate use (primarily heroin) among white activists and nonwhite militants and the frequency

TABLE 21-V
OPIATE USE BY WHITE ACTIVISTS AND NONWHITE MILITANTS

Ethnicity of Activists/Militants	Incidence of Use		Among Users—Extent of Use*							
			Regular		Frequent		Occasional		Total	
	N	%	N	%	N	%	N	%	N	%
White activists (N=20)	8	40.0	—	—	1	12.5	7	87.5	8	100.0
Nonwhite militants (N=66)	8	12.1	2	25.0	3	37.5	3	37.5	8	100.0
Total	16	18.6	2	12.5	4	25.0	10	62.5	16	100.0

*Regular use—daily.
Frequent use—several times/week or once/week.
Occasional use—about once/month or less often than once/month or not regularly.
Incidence of use $\chi^2 = 7.87775$ P < .01.

of use among those activists and militants currently "using." White activists reported significantly more current opiate use than nonwhite militants but the extent of their use was more likely to be occasional. Seven of eight white activist current users of opiates used the drug occasionally which was once a month or less frequently. Nonwhite militant current opiate users were few (12 percent of all nonwhite militants) but were more likely to report greater frequency of use. Regular or daily use was indicated by only two students, both nonwhite militants. Also in terms of freqeuent use, we find three times as many nonwhite militants as white activists using opiates once or several times a week (37.5 to 12.5 percent respectively).

Hard Hallucinogens

Table 21-VI clearly shows that the use of LSD-type drugs is primarily a white activist "bag" not shared by nonwhite militants. A substantial 60 percent of white activists reported at least

TABLE 21-VI

HARD HALLUCINOGEN USE BY WHITE AND NONWHITE ACTIVISTS

| Use of Hard Hallucinogens | Ethnicity | | | |
| | White Activists | | Nonwhite Militants | |
	N	%	N	%
Use hard hallucinogens currently	9	45	4	6
Used hard hallucinogens in past but not currently	3	15	2	3
Used drugs but never used hard hallucinogens	3	15	32	49
Never used any drugs	5	25	28	42
Total Activists	20	100	66	100

some experience with these drugs compared to only 9 percent of the nonwhite militants. Forty-five percent of the white activists reported that they were *currently* using one of the hard hallucinogens at the time of this study while only 6 percent of the nonwhite militants so reported.

Table 21-VII emphasizes the notion that there is a significant difference in the frequency of current use of hard hallucinogens among white activists and nonwhite militants. Hallucinogens are more likely to be used *occasionally* by both white activists and nonwhite militants (66.7 and 75.0 percent respectively). The only incident of *regular* use was reported by one nonwhite militant,

TABLE 21-VII

HARD HALLUCINOGEN USE BY WHITE ACTIVISTS AND NONWHITE
MILITANTS

Ethnicity of Activists/Militants	Incidence of Use		Among Users—Extent of Use*							
			Regular		Frequent		Occasional		Total	
	N	%	N	%	N	%	N	%	N	%
White activists (N=20)	9	45.0	—	—	3	33.3	6	66.7	9	100.0
Nonwhite Militants (N=66)	4	6.1	1	25.0	—	—	3	75.0	4	100.0
Total	13	15.1	1	7.7	3	23.1	9	69.2	13	100.0

*Regular use—daily.

Frequent use—several times/week or once/week.

Occasional use—about once/month or less often than once/month or not regularly.

Incidence of Use $\chi^2 = 18.1378$ P $<$ .001.

whereas one third of the white activists but no nonwhite militants reported use of hard hallucinogens *frequently,* or once or several times a week.

Soft Hallucinogens

Although our data suggests that black militants tend to avoid the severe mind-altering drugs such as LSD, Table 21-VIII shows that they do not have the same restraints with the milder hallucinogens such as marijuana and hashish. Nevertheless, the white

TABLE 21-VIII

SOFT HALLUCINOGEN USE BY WHITE AND NONWHITE ACTIVISTS

Use of Soft Hallucinogens	Ethnicity			
	White Activists		Nonwhite Militants	
	N	%	N	%
Use soft hallucinogens currently	12	60	31	47
Used soft hallucinogens in past but not currently	3	15	6	9
Used drugs but never use soft hallucinogens	—	—	1	2
Never used any drugs	5	25	28	42
Total Activists	20	100	66	100

activists continue to maintain their substantial lead in this area also. Sixty percent of the white activists reported current use of marijuana (including hashish) compared with 47 percent of the nonwhite militants. When one considers the category "Used soft hallucinogens in past but not currently," the ratio of positive responses for white activists over nonwhite militants was almost 2 to 1 (15 to 9 percent, respectively). Seventy-five percent of the white activists had had some experience with the soft hallucinogens, primarily marijuana, compared with 56 percent of the nonwhite militants.

Table 21-IX shows the extent of current use of soft hallucinogens among white activists and nonwhite militants. White acti-

TABLE 21-IX

SOFT HALLUCINOGEN USE BY WHITE ACTIVISTS AND NONWHITE MILITANTS

Ethnicity of Activists/Militants	*Incidence of Use*		*Among Users—Extent of Use**							
			Regular		*Frequent*		*Occasional*		*Total*	
	N	%	N	%	N	%	N	%	N	%
White activists (N=20)	12	60.0	5	41.7	6	50.0	1	8.3	12	100.0
Nonwhite militants (N=66)	31	47.0	6	19.4	15	48.4	10	32.2	31	100.0
Total	43	50.0	11	25.6	21	48.8	11	25.6	43	100.0

*Regular use—daily.
  Frequent use—several times/week or once/week.
  Occasional use—about once/month or less often than once/month or not regularly.
  Incidence of Use $\chi^2 = 1.0424$ .30 <P <.40 not significant at .05 level.

vists are more inclined to be heavy users of marijuana and/or hashish than are the nonwhite militants. For example, daily or *regular* use was reported by 41.7 percent of the white activists, over twice as many as nonwhite militants (19.4 percent). Nonwhite militants were more likely than white activists to use soft hallucinogens only occasionally (32.2 to 8.3 percent respectively).

DISCUSSION

Our data appears to confirm the notion that white activist college students are markedly more drug involved than are nonwhite militant college students. In terms of opiate use, allegedly increasing at a rapid rate on college campuses, white activists reported much greater involvement than nonwhite militants though their use was most likely to be occasional. We found that the use of hard hallucinogens such as LSD was reported to a significantly greater extent by white activists than nonwhite militants. Only when comparisons were made on the basis of marijuana use did we find a substantial incidence among nonwhite militants (47 percent currently using). However, even at this level of drug use, white activists maintained their advantage (60 percent currently using). Nonwhite militants "play around" with marijuana (and hashish) but do not tend to exhibit the "head activity" of white activists.

Baseline data useful in the interpretation of the findings presented here were obtained in a subsequent study based upon a stratified, random sample of students at the same university (N = 491). Almost one half of these respondents (47.9 percent) reported illicit experiences with one or more of the drugs of immediate concern. Again, almost one half of this larger sample (46.9 percent) reported some experience with marijuana. Finally, over 8 percent reported one or more illicit experiences with an opiate (primarily heroin).

There are widespread feelings that heroin use among college students is rapidly increasing. However, there is little evidence that white college student "joy popping" is resulting in a substantial amount of primary drug addiction.*

To the extent that the college population reflects the various segments of the larger society, the university may be considered as

---

*Primary drug addiction[1] is defined as a complex behavior system associated with the compulsive use of an opiate—opium, morphine, heroin, codeine, dilaudid and the "synthetic equivalents," Demerol®, methadone, etc. Its "active stage" is characterized primarily by an intense conscious desire for the drug, 24-hour-a-day dependence on it to avoid withdrawal distress and the tendency to increase the dosage and frequency of use far beyond physiological necessity. Its "inactive stage" is characterized by a tendency to relapse, evidently a function of the intensification of pre-addiction personality patterns and conflicts, and the presistence of attitudes established during the early phases of the addiction process. Both the active and the inactive stages are characterized by the person's definition of himself as an addict.

a microcosm of that society. With the expansion of "open enrollment procedures" obviously more and more nonwhite minority
groups are becoming increasingly represented in the student population. Many of these representatives of nonwhite minorities
come from ghetto areas characterized by slum conditions, high
crime rate and primary drug addiction. Thus, one might expect
some increase in the percentage of student addictions (primary
addiction) among the minority group individuals as well as some
contagion potential.

However, it must be emphasized that these same minority-
group student populations are bringing with them, particularly
the militants, a hostile antiheroin subculture. In fact, these anti-
drug values frequently border upon reactive violence. For example, one female black militant respondent indicated "they
should kill every dope pusher in Harlem."

So, generally, black militants feel less of a need for heavy, continuous and varied drug involvement than white activists. They
may smoke marijuana or use hashish occasionally "for kicks," but
they do not become involved in either Keniston's "head" or
"seeking" types of motivation for drug use.[3] Whereas white activists are apparently in the process of rebelling against the values
of their culture of orientation as well as seeking a substitute of
identities, nonwhite militants are in the process of incorporating
both new value systems and new identities based upon an ego-en-
hancing ideology which provides little stimulus for "escape" from
the "real world of their involvement" into a life of heavy "head"
or "seeker" type drug involvement.

REFERENCES

1. Bailey, Walter C.: Primary drug addiction. *Med Opinion and Rev,* July
   1967, p. 83.
2. Blum, Richard H.: *Students and Drugs (Vol. II).* San Francisco, Jossey-
   Bass, 1969.
3. Keniston, Kenneth: Heads and seekers. Drugs on campus, counter cultures
   and American society. *Ment Hlth Dig, 1:*8, 1969.

Chapter 22

Patterns of Drug Usage Among University Students
Multiple Drug Usage

Doris H. Milman and Jeffrey L. Anker

A STUDY OF NONMEDICAL DRUG USAGE among university students by means of a questionnaire survey was undertaken in May 1969. The purpose was twofold: to gather up-to-date information on a rapidly changing problem and to pursue in depth some hitherto unstudied or unreported aspects of drug usage. The method of study, the demography of the sample and the results with respect to trends of drug usage by calendar year and usage of marijuana are the subject of a previous communication.[1] The subject of this communication will be the use of multiple illicit drugs (i.e. illegal drugs or medically approved drugs used for nonmedical purposes). The relation of illicit drug usage to practices with respect to tobacco and alcohol is also included.

METHOD

A questionnaire of 220 items embracing 74 postulates was employed. The illicit drugs studied were marijuana, hashish, amphetamines, barbiturates, LSD, opium, glue, heroin and cocaine. A detailed inquiry was made of past and present drug practices, frequency of usage, demographic data, personal and social factors, the use of tobacco and attitudes toward drug usage. The questionnaire was presented at two university centers, two agriculture and technical colleges, six liberal arts colleges and three medical schools of a large eastern state university. The campuses studied had a combined enrollment of about 75,000 students.

Note: This study was conducted with financial assistance from USPHS Grant FR-00291 and the State University of New York Faculty Senate Committee on Drug Abuse.

The undergraduate sample was drawn from randomly selected morning classes, approximately 600 students being surveyed at each school. The administration of the questionnaire was supervised by one of us (J.A), then a medical student, with the assistance of other senior medical students. Student volunteers were enlisted locally at each campus to ensure simultaneous administration as well as to exclude any involvement of university personnel. There was no prior announcement of the subject of the questionnaire so as to ensure that students' responses would be uninhibited and unrehearsed. The students were urged not to respond to the questionnaire unless they could comply honestly and willingly. By this means a response rate of 100 percent and a total undergraduate sample of 6174 responses were obtained. Of these 6110 were deemed suitable and were pooled for statistical analysis.

Because of their relatively small enrollment, the entire population of each medical school was surveyed rather than a random sample. A total of 927 graduate students was surveyed, 738 by direct classroom administration and 189 by mail (owing to the nature of their academic assignment). The rate of return of the mailed questionnaires was 30 percent in contrast to the 100 percent rate of response in the classrooms. Of the total, 922 graduate questionnaires were acceptable for analysis.

The data were quantitated by tabulations and cross-tabulations. Those variables were eliminated from subsequent analysis where there was an insufficient quantity of data (QNS) or where no differences in distribution (chi square, $p > .01$) were observed. Intra-questionnaire reliability was estimated to be $\geq 95\%$ for non-drug questions and $\geq 85\%$ for drug-related questions.

RESULTS

Demography

Demographic differences between the graduate and undergraduate samples are described in the previous communication.[1] In summary, the chief differences are in age, sex distribution, religious background, marital status and parental income and education.

Prevalence of Individual Drugs

The lifetime use (i.e. past as well as present use) of individual drugs is listed (Table 22-I and Figure 22-1) in order of de-

TABLE 22-I

PREVALENCE OF INDIVIDUAL DRUGS

	Undergraduates			Graduates		
	N	*% of Sample*	*% of Users*	*N*	*% of Sample*	*% of Users*
Alcohol	5958	98		911	97	
Marijuana	1657	27	81	392	42	87
Hashish	1095	18	55	191	20	42
Amphetamines	631	10	32	143	14	32
Opium	386	6	19	20	2	5
Barbiturates	242	4	12	41	4	9
LSD	241	4	12	25	3	6
Glue	91	1	5	4	<1	1
Cocaine	62	1	3	2	<1	<1
Heroin	29	<1	1	1	<1	<1
Other drugs	334	5	17	41	4	9

creasing frequency. Alcohol is by far the most commonly used drug and is virtually universally the first drug used.

There are several noteworthy differences between the undergraduate and graduate samples with respect to individual drugs. Marijuana and amphetamines have a greater prevalence among graduates than among undergraduates. On the other hand, opium, glue, cocaine and heroin have a substantial representation among the undergraduates and are used little or not at all by the graduates. The reasons for these differences can merely be inferred since no questions were directed at the reason for choosing a particular drug or drugs. The wider range of drugs used by undergraduates suggests that younger people are more experimental and less discriminating, an observation also made by Mizner et al.[2] Medical students, on the other hand, being conversant with the pharmacology of drugs because of the nature of their studies or being more prudent by virtue of their age are more inclined to restrict themselves to "safe" or less exotic drugs. The increased use of amphetamines by medical students, noted here, has been documented also by Mizner et al.[2] and by Smith and Blachly.[3]

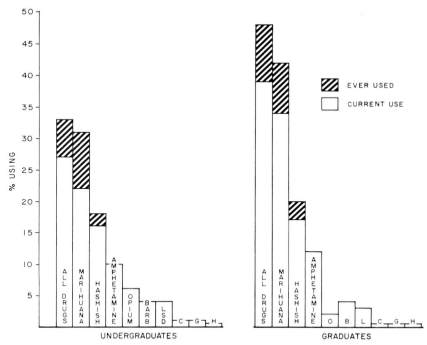

Figure 22-1. Prevalence of individual drugs.

Familiarity, accessibility and the pressure of studies have been offered in explanation of this increased use. The increased prevalence of marijuana among medical students noted by us has also been reported by Mizner *et al.*[2] He ascribes it to demographic factors, for example upper socioeconomic stratum and geographic origin (east and west coasts) of the medical school sample. Similarly in our survey, sampling factors appear to account for the higher prevalence of marijuana, our medical student population being comprised predominantly of men from higher socioeconomic backgrounds and with a large representation of Jewish students, all factors highly correlated with drug usage.[4,5]

Use of Multiple Drugs

Use of multiple drugs is a pattern which has been substantiated many times in clinical observation.[2,4,6-9]

Drug Abuse

Thirty-three percent of undergraduates and 48 percent of graduates report having used at least one illicit drug at least one time (Table 22-II and Fig. 22-2). Somewhat less than two thirds

TABLE 22-II
USE OF MULTIPLE DRUGS

	Undergraduates (N=6110)			Graduates (N=922)		
	N	% of Sample	% of Users	N	% of Sample	% of Users
Use no drug	391	6		38	4	
Alcohol as first drug	5602	91		882	95	
Illicit drug as first drug	121	2		4	<1	
Illicit drug as second drug	1874	31		447	48	
Use at least one illicit drug	1995	33		451	48	
Use at least two illicit drugs	1225	20	61	305	33	68
Use at least three illicit drugs	690	11	35	140	15	31

of undergraduate users and slightly more than two thirds of graduate users have used at least three illicit drugs.

Another clinical impression, born out statistically in this study, is that marijuana is the most widely used of the illicit drugs. Eighty-one percent of undergraduate users and 87 percent of graduate users use marijuana. The graduate students' greater use of marijuana is consistent with their greater total use of illicit drugs combined with their lesser use of opium, glue, cocaine and heroin.

Order of Introduction of Individual Illicit Drugs

After alcohol, the drug first to be introduced (Table 22-III and Fig. 22-3) is marijuana.Among users, more than 90 percent use it as their second drug and first illicit drug. Hashish follows as the third drug and second illicit drug for both undergraduate and graduate students. Differences between the two student groups emerge in respect to amphetamines, which appear earlier in the spectrum of graduate drug use and later among undergraduate drug use. As stated above, the pressure for achievement by medical students leads to an early and preferential use of this drug. Among LSD users, where the data are sufficient for analysis,

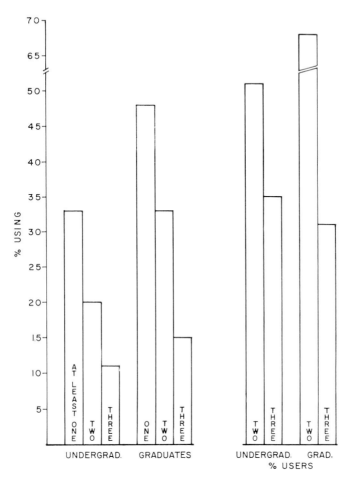

Figure 22-2. Use of multiple drugs.

this drug is their fourth in order of introduction. No specific inquiry was made about the order of introduction of opium, cocaine and heroin. If we had anticipated, which we did not, the frequency with which opium was used by undergraduates, we would have included a question about the timing of its introduction.

TABLE 22-III

ORDER OF INTRODUCTION OF INDIVIDUAL DRUGS

	% of Users							
	Using as 1st Drug		*Using as 2nd Drug*		*Using as 3rd Drug*		*Using as 4th Drug*	
	UG	G	UG	G	UG	G	UG	G
Alcohol	91	95	3	2	3	1	No Information	
Marijuana	4	<1	82	84	13	13	2	2
Hashish	1	0	21	7	68	77	10	16
Amphetamines	1	<1	23	60	25	23	51	16
Barbiturates	2	0	37	20	27	49	35	31
LSD	5	4	8	4	25	30	62	61
Glue	13	QNS	55	QNS	22	QNS	10	QNS

UG = graduates.

G = undergraduates.

QNS = insufficient quantity.

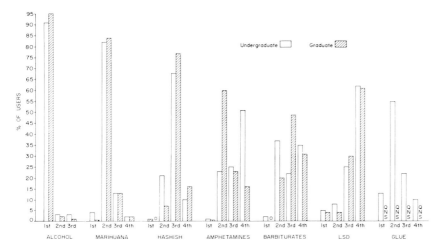

Figure 22-3. Order of introduction of individual drugs.

Glue, which is used only by undergraduates, has a significant representation as a first drug and is most commonly employed by its users as a second drug. Its ready availability and cheapness probably account for its early use, at an age when the cost, the legal restrictions, and the logistics of procurement preclude the use of more sophisticated drugs.

Relation to Tobacco

The use of four illicit drugs—marijuana, amphetamines, opium and LSD—was correlated with the use of tobacco (Fig. 22-4). There is a clear difference between nonsmokers and smokers, the smokers indicating much greater usage of the drugs studied. This association is understandable for marijuana and opium since these drugs are usually smoked. LSD and amphetamines, however, are taken by other routes and yet the association with tobacco exists. It would appear that the motivation for drug usage is broadly based and is determined by a variety of factors that embrace both licit and illicit substances.

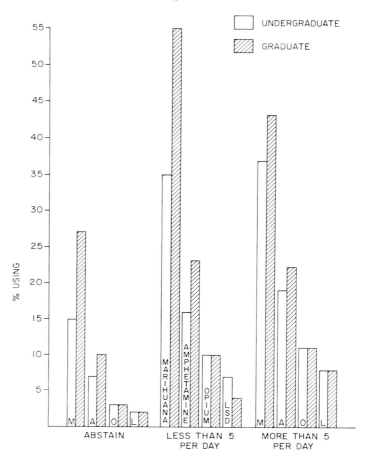

Figure 22-4. Prevalence of drug usage among tobacco users.

Relation to Alcohol

Marijuana, amphetamines, opium and LSD usage were correlated with the use of alcohol (Fig. 22-5). Certain interesting
facts emerge. There is a group of abstainers from alcohol among
whom a significant percentage of drug users are found, the prevalence being roughly equivalent to that of those alcohol users
who occasionally become intoxicated. Among drinkers there is a
positive correlation between use of drugs and degree of use of al-

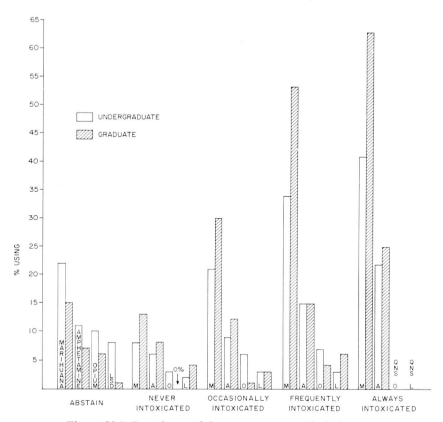

Figure 22-5. Prevalence of drug usage among alcohol users.

cohol. Only the very limited drinkers are limited in use of other drugs. As with tobacco, heavy use of alcohol is correlated with a high incidence of illicit drug usage. This suggests that the motivation for drug usage is based not only on the specific pharmacological properties of the given drug but on a general need to alter consciousness or achieve intoxication.

COMMENT

The results of this survey are consistent with the findings of others. Differences can be accounted for by the methods of gathering data, the populations studied, and the year when the study was undertaken. The reliability of this study is, we believe, enhanced by the fact that it was in part designed and wholly administered by students.

Certain facts emerge which have important implications with respect to education, therapy and control of drug abuse. Student drug use is a well-established practice, embraced by almost half of the graduate sample and one third of the undergraduate sample. The drug of choice, after alcohol, is marijuana, with hashish ranking second in prevalence. Heroin use is insignificant unless one feels that even one user is too many. Multiple drug use is the rule rather than the exception. Moreover, the younger users employ a greater variety of drugs and with less discrimination, including heroin and, surprisingly, opium.

Educational measures aimed at combating drug usage must take into account the lack of specificity in choice of drug and the tendency to experiment. It appears from these data as well as from practical experience that drug choices are determined by fads, novelty, publicity and expediency as much as by the intrinsic psychotropic properties of the given drug. Hence, education should be directed at the potential dangers to the developing personality of escape through drugs or dependence upon drugs, rather than a caveat against the specific undesirable effects of specific drugs.

Treatment of addiction by means of a substitute drug must be approached with caution lest the substitute become yet another choice in the user's spectrum of intoxicants. As we have seen, the trend is toward multiple usage and it cannot be assumed that a new therapeutic agent will long remain immune from abuse, especially in view of the fact that two of the most commonly abused drugs, amphetamines and barbiturates, have been preempted from legitimate therapeutic status.

Control of commerce in drugs must be sufficiently broad, flexible and alert to accommodate to changing fads. Also, account must be taken of the popularity of hashish, which ranks second in prevalence among illicit drugs. If marijuana were to be legalized, for example, what would be the status of hashish, a vastly more potent cannabis preparation? Are we prepared for the widespread usage hashish would enjoy in the wake of a social acceptance of marijuana? What other Eastern variants of cannabis would come into vogue in the wake of the legalization of marijuana?

Finally, these data tend to refute the popular contention that the use of marijuana does not lead to the use of other drugs. The following facts—namely that marijuana is the most widely used drug, that it is the first illicit drug employed and that multiple drug usage is the rule for two thirds of users—lead inescapably to the conclusion that marijuana is the first step in the direction of drug abuse.

In summary, the pattern of multiple drug usage by young people raises new and unsettling questions for the future of this very thorny problem.

ACKNOWLEDGMENTS

We are indebted to Dr. Stuart A. Kahan for the processing and statistical evaluation of the data. Drs. Victor Tesoriero, Leslie Elkind and Mark Bennett assisted in the survey during their fourth year as medical students.

REFERENCES

1. Anker, J. L., Milman, D. H., Kahan, S. A., and Valenti, C.: Drug usage and related patterns of behavior in university students: I. General survey and marihuana use. *J Amer Coll Health Ass, 19:*178-186, 1971.
2. Mizner, G. L., Barter, J. T., and Werme, P. H.: Patterns of drug use among college students: A preliminary report. *Amer J Psychiat, 127:* 15-24, 1970.
3. Smith, S. N., and Blachly, P. H.: Amphetamine usage by medical students. *J Med Educ, 41:*167-170, 1966.
4. Hinckley, R. G. *et al.:* Nonmedical drug use and the college student. *J Amer Coll Health Ass, 17:*35-51, 1968.
5. Suchman, E. A.: The "hang-loose" ethic and the spirit of drug use. *J Health Soc Behav, 9:*146-155, 1968.
6. Imperi, L. L., Kleber, H. D., and Davie, J. S.: Use of hallucinogenic drugs on campus. *JAMA, 204:*1021-1024, 1968.
7. Eells, K.: Marijuana and LSD: A survey of one college campus. *J Counsel Psychol, 15:*459-467, 1968.
8. Rand, M. E., Hammond, J. D., and Moscou, P. J.: A survey of drug use at Ithaca College. *J Amer Coll Health Ass, 17:*43-51, 1968.
9. Robbins, E. S., Robbins, L., Frosch, W. A., and Stern, M.: College student drug use. *Amer J Psychiat, 126:*1743-1750, 1970.

Chapter 23

Patterns of Nonmedical Drug Usage Among University Students
Student Attitudes Toward Drug Usage

Jeffrey L. Anker and Doris H. Milman

A N INVESTIGATION by means of an anonymous self-administered questionnaire was undertaken in May 1969 to determine patterns of and attitudes toward drug usage among undergraduates (UG) and graduates (G) of the State University of New York. A sample of 7,032 students (UG 6110, G 922) was surveyed. The details of the method of this study have been presented in other articles,[1,2] which focused on patterns of usage. This chapter focuses on student attitudes.

PURPOSE

It is our conviction that one must have a perspective of student attitudes toward drug usage in order to understand the drug scene and anticipate future developments within it. As educated and potentially influential members of society, the opinions of students inevitably must be reckoned with. If our goal is to develop an approach and attitude toward drug usage which is viable for our society it must be realistic, in which case we must take into account the fact that the drug-oriented generation has its own views about drug use. Their views cannot be denied if we hope to maintain open avenues of communication.

With this in mind, a major portion of this study was devoted to learning the students' opinions about drug use. Three facets

Note: This study was conducted with financial assistance from USPHS Grant FR-00291 and the State University of New York, Faculty Senate Committee on Drug Abuse.

of the student perspective were focused on. First, we tried to gain insight into the extent to which students accept and are open to drug use. Second, we tried to learn the extent to which students consider drugs to be potentially harmful. Finally, we tried to learn how drug users view their drug use as having affected their lives.

We define acceptance as willingness to use drugs personally and/or approval of use by others. Openness to drug use is a more encompassing concept, including those who have neither definitely accepted nor rejected drugs and who therefore are both open to drugs and susceptible to their use. As parameters of acceptance we considered student attitudes toward legalization, their own potential use, use by their own children in the future and use by their younger siblings. We believe that those people who said they "don't know" whether they would try a drug or whether they would approve of a drug's use by others are ones who might, being susceptible individuals who are open to the general climate of opinion about drugs. For the older generation, concern over potential harm has been a restraining influence. Knowing student sentiment about potential harm of drugs can give us an idea of what checks exist on students' acceptance of drug use. Also, we can infer something about their understanding of these drugs. Knowing users' subjective evaluation about the effect of drug use on their lives may be useful in anticipating future developments within the drug scene.

RESULTS

Opinions of Students on Possible Legalization of Drugs

Students were considered to be open to the idea of the legal availability of drugs if they indicated they would or might ("don't know") like it to be available for use without a doctor's prescription (Table 23-I). The greatest number of students indicated that they would or might like alcohol to be legally available. Of the illicit drugs, students were most open to legalization of the cannabis preparations, but clearly they were more so for marijuana than for hashish. A sizeable number were also open to legalization of amphetamines, barbiturates, glue and LSD. Increases in the number of students definitely approving of legaliza-

TABLE 23-I
OPINIONS OF STUDENTS ON POSSIBLE LEGALIZATION OF DRUGS

	Undergraduates*						Graduates*					
	Yes						Yes					
	Any Age	Undecided Whether Any Age or Over 18	Over 18	Don't Know	Total Approving of Legal Availability	Total Open to Legal Availability	Any Age	Undecided Whether Any Age or Over 18	Over 18	Don't Know	Total Approving of Legal Availability	Total Open to Legal Availability
Alcohol	11	1	85	1	97	98	12	1	84	1	97	98
Marijuana	7	4	33	17	44	61	8	4	52	13	64	77
Hashish	5	4	20	18	29	47	6	5	28	16	39	55
Amphetamines	2	5	7	19	14	33	1	4	7	8	12	20
Barbiturates	2	5	9	18	16	34	1	3	7	6	11	17
Glue	7	5	4	14	16	30	10	3	6	7	19	26
LSD	1	5	4	10	10	20	2	3	5	7	10	17
Opium	1	5	3	9	9	18	1	3	3	5	7	12
Cocaine	1	5	2	9	8	17	1	3	3	5	7	12
Heroin	1	5	1	7	7	14	1	2	2	3	5	8

*Numbers are in percent of total undergraduate and graduate samples respectively.

tion from drug to drug were mostly due to increases in the number
with a moderate position. Thus, the bulk of students who favored
the legal availability of hashish, marijuana and alcohol felt they
should be legally available over the age of 18 only.

TABLE 23-II
SHOULD MARIJUANA BE LEGALLY AVAILABLE?
DEMOGRAPHIC BREAKDOWN OF UNDERGRADUTES

	N	Total Yes*	Total Yes** + Don't Know
Sex			
Male	2665	49	63
Female	3421	41	61
Age			
17	64	72	86
18	1199	48	65
19	1806	44	62
20	1319	47	64
21	915	42	60
22	385	44	64
23	100	35	46
24	265	29	44
Religion			
Jewish	926	60	76
Mixed	523	43	61
Catholic	2427	41	59
Protestant	2010	38	56
Family Income			
$0–1,000	71	39	48
$1–5,000	515	42	57
$5–10,000	2573	41	58
$10–20,000	2317	48	66
$20–30,000	353	52	69
$30,000 or more	144	56	75
Father's Education			
Grade 8	656	40	55
Some H.S.	1093	41	56
H.S. grad	2072	43	61
Some college	1076	48	67
College grad	679	49	68

*The percent of N approving of (accepting) legal availabiliy of marijuana.
**The percent of N open to marijuana being legally available.

The undergraduates were broken down into demographic subgroups and attitude toward legalization of marijuana was studied (Table 23-II). Males, younger students, Jewish students and students from higher income and more educated families were most accepting of and open to the idea of marijuana being legally available.

Attitudes of Students Towards Personal Use of Drugs

Students were considered to be open to personal use of a drug if they reported they did, would or might ("don't know") try that drug (Table 23-III). Far more students were open to the use of marijuana than any other drug studied. More than two thirds of graduates and more than one half of undergraduates indicated they did, would or might try marijuana. Students were next most open to use of the other cannabis derivative, hashish. A considerable number of students also indicated an openness to personal use of amphetamines, barbiturates and LSD.

The undergraduates were broken down into demographic subgroups and openness to use of marijuana was studied. Though differences in actual use of marijuana existed among these groups, the proportion who said they "would try" it was close to being the same across all groups, except for family income where it was noted that as income increased, both use and the proportion who said they would try it increased (Table 23-IV). Also, those groups with a lower prevalence of actual use had a greater proportion of students who said they "would not try" it.

Attitudes of Students Toward Introducing Own Children to Use of Drugs

Far more students indicated they would or might ("don't know") introduce their own children to use of alcohol than any of the illicit drugs studied (Table 23-V). Of the illicit drugs, by far the greatest number of students reported they would or might introduce their children to use of marijuana. Hashish was clearly next, with other illicit drugs grouped considerably below these two cannabis preparations. Of those students who said they would introduce their children to the use of drugs, most indicated they

TABLE 23-III
ATTITUDES OF STUDENTS TOWARDS PERSONAL USE OF DRUGS

	Undergraduates*					Graduates*				
	Tried	Would Try	Don't Know	Total Willing to Use	Total Open to Use	Tried	Would Try	Don't Know	Total Willing to Use	Total Open to Use
Marijuana	23	22	10	45	55	36	26	7	62	69
Hashish	17	12	8	29	37	21	20	7	41	48
Amphetamines	9	7	9	16	25	15	11	6	26	32
Barbiturates	4	7	10	11	21	6	11	6	17	23
LSD	4	6	7	10	17	3	10	10	13	23
Opium	3	5	4	8	12	0	10	4	10	14
Cocaine	1	5	4	6	10	0	10	4	10	14
Glue	1	3	5	4	9	0	5	3	5	8
Heroin	0	4	3	4	7	0	6	2	6	8

*Numbers are in percent of total undergraduate and graduate samples respectively.

TABLE 23-IV

WOULD TRY MARIJUANA — DEMOGRAPHIC BREAKDOWN OF UNDERGRADUATE.

	N^*	Tried	Would Try	Total Willing To Use	Don't Know	Total Open To Use	Would Not Try
Sex							
Male	2645	30	24	54	8	62	38
Female	3419	19	23	42	12	54	46
Age							
17	64	47	23	70	5	75	25
18	1194	27	22	49	12	61	39
19	1806	24	25	49	10	59	41
20	1316	24	24	48	9	57	43
21	908	23	21	44	11	55	45
22	385	21	25	46	8	54	46
23	99	21	19	40	8	48	52
24	263	14	18	32	6	38	62
Marital Status							
Single	5541	25	23	48	11	59	41
Married	486	16	21	37	7	44	56
Religion							
Jewish	919	49	23	72	10	82	18
Mixed	521	24	23	47	11	58	42
Catholic	2418	20	24	44	11	55	45
Protestant	2007	17	22	39	10	49	51
Family Income							
$0–1,000	71	20	11	31	10	41	59
$1–5,000	517	21	20	41	7	48	52
$5–10,000	2569	20	22	42	11	53	47
$10–20,000	2296	27	24	51	11	62	38
$20–30,000	352	31	25	56	12	68	32
$30,000 or more	144	35	34	69	7	76	24
Father's Education							
Grade 8	655	18	21	39	11	50	50
Some H.S.	1092	20	22	42	9	51	49
H.S. grad	2064	22	24	46	10	56	44
Some college	1066	26	23	49	12	61	39
College grad	678	30	22	52	13	65	35
Grad degree	474	33	26	59	12	71	29

*N = an absolute number.

The other columns are in percent of the respective N's.

Total willing to use = tried + would try.

Total open to use = tried + would try + don't know.

TABLE 23-V

ATTITUDES OF STUDENTS TOWARDS INTRODUCING OWN CHILDREN TO USE OF DRUGS

| | Undergraduates* | | | | | | Graduates* | | | | | |
| | Yes | | | Total Willing to Introduce Children | Don't Know | Total Open to Introducing Children | Yes | | | Total Willing to Introduce Children | Don't Know | Total Open to Introducing Children |
	Any Age	Any Age if Mature	Over 18				Any Age	Any Age if Mature	Over 18			
Alcohol	15	53	19	87	5	92	19	60	9	88	3	91
Marijuana	3	19	6	28	12	40	5	35	6	46	12	58
Hashish	2	12	3	17	10	27	3	22	4	29	11	40
Amphetamines	1	2	1	4	10	14	3	6	3	12	7	19
Barbiturates	0	2	1	3	10	13	2	6	2	10	6	16
LSD	0	2	1	3	7	10	1	3	2	6	6	12
Opium	0	1	0	1	6	7	1	1	1	3	4	7
Glue	0	1	0	1	6	7	2	1	0	3	4	7
Cocaine	0	0	0	0	5	5	1	2	0	3	4	7
Heroin	0	0	0	0	5	5	1	1	0	2	2	4

*Numbers are percent of total undergraduate and graduate samples respectively.

Total willing to introduce children = sum of the three "yes" categories.

Total open to introducing children = "yes" + "don't know."

would do this when their children were mature enough, regardless of age.

Attitudes of Students Towards Permitting Younger Siblings to Try Drugs

The greatest number of students reported that they would permit their younger siblings to try alcohol (Table 23-VI). The

TABLE 23-VI

ATTITUDES OF STUDENTS TOWARDS PERMITTING YOUNGER
SIBLINGS TO TRY DRUGS

	Undergraduates* Yes	Graduates* Yes
Alcohol	78	84
Marijuana	27	47
Hashish	17	29
Amphetamines	4	11
Barbiturates	4	9
LSD	4	5
Opium	4	5
Cocaine	3	5
Glue	3	4
Heroin	1	4

*Numbers are in percent of those undergraduate (N = 4,612) and graduate (N = 518) students respectively with younger siblings between the ages of 12 and 18

two cannabis preparations were next, with marijuana being considerably higher than hashish and hashish being considerably higher than the other illicit drugs.

Opinions of Students About Potential Harm (Psychological and/or Physical) of Drugs

All drugs studied were generally viewed as potentially harmful by these students (Table 23-VII). The number of students with this view varied for the specific drugs. At one extreme heroin was considered by almost all students to be potentially harmful. Cannabis derivatives, especially marijuana, were perceived by fewer students than any other drug studied, including alcohol, as potentially harmful.

TABLE 23-VII

OPINIONS OF STUDENTS ABOUT POTENTIAL HARM
(PSYCHOLOGICAL AND/OR PHYSICAL) OF DRUGS

	Undergraduates* Potentially harmful	*Graduates* Potentially harmful*
Heroin	96	98
Opium	92	96
Cocaine	92	95
LSD	92	94
Glue	87	94
Barbiturates	84	92
Amphetamines	81	92
Alcohol	67	85
Hashish	65	75
Marijuana	59	68

*Numbers are in percent of total undergraduate and graduate samples respectively

Opinions of Drug Users About the Effect of Drug Use on Their Lives

Most users felt that drugs had not affected their lives (Table 23-VIII). Of the remainder, most felt that drugs had made their lives better. A small number of users did not know what effect drug use had had on their lives. Virtually none believed that use of drugs had made their lives any worse.

TABLE 23-VIII

OPINIONS OF DRUG USERS ABOUT THE EFFECT OF DRUG USE ON THEIR LIVES

	Undergraduates*	*Graduates**
No change	66	71
Made better	20	20
Don't know	14	9
Made worse	0	0

*Numbers are in percent of undergraduate $(N = 1844)$ and graduate $(N = 424)$ drug users.

COMMENT AND SPECULATION

In support of the concept that the present state of drug use is of a contagious nature, we propose a model of a self-escalating system. We submit that students are chronically exposed to the presence of drugs and to users,[3,4] to the widespread acceptance of and openness to drug use, and to the operation of peer group pressures.[5] In this milieu, the nonusing highly susceptible students become users. Usage increases but acceptance and openness exceed actual usage as moderately susceptible students become highly susceptible ones and tentatively unsusceptible students become moderately susceptible ones. If one projects ahead, openness will continue to exceed acceptance which will continue to exceed use. When the contagion in use reaches the phase of exponential rise, the self-escalating quality of the system begins to operate. Ultimately openness will approach 100 percent; shortly thereafter acceptance will approach 100 percent and then it will become only a matter of time until use will catch up.

The results of our study are supportive of such a model. Use, acceptance and openness increase together. For illicit drugs, openness greatly exceeds use and acceptance exceeds use, but by lesser amounts. These findings, observed by us, are consistent with the experiences of others.[3-6] For alcohol, however, openness, acceptance and use are approximately the same, approaching 100 per cent. It is therefore hypothesized that alcohol is now at the end point of the aforementioned self-escalating system.

We suggest that students who reported they "would try" cannabis are highly susceptible to use of that drug. Those who indicated they might ("don't know") try cannabis are considered moderately susceptible and those who said they "would not try" it are considered tentatively unsusceptible. In any event, if one considers the ten-year use curves reported in a previous article[1] for marijuana and hashish, one sees that if they are extrapolated to the future the increase in the number of cannabis users is striking. Such hypothesizing cannot be done for the other illicit drugs since they are not presently in the exponential stage of the contagion.

The data show that for marijuana, where use has passed into an explosive phase, demographic subgroups, regardless of differences in actual use, tended to have comparable numbers of highly susceptible individuals who said they would try it. This can be interpreted to mean that once the contagion has taken a foothold, demographic subgroups, regardless of original resistance, tend to become equally susceptible. The one notable exception is for family income and it may be that this is the most basic parameter for determining predisposition to drug use. It also may be that some students who said they "would try" marijuana are more susceptible than others, depending on background.

The students' view that marijuana is potentially less harmful than alcohol will support and stimulate their acceptance of an openness to this drug. Their view that the illicit drugs other than cannabis are potentially harmful will act as a restraint on their acceptance of and openness to these drugs. The opinion of users that drug use has had no effect or a beneficial effect on their lives, as has also been found by Imperi[3] and Eells,[6] will stimulate nonusers toward openness, acceptance and use, as users come into contact with nonusers, as drugs remain a part of the student culture and as the dynamics of peer group acceptance operate. The relative willingness of many students to allow their younger siblings to try cannabis can be expected to have a reinforcing effect on the growth of cannabis use as the contagion in cannabis use spreads downward to this age group. The relative willingness of these students to introduce their own children to the use of cannabis could have a sustaining effect in terms of long-range evolution.

These students' attitudes show that they are doubting and questioning Establishment taboos against drug use, primarily the cannabis drugs. Of those who have definitely rejected the Establishment position, most are moderate, favoring legalization of cannabis only for people over 18 and intending to introduce their children to cannabis use only when they feel their children are mature. This is their thinking for alcohol as well and it probably is consistent with the older generation's position with respect to alcohol. These students are aware of the potential danger of all drugs, their awareness being generally consistent with medical judgments of the potential dangers of the various drugs. But the data show that they are beginning to question Establishment taboos against the more dangerous drugs as well.

These students' views present us with many critical and complex questions. For example, is it too late to prevent marijuana and even hashish from becoming endemic in our student culture, regardless of whether we think such a development is good or bad? Perhaps it is not too late to stop the spread of the more potent and more dangerous drugs. But are openness, acceptance and use of these other drugs about to explode the way they did for cannabis in the middle 60's? Serious attempts at education, treatment and control of drug use must take into account students' views and the dynamics that are operating if they are to be successful.

ACKNOWLEDGMENTS

We are indebted to Dr. Stuart A. Kahan for the processing and statistical evaluation of the data. Drs. Victor Tesoriero, Leslie Elkind and Mark Bennett assisted in the survey during their fourth year as medical students.

REFERENCES

1. Anker, J.L., Milman, D.H., Kahan, S.A., and Valenti, C.: Drug usage and related patterns of behavior in university students: I. General survey and marihuana use. *J Amer Coll Health Ass* (in press).
2. Milman, D.H., and Anker, J.L.: Patterns of drug usage among university students: multiple drug usage. In *Drug Abuse: Current Concepts and Research,* edited by W. Keup. Springfield, Charles C Thomas, 1971.
3. Imperi, L.L., Kleber, H.D., and Davie, J.S.: Use of hallucinogenic drugs on campus. *JAMA, 204:*1021-1024, 1968.
4. King, F.W.: Users and nonusers of marihuana: some attitudinal and behavioral correlates. *J Amer Coll Health Ass, 18:*213-217, 1970.
5. Suchman, E.A.: The "hang-loose" ethic and the spirit of drug use. *J Health Soc Behav, 9:*146-155, 1968.
6. Eells, K.: Marihuana and LSD: A survey of one college campus. *J Counsel Psychol, 15:*459-467, 1968.

Chapter 24

Exploration of the Attitudes of Students Involved with Drugs

Robert E. Stoessel

I N COMMUNITIES across the nation, fear is spreading over the increase in the use of narcotics among teenagers and younger children. One reason for the growing concern is the increase in drug-related deaths in the past few years. Last year, in New York City alone, there were 900 deaths directly related to drugs. Local experts estimate that there are at least 25,000 teenage heroin addicts in New York, and there is little reason to believe that other cities and suburban areas are any more immune.

It is evident that schools have not escaped this alarming problem and that educators have a responsibility to both students and society to formulate a preventive drug education program. But not all educators feel their responsibility should be so profound. Some are unwilling to recognize the extent of the problem and tend to minimize its effect. Some are satisfied with an isolated kind of teaching based on warnings, even though past experience supports its ineffectiveness. There are still others who receive support from parents in abdicating the school of its responsibility by attributing the drug problem to the lack of policing and isolating its effect to "other schools."

Fortunately, not all educators are apathetic and many have attempted to assess the extent of drug use in their schools. But the only methods presently available require the use of burdensome questionnaires which ultimately rely on the honesty of the students to directly state whether or not they use drugs. While this assessment is necessarily the first step, if not done accurately, hysterics may replace apathy, which would be equally dangerous.

Accurately assessing the extent of drug use may be accomplished in another way. Referring to social psychology and one of its major issues, attitude formation, Krech[3] states:

> As man in his finite world is repeatedly forced to cope with the same object, the repeatedly evoked cognitions, feelings and response dispositions become organized into a unified and enduring system—for man is an organizing and conserving animal. This entire "package" of particular beliefs, feelings, and response tendencies is henceforth always there, on the ready, whenever the individual is confronted by the appropriate object.
>
> The social actions of the individual reflect his attitudes—enduring systems of positive or negative evaluations, emotional feelings and pro or con action tendencies with respect to social objects.

Making use of these concepts regarding attitudes, it may be possible to differentiate drug users from nonusers by their attitudes towards drugs. If the responses of drug users and nonusers are compared, it is hypothesized that their attitudes regarding drugs will differ significantly.

SUBJECTS AND PROCEDURES

One hundred and forty junior high-school students, half of whom were admitted drug users, and fifteen clinical patients in various stages of psychotherapy for drug abuse were used. The subject's use and nonuse of drugs was substantiated by biographical data, hospital records and peer group collaboration.

The drug attitude inventory used (Table 24-I) consisted of twenty-five statements regarding drugs with which each subject was asked to indicate whether he "strongly agreed," "agreed," was "undecided," "disagreed" or "strongly disagreed." The author chose the statements from his experience in their ability to discriminate between drug users and nonusers.

Each subject was given the Drug Attitude Inventory and asked to respond to every statement. An item analysis was used to ascertain the most discriminating statements and a chi-square analysis was computed to evaluate the probability that discrepancies as great or greater than those would have resulted from sampling fluctuations.[4]

The clinical patients were grouped according to their length

TABLE 24-I
ATTITUDE INVENTORY

Strongly Agree	Agree	Undecided	Disagree	Strongly Disagree
A	B	C	D	E

1. Sometimes a person needs drugs even when he is not sick. _____
2. It is "chicken" to refuse to try a drug. _____
3. Drugs are an important part of the social scene. _____
4. I would never use drugs for kicks. _____
5. We need stricter control of drugs. _____
6. Narcotics are OK for a quick kick. _____
7. It's hard being the only person in the group not using drugs. _____
8. Drug dependence affects all of society. _____
9. Marijuana should be legalized. _____
10. Self-medication is a dangerous practice. _____
11. People who use marijuana are looking for an easy way out of responsibilities. _____
12. Too much fuss is being made about drug abuse. _____
13. Education is necessary to deal with the drug problem. _____
14. Marijuana users are likely to try other drugs. _____
15. Kids make fun of others not using drugs. _____
16. "Pot" parties are groovy. _____
17. Drugs are necessary for courage. _____
18. I could not care less if people use drugs. _____
19. Kids have adequate knowledge about drugs. _____
20. Kids who give drugs to their friends are not drug pushers. _____
21. Drug users are not successful in school. _____
22. Most kids learn about drugs from their friends. _____
23. I wish they would do more to publicize information about drugs. _____
24. Using LSD is a good way to gain insight. _____
25. It is OK to use "goof balls" (barbiturates) for kicks. _____

of time in therapy, and their responses were scored in a procedure similar to that developed by Likert.[2] The total score was obtained by summing all the responses of the discriminating statements, scoring the response categories 5, 4, 3, 2, and 1 respectively for favorable statements and reversing the scoring for unfavorable statements.[1]

RESULTS

Results of the item analysis, combining the agreement and disagreement categories, are found in Table 24-II. Except for six

TABLE 24-II

ITEM ANALYSIS AND CHI-SQUARE VALUES FOR RESPONSES OF DRUG
USERS AND NONUSERS ON ATTITUDE INVENTORY

		Agree	*Undecided*	*Disagree*	*Chi-square*
1.	User	46	8	16	
	Nonuser	19	12	39	20.71*
2.	User	10	6	54	
	Nonuser	1	6	63	1.88
3.	User	26	15	29	
	Nonuser	3	10	57	22.11*
4.	User	17	19	34	
	Nonuser	64	1	5	44.49*
5.	User	34	21	15	
	Nonuser	62	5	3	10.12*
6.	User	20	18	32	
	Nonuser	0	3	67	24.61*
7.	User	47	6	17	
	Nonuser	42	14	14	.02
8.	User	42	14	14	
	Nonuser	37	20	13	.00
9.	User	50	9	11	
	Nonuser	8	14	48	53.53*
10.	User	33	18	19	
	Nonuser	53	9	8	8.45*
11.	User	15	13	42	
	Nonuser	43	13	14	30.12*
12.	User	32	14	24	
	Nonuser	4	5	61	34.67*
13.	User	33	8	29	
	Nonuser	62	1	7	20.24*
14.	User	32	8	30	
	Nonuser	61	8	1	24.88*
15.	User	23	16	31	
	Nonuser	47	16	7	23.38*
16.	User	30	30	10	
	Nonuser	0	11	59	46.18*
17.	User	9	8	53	
	Nonuser	0	5	65	1.49
18.	User	16	17	37	
	Nonuser	11	15	44	1.49
19.	User	42	8	20	
	Nonuser	14	7	49	26.20*
20.	User	42	10	18	
	Nonuser	5	12	53	46.40*
21.	User	15	15	40	
	Nonuser	40	18	12	26.38*

22.	User	49	8	13	
	Nonuser	47	14	9	.47
23.	User	32	13	25	
	Nonuser	52	11	7	14.83*
24.	User	15	21	34	
	Nonuser	3	9	58	9.21*
25.	User	24	15	31	
	Nonuser	1	3	66	20.98*

*Significant at the 1% level.

statements—2, 7, 8, 17, 18 and 22—all the statements differentiated the user from the nonuser. The two groups responded differently to eight statements and one group consistently favored one response while the other group showed an inconsistency in responding to the remaining eleven statements.

Results of the chi-square analysis are also found in Table 24-II. In all statements, except the six previously mentioned, the discrepancies found would be expected in less than 1 percent of the samples if there were no differences in the way drug users and nonusers responded.

The total scores and means obtained by the clinical patients are found in Table 24-III. Results indicated that the mean in-

TABLE 24-III

ATTITUDE INVENTORY SCORES AND MEANS FOR GROUPS IN THREE STAGES OF PSYCHOTHERAPY FOR DRUG ABUSE

	One Month	Six Months	One Year
	+10	+75	+120
	− 5	+55	+ 90
	−10	+20	+ 50
	−25	+20	+ 45
	−60	+ 5	+ 40
	−60	+35	+ 69
Total	−90	+175	+345
Mean	−18	+ 35	+ 69

ventory score for each group was a positive function of the length of time in therapy. Scores showed a positive increase as time in therapy increased.

DISCUSSION

As the individual develops, his cognitions, feelings and action tendencies with respect to objects in his world become crystallized into enduring systems called attitudes. Krech[3] states, "The action tendency component of an attitude includes all the behavioral readinesses associated with an attitude. If an individual holds a positive attitude toward a given object, he will be disposed to help or reward or support the object; if he holds a negative attitude, he will be disposed to harm or punish or destroy the object."

Students develop attitudes and action tendencies toward drugs very early in their lives. Determining which came first or whether a causal relationship existed was not the object of this investigation. However, that both attitude and action tendency existed concurrently and that attitudes can be used to differentiate drug users from nonusers was substantiated. Likewise, a successful rehabilitation program, though not limited to attitude modification, should result in a change in attitudes towards drugs.

The implications for a drug education program can be gleaned from question 19, in which drug users, contrary to nonusers, agree that they have an adequate knowledge of drugs. Many attitudes held by people lack validity because they are not sufficiently well informed. In most cases, the information possessed by drug users is sadly inadequate, and as long as they fail to include certain of the essential facts of drugs, their knowledge may be distorted and their beliefs wrong.

While this research was limited in its population and statistical data, it is presented as the beginning of further research in attitude formation and modification, and its relation to drug abuse.

REFERENCES

1. Anastasi, A.: *Psychological Testing*. London, Macmillan, 1969, p. 486.
2. Hilgard, E., and Atkinson, R.: *Introduction to Psychology*. New York, Harcourt, Brace & World, 1967, p. 522.
3. Krech, D., Crutchfield, R., and Ballachey, E.: *Individual in Society*. New York, McGraw-Hill, 1962, p. 137, 140.
4. Wert, J., Neidt, C., and Ahmann, J.: *Statistical Methods in Educational and Psychological Research*. New York, Appleton-Century-Crofts, 1954, p. 627.

Chapter 25

Diffusion Paths for a Drug of Abuse

Carl D. Chambers, Barbara K. Sheridan and Thomas Willis

WHILE MOST BEHAVIORAL SCIENTISTS have referred to contagion aspects of drug misuse, there have been few empirical attempts to describe the diffusion paths for a drug of abuse. During the course of a series of investigations designed to assess various types of propoxyphene abuse, the diffusion paths for this specific drug were isolated. Three examples of the illicit diversion of this legally prescribed drug will be depicted: first, the diffusion within a black Philadelphian ghetto among adolescents with histories of prior drug experimentation; second, the diffusion within a predominantly white, middle-class, southern, suburban community among adolescents with no history of prior drug experimentation; and finally, the diffusion among adult abusers of multiple soft drugs who reside in Greenwich Village. The description of the diffusion paths will include means of initiation, rapidity of diffusion and the characteristics and consequences of abuse.

Propoxyphene hydrochloride (Darvon®) was first synthesized by Pohland and Sullivan in 1953. A major thrust of the advertising for this drug has been that it is equal to codeine in intensity and duration of analgesic action, but as having fewer side effects and without codeine's potential for abuse and addiction.[6] Since that time, Darvon has become one of the most widely prescribed analgesics. In 1967, Darvon was among the fifty most prescribed drugs which comprised 33 percent of all prescriptions.[1]

The results of extensive studies dealing with the nature of propoxyphene abuse have been reported by Chambers and Wieland,[4] Chambers and Taylor[3] and Chambers, Moffett and Cuskey.[2] The authors have examined the addiction liability, prevalence and type of abuse among addict and nonaddict populations.

ILLICIT DIVERSION WITHIN A BLACK GHETTO
IN PHILADELPHIA

There are a small number of people who choose propoxyphene as a primary drug of abuse. Both the preference for the drug's effects and its ready availability contribute to this choice. Typically, four abusers were located who reported using propoxyphene to seek euphoric effects, who used the drug a minimum of twice weekly for at least a two-month period and who had access to other drugs but did not use them. The propoxyphene abuse among the four dates back to 1962 (Chart 1).

CHART 1.

PROPOXYPHENE DIFFUSION AMONG PREFERENCE USERS

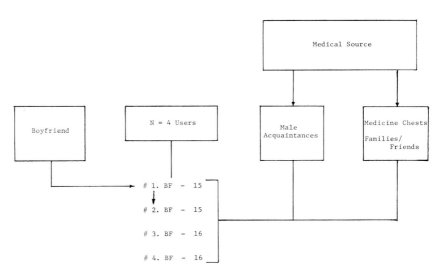

The four abusers reported that they had received some euphoric effects from the propoxyphene, but it was not until the abuse doses got into higher ranges that craving, dependency and tolerance were reported with any regularity (Table 25-I). Most of these preference abusers took the drug by mouth and did so without preparing the drug in any manner.

TABLE 25-I

PROPOXYPHENE ABUSE CHARACTERISTICS AND EFFECTS BY AGE, RACE AND SEX OF PREFERENCE ABUSERS

Preference Abusers (Age-Race-Sex)	Abuse Characteristics				Self-reported Effects			
	Abuse Dose (mgm)	Months of Abuse	Primar-ily Oral Route	Drug Prepara-tion	Euphoria	Crav-ing	Depend-ency	Toler-ance
1. 15—BF	325	4	Yes	No	Yes	No	No	No
2. 15—BF	325	4	Yes	No	Yes	No	No	No
3. 16—BF	325	4	Yes	No	Yes	No	No	No
4. 16—BF	325	4	Yes	No	Yes	No	No	No

These four abusers were members of the same gang of juvenile females in a black ghetto of North Philadelphia. All four had histories of prior drug abuse—principally with Seconal® capsules which they were able to purchase on the street for 50¢ and cough syrups containing codeine which they purchased illegally from pharmacists. One of the girls (subject #1) introduced the others to propoxyphene after she was initiated into its abuse by her boyfriend. The boyfriend had learned how to abuse the drug while in jail. Almost all of the propoxyphene used by these four girls was stolen medicine either given to them by males or stolen by the girls themselves from the medicine cabinets of their families and friends.

The route was oral and the entire capsule was swallowed. The girls normally took five capsules (325 mg) at a time and reportedly received a euphoric reaction each time. After approximately four months of regular abuse, three or four times a week, one girl ingested ten capsules (650 mg) and received what can only be described as a narcotic-like overdose. An older male opiate addict who was present recognized the symptoms and successfully treated the overdose with milk, ice packs and walking—as though it were an overdose of narcotics.

This 15-year-old black female stated her overdose was an attempt at suicide. The attempt was made because of difficulties she was having with the boyfriend who had introduced her to the euphoric effects of propoxyphene. At the 650 mg dose, drowsiness and "drunkenness" occurred rapidly, within fifteen minutes, and unconsciousness occurred shortly thereafter within another fifteen minutes. Convulsions did not occur although they have sometimes been associated with toxic overdose.[5]

After this episode, regular abuse of propoxyphene ceased in all four girls. The one who experienced the overdose has abstained from all drug use for over one year, and the other three only infrequently use propoxyphene.

TABLE 25-II
DRUG HISTORIES OF PREFERENCE ABUSERS

Preference Abusers	Drugs Abused Prior to Propoxyphene	Time of Propoxyphene Preference	Subsequent or Current Drugs of Abuse
1. 15—BF	Codeine C.S.—Seconal	1969	None
2. 15—BF	Codeine C.S.—Seconal	1969	Codeine C.S—Propoxyphene
3. 16—BF	Codeine C.S.—Seconal	1969	Codeine C.S.—Propoxyphene
4. 16—BF	Codeine C.S.—Seconal	1969	Sedatives—Propoxyphene

Although all four of these juvenile abusers stated they had received euphoric effects from the drug at 325 mg, and one overdose reportedly occurred at 650 mg, *none* of the four developed a tolerance or reported experiencing any of the physical symptoms associated with a dependence.

This process of the introduction of a new drug, the eruption of its abuse and the disenchantment with the drug or the introduction of a new drug seems to be fairly typical in juvenile deviant gangs. Interview data is available, at least for adolescents in Philadelphia, which suggests that alcohol, various sedative-hypnotics, amphetamines and, in some cases, marijuana have been introduced at a group level but have enjoyed only short periods of popularity, for example, three to six weeks. After the transitory eruption phase, the members of the group usually revert to drugs that they individually prefer until a "newer" drug is introduced. While availability is a key factor, it alone will not explain the process, as most of the drugs used by those younger abusers are available most of the time.

ILLICIT DIVERSION WITHIN A WHITE, MIDDLE-CLASS, SUBURBAN COMMUNITY IN THE SOUTH

A second instance of diffusion involves propoxyphene as a drug of chance experimentation. In contrast with abuse by preference, chance experimentation for illustrative purpose involves use of the drug at least three times, but without the extent or regularity associated with the preference abusers. Three times was selected in an attempt to exclude those persons who took the drug solely out of curiosity. By the third time it was assumed that the person would know what to expect and what the drug would do.

The chance experimentation that was observed involved drug-naive adolescents who did not routinely have other drugs readily accessible. They tended to abuse the propoxyphene at very irregular intervals only. Data collected at a private resident high school for females, located in a suburban community of less than 5,000 population, illustrate this pattern. Of the 112 female residents of this private high school, 11 (9.8 percent) had abused propoxyphene (Table 25-III).

TABLE 25-III

PROPOXYPHENE EXPERIMENTATION AND ABUSE CHARACTERISTICS AMONG FEMALES IN A PRIVATE RESIDENCE HIGH SCHOOL

I.	Legitimate medical use only	79	70.5%
II.	No use or abuse	22	19.6%
III.	Some abuse experimentation (chance abusers)	11	9.8%
	A. *Sources of propoxyphene*		
	School nurse	11	100.0%
	Parents provided from physician	4	36.4%
	Prescription from local physician	1	9.1%
	B. *Setting of propoxyphene abuse*		
	Alone	1	9.1%
	Social group	10	90.9%
	Off campus	2	18.2%
	With member of opposite sex	2	18.2%
	C. *Route of Propoxyphene Abuse*		
	Oral	11	100.0%

Several factors suggest the uniqueness of this pattern of abuse. The propoxyphene abuse was integrated into what appeared to the investigators to be a larger pattern of adolescent rebellion against the authority within this resident school. For example, the taking of three to five propoxyphene capsules or the propoxyphene balls from the compound capsules was almost always in the context of the girls gathering in one room after the required hour for retiring, where they would smoke cigarettes, take the propoxyphene and drink any alcohol they had smuggled into the school in mouthwash bottles. During these gatherings, the conversations reportedly centered around the recounting of recent or anticipated sexual experimentations.

Only two of these high school girls had any experience with other drugs. Both had smoked "some" marijuana and one had, on two occasions, experimented with propoxyphene prior to coming to the school. The one girl who initiated the other ten in the abuse of propoxyphene reported she had learned it could be done by observing her mother abuse the drug. From the girl's account, her mother was being treated by their family physician for a "drinking problem" with sleeping pills and propoxyphene, both of which were taken in large quantities.

> ". . . .If they made Mother feel so good and act so
> drunk, I knew they would do the same for me."

The girl's mother had provided her with a bottle of one hundred 65 mg capsules when she left for school, ostensibly to alleviate menstrual cramps. She first shared the drugs with her roommate and then, in turn, with receptive persons as they became members of the nucleus peer group. Once the original one hundred capsules were gone, they began accumulating capsules which were dispensed quite readily to any girl by the school nurse. Six of the girls also wrote to their families for supplies and four reported that their parents had mailed them propoxyphene which had been obtained through their family physician. The girl who introduced this pattern of abuse also secured a supply of the drug from a local physician (Chart 2).

All of the girls used the drug orally, ten of the eleven had abused it only in the company of other people who were also abusing it and nine of the eleven abused it only on the school campus. The two who admitted to abusing the drug off campus

CHART 2.

PROPOXYPHENE DIFFUSION AMONG CHANCE ABUSERS

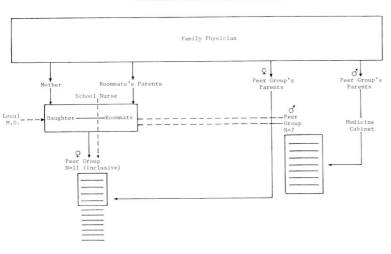

did so in the company of boys whom they had met in the local community.

In an attempt to further trace the diffusion of the propoxyphene, the two girls who had experimented off campus were persuaded to introduce one of the investigators to their male partners. From this point of entry, a total of twenty-three males in the same general educational-social peer group were interviewed. Six (26.1 percent) of these twenty-three male high-school students reported themselves to be chance experimenters with propoxyphene. An additional seven "knew" you could get high on propoxyphene but felt that beer was all anyone really needed to get high. None of these six males had a history of abusing any drug before being introduced to propoxyphene. Once initiated, however, their experimentation differed in one respect from that of the females. Five of the six males did attempt to get "high" while they were alone, and four of them indicated that they were almost always at home and alone when they experimented with the drug. All six indicated their *major* source of propoxyphene was from the family medicine cabinets. The only other source was from the two girls who, on occasion, provided the propoxyphene which was consumed during "parking" sessions. The abuse of propoxyphene on dates appears to have been an acceptable end product in itself. Although petting and sexual intercourse were reported common on dates, the use of propoxyphene did not appear to be positively or negatively associated with this behavior.

This experimentation had occurred between September, 1968, and February, 1969. At the time of the interview, all seven of the females and five of the six males indicated that they would probably continue to "use some propoxyphene." Whether this indeed has occurred or whether the experimentation progressed to some other level of abuse or to other drugs is unknown.

ILLICIT DIVERSION WITHIN THE GREENWICH VILLAGE AREA OF NEW YORK CITY

A third form of episodic abuse, in contrast to the previously discussed adolescent experimenters who were drug naive and without ready access to other drugs, consisted of adults who abused multiple drugs with ready access to all types of drugs.

TABLE 25-IV
BACKGROUND CHARACTERISTICS OF SPREE ABUSERS
BY AGE, RACE AND SEX

Spree Abusers (Age-Race-Sex)	Father's Occupation	Social Class	Formal Education
1. 21—WF	Lawyer	Middle	14
2. 21—WF	Bus. Exec.	Upper	13
3. 23—WF	Bus. Exec.	Upper	16 (B)
4. 23—WF	Bus. Exec.	Upper	13
5. 24—WF	No Data	Lower	12
6. 25—WF	Bus. Exec.	Middle	13
7. 25—WF	Artist	Middle	12
8. 26—WF	Bus. Exec.	Middle	18 (M)
9. 28—WF	No Data	Middle	16 (B)
10. 28—WF	No Data	No Data	12
11. 24—WM	Bus. Exec.	Middle	12
12. 24—WM	Bus. Exec.	Middle	15

Twelve propoxyphene abusers were followed from June, 1966, to June, 1970, to show the routes of diffusion as well as significant changes in abuse pattern over time. Because of the availablity of the drug and the ease with which refill prescriptions could be obtained, a broad pattern of abuse materialized within a relatively short period of time.

A typical coffee house setting in Greenwich Village, New York, provided the initial reference point of study of the group. Eight of the subjects had been employed there at some time during a period of three years. It was found that propoxyphene was given away quite freely. Sale of the drug by street dealers is a rare phenomenon. Only the uninitiated seeker of drugs will purchase the drug from a dealer, but dealers generally handle small quantities and sell propoxyphene only as a favor for any of their clients who may desire the drug. While they may "push" the other drugs, they "carry" propoxyphene.

Of the twelve subjects who were studied, seven had procured propoxyphene by medical prescription. Six of the seven obtained the drug from other sources as well. Five subjects received the drug from dealer sources, two of whom received it exclusively from dealers. Of the twelve, eleven provided propoxyphene to

Marital Status	Primary Occupation	Rationale for Abuse	Deviancy Characteristics	
			Therapy	Arrests
Single	Musician	Stress	Private	—
Remarried	Housewife	Stress	Private	—
Single	Writer	Stress	Private	—
Single	Designer	Stress	Private	—
Single	Waitress	Euphoria	Private	(1) Drugs
Remarried	Housewife	Euphoria	Private	—
Single	Welfare	Euphoria	Institution	(1) Drugs
Separated	Teacher	Euphoria	Private	—
Single	Social Worker	Stress	Private	—
Married	Waitress	Euphoria	Private	(1) Drugs
Single	Musician	Euphoria	—	—
Single	Bus. Exec.	Euphoria	—	—

other persons. Other drugs such as marijuana, LSD, cocaine or heroin were not permitted on the premises of the club; however, amphetamines were acceptable, as hours were long and work tiring. All twelve subjects were white and mostly from upper middle to upper income brackets, with parents of professional background. Their educational attainment ranged from high school graduate to Master's Degree. All but two of the subjects were involved in some form of psychotherapy. The majority of the group had been in private therapy.

There was no indication of any major criminal involvement —the only arrests for the group having been for possession or sale of drugs. Only three of the subjects had ever been arrested, and in each instance the case was either dismissed or found in favor of the defendant.

The major reasons given for propoxyphene use by these subjects were (a) as substitutes for aspirin when they did not wish to use codeine (codeine was known to the group to have unpleasant side effects) and (b) as relievers of emotional stress.

The degree of experimentation with other drugs was found to be extremely high. From this group only two addictions—both to heroin—developed during the period of observation. It should be noted that eight of the twelve had at one time experimented with heroin. The rank order of use of these drugs is not known (Table 25-V).

The initiator of propoxyphene abuse in this matrix was a 21-year-old white female (subject #1). She had managed the coffee house from time to time and had been "on the scene" for approximately five years. Her source of the drug had been from a private physician who prescribed the drug for menstrual cramps. She also had obtained the drug from a dentist who had performed major cosmetic dental surgery on her for over a $1\frac{1}{2}$ year period. Both prescriptions had no refill limits, and therefore, unlimited amounts of the drug were readily available.

At one point a relationship developed between subject #1 and #12. They lived together for several months. He was a 24-year-old white male musician performing at the club. She provided him with the drug as he requested it. This relationship did not last,

TABLE 25-V

PROPOXYPHENE ABUSE CHARACTERISTICS AND OTHER DRUG INVOLVEMENT BY AGE, RACE AND SEX

Spree Abusers (Age-Race-Sex)	Abuse Dose	Years of Abuse	Route	Illegal Source	Source For Others	Concurrent Drug Abuse During Sprees	Other Drug Involvement	Ever Addicted Any Drug
1. 21—WF	390	4.5	Oral	No	Yes	None	1-2-5-6-8-9	No
2. 21—WF	390	3.5	Oral	Yes	Yes	None	5-6-7-8-9	No
3. 23—WF	585	5.0	Oral	Yes	Yes	None	1-2-3-5-6-7-8-9	No
4. 23—WF	585	2.0	Oral	Yes	Yes	None	3-5-6-7	No
5. 24—WF	585	3.0	Oral	Yes	Yes	5	5-7-8-9	No
6. 25—WF	780	3.0	Oral	Yes	Yes	None	1-3-5-7-8-9	1
7. 25—WF	1040	2.0	Oral/IV	Yes	Yes	None	1-2-5-6-7-8-9	1
8. 26—WF	585	4.0	Oral	Yes	Yes	None	1-2-5-6-7-8-9-10	No
9. 28—WF	585	1.0	Oral	No	Yes	5	5-6-7-8-9	
10. 28—WF	780	1.0	Oral	Yes	Yes	5	1-5-6-7-8-9	No
11. 24—WM	390	3.0	Oral	Yes	No	None	1-5-6-7	No
12. 24—WM	780	4.0	Oral	Yes	Yes	5	1-2-3-5-6-7-8-9-10	No

1. Narcotic Analgesics
2. Sedative-Hypnotics
3. Tranquilizers
4. Antidepressants
5. Marijuana
6. LSD
7. Other Psychotogens
8. Methedrine
9. Other Stimulants
10. Organic Solvents and Inhalants

as such, but subject #1 on occasion continued to supply him with the drug. He subsequently acquired a prescription for propoxyphene and also obtained it from dealers from whom he purchased other drugs.

CHART 3.
PROPOXYPHENE DIFFUSION AMONG SPREE ABUSERS

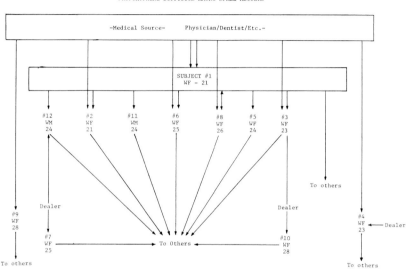

Occasionally other employees at the coffee house would seek propoxyphene and would ask subject #1 for it. She would provide them with the drug whenever asked, if it was available to her. These subjects were #2, 3, 5, 6, 8, 11, and 12. The schematic representation of this diffusion pattern is indicated on Chart 3.

SUMMARY AND CONCLUSIONS

This chapter has presented the illicit diversion of propoxyphene (Darvon) as a drug of abuse, exemplified by three separate paths of diffusion. The abuse of the drug has been depicted as a drug of preference, as a drug of chance experimentation and as a drug of spree abuse. Propoxyphene was abused as little as only once to as much as over a four-year time period. Abuse of the drug was recorded for adolescents as well as adults, for both blacks and whites, and for males and females. Abuse of the drug was also found to be present among persons from all socioeconomic strata as well as in persons having various prior drug histories. Some of the abusers reported experiencing euphoric effects, both orally and by injection. Reports indicated use of the propoxyphene to alleviate stressful situations. A suicide attempt by toxic overdose of the drug was also isolated.

The primary channel for propoxyphene diffusion originates from the manufacturer who provides it to medical professionals and pharmacies. Subsequently, individuals are initiated into its use with existing options for abuse—as illustrated in the previously mentioned patterns.

While these are but a few examples of the illicit diversion of propoxyphene, in all three instances they represent diffusion of the drug from a single legal source—physicians. While propoxyphene was prescribed for various reasons to legitimate users, once they developed into abusers, they continued to tap the medical source for the drug as well as to supplement their supply from dealers and friends.

The basic source of the propoxyphene which is being abused in the United States is by overprescription—physicians who write prescriptions for large numbers of capsules which are easily refillable, and while propoxyphene is readily available from many sources, legal as well as illicit, the medical source appears to be utilized with the highest frequency.

The fact that propoxyphene is readily available from legal sources and that prescriptions are open-ended may enhance its abuse. Stricter controls on dispensation of propoxyphene will not eliminate its existence or diffusion due to the availability of other sources but may indeed contribute to less abuse of the drug.

REFERENCES

1. Burack, Richard: *The New Handbook of Prescription Drugs.* New York, Ballantine Book, 1970.
2. Chambers, Carl D., Moffett, Arthur D., and Cuskey, Walter R.: Five patterns of Darvon abuse. *Int J Addiction,* Vol. 5, 1970.
3. Chambers, Carl D., and Taylor, W. J. Russell: Patterns of propoxyphene abuse. *Int J Clin Pharmacol Ther Toxicology,* 1971.

4. Chambers, Carl D., and Wieland, William: *Patterns of Darvon Abuse.* Reported to the Committee on Problems of Drug Dependence, National Academy of Sciences, National Research Council, February, 1970.
5. McCarthy, W., and Keenan, R.: Propoxyphene hydrochloride poisoning: Report of the first fatality. *JAMA, 187:*460-461, 1964.
6. *Physicians' Desk Reference,* Twenty-fourth edition Medical Economics, Inc., Oradell, New Jersey, 1970, p. 831.

Chapter 26

The Alienating Influence of Marijuana

Andrew I. Malcolm

I N A RECENT paper I hypothesized that the use of certain illusion-ogens might facilitate the diffusion and persistence of the alienated life style.[1] It was proposed that there were similarities between the procedures and effects of such apparently diverse social phenomena as religious revivalism, brainwashing, dance trance rituals in many parts of the world, political demagoguery and indoctrination into the modern drug-using community.

In all of these circumstances the altered state of consciousness (ASC) is a condition that develops in a variable number of people in the population at risk. Such an acute mental aberration, caused by a variety of means, appears to result in marked hypersuggestibility and, in some cases, major and persisting personality changes. The idea that there may be some relationship between the penitent who rushes forward to make a decision for Christ and the seeker after mind expansion who ingests an illusionogen and achieves the conviction that the ideas subscribed to by his peers are utterly valid will seem, at first sight, to be highly unlikely. It will be my purpose in this chapter to show that such a relationship may indeed exist and that, depending on the relative contributions of three variables in any particular case, the processes of social alienation and social affiliation may be profoundly influenced by the ASC experience. It will be my further purpose to indicate various elements of this hypothesis that might be objectively tested.

ALIENATION

To be alienated is to have been excluded from, or to have withdrawn one's attachment to, one or more of the several institutions of social control that exist in the inclusive society. For such a person the judicial, economic, educational, religious, political and other systems that prevail in the larger society are institutions whose values he cannot espouse and whose further interference in his life he resents. But this sense of estrangement is not ordinarily something that develops very suddenly. More often the person is affected over some period of time by numerous influences that tend to promote further withdrawal on the one hand or renewed affiliation on the other.

There has been, nevertheless, a particular tendency in recent time to honor progressively more vigorous criticism of all of the institutions of the society. It must be that very few people have been entirely unaffected by the questioning spirit of the age. Yet it may also be that there is much variation in the ability of people to withstand the loneliness and isolation that follow upon separation from previously respected institutions. In any case, a sense of meaninglessness is not conducive to security; and we may assume that a person who lacks core values is probably a seeker after attachment of some kind.

Now a number of studies have shown that the more closely a person is affiliated with the values of the drug-using subculture, the more alienated he is from the values of the inclusive society.[2] This is really what one would expect. However the explanations for the intensity and persistence of the attachment to the alienated subculture have consistently failed to refer to what I have called the conversion factor.

How is it that a person who is only marginally alienated can come to accept uncritically in a relatively short period of time the notion that some view of reality that is antithetical to that of the inclusive society is utterly right? We know from the study of religious experience, for example, that attitudinal reorientation can occur with dramatic suddenness. It will now perhaps be useful for us to consider why it is that many users of psychoactive drugs are similarly convinced that they have died and been reborn, that they are rejuvenated, that the way of life advocated by their peers is enlightened and that the way of life persisted in by their former friends and relatives is irredeemably evil. It may be that to fully explain this phenomenon we will have to consider the nature of the altered state of consciousness.

It is interesting that regardless of the means by which the ASC is produced the experience presents certain common characteristics. Thus the Bushman in a condition of marked sensory over-stimulation achieves the ASC with its attendent disturbances of perception, cognition and volition. He becomes euphoric, he sees God, he is given the magical power to heal; and his affiliation to the cult is strongly reinforced. Similarly the Zen monk after many years of training, periodic fasting and meditation may, in a condition of marked sensory deprivation, be rewarded with divine enlightenment. In both cases the experience is socially integrative and it is achieved without the use of chemicals. The immature person in our society who gains admission to an admired circle of drug users is already disenchanted with his society of orientation. In this there may be little resemblance to the examples given above. However he may be fascinated by the values of the alternate society, and in the course of time it is to this society that he desires to affiliate. He may protest that his primary interest is pleasure but to the extent that he is actually alienated from the inclusive society and genuinely interested in the style of the smaller group his resistance to the techniques that might produce the ASC is lowered. Finally the illusionogen is offered to him; and he ingests it in the company of his friends.

PERSONALITY, CHEMICAL AND MILIEU

Now here three important variables must be introduced. These are the personality of the user, the nature of the chemical, and the values inherent in the milieu in which the drug experience occurs.[3] It could probably be shown, for example, that a person who has not yet established a sense of identity and a system of values would be much more vulnerable than would be a person who had lived longer and who had achieved some understanding of what he believed in. This might be especially the case in our society today. A person born in the 1950's might well reach adulthood without ever having been assured that any of the institutions that surrounded him had any validity or relevance for him at all.

The second variable is the drug itself, the dose in relation to body weight and its pharmacologic properties. A brief exposure to a mild form of cannabis might have virtually no intoxicating effect; a massive dose might be markedly disruptive to the processes that maintain normal waking consciousness. Much additional research must be undertaken in the matter of the dose-response aspects of cannabis intoxication.

The third variable is the nature of the milieu. Techniques of sensory bombardment or of sensory deprivation are commonly found in situations in which the ASC is an intentional goal. Moreover there is frequently a prevailing ideological or religious system the values of which are understood by all the participants. Finally there is often the presence of some strong figure: a shaman, an interrogator, a revivalist, a demagogue or a guru. The role of this strong man is to act as guide as the ego boundaries of the subject dissolve and as his judgment and ability to test reality are degraded. In most such cases the subject's dependence on the guide develops in direct ratio with his own sense of powerlessness. The result, of course, can be a strong and entirely nonrational conviction that the system of belief offered by the authority is valid and that the system of belief condemned by him must be denounced.

Now it would be of the greatest interest to determine experimentally to what extent a wide range of people would become suggestible under the influence of various doses of cannabis.

This could be objectively studied. It would be my prediction that a mature person who ingests a moderate dose of the loose form of cannabis in a setting that is socially integrative would experience nothing more injurious to himself and to society than pleasureable intoxication. On the other hand, an immature or psychiatrically ill person who ingests a heavy dose of cannabis in a setting that is intricately designed to facilitate the appearance of the ASC might, in fact, have that experience and might, accordingly, become intensely suggestible, dependent on the guidance of the enveloping authority and, in due course, persuaded. It is interesting that many of the experimenters, with marijuana especially, emphasize their free will and independence. I think it could be shown that the ASC, should it occur, does not confer freedom of choice. On the contrary, the consequences of the experience are determined, in large part, by exterior influences during a period when the subject's rationality is suspended and he is in a state of marked hypersuggestibility.

It is known, however, that in the case of religious conversion, brainwashing and other phenomena that seem to depend on the appearance of the ASC, the persistence of the conviction that the new view of reality is unassailably correct may be short lived. Reinforcement appears to be necessary. In the case of the disaffiliated and immature person whose withdrawal has been facilitated by the many techniques practiced in the drug-using subculture such reinforcement commonly occurs. He may be brought repeatedly to that point at which the ASC supervenes and at which he is rendered dependent and suggestible. Thus we may now ask several questions.

1. Depending on particular mixes of personality, drug and environmental influences, can cannabis produce the distortions of perception, changes in emotion and aberrations of thought processes that characterize the altered state of consciousness?

2. Is a person who is intoxicated with marijuana demonstrably more suggestible than he would be in the drug-free state?

3. Does the repeated use of marijuana tend to create a receptive attitude toward the use of such drugs as LSD that undoubtedly are capable of producing the ASC?

4. Is there a common neurophysiological basis for altered states of consciousness developed under such widely divergent conditions as drug intoxication and demoniacal possession states?

5. Is there a relationship between the degree of social withdrawal and the intensity and frequency of exposure to the drug experience?

6. Finally, if it can be shown that to the many known variables that facilitate alienation we must now add the conversion factor noted in this chapter, what are the legal, social and therapeutic implications?

REFERENCES

1. Malcolm, Andrew I.: Alienation and the Use of Psychoactive Drugs. AOA 47th Ann. Mtg., San Francisco, March 1970.
2. Holmes, Douglas, and Solomon, Theo.: Drug Use and Alienation: A Report of Preliminary Study Findings. AOA 47th Ann. Mtg., San Francisco, March 1970.
3. Malcolm, Andrew I.: *The Pursuit of Intoxication*. Addiction Research Foundation, Toronto, 1971, pp. 223-239.

SECTION IV

PSYCHOPHARMACOLOGICAL ASPECTS

Chapter 27

From Soft to Hard Drugs—Progression, Regression or Digression?

C. R. B. Joyce

I HAVE DELIBERATELY used several vague concepts in the title of this chapter, not in order to spend the brief time available in a semantic exercise, nor to show the difficulties of a field that all of us here know to be extremely difficult anyway, but as a reminder of the need for the study of language as a basic technique of this kind: one we all use, one to which most of us pay less attention than the surgeon to his scalpel or the nurse to her needle.

First, there are few clear distinctions between "soft" and "hard" drugs; the adjectives themselves are emotive, but in an ambiguous way, and not clearly related, as some might think, to the subcategories of psychological and physical dependence respectively. For example, EEG changes are produced by and following withdrawal from drugs normally considered "soft."[1] Is this a sign of physical dependency or only evidence that the information provided by such techniques is itself soft? For the present purpose, we are reviewing the possible relationships between two or more kinds of drugs that are considered to differ in the degree of personal and social dangers that they present to the individual who consumes them.

Second. I do not propose to define "progression." The term is the one usually chosen to discuss the relationship between the use of different kinds of drugs, whether the discussants believe that progression occurs or whether they deny this. Instead of definitions, again, I would prefer that we should think about some of the many other possible kinds of association, and so I have chosen to discuss regression, with its deliberate ambiguities drawn from

243

fields as diverse and in general unknown to each other as statistics and psychoanalysis, and the literary term "digression." The element that these three terms have in common is a relationship to the one experimental variable that man has so far found no way to control—TIME!

My title therefore poses two questions about observations upon the drug-taking behavior of an individual, or of a group of in-dividuals, with the passage of time: first, what is the likelihood that each individual will at different times be using a drug that presents a different degree of danger, in the sense just defined? More precisely, what is the chance that he will be using the same class of drug, using a class presenting a greater danger or using a less dangerous drug? It is to be noted that, for reasons which will appear if they are not already obvious, the question must be asked *and answered,* in terms of individuals and not groups. Second, if answers to the first question suggest that variations in drug-taking behavior occur other than at random, then and only then is it worth considering what kinds of hypotheses can be advanced to ac-count for this and, of course, how the appropriate experiments may be set up to choose between them.

Although, or more likely because, all the evidence was soft even if some drugs were hard, many people have been voicing certainties and not hypotheses. Only in very recent years has in-formation begun to be available which was even remotely appro-priate to the first question: the very simple question whether changes in drug-using behavior are nonrandom. In general, all studies until recently have been retrospective; that is to say, no information about the drug-taking behavior of an individual was collected at the time of the behavior itself rather than as his re-collection of his behavior at earlier times. Not only are such retro-spective studies notoriously unreliable, but they are particularly subject in the case of drug studies to errors of measurement in-duced by the very phenomenon that they are trying to estimate. Even now, the necessary information is not really available: the various estimates of the incidence of cannabis smoking, heroin taking, LSD tripping, even alcohol misuse (probably the hardest data we possess), are all subject to errors of estimation the magnitudes of which are themselves uncertain but may vary from a factor of two to ten fold or more; they refer to completely different populations, both in place and time; and if they are histories at all, they are not histories of individuals, but of groups. We must now consider the irrelevance of such data to our problem, even in prospective and not retrospective studies. Suppose that of a group of one hundred individuals studied at time t_1, fifty were using cannabis, and at time t_2 fifty were found to be using heroin. Amongst others, one may hypothesize (a) that the prior use of cannabis predisposes to the subsequent use of heroin in the same individuals; (b) that a nucleus of cannabis users creates a reservoir of heroin users; or (c) that the smoking of cannabis is an effective prophylactic against the development of the heroin habit. However no scientific choice, not even a faint one, could be made on the basis of the information provided. It is also obviously necessary to know, amongst many other usually unavailable facts, whether the fifty using heroin at t_2 included all the fifty who had previously used cannabis, which would support *(a)*, or none of them, which would support *(c)*. The argument has to be framed in terms of t_2: the only point, but it is a vital one, of the data from t_1 is to provide a reliability check. It is not, however, in this way that it is commonly used. Even people who might be expected to know better argue that an increase in the *incidence* of both heroin and cannabis use between t_1 and t_2 indicates that one causes the other. From the logical point of view, it is worth noting the uncertainty in the direction of the relationship: logically, heroin use might cause cannabis smoking. It is also worth noting, in passing, observations that while 13 percent of a cross-sectional sample admit to the use of cannabis, only 0.5 percent admit to heroin use; also observations of Blum and his associates on an eleven- to thirteen-year-old San Franciscan Negro group show that members progress directly to intravenous barbiturate injection, with no previous use of cannabis but plenty of tobacco and alcohol use, however. At the moment, I only wish to emphasize certain fundamental disparities. As another source of evidence, the *Sacramento Good News* puts it, 201 million Americans did *not* take drugs in 1969. Alas, the estimate is certainly in error; the question is rather what drugs we are talking about. Dr. Blum, again, has shown, as has Dr. Smart,[2] that drug-using parents (in the widest sense) tend to have drug-using children (in a narrower sense). In this connection, we can remind ourselves of Vaillant's demonstration that physicians use significantly more mind-altering drugs than matched controls.[3] We have always had expectations of drugs and expectations of doctors as Dr. Schultes reminded us[4]: expectations which Madison Avenue capitalized but did not create. I have just expressed considerable scepticism, but we can indeed take it to be the case that nonrandom associations in drug-taking behavior have been adequately shown. We have therefore now to ask whether such an association implies causation, whether it is due to dependence of both variables upon one or more intervening phenomena or whether it is merely a fortuitous association and nothing more. For example, the current explosive rise of interest in experiments with drugs in Great Britain can be dated to within a year or two of 1955, the year in which commercial television also made its appearance. No one, so far as I know, has suggested that watching commercial television in those early days actually caused drug taking, although despite the failure of certain enquiries to demonstrate a causal relationship between the exhibition of violence by the mass media and the practice of violence, there are at least two bases for a belief that such a relationship does exist. One, not scientific, is the testament of Jerry Rubin[5] to the value of television in getting out the street guerrilleros once the trouble has started; the other, scientific but related as yet neither to violence nor to drug taking, that of Zajonc[6] that merely repeating exposure to the same stimulus, with no value judgments or explicit rewards attached, or implicit either, increases preferences for that stimulus. Rats and, I suspect, pigeons, reared to a background of Mozart only, prefer to work for Mozart as an operant reinforcer in comparison with Schoenberg—but wait —the reverse is also true. It is not only Mozart who is strictly for the birds. What commercial television may have done was to demonstrate a wider variety of alternative behavior in general. It is also well known that other social changes, themselves perhaps related to this and affecting the socioeconomic status of British adolescents, were occurring at the same time. The two phenomena may therefore have shared dependence upon an intervening variable. On the other hand, the reputedly simultaneous increase between the two world wars of the per capita consumption of bananas in Great Britain and of first admissions to mental hospitals with a diagnosis of acute schizophrenia were probably not associated in anything but a random way. However, it is worth noting that for a short time, and quite recently, it looked as if a causal explanation might be forthcoming. But it turns out that bananas, whether eaten with their 5-hydroxytryptamine-containing skins or not, whether dried, roasted, grated or thrown away, do not in fact lead to trips either in an ambulance or in the realms of mind. Nevertheless, we should remember that hypotheses about causal relationships, as Bronowski has said about the gravitational constant, need to be frequently tested and in different places.

However, one kind of causal relationship is absolute. There is no doubt that dependence on drugs cannot occur in the absence of access to the drug in question. Given a model nearer to reality, in which there is access to both cannabis and heroin, access to one is also contaminated by access to the other, just as it is more likely that your five-year-old daughter will swallow her mother's pill or a sublethal dose of iron if they are kept in the icebox rather than in the bathroom closet. In some countries, coffee, wine and spirits are dispensed in separate establishments. It requires a definite effort to move from one such establishment to another. This kind of "progression," a very real, physical one, is more likely to occur if coffee, beer and whisky can be had at the same counter. Remember Schachter's experiments in suggestibility: in comparison with normals, obese subjects were more likely to help themselves to plates of sandwiches placed at their disposal, during work at a long, demanding task, and were much more likely to get up and go to an icebox that they had been told contained food, as well as to go and open an icebox about whose contents they had not been informed at all.[7] What we may call associated access is undoubtedly a factor in the migration of drug users between different groups of drugs: it is still a more likely factor than pharmacological association, despite suggestions that the cannabidiol nucleus if looked at at the correct angle from a point slightly southeast of Basel, Switzerland, takes on features of distinct similarity to that of the morphine nucleus.[8]

The arguments against the occurrence of causal progression have been excellently summarized by Kaplan.[9] I would like only to add a reminder of Blum's demonstration that if you use the drugs "highest" in the danger scale—heroin or LSD—you are certain to have used all the drugs lower—barbiturates, amphetamines, aspirins and caffeine.[10] If you have never used aspirins—and there are some such people—you won't be using heroin or even barbiturates either. There are psychological reasons why people who have experimented with one drug will want to experiment with another. The validity of these also seems to me to be *a priori* greater than that of similar pharmacological arguments. They depend heavily upon the predisposition of the individual, his access not only to the drugs in question but to information about them, both of a positive and negative character, his evaluations of the sources of his information and the interaction between all these: there is a temporal progression, from aspirin, tobacco and beer onwards. There are checkpoints in this process, some set by society, some by parental, some by individual control—such as the last (or almost last) decision to use the needle, to break the integrity of the body wall against the not-I, to take that decisive step that is usually so indecisively taken.

Having said something about progression as well as about regression in its statistical, although not in its psychoanalytic, sense, I would like, finally, to take up the question of digression, and to end, as I began, with an aspect of the linguistic contribution to the problem.

Why is it that so many people are concerned about drug dependence? It exists, it has certain dimensions, it is certainly increasing in size. It is also selective in that particular age and other groups are apparently susceptible. Yet those who protest about drug misuse are not in general those who misuse drugs—not, at least, the drugs in question. It seems that the protesters—for once on the other side of the generation gap—have their problems as well. One notes with extreme sympathy the frequent occurrence of drug tragedies in the families or intimate circles of those who pronounce with genuine horror against drug misuse. Understandable though it may be, one may guess, still with sympathy, at other kinds of motivation and association than the obvious ones. It is also notable in this connection how frequently those who are eminent in their own subject but know little about this one are moved by the strength of their emotions to pronounce with emphasis upon it, as well as to consider as "evidence" materials to which they would pay no attention in their own expert fields.

The relationship between the social phenomenon and those who tend it in their various capacities resembles, in its ambiguity and perhaps in its consequences, that which exists between the alcoholic and his spouse or best "friend." Its existence ministers to a need in those who apparently seek to eradicate it. The relationship of society as a whole to drug dependence is perhaps such a symbiosis, or perhaps one should say parasitosis. To what needs of the parasite does the relationship minister? As one such parasite, I am aware of some of my own needs, but probably not of all of them.

Drug dependence can be considered as one of many successors to other phenomena of growth and development that have afflicted earlier ages: adolescence is a stormy time and generates stormy behavior. It is also a time of heights and depths in experience, some of which are not attained so easily later. Our subsequent attitudes to this period through which we have most of us (unbelievably) passed, remain, therefore, ambivalent. Our inability to return to the good times can often be helpfully exorcised by emphasizing our rejection of its unsatisfactory aspects. Our forefathers did this with noteable success by their projections of the deplorable nature of adolescent auto-erotic experience, and we may have done the same more recently in regard to motorbicycles, pop music, strange dress, language altogether too familiar, and the use of other even more vigorous methods of expression (such as bombs and highjackings) that an ambiguous technology places within our grasp. A few years ago, I predicted the next fashion. Last week I learnt that it already exists. Fortunately, I did not publish the prediction then, and I shall not do so now.

Dependence can also be regarded as a kind of environmental pollution.[11] I suspect that this may be an unconscious attitude: it certainly does not seem to be a conscious one. It may be that although for some of us its size (which in this context can be regarded as small) creates the illusion that this is one kind of pollution that we can do something about, others, the pessimists, may regard our inability to do anything about it as an indication of the futility of trying to solve the problems presented by pollutions of a larger kind. Whether there is social, psychological or pharmacological progression, statistical or psychological regression, I think there is little doubt that the "soft-drug–hard-drug" debate provides a most valuable digression but one that is largely inhibitory to further progress.

REFERENCES

1. Oswald, I., and Thacore, V.R.: Amphetamine and phenmetrazine addiction. Physiological abnormalities in the abstinence syndrome. *Brit. Med J, 2:*427, 1963.
2. Smart, R.: In *Drug Abuse: Concepts and Research,* edited by W. Keup. Springfield, Charles C Thomas, 1972.
3. Vaillant, G.E., Brighton, J.R., and McArthur, C.: Physicians' use of mind-altering drugs. *New Eng J Med, 282:*365-370, 1970.
4. Schultes, R.E.: In *Drug Abuse: Concepts and Research,* edited by W. Keup. Springfield, Charles C Thomas, 1972.
5. Rubin, J.: *Do It!* New York, Simon & Schuster, 1970.
6. Zajonc, R.: Brainwash: Familiarity breeds comfort. *Psychology Today,* Feb. issue, 1970.
7. Schachter, S.: In *Psychological Approaches to Social Behavior,* edited by P.H. Leiderman and D. Shapiro. Stanford, Stanford University Press, 1964.
8. Joyce, C.R.B., and Curry, S.H. (Eds.) : *Cannabis: Botany and Chemistry.* London, Churchill, 1970.
9. Kaplan, J.: *Marijuana: the New Prohibition.* Cleveland, World Publishing, 1970.
10. Blum, R.H., Braunstein, L., and Stone, A.: Normal drug use: an exploratory study of patterns and correlates. In *Drug Abuse: Social and Psychopharmacological Aspects,* edited by J.O. Cole, and J.R. Wittenborn. Springfield, Charles C Thomas, 1969.
11. Joyce, C.R.B.: Basic and applied research on drug dependence—the need for cooperation. I.C.A.A. Institute on Prevention and Treatment of Drug Dependence. 1970, pp. 173-182.

Chapter 28

Alcohol As It Compares to Other Addictive Substances

Benjamin Kissin

THE PURPOSE of this chapter is to compare alcohol with other addictive drugs and alcoholism with other drug addictions. Our special interest is to explore the mechanisms by which the social use of some of these drugs is converted by certain individuals into social abuse—that is, into a drug addiction. Toward that end, we shall review some of the social, psychological and pharmacological mechanisms invloved in these processes.

Table 28-I shows a comparison of the social determinants and characteristics of alcoholism and of other types of drug dependence.

The estimated incidence of dependence upon these various agents is at best an educated guess with possible exceptions in the cases of alcoholism and heroin addiction. Alcoholism incidence has been estimated traditionally on the basis of number of autopsy reports of alcoholic cirrhosis (so called Jellinek formula)[1] and more recently on the basis of nationwide surveys.[2] Heroin addiction estimates are based on police records and other official counts multiplied by some arbitrary factor. The numbers for the other categories are blind guesses based on general clinical impressions.

An interesting statistic that should be on the chart relates to the question: what percentage of all individuals taking a drug tend to become addicted. For alcohol the figure is 5 to 7 percent, for heroin probably 80 to 90 percent, for marijuana in the United States about 5 to 7 percent (it may be higher in North Africa), for

Note: This chapter was supported in part by Grant #MH16477 from the National Institute of Mental Health, USPHS.

TABLE 28-I

COMPARISON OF SOCIAL DETERMINANTS AND CHARACTERISTICS OF ALCOHOLISM AND OTHER TYPES OF DRUG DEPENDENCE

Influence	Alcoholism	Opium (morphine, heroin) Dependence	Marijuana (hashish, bangh) Dependence	Stronger Hallucinogens (LSD, mescaline, DMT and IV amphetamines)	Barbiturates, Sedatives, Tranquilizers and Oral Stimulants
1. Cultural dominance (worldwide)	Western civilization	China	India and North Africa	Primitive societies ("hippies" and modern intellectuals)	Modern Western Societies
2. Estimated incidence (U.S.)	6,000,000	250,000 (?)	200,000 (?)	25,000 (?)	10,000,000 (?)
3. Ethnic predominance (U.S.)	Irish-Americans Scandinavians Negroes	Negroes Puerto Ricans	All groups	Whites	All groups
4. Socioeconomic predominance (U.S.)	All groups	Lower	All groups	Middle and upper	Middle and upper
5. Urban predominance over rural (U.S.)	Slight	Marked	Marked	Marked	Slight (?)
6. Dominant age group U.S.	35 to 50	17 to 25	17 to 25	20 to 25	All ages
7. Dominant sex pattern (U.S.)	Males 3.5:1	Males 2:1	Males 2:1	Males 2:1	Females 2:1
8. Characteristic life style (U.S.)	Bars Solitary drinking	Street life	College student life	"Hippie" subculture	Children— street life Adults—middle class life
9. Legality (U.S.)	Legal	Illegal	Illegal	Illegal	Legal

the stronger hallucinogens probably 70 to 80 percent, and for tranquilizers and sedatives probably 5 to 10 percent. These figures are obviously important in describing the addictive potential of a drug and in determining the level of social acceptability. In these terms, alcohol, marijuana and tranquilizers are socially acceptable; heroin and the stronger hallucinogens are not.

The important role of culture in determining each of these categories of drug dependence is illustrated here. Each of the first four drug addictions represents a disease that is as old as the civilization in which it is found. The last category, the newer synthetic tranquilizers, sedatives and stimulants, are probably less socially determined than any of the other groups, possibly because of the absence of a long cultural tradition. Each of the "ancient" drugs is identified with a particular cultural pattern and, in an odd way, this ancient pattern is brought forward to modern times. For example, in Ireland and Scandinavia, drinking whiskey and beer is a normal part of daily masculine activity; Irish American and Scandinavian American alcoholics tend to be daily drinkers. On the other hand, in Africa, among the native tribes, heavy drinking is generally reserved for holidays and feasts. Among American Negroes, weekend drinking is a more common pattern. In both cultures, drinking alcohol is predominantly a masculine activity and this pattern persists in our country.

The impact of cultural forces on patterns of drug taking is clearly demonstrated by a recent informal survey of an area of Brooklyn which is sharply divided by a broad avenue running through it. On one side of the avenue, the population is almost entirely Puerto Rican and poor; on the other side, it is heavily Italian and Irish and middle class. In the Puerto Rican area the dominant addiction by far among teenagers is heroin; in the other area it is predominantly hallucinogens, barbiturates and amphetamines with very little heroin used. The clear-cut cultural distribution of different types of drug abuse in this area suggests that culture may indeed be the most important element in determining type of drug dependence.

Alcohol abuse differs from the other forms of drug dependence in four other ways; it usually occurs in an older population, the predominance among males tends to be greater than with other drugs, the life style associated with alcohol abuse is different and, finally, it is legal. The first of these differences, age, can be accounted for by the fact that psychological dependence and physical dependence appear to develop quite slowly with alcohol. It probably takes three to five years of heavy drinking to become an alcoholic. Psychological dependence probably develops more rapidly with almost all the other drugs. The next two differences—dominant male ratio and characteristic life style—are probably part of the cultural heritage previously described. But certainly not unimportant in differentiating the life style of the alcoholic from that of other drug abusers is the fact that alcoholism is essentially the only legal form of drug dependence there is. All other forms, even dependence on tranquilizers, are basically illegal; you cannot walk into a drugstore and ask for a quart of Librium.® Consequently, the political action of a society may determine in large part the incidence of a given form of drug abuse. The fact that the drugs with the highest incidence of abuse in Table 28-I—that is, alcohol and tranquilizers—are also the only legal drugs is of interest.

The psychological characteristics of alcoholics and other drug abusers are illustrated in Table 28-II. Many of the special psychological characteristics that differentiate alcoholics from other drug abusers are almost certainly related, at least in part, to the social determinants of drug dependence we have just discussed. Others are probably related to the specific psychopharmacological effects of the drugs involved. If we consider the spectrum of influences to run from sociological to psychologic to physical, it is certainly at the psychological level that the greatest interaction of all three forces occurs.

This is well illustrated with our first item—what we have chosen to call character structure. Passive dependence is a characterologic quality which has been experimentally related to personality differentiation. Witkin and his group[3] have developed a group of experimental perceptual test situations which appear to discriminate quantitatively among various levels of personality differentiation ranging from the markedly field dependent to the

TABLE 28-II

PSYCHOLOGICAL CHARACTERISTICS OF ALCOHOLICS AS COMPARED WITH OTHER DRUG ABUSERS

	Alcoholics	Heroin Addicts	Cocaine and IV Amphetamine Abusers	Heavy Marijuana Users	Hallucinogen Abusers	Oral Stimulant Abusers	Sedative and Tranquilizer Abusers
Character Structure							
1. Passive dependence	++++	++				++	++
2. Impulsivity	++++	++++	++	++	++	++	++
3. Low frustration tolerance	++++	++++	++	++	++	++	++
Affective Disorder							
1. Boredom	++	++	++++	++++	++++	++++	+
2. Depression	++	+	++++	++++	++++	++++	++
3. Anxiety	+++	+++	++	+	+++	+	++++
4. Repressed hostility	+++	+++	++	+	++	+	++++
Sociopathy							
1. Antisocial behavior	0 to ++++	++	++++	+	+	+	+
2. Psychopathy	++	++	++++	+	+	+	+
Thought Disorder							
1. Schizoid	++	++	++++	++	++++	+	+
2. Psychosis	+	+	++++	+	++++	+	+
Drive Toward							
1. Euphoria (excitement)	+	++	++++	++++	++++	++++	+
2. Psychedelic experience (thrill)	++	++	++++	++	++++	++	+
3. Grandiosity	++++	++	0	++	+	++	+
4. Oblivion	++++	++++	0	+	0	0	++++

definitely field independent. Although field dependence is not entirely equivalent to passive dependence, we may use them as strongly related for the purposes of this discussion.

In a recent study of field dependence in four groups of severe drug abusers (heroin, barbiturates, hallucinogens and amphetamine), Beca Tomim,[4] a co-worker of Witkin, found heroin users to be the most field dependent, barbiturate users next, hallucinogens users less dependent, and amphetamine users somewhat field independent. The value of this study is somewhat limited in that all patients studied were psychotic; nevertheless, the patterns described are in keeping with the clinical impressions of other investigators. However, Tomim's most field dependent group, the heroin users, were not nearly so dependent as several other studies[5] have demonstrated alcoholics to be. Consequently a sequence exists for the drug users, with alcoholics at the most dependent end and amphetamine users at the relatively independent end.

It is psychodynamically logical that markedly field dependent passive individuals should seek depressant drugs which, by providing oblivion, should satisfy underlying passive needs. It makes equal sense that active field independent individuals should seek stimulant drugs which would satisfy their active aggressive needs.

In the area of affective disorders, Kissin and Platz[6] have shown alcoholics to have a significantly higher level of anxiety and depression than a matched group of controls with anxiety somewhat more marked. Anker *et al.*[7] found a high level of boredom and depression among marijuana users with anxiety less evident. The presence of underlying boredom and depression in hallucinogen, amphetamine and marijuana abusers is suggested by the work of Zuckerman,[8] who found a high level of "sensation-seeking activity" in these three groups.

The data reported here on levels of sociopathy, thought disorder and drive toward euphoria, psychedelic experience and oblivion is based largely on clinical observation and requires experimental validation. When these general personality types are related to the specific pharmacodynamic actions of the various drugs, one can make out a fair case for the reasons that certain types of individuals take certain types of drugs. However, the exceptions at this point are as numerous as the examples so that, much as we would like to, we cannot make a strong case for the specific interaction of a given type of individual with a given drug. The overriding influence of social and cultural influences has already been mentioned. There are, in addition, certain direct pharmacological effects of the drugs themselves which may be the determining factors.

The psychopharmacological effects of various drugs are described in Table 28-III. The first item dealing with dose-related effects of different drugs is of interest. With most drugs—heroin, amphetamines, cocaine and hallucinogens—there is a quantitative relationship of dosage to effect, but the effects at all dosage levels are qualitatively similar. With alcohol particularly, and with tranquilizers and marijuana in part, there is a qualitative dissociation between dosage and effect, with disinhibiting effects at low dosage and often excitatory effects at moderate dosages. In high doses, alcohol and tranquilizers are markedly depressant, while marijuana becomes hallucinogenic. The fact that these drugs have a wider range of activities probably accounts in part for their greater popularity. They are indeed the three most widely abused groups of psychotropic drugs in the United States (see Table 28-I). This may be true because the broader spectrum of effects permits them to be egosyntonic to a larger segment of the population at any one time and to any given individual at all times.

The dose-related qualitative differences built into these drugs contribute to their social acceptability in still another way. When one is drinking for the mild disinhibiting effect of alcohol (social drinking), the individual often becomes aware that he has drunk too much: he either becomes too loud or too sleepy. He is able to recognize the change because it is sharp and qualitative. On the other hand, if he takes heroin, amphetamines, cocaine or LSD, there is no sharp qualitative change in effect from a low to a high dose; it is merely more of the same. This pharmacologic characteristic can be expressed in the ratio between the toxic dose of a drug and its lowest effective dose. The ratio is high with alcohol and tranquilizers, moderate with marijuana, and low with most

TABLE 28-III

PSYCHOPHARMACOLOGIC EFFECTS OF ALCOHOL AND OTHER DRUGS

	Alcohol	Barbiturates, Sedatives and Tranquilizers	Heroin	Amphetamine	Cocaine	Marijuana	Hallucinogens (LSD, DMT, etc.)
1. Central Nervous System Effect							
Low dose	Disinhibiting	Disinhibiting	Depressant	Excitatory	Excitatory	Disinhibiting	Hallucinogenic
Moderate Dose	Excitatory or Depressant	Excitatory or Depressant	Depressant	Excitatory	Excitatory	Hallucinogenic	Hallucinogenic
High dose (toxic)	Depressant	Depressant	Depressant	Excitatory	Excitatory	Hallucinogenic	Hallucinogenic
2. Ratio—*toxic dose / Lowest effective dose*	High	High	Low	Low	Low	Low to Moderate	Low
3. Rapidity of Effect (usual route of administration)	Rapid (oral)	Slow (oral)	Rapid (IV)	Slow (oral)	Rapid (sniffing)	Rapid (smoking)	Moderate (oral)
4. Development of Tolerance	Mild	Moderate	High	High	None	None	High
5. Psychological Dependence	Variable	Variable	High	Variable	High	Moderate to Strong	Mild
6. Physical Dependence	Moderate	Moderate	High	None	None	None	None
7. Psychopharmacologic Effect							
Euphoria (excited)	++	++	+++++ (boxed)	++++ (boxed)	++++ (boxed)		
(relaxed)	++	++	++	+++ (boxed)	+++ (boxed)	+++ (boxed)	
Repression	++	++	+				
Excitability and Aggressivity	+ to ++++ (boxed)	+ to ++++ (boxed)		+ to ++++ (boxed)	+ to ++++ (boxed)	+ to ++++	++++ (boxed)
Hallucinogenic and Psychotomimetic	++	++	+			+ to ++++	++++ (boxed)
Paranoid Reactions	+ to ++++ (boxed)	+ to ++++ (boxed)	+	+ to ++++ (boxed)	+ to ++++ (boxed)	+ to ++++	++++ (boxed)
Interpersonal Relatedness							++++ (boxed)
Low Dose	Good	Good	Poor	Good	Good	Fair	Poor
High Dose	Poor	Poor	Poor	Poor	Poor	Poor	Poor
8. Organic Brain Damage	High	Low	Low	Low	Low	Low (?)	(?)
9. Systemic Organic Damage	High	Low	Low	Low	Low	Low	Low

of the other drugs. In a sense it may be one index of the social acceptability of a drug.

The rapidity of onset of effect by the usual route of administration is of significance in the development of dependence. The usual dependency-prone individual is impulsive and has a low frustration tolerance; he is unwilling to wait long for the desired effect. Consequently, it is not surprising that the drugs that cause the strongest dependencies are those that have the most rapid onset of effect, while slow-acting drugs (barbiturates, tranquilizers and sedatives) tend to cause less psychological dependence.

The evaluation for each of the drugs on the next three items —tolerance, psychological dependence and physical dependence— is taken from the WHO Report on Drug Dependence.[9] Physical dependence occurs only among the depressant drugs—alcohol, barbiturates and sedatives, and heroin. Psychological dependence occurs to a greater or lesser degree among all drugs and is the *sine qua non* of "drug addiction." It is interesting to note that psychological dependence is highest with heroin, cocaine and marijuana, and probably mildest with LSD. There is much evidence that psychological dependence is a more important element in addiction than is physical dependence.

The psychopharmacologic effects of different drugs is largely a function of their CNS effects as described in item 1. Of interest is the element of interpersonal relatedness. At high doses all drugs interfere with personal contact. At low doses alcohol, tranquilizers, amphetamines and perhaps marijuana often improve interpersonal contact. This is probably another index of social acceptability of a drug together with those previously mentioned.

Finally, we come to the questions or organic brain damage and other forms of system organic damage. In this area, alcohol is uniquely the most severe. This is, of course, due to the fact that alcohol has so many general systemic metabolic effects as opposed to most other drugs whose effects are mainly limited to the central nervous system. The severity of the organic complications of alcoholism should not be minimized. On the other hand, it is clear that they occur not with the social use of alcohol but only with its pathological abuse.

At this time in history, when the possibility of switching from an alcohol-oriented society to a marijuana-oriented society has become a topic for discussion, it may be of interest to compare these two drugs from the point of view of social acceptability. Both are mildly disinhibiting in low dosages and relatively nontoxic. Alcohol is somewhat more toxic in moderate doses (hangovers, et cetera), and it is much more toxic in high doses. It produces more violent behavior, it causes physical dependence, it more seriously impairs performance, causing auto accidents, etcetera, and, in the long run, produces more serious physical deterioration.

Is marijuana, then, perhaps a more socially acceptable drug than alcohol? Probably not. Its ratio of "toxic dose to lowest effective dose" is lower than that of alcohol, it causes stronger psychological dependence much more rapidly, it is more euphoriant, it is hallucinogenic, and even at low doses it may inhibit rather than facilitate social intercourse. It can precipitate acute and perhaps even chronic psychosis.[10] From a social viewpoint it is probably an equally dangerous drug to alcohol, even though pharmacologically it may be safer.

The key question is, What is the potential for severe drug abuse with these two drugs? We know from many studies that about 5 to 6 percent of all individuals who take alcohol become alcoholic that is, personally and socially incapacitated. The figures for marijuana appear quite similar. In a recent study, Anker *et al.*[7] found between 4 and 13 percent (depending on the sample) of all marijuana smokers to be heavy users—that is, to smoke regularly more than twice a week. In another recent study at Brown University, where heavy smoking was defined as almost daily smoking, heavy smokers constituted about 7 percent of all individuals on marijuana. If we accept this latter figure, it would seem that about the same percentage of those who use alcohol and of those who use marijuana tend to become addicted.

Now this would not be too serious if these were the same 5 to 7 percent. Instead of having six or seven million alcoholics in the United States we might have six or seven million marijuana addicts and perhaps this would constitute a lesser hazard. Unfortunately, the present evidence that we have, skimpy as it is, suggests that the alcoholism-prone and the marijuana-addiction–prone populations are not the same. In the previously mentioned study by Anker *et al.*,[7] the authors found the demographic pattern of the heavy college drinkers to be quite different from that of the heavy marijuana users. The latter had a high incidence of well-educated young people of Jewish extraction, whereas few of these were heavy drinkers. There was little correlation between heavy drinking and heavy marijuana use—if anything the correlation tended to be a negative one. The results in Zuckerman's study[8] had a similar pattern: heavy drinkers tended not to be heavy drug users. There is other evidence that there are different populations, for example, the field dependency studies of Tomim,[4] which showed hallucinogen abusers to be relatively field independent as opposed to alcoholics who are markedly field dependent. If, then, the use marijuana were to become as widespread as the use of alcohol, we might very well have six to seven million marijuana addicts in the country in addition to our present six to seven million alcoholics.

This possibility becomes all the more serious when we consider the relationship established clinically, if not experimentally, between heavy marijuana abuse (daily or almost daily) and the use of the stronger hallucinogens. The social implications of such a development would of course be immense, perhaps no worse than those of alcoholism but at least as great.

Much of the social, psychological and pharmacological data described in this chapter is tentative. There is much we do not know, and even what we do know, we do not know very well. Nevertheless, it is on the basis of information such as this that we will be able to make more intelligent legal and social decisions about the use of these drugs.

REFERENCES

1. Jellinek, C.M.: Recent trends in alcoholism: Alcoholism consumption. *Quart J Stud Alcohol, 8*:1-42, 1947.
2. Cahalan, D., Cisin, I.H., and Crosley, H.M.: *American Drinking Practices.* Publications Division, Rutgers Center of Alcohol Studies, New Brunswick. N.J., 1969.

3. Witkin, H.A., Dyk, R.B., Faterson, H.F., Goodenough, D.R., and Karp, S.A.: *Psychological Differentiation*. New York, Wiley, 1962.

4. Tomin, B.: Perceptual Style in Drug Abusers. Unpublished data.

5. Witkin, H.A., Karp, S.A., and Goodenough, D.R.: Dependence in alcoholics. *Quart J Stud Alcohols, 20:*493-504, 1959.

6. Kissin, B., and Platz, A.: *The Use of Drugs in the Long Term Rehabilitation of Chronic Alcoholics. Proceedings 3rd Neuropsychopharmacology Congress.* 1969, p. 835-851.

7. Anker, J.L., Milman, D.A., Koheen, S.A., and Valenti, C.: Drug usage and related patterns of behavior in university students: 1. General survey and marihuana use. *Amer J Coll Health* (in press).

8. Zuckerman, M.: Drug usage as one manifestation of a 'sensation seeking' trait. In *Drug Abuse; Current Concepts and Research,* edited by W. Keup. Springfield, Charles C Thomas, 1971.

9. Eddy, N.B., Halbach, H. Isbell, H., and Seevers, H.M.: Drug dependence: Its significance and characteristics. *Bull WHO* 37, 1965.

10. Talbott, J.A., and Teague, J.W.: Marihuana psychosis. *JAMA, 210:*299-302, 1969.

Chapter 29

Structure-Activity Relations of Analgesic and Addictive Potentials

Arthur E. Jacobson

SCORES OF MEDICINAL CHEMISTS have, during the last forty years, been involved with the synthesis of analgetics; literally thousands have been prepared.[1-3]

We will attempt to look at the relatively few clinically accepted ones which are commercially available and shall restrict the discussion even more by choosing to look at those which have analgetic activity somewhat comparable to morphine, excluding the innumerable codeine-like compounds.

Morphine itself, of course, is a widely used and abused analgetic. There are several reasons why medicinal chemists seek a better one. Morphine, as you all know, is dependence producing, induces respiratory depression and an unfortunate tolerance is developed to it.

Perhaps we seek the improbable magic bullet. We would like to synthesize a compound which blocks pain transmission or perhaps the awareness of pain, without any untoward alteration of a normal state of consciousness, enzyme system or metabolism. Indeed, there have been times when the near-perfect analgetic was presumed found. Heroin was at first believed to be such a drug. Similar errors in judgment have been made many times since— magic bullets are quite hard to find.

The following are five main classes of clinically useful analgetics for man, in order of their historical rise. (a) the opium alkaloids and their derivatives,[4] (b) Pethidine® (meperidine) and its congeners, due to Eisleb and Shaumann,[5] (c) methadone and its congeners, due to Bockmuhl and Erhart,[6] (d) the morphinans and relatives, due to Grewe,[7] and (e) the 6,7-benzomorphans, due to E. L. May.[1]

Medicinal chemists have made many modifications of class 1 through 4, but the parents remain the best of their class although other useful analgetics have appeared from the modifications. All of them, to a large degree, suffer from the defects associated with the opium alkaloids; they are dependence producing in man, man develops tolerance to them and they are respiratory depressants.

It is only in class 5, the benzomorphans represented by phenazocine (2′-hydroxy-5,9-dimethyl-6,7-benzomorphan), that any separation of analgetic effect from the various defects has been found and then only in animals, the carry-over to man has been disappointing.

Thus, it would appear that things are rather grim and medicinal chemistry has "flopped" rather badly. However, let me quickly state that we have yet to mention, among other possibilities, the narcotic antagonists.

Before we get to these Elysian fields, let us take the *ex post facto* look at the classes of compounds mentioned. Medicinal chemists and pharmacologists desire to correlate biological data with structural analysis. The most successful of these rationalizations is, indeed as is quite common, an *ex post facto* affair. The question which we should like to answer is, what do all of these compounds have in common? In fact, they all have three or four similar structural features although at first glance this may not have seemed likely.

They all have (a) a quaternary carbon; (b) a benzene nucleus linked to this carbon; (c) a tertiary amino group two saturated carbon atoms away from the quaternary carbon; and (d) a phenolic hydroxyl group situated meta to the quaternary carbon —if the tertiary nitrogen is a part of a six-membered ring.

With very few exceptions, all clinically accepted commercially-available strong analgetics have these features. We will return to an exception a bit later.

A fifth structural feature in some, but not all, of these classes of compounds has produced the narcotic antagonists.[8] This involves a change in the nitrogen substituent. When an N-CH3 is replaced by an N-allyl, N-3,3-dimethylallyl, N-cyclopropylmethyl or perhaps just N-n-propyl, then we may obtain a drug which can cancel or reverse most of the pharmacologic effects of morphine-like compounds.

An N-allyl derivative of normorphine produced the well-known narcotic antagonist N-allylnormorphine, or nalorphine. The pharmacologic effect of nalorphine, as an antagonist to morphine, and others was demonstrated in 1943.[9] More recently, (-)-3-hydroxy-N-allylmorphinan (or levallorphan) among the morphinans and alpha(+/-)-2-allyl-5,9-dimethyl-2'-hydroxy-6,7-benzomorphan[1] were also found to be narcotic antagonists. These compounds displayed little or no analgetic activity in the usual animal tests (although animal test procedures are now available which do enable us to routinely examine antagonists for analgetic activity). The latter two compounds have twice the potency of nalorphine as antagonists. Further, in man, nalorphine is comparable to morphine in analgetic potency. This fact, that nalorphine could be both agonist and antagonist, was the beginning of the new generation of agonist-antagonists. It was an accidental discovery of Lasagna and Beecher,[10] and later, Keats and Telford.[11] Although nalorphine is without abuse liability, its high incidence of side effects precludes its use as a substitute for morphine.

The quite remarkable fact that nalorphine had both agonist and antagonist characteristics led first the Smith, Kline & French pharmaceutical company, and then S. Archer at Sterling-Winthrop to synthesize over twenty N-substituted derivatives of the 6,7-benzomorphans.[12] The benzomorphan class was chosen because this was the only class in which previous dissociation of analgetic effect and dependence liability had been shown to occur in animals, by E. L. May and associates. Thus, pentazocine (Talwin®) appeared, a weak antagonist. At a dose of 40 mg/70 kg (man) it appears to be comparable to 10 mg/70 kg (man) of morphine in controlling pain of various origins and it is being used clinically without narcotics control.

It should be mentioned that the agonist-antagonists exemplified by pentazocine are not totally free of dependence properties. It has been said, however, that the dependence which might develop to some of these drugs is not of the opiate-type. It is a qualitatively different sort of dependence. Dr. Martin's studies at Lexington appear to indicate that the agonist-antagonists may or may not be sought after by individuals dependent on the drug, depending on the particular agonist-antagonist, and that physical withdrawal from these drugs is far easier than that from the morphine-type.[13]

Cyclazocine,[12] a rather interesting agonist-antagonist, is an N-cyclopropymethyl derivative of the benzomorphan. It is a very strong antagonist and is forty times as potent as morphine in post-operative pain. It is presently under study as a rehabilitation agent and deterrent to illicit narcotics use. It is being tried in combination with naloxone,[14] the only pure antagonist known. Evidently, naloxone (N-allyl-7,8-dihydro-14-hydroxynormorphinone) supresses the analgetic effect (or agonist activity) of cyclazocine. Thus, where nalorphine evidently occupies the "agonist receptor sites" presumably blocking further euphoria acquisition by a later heroin inoculation, the cyclazocine-naloxone combination blocks euphoria occurring after a later heroin inoculation by a somewhat different mechanism. It would be easy to say that the "agonist" receptor site and the "antagonist" receptor sites are identical, and therefore the antagonists cyclazocine and naloxone are blocking the sites previously available to heroin. However, this is still on contention; many investigators seem to think that these receptor sites are not the same.

So far we have mentioned four criteria for structure-activity correlations of analgetics and a fifth (N-substitution) for antagonist activity. Recently, E. L. May and associates have found another factor of importance in the benzomorphan class of compounds—optical resolution. This is the first known instance where certain N-methyl compounds, as their levo-isomers, are found to retain all of the analgetic activity of the original racemic mixture and also act as narcotic antagonists. Thus we have a sixth criterion for structure-activity correlation, optical resolution of some of the compounds of class 5, the benzomorphans, produces the agonist-antagonist.[15-17]

Here then is our silver lining, if not our magic bullet. The agonist-antagonist produced in adherence with (if only *ex post facto* adherence) the listed six correlations. Thus far, only pentazocine has found clinical applicability. Undoubtedly, many more will be forthcoming in the future.

Let me just mention, at this point, that the evolved structure-activity correlations are quite limited in utility. In fact they are very unsatisfactory from a scientific point of view. It is not difficult to find compounds which meet these criteria which are neither analgetics nor antagonists. It is also possible to find exceptions to the criteria which are analgetics. One of these is fentanyl (N-(1-phenethyl-4-piperidyl) propionanilide).

Fentanyl is clinically used. It is a powerful analgetic. It is also highly dependence producing. It meets almost none of the criteria for structure-activity correlation. It is our exception to the rule.

A further source of difficulty is that the structure-activity correlations tell us very little about receptor sites, to say nothing of molecular mechanism of activity.

In fact, little is known about receptor sites although hypotheses have been advanced and withdrawn. Biochemists seek receptor sites among their multitude of enzymes and proteins. It is a field that is being actively pursued. Medicinal chemists are choosing a different approach amenable, hopefully, to this analgetic field.

The relatively recent emergence of the techniques of nuclear magnetic resonance spectroscopy and electron paramagnetic resonance spectroscopy have served to enliven the interface of biology and chemistry. Several groups are looking at the interactions of small and large molecules (drugs and enzymes, etcetera) in this way, claiming to observe a site of interaction and the type of interaction which occurred.[18,19]

Other groups have chosen to examine biological data from a different physical-chemical point of view. Quantum mechanics is being utilized to pick out energetically favorable conformations of drug molecules, and receptor site interaction is inferred from these data.[20] The quantum mechanics used is usually a simplified version, for further progress using larger molecules and more precise calculations, larger capacity and higher speed computers will have to be developed.

A third significant development is that due to C. Hansch at Pomona College, California.[21] He has combined partition coefficients (which simulate transport phenomena to an active site), steric factors and electronic factors in a series of equations which he submits to computerized regression analysis. He has looked at perhaps a thousand series of drugs and found he could correlate the biological activity with all or some of these physical-chemical parameters in about seven hundred of them. We are now attempting to do this with analgetics.

The hope in all of this is to relate an experimentally measurable or calculable physical-chemical property or mathematically derived term, to an experimentally measured biological activity. This will enable medicinal chemists to predict the activity of theoretical compounds.

This pursuit is still in its infancy but contemporary medicinal chemistry is becoming increasingly involved with them. This may, or may not, turn out to be an improvement over former structure-activity correlations. At the least, they promise to be better rationalizations.

REFERENCES

1. Jacobson, A.E., May E.L., and Sargent, L.J.: In *Medicinal Chemistry*, 3rd ed., edited by A. Burger. New York, John Wiley, 1970, Part II, pp. 1327-1350.
2. DeStevens, G. (Ed.): *Analgetics (Vol. 5)*. New York-London, Academic Press, 1965.
3. Eddy, N.B., and May, E.L.: In *Synthetic Analgesics*, edited by J. Rolfe, London, Pergamon, 1965, part II.
4. Small, L.F., Eddy, N.B., Mosettig, E., and Himmelsbach, C.K.: *Studies on Drug Addiction*, Suppl. No. 138 to the Public Health Reports, Washington, D.C., U.S. Govt. Printing Office, 1938.
5. Eisleb, O., and Shaumann, O.: Dolantin, ein neuartiges Spasmolytikum und Analgetikum. *Deutsch Med Wschr, 65*:967, 1939.
6. Bockmühl, M., and Ehrhart, G.: Über eine neue Klasse von spasmolytisch und analgetisch wirkenden Verbindungen. *Ann Chem Liebigs, 561*:52, 1948.
7. Grewe, R.: Das Problem der Morphin-Synthese. *Naturwissensch, 33*:333, 1946.
8. Martin, W.R.: Opioid antagonists. *Pharmacol Rev, 19*:463, 1967.

9. Unna, K.: Antagonistic effect of N-allylnormorphine upon morphine. *J Pharmacol Exp Ther, 79:*27, 1943.

10. Lasagna, L., and Beecher, H.K.: The analgesic effectiveness of nalorphine and nalorphine-morphine combinations in man. *J Pharmacol Exp Ther, 112:*356, 1954.

11. Keats, A.S., and Telford, J.: Nalorphine, a potent analgesic in man. *J Pharmacol Exp Ther, 117:*190, 1956.

12. Archer, S., Albertson, N.F., Harris, L.S., Pierson, A.K., and Bird, J.G.: Pentazocine. Strong analgesics and analgesic antagonists in the benzomorphan series. *J Med Chem, 7:*123, 1964.

13. Eddy, N.B., and Martin, W.R.: Drug dependence of specific opiate antagonist type. *Pharmakopsychiat Neuro-Psychopharmakol, 3:*73, 1970.

14. Kallos, T., and Smith, T.C.: Naloxone reversal of pentazocine-induced respiratory depression. *JAMA, 204:*932, 1968.

15. May, E.L., and Eddy, N.B.: Interesting pharmacological properties of the optical isomers of α-5,9-diethyl-2'-hydroxyl-2-methyl-6,7-benzomorphan. *J Med Chem, 9:*851, 1966.

16. Ager, J.H., Jacobson, A.E., and May, E.L.: Separation of morphine-like effects by optical resolution. Levo-isomers as strong analgetics and narcotic antagonists. *J Med Chem, 12:*288, 1969.

17. May, E.L., and Takeda, M.: Optical isomers of miscellaneous strong analgetics. *J Med Chem, 13:*805, 1970.

18. Rose, P.I.: Protein-metal ion binding site: Determination with proton magnetic resonance spectroscopy. *Science, 171:*573, 1971.

19. Jost, P., and Griffity, O.H.: Electron spin resonance and the spin-labelling method. In *Methods in Pharmacology (Vol. 2), edited* by C. Chignell. New York, Appleton-Century-Crofts, 1971 (in press).

20. Kier, L.B., and George, J.M.: Molecular orbital conformation of phenylcholine ether. *J Med Chem, 14:*80, 1971.

21. Hansch, C.: A quantitative approach to biochemical structure-activity relationships. *Accounts Chem Res, 2:*232, 1969.

Chapter 30

Studies on the Subjective Effects of Narcotic Antagonists

Donald R. Jasinski

IN RECENT YEARS a number of compounds which have the ability to antagonize morphine have been studied extensively in man and animals. Impetus for production and study of the narcotic antagonists stems from observations of Lasagna and Beecher[13] that nalorphine had analgesic activity in man and those of Wikler *et al.*[20] and Isbell[6] indicating that nalorphine had low abuse potential.

This chapter will describe the subjective effects of the antagonists nalorphine, cyclazocine, naloxone, profadol and pentazocine (Fig. 30-1) and relate these to the two-receptor hypothesis formulated by Martin in his extensive review of the opioid antagonists.[14] Aspects of the human pharmacology of antagonists related to developing an analgesic of low abuse potential have recently been discussed.[7]

The first detailed study of the subjective effects of the narcotic antagonists was that by Martin and collaborators,[16] who utilized the single dose opiate questionnaire[2,15] to document the subjective effects of cyclazocine and nalorphine and to contrast these with the effects produced by morphine. It was observed that with small doses of cyclazocine and nalorphine, subjects identified the drugs as an opiate and reported subjective feelings of well-being, relaxation, elation and certain other symptoms similar to those produced by morphine. With increasing doses, subjects re-

Note: This study was presented at the 14th Annual Meeting of the Eastern Psychiatric Research Association, New York, November 1969, and won the 1969 Best Paper Award, donated by the Gralnick Foundation, Port Chester, New York.

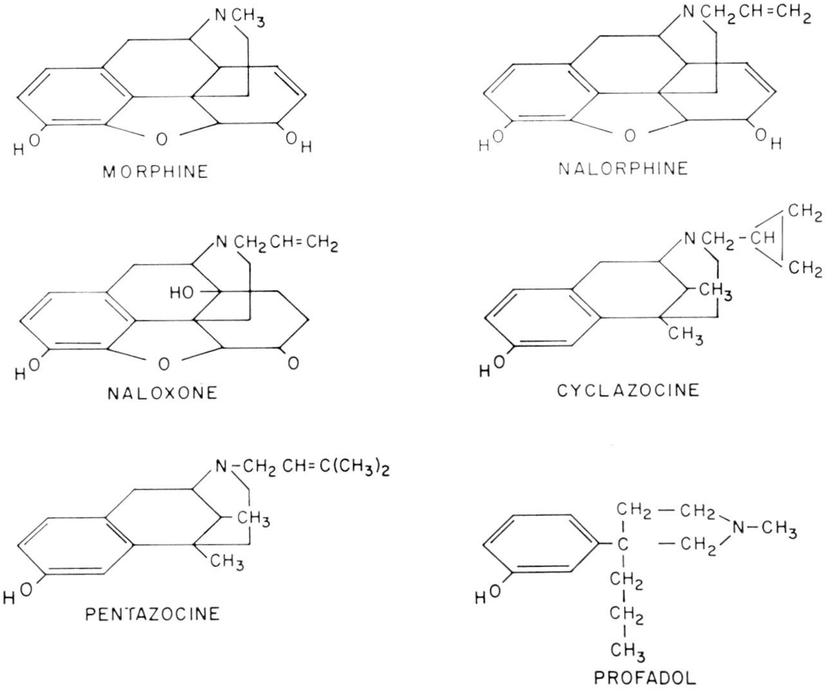

Figure 30-1.

ported two additional types of subjective changes and no longer identified the drugs as opiates. One set resembled the effects produced by sedative hypnotics and tranquilizers such as tiredness, lethargy, sleepiness, loss of energy and drunkenness. The other set resembles those produced by psychotomimetic agents such as feelings of irritability, racing thoughts, difficulty in concentrating and, in the extreme, a toxic psychosis with depersonalization, derealization, delusions and hallucinations, With chronic administration of cyclazocine, subjects became tolerant to the subjective effects, were cross-tolerant to the effects of nalorphine, and, upon abrupt withdrawal, exhibited an abstinence syndrome distinguishable from the morphine abstinence syndrome. Subsequently, Martin and Gorodetzky demonstrated that nalorphine produces dependence which more closely resembles cyclazocine than morphine dependence.[17]

These studies fostered studies by Haertzen,[4] who evaluated
the subjective effects of cyclazocine and nalorphine with the Addiction Research Center Inventory (ARCI). The ARCI is a 550-
item structured questionnaire which contains a number of empirically derived scales. Initially, scales were developed which
distinguish certain drug-induced subjective states from placebo
and no-drug conditions.[5] Scales were also developed which characterized similarities or differences among the subjective states of
no-drug, placebo, morphine, pyrahexyl, pentobarbital, chlorpromazine, alcohol, LSD and amphetamine.[3] Haertzen confirmed
the observations of Martin *et al.* that nalorphine and cyclazocine
produced similar subjective effects that could be distinguished
from those of morphine. Of primary importance was their observation that unlike morphine, nalorphine and cyclazocine produced dose-related responses on the LSD (LS) and pentobarbital-
chlorpromazine-alcohol group (PCAG) scales. No significant responses were observed on the morphine-benzedrine group (MBG)
scale, which further differentiated nalorphine and cyclazocine
from morphine.

Subsequently a lesser number of items from the MBG, LS and
PCAG scales have been used in shorter questionnaires, along with
the single dose opiate questionnaire, in a number of studies to
differentiate nalorphine-like subjective effects from morphine-like
subjective effects.[8-12]

Based on studies of morphine and morphine antagonists in
man and the chronic spinal dog, Martin proposed that nalorphine
exerts certain of its agonistic activities such as analgesia and subjective effects through a receptor which is distinct from the morphine receptor (receptor dualism).[14] The morphine antagonistic
effect of nalorphine is due to reaction of nalorphine with the
morphine receptor, where nalorphine exerts little or no agonistic
activity but acts as a competitive antagonist. Within the context
of the two receptor hypothesis, Martin further proposed that
agonists of either the morphine or nalorphine type could exist.

More recently studies of other narcotic antagonists have demonstrated agonistic activities which differ markedly from the
nalorphine type. Three compounds which have been extensively

studied with consequent practical and theoretical importance are naloxone, profadol and pentazocine.

The narcotic antagonist naloxone in man is seven times as potent as nalorphine as a morphine antagonist but produces no significant subjective or physiological changes when administered acutely or chronically.[8] Naloxone, therefore, has little or no agonistic activity and is regarded as a pure competitive antagonist.

Not only will naloxone antagonize the agonistic effects of morphine, but it will also antagonize the agonistic effects of antagonists. After demonstration in the chronic spinal dog that naloxone antagonizes the flexor reflex depression[18,19] produced by cyclazocine and the antinociceptive effect of a number of narcotic antagonists in the mouse and rat phenylquinone-writhing test,[1] studies were conducted to determine if naloxone would antagonize the effects of cyclazocine in man. Naloxone antagonizes both those effects of cyclazocine which resemble morphine, such as pupillary constriction and respiratory depression, and those which do not, such as subjective effects.[12] One implication of these studies is that the morphine and nalorphine receptors, although distinct, must be stereochemically similar since naloxone is an effective antagonist at both types of receptors.

Another type of agonistic effect of narcotic antagonists is typified by those produced with profadol. Profadol is 1/50th as potent as nalorphine in precipitating abstinence in man, yet produces subjective effects which are morphine-like rather than nalorphine-like. On the basis of substitution studies in morphine-dependent subjects and chronic intoxication, it was concluded that profadol was a partial agonist of the morphine type that is a competitive dualist of morphine.[9,10]

Recently the effects of the analgesic pentazocine have been reinvestigated to determine whether pentazocine, like profadol, could be considered a partial agonist of morphine. Pentazocine produces subjective effects which, depending upon dose, resemble both morphine and nalorphine.[11] In doses up to 40 mg/70 kg, pentazocine produces typical morphine-like subjective effects which can be equivalent to those produced by 10 mg/70 kg of morphine, as evidenced by the type of responses on the single-dose opiate questionnaire, accompanied by elevated responses on the MBG items. With a dose increase to 60 mg/70 kg, pentazocine produces subjective effects which more closely resemble those produced by nalorphine, since at this dose the response on the single-dose opiate questionnaire resembled those produced by nalorphine, with no significant response on the MBG items but with responses on the LS and PCAG items equivalent to those produced by 10 mg/70 kg of nalorphine. One explanation offered for this effect is that pentazocine has agonistic activity at both types of receptors, with relatively higher affinity and lesser intrinsic activity at the morphine receptor and lesser affinity and higher intrinsic activity at the nalorphine receptor. Thus, with low doses of pentazocine weak, nonpsychotogenic nalorphine-like subjective effects are combined with morphine-like subjective effects, but as the dose is increased the effects become predominantly nalorphine-like.

Thus, narcotic antagonists produce distinct types of subjective effects. These subjective effects may be classified as morphine-like as with profadol, nalorphine-like as with nalorphine and cyclazocine, or may be a mixture of both morphine and nalorphine effects as with pentazocine. Narcotic antagonists may also be lacking in the production of subjective effects as is seen with the pure antagonist, naloxone. The relationship of these diverse agonistic effects to antagonistic activity is consistent with the concepts of receptor dualism and competitive dualism.

REFERENCES

1. Blumberg, H., Dayton, H. B., and Wolf, P. S.: Counteraction of narcotic antagonist analgesics by the narcotic antagonist naloxone. *Proc Soc Exp Biol, 123:*755-758, 1966.

2. Fraser, H. F., Van Horn, G. D., Martin, W. R., Wolbach, A. B., and Isbell, H.: Methods for evaluating addiction liability. (A) "Attitude" of opiate addicts toward opiate-like drugs. (B) A short-term "direct" addiction test. *J Pharmacol Exper Ther, 133:*371-387, 1961.

3. Haertzen, C. A.: Development of scales based on patterns of drug effects, using the Addiction Research Center Inventory (ARCI). *Psychol Reports, 18:*163-194, 1966.

4. Haertzen, C. A.: Subjective effects of narcotic antagonists cyclazocine

and nalorphine on the Addiction Research Center Inventory (ARCI). In preparation.

5. Hill, H. E., Haertzen, C. A., Wolbach, A. B., Jr., and Miner, E. J.: The Addiction Research Center Inventory: Standardization of scales which evaluate subjective effects of morphine, amphetamine, pentobarbital, alcohol, LSD-25, pyrahexyl, and chlorpromazine. *Psychopharmacologia, 4:*167-183, 1963.

6. Isbell, H.: Attempted addiction to nalorphine. *Fed Proc, 15:*442, 1954.

7. Jasinski, D. R.: Narcotic antagonists as analgesics of low dependence liability—theoretical and practical implications of recent studies. In *Yearbook of Drug Abuse,* edited by L. Brill and E. Harms. In press.

8. Jasinski, D. R., Martin, W. R., and Haertzen, C. A.: The human pharmacology and abuse potential of N-allylnoroxymorphone (naloxone). *J Pharmacol Exp Ther, 157:*420-426, 1967.

9. Jasinski, D. R., Martin, W. R., and Hoeldtke, R.: Studies on the ability of m- (1-methyl-3-propyl-3-pyrrolidinyl) phenol (profadol, CI-572) to produce morphine-like dependence. *Fed Proc, 28:*735, 1969.

10. Jasinski, D. R., Martin, W. R., and Hoeldtke, R.: Studies of the ability of the "weak" narcotic antagonists GPA-1657, profadol (CI-572), and propiram (BAY-4503) to produce dependence of the morphine type in man. In preparation.

11. Jasinski, D. R., Martin, W. R., and Hoeldtke, R.: Effects of short- and long-term administration of pentazocine in man. *Clin Pharmacol Ther, 11:*385-403, 1970.

12. Jasinski, D. R., Martin, W. R., and Sapira, J. D.: Antagonism of the subjective, behavioral, pupillary, and respiratory depressant effects of cyclazocine by naloxone. *Clin Pharmacol Ther, 9:*215-222, 1968.

13. Lasagna, L., and Beecher, H. K.: The analgesic effectiveness of nalorphine and nalorphine-morphine combinations in man. *J Pharmacol Exp Ther, 112:*356-363, 1964.

14. Martin, W. R.: Opioid antagonists. *Pharmacol Rev, 19:*463-521, 1967.

15. Martin, W. R., and Fraser, H. F.: A comparative study of physiological and subjective effects of heroin and morphine administered intravenously in postaddicts. *J Pharmacol Exp Ther, 133:*388-399, 1961.

16. Martin, W. R., Fraser, H. F., Gorodetzky, C. W., and Rosenberg, D. E.: Studies of the dependence-producing potential of the narcotic antagonist 2-cyclopropylmethyl-2'-hydroxy-5,9-dimethyl-6,7-benzomorphan (cyclazocine, Win-20,740, ARC II-C-3). *J Pharmacol Exp Ther, 150:*426-436, 1965.

17. Martin, W. R., and Gorodetzky, C. W.: Demonstration of tolerance to and physical dependence on N-allylnormorphine (nalorphine). *J Pharmacol Exp Ther, 150:*437-442, 1965.

18. McClane, T. K., and Martin, W. R.: Antagonism of the spinal cord

effects of morphine and cyclazocine by naloxone and thebaine. *Int J Neuropharmacol, 6*:325-327, 1967.

19. McClane, T. K., and Martin, W. R.: Effects of morphine, nalorphine, cyclazocine, and naloxone on the flexor reflex. *Int J Neuropharmacol, 6*:89-97, 1967.

20. Wikler, A., Fraser, H. F., and Isbell, H.: N-allylnormorphine: Effects of single doses and precipitation of acute "abstinence syndromes" during addiction to morphine, methadone or heroin in man (postaddicts). *J Pharmacol Exp Ther, 109*:8-20, 1953.

Chapter 31

Electrophysiological and Behavioral Interrelationships of Various Hallucinogens and Depressants in Animals

Murray A. Cowen

THERE ARE two major problems in investigating the physiological effects of hallucinogenic substances and their possible relationships with human psychoses. Firstly, it is difficult to elicit notable behavioral abnormalities with them in laboratory animals in doses comparable to those which are psychotogenic in humans. Secondly, it is very difficult to detect biochemical or electrophysiological changes in the brain associated with these dose levels. This chapter will describe how the use of TCDC techniques[9,11] makes it possible to detect minute doses of hallucinogens in animals, will estimate the relative potency of these substances and then will derive novel empirical results which may be translated into behavioral studies on animals.

The transcephalic direct current (TCDC) potentials are the slowly changing voltages measured between specified diploic-emissary vein distributions on the intact surface of the head (Figs. 31-1 and 31-2). It has been shown that these potentials are principally generated by the subjacent cortex and transmitted to the surface via communicating vascular channels. The charges so generated are stored, hence the potentials are partly amplified by mechanisms operating at the surface.[8]

On the basis of many diverse studies including autoradiography and enzyme localization, it appears that the potentials are generated principally by glial cells which participate in the so-

Note: This research was supported partly by the Syracuse Veterans Administration Hospital and partly by Marcy State Hospital.

BASELINE

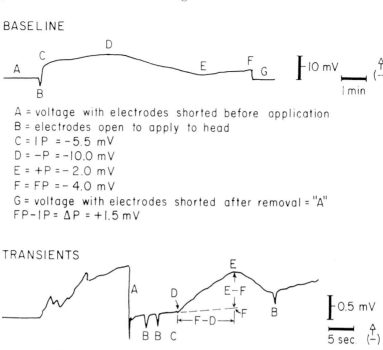

A = voltage with electrodes shorted before application
B = electrodes open to apply to head
C = I P = -5.5 mV
D = -P = -10.0 mV
E = +P = -2.0 mV
F = FP = -4.0 mV
G = voltage with electrodes shorted after removal = "A"
FP - IP = ΔP = +1.5 mV

TRANSIENTS

A = rebalance channel
B, B, B = eye closures = +.250 mV
C = stimulus administered
D-C = lag time = 0.9 sec.
F-D = persistence = 11 sec.
E-F = peak magnitude of response = 0.75 mV
D-E = sign of response = (-)

Figure 31-1. Scoring technique.

called blood brain barrier. Further studies involving the injection of numerous substrates and enzyme-blocking agents have shown that the voltages are generated by membrane permeability changes which accompany nucleotide metabolism in these cells.[8]

These potentials are modulated by vascular mechanisms, plasma constituents, and also respond to neuronal activity since the extracellular potassium and glutamate concentrations, which increase locally in conjunction with calcium decreases, due to

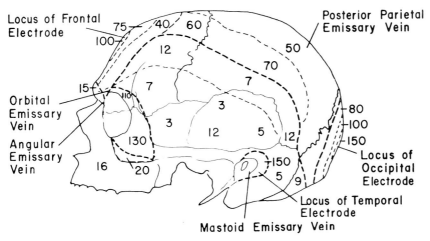

Figure 31-2 A.

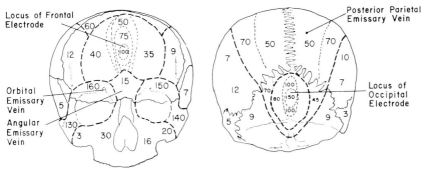

Figure 31-2 B. Isopotential zones projected on the skull are isomorphic with relative density of vascular emissary channels in skull. The major emissary veins are named. The relative concentration of microvascular channels are given in relative percent per centimeter squared of bone surface. There is a comparable distribution of vascular channels in the subjacent inner table of the skull. Those corresponding to the frontal, occipital and temporal concentrations are found in the bony impressions of the superior saggittal and lateral extremity of the transverse sinuses respectively.

neuronal activity, appear to initiate both glial purine synthesis and TCDC potential negativity over the area.[10,14]

Functionally, frontal negativity correlates with "orienting processes" whereby the brain reprograms itself to deal with novel and complex external situations.[5,6] Frontal positivity correlates with defensive reflexes and withdrawal from the environmental stimuli.[4-6] Left temporal TCDC electronegativity correlates with intensive recall and reprocessing of complex information.[10] Differential characteristic TCDC abnormalities have now been found for various human psychotic states including senility,[12] childhood autism,[10] and schizophrenia.[8,12] In the latter, a correlation has been found between excessive frontal negativity and hallucinations of an auditory, visual or tactile nature.[7]

The studies reported below were specifically prompted by three considerations: first, the possibility that these schizophrenic potentials were due to an endogenous hallucinogen[8]; second, a recent TCDC study on college students revealed that five out of ten who had taken "drugs" showed abnormally high frontal TCDC potentials[18]; and finally a report that a group of normal (and TCDC normal) Canadian youth showed TCDC frontal abnormalities after injestion of 100 μg LSD-25 and that these TCDC abnormalities were still discernible in some up to four months after taking the drug once.[1]

METHODS

The first series of studies involved TCDC recording between frontal and occipital sites in a group of pentobarbital (50 mg/kg intraperitoneal) anaesthetized rats of various breeds. Following anaesthesia, the left internal carotid artery was cannulated for test injections. These injections always consisted of the test substance dissolved in 0.2 cc of physiological saline administered in ten seconds via the catheter. The number of animals and specifics of the hallucinogens tested are shown on Tables 31-I, 31-II and 31-III. TCDC recordings were made with non-polarizing Ag/Ag Cl wick electrodes and a saline scalp contact using a dynograph type R with dc input couplers. The rats were grounded to the machines by rectal leads. TCDC output was split and recorded simultaneously on two channels set at 10 mv/cm and 0.5 mv/cm gain respectively and polarization were checked and controlled in a standard manner.[11] After data had been collected on the relative dose effects of the hallucinogens (Table 31-I), further studies

TABLE 31-I

TCDC (FO) EFFECTS OF HALLUCINOGENS INJECTED INTO THE
INTERNAL CAROTID ARTERY OF PENTOBARBITAL-ANAESTHETIZED
RATS

Dose	Compound	N	lag (sec)	Sign (%) +	—	0	Peak Magni- tude (mv)	Persis- tence (sec)	Relative TCDC Effect
5µg	DMPEA	5	6.4	20,	80,	0	—.218**	27.70	—6.04
5µg	Bufotenine	12	3.5	8,	84,	8	—.241*	10.36	—2.50
5µg	DET	5	1.00	0,	100,	0	—.090***	11.80	—1.06
5µg	5-MOT	5	1.20	40,	60,	0	—.050°	11.40	—0.57
0.5µg	LSD 25	13	3.54	8,	92,	0	—.470***	30.55	—14.36
0.5µg	Adrenochrome	6	1.20	0,	83,	17	—.192**	14.00	—2.80
0.5µg	Bufotenine	27	3.7	19,	67,	14	—.120*	11.04	—1.32
0.5µg	DET	6	3.0	0,	100,	0	—.113**	11.50	—1.30
0.5µg	5-MOT	7	2.6	43,	57,	0	+.013°	11.00	+0.14
80 ng	DET	6	1.8	0,	83,	17	—.150*	12.35	—1.85
30 ng	LSD 25	7	1.6	0,	100,	0	—.286***	26.70	—7.64
30 ng	DMT	9	1.5	0,	100,	0	—.378***	9.50	—3.59
30 ng	DET	5	1.5	0,	100,	0	—.127*	11.30	—1.44
5 ng	LSD 25	7	1.8	14,	72,	14	—.350*	17.70	—6.20
5 ng	DMT	8	1.8	13,	87,	0	—.159**	8.00	—1.27
5 ng	DET	6	1.7	33,	67,	0	—.033°	5.67	—0.19

°=p>.05 by t-test, two tailed.
*=p<.05 by t-test, two-tailed.
**=p<.01 by t-test, two-tailed.
***=p<.005 by t-test, two-tailed.

were done in animals whose blood brain barrier permeability had been increased by prior internal carotid injection of a ph neutral solution of lactate in physiological saline (1:40 dilution). The number of animals and test injections are shown in Table 31-II.

A last group of TCDC studies involved testing of the effect of pretreatment with a number of compounds including chlorpromazine, spermidine, Diamox®, and zinc on various hallucinogens (Table 31-III).

RESULTS OF TCDC STUDIES

The relative TCDC potency of the compounds tested are shown in Table 31-I, and the relative halilucinogenic potency are shown in Table 31-IV.[2,3,15-17,19-26] It is obvious that the two are

TABLE 31-II

TCDC (FO) EFFECTS OF HALLUCINOGENS INJECTED INTO INTERNAL
CAROTID ARTERY OF PENTOBARBITAL-ANAESTHETIZED RATS PRE-
TREATED WITH LACTATE (PH 7.0) TO INCREASE PERMEABILITY OF
THE BLOOD BRAIN BARRIER

Dose	Compound	N	lag (sec)	Sign (%) + — 0	Peak Magni- tude (mv)	Persis- tence (sec)	Relative TCDC Effect
5 μg	Bufotenine	7	4.2	0, 86, 14	—.200**	16.6	—3.31
5 μg	DET	7	2.00	0, 100, 0	—.107***	11.2	—2.35
5 μg	5-MOT	7	1.14	43, 57, 0	+.021°	9.9	+0.21
0.5 μg	DET	7	2.00	0, 100, 0	—.375*	16.7	—6.26
0.5 μg	Bufotenine	15	1.7	13, 80, 7	—.132*	15.2	—2.00
0.5 μg	5-MOT	6	2.8	67, 33, 0	+.292°	19.35	+5.65
80 ng	DET	15	1.7	7, 93, 0	—.082***	10.75	—0.88
30 ng	LSD25	5	1.8	0, 100, 0	—.381***	28.3	—10.78
30 ng	DET	5	2.5	20, 80, 0	—.075*	11.50	—.86
5 ng	LSD25	7	2.4	0, 100, 0	—.289***	16.7	—4.83
5 ng	DMT	6	1.8	0, 100, 0	—.225***	9.7	—2.17
5 ng	DET	7	1.3	14, 86, 0	—.046*	8.43	—.39

°=p>.05 by t-test, two-tailed.
*=p<.05 by t-test, two-tailed.
**=p<.01 by t-test, two-tailed.
***=p<.005 by t-test, two-tailed.

highly correlated and that the TCDC circuit responds to extremely small amounts of truly potent hallucinogens such as DMT
and LSD-25. Table 31-II shows that pretreatment with lactate
generally potentiates the TCDC effects of all true hallucinogens.
From Table 31-III, it may be seen that chlorpromazine effectively
blocks the TCDC effects of bufotenin as does spermidine. This
may be of importance since both chlorpromazine and spermidine
inhibit the TCDC abnormalities in schizophrenia.[8,13]

It may also be seen that Diamox, which inhibits carbonic
anhydrase, which is found in glia but not neurons, markedly
diminishes the TCDC effects of a typical hallucinogen, DMT.

Finally, it may be seen (Table 31-III) that minute amounts of
zinc block the TCDC effects of relatively enormous doses of LSD-
25.

To see if this hitherto unreported antagonism between Zn and
LSD-25 would also apply to behavioral studies, the following experiment was performed on naive and unmedicated rats.

TABLE 31-III

STUDIES OF CHEMICAL MODULATION OF THE TCDC (FO) EFFECTS OF
HALLUCINOGENS

Dose	Compound	Modulator	N	Lag (sec)	Sign (%) + — 0	Peak Magnitude (mv)	Persistence (sec)	Relative TCDC Effect
0.5 μg	Bufotenine	None	27	3.7	19, 67, 14	—.120	11.04	—1.32[a]
0.5 μg	Bufotenine	20 min after 5 mg spermidine IP	14	1.72	14, 50, 36	—.073	7.20	—0.53[b]
0.5 μg	Bufotenine	20 min after 5 mgm chlorpromazine IP	12	1.80	8, 34, 58	—.015	5.10	—0.08[c]
30 ng	DMT	None	9	1.5	0, 100, 0	—.378	9.5	—3.59[d]
30 ng	DMT	5 min after 5 mgm Diamox IC	10	1.7	0, 100, 0	—.090	9.1	—0.82[e]
500 ng	LSD25	None	13	3.5	8, 92, 0	—.470	30.55	—14.36[f]
500 ng	LSD25	Up to 15 min after 30μg 2n++ IC	19	2.3	37, 76, 37	—.016	5.74	—0.09[g]

t (a = b) 1.70, p < .10;

t (a = c) 2.75, p < .01;

t (d = e) 5.63, p < .0001;

t (f = g) 7.68, p < .00001.

TABLE 31-IV

RELATIVE HALLUCINOGENIC POTENCY OF COMPOUNDS TESTED

Compound	Hallucinatory Dose	Comment
5-Methoxytryptamine	behavior in rat altered at 22 mg/kg/IV	Doubtfully hallucinogenic
DMPEA	doubtful even at 20 mg/kg in cat	Mainly of theoretical interest
Bufotenine	2–16 mg/kg/i.v.	Some dispute
Diethyltryptamine	0.5 to 1.0 mg/kg/i.m.	Undoubted hallucinogen
Adrenochrome	7μg/kg/IV	Potency disputed
Dimethyltryptamine	7 to 14μg/kg/i.m.	Short acting
LSD-25	2 to 7μg/kg/p.o.	Most potent

METHOD OF BEHAVIORAL STUDY

A total of twenty-four male rats were maintained in separate cages for two weeks prior to testing. This N was divided randomly into four groups of six animals with each group receiving an intraperitoneal injection of one of four substances selected for testing. Two animals of a group were placed together in an observation box equipped with photocells for automatic counting of movements. For three 10-minute intervals, the animals had their motor activity registered and the number of preening and rearing episodes counted. In addition, their startle and orienting responses, to standardized loud and soft sounds respectively, were noted and rated on a 0 to 3 scale of intensity by a group of naive and independent raters. After this 30-minute interval, the rats of group 1 received a 1.0 cc injection of physiological saline IP, group 2 were injected with 0.5 mg Zn acetate in 1.0 cc NaCl IP, group 3 with 1μg LSD-25, in NaCl (1.0 cc/IP) and group 4 with both Zn and LSD by separate injections. The raters were blind to the nature of the injections given any pair of animals. Following injection, the same behavioral parameters noted above were observed for six succeeding 10-minute intervals. The ratio of behavioral events noted in the postinjection periods to preinjection periods were calculated to determine the relative behavioral effects of the various injections.

RESULTS OF BEHAVIORAL STUDY

The results are summarized in Table 31-V. As may be seen, the rats given LSD-25 injections showed the greatest relative activity in each of the five behavior parameters studied ($p<.001$). In each instance, the effects following Zn injections are very similar to those following the control, NaCl, injection. In particular, the Zn effect on motor activity per se was negligible as compared with the NaCl control groups so that any Zn interaction with LSD-25 can hardly be explained on the basis of some peripheral motor inhibitory effect of the cation.

It may be seen that the combined administration of Zn with LSD-25 resulted in the greatest inhibition of three parameters: motor activity, preening and rearing of any injection ($p<.01$).

TABLE 31-V

BEHAVIORAL CHANGE NOTED IN RATS GIVEN VARIOUS INJECTIONS INTRAPERITONEALLY

Behavior	Number of Observation Periods for Each of the Compounds Tested		Relative Change After Injection			
	Before Injection	After Injection	NaCl*	2n**	LSD-25***	2n** and LSD-25***
Startle	18	36	2.37	2.14	2.73	2.62
Orienting	18	36	1.80	1.88	2.92	1.86
Rearing	18	36	0.27	0.07	0.38	0.04
Preening	18	36	1.80	0.75	1.92	0.34
Motor activity	15	36	0.45	0.55	0.71	0.25

Rank ordering of injection effects

Startle: LSD>2n+LSD>NaCl>2n

Orienting: LSD>2n>2n+LSD>Nacl

Rearing: LSD>NaCl> 2n>2n+LSD

Preening: LSD>NaCl> 2n>2n+LSD

Motor activity: LSD>2n>Nacl> 2n+LSD

*1 cc physiological NaCl.

**0.5 mg $2n^{++}$ as 2n Acetate

***1.0μg LSD-25.

The zinc not only inhibited each behavioral effect of LSD-25 noted in this study (p<.001) but in four of the five instances the extent of inhibition due to the combined injection "overshot" the relative inhibition found after the zinc alone was administered (p<.005).

DISCUSSION AND CONCLUSIONS

These experiments clearly show that the TCDC circuit is extraordinarily sensitive to hallucinogens and that the electrophysiological effects of these compounds parallel their behavioral effects. It is also apparent that the relative ability of three compounds—chlorpromazine, spermidine and zinc—to modulate the TCDC effects of hallucinogens is paralleled by their ability to modulate the behavioral effects of these psychotogens as well.

The TCDC potentials certainly appear to be generated by glial cells, but the mechanisms respond to both neural and vascular controls. Thus it is possible that the hallucinogens act primarily at neuronal sites which, in turn, modulate TCDC potentials. Studies, now in progress, may further clarify the nature of the neuronal input to the TCDC circuit and help to resolve this uncertainty.

It is safe to conclude the TCDC techniques are most useful in studying the physiology of hallucinogens and that the hypothesis linking endogenous production of psychotogens to schizophrenia has been significantly strengthened by the above findings.

ACKNOWLEDGMENTS

The hallucinogens used in this study were administered under the kind collaboration of Dr. F. Grant, Marcy State Hospital, Marcy, New York, and Dr. A. Bolton, University of Saskatchewan, Regina, Saskatchewan, Canada. Acknowledged, too, is the fine collaboration of A. Wilson in the animal experiments of this study.

REFERENCES

1. Auerbach, A.: Personal communication.
2. Boszormenyl, Z., Der, P., and Nagy, P.J.: Observations on the psycho-togenic effect of N-N diethyl tryptamine. *Ment Sci, 105:*171-181, 1959.
3. Buday, P.V.: Pharmacologically active substances present in the central nervous system. *Nature, 19:*245-247, 1961.
4. Cowen, M.A.: Elementary functional correlates of the transcephalic dc circuit. *Psychophysiol, 3:*262-272, 1967a.
5. Cowen, M.A.: The baseline transcephalic dc potential in normals. *J Psychiat Res, 5:*307-315, 1967b.
6. Cowen, M.A.: Some higher functional correlates of the TCDC circuit. *Psychiat Quart, 42:*409-429, 1968a.
7. Cowen, M.A.: Schizophrenic hallucinations and the transcephalic dc potential. *Arch Gen Psychiat (Chicago), 18:*114-116, 1968b.
8. Cowen, M.A.: Electrophysiological studies on the brain effects of nucleo-tide and tryptophan metabolites. *Dis Nerv Syst, 31:*772-780, 1970.
9. Cowen, M.A.: A review of current concepts of the TCDC circuit. *Psychophysiol,* 1971, in press.
10. Cowen, M.A.: The substrate biochemistry of the TCDC circuit. Manu-script in preparation.
11. Cowen, M.A., Ross, J., and McDonald, R.D.: Some aspects of the trans-cephalic dc circuit. *Psychophysiol, 4:*207-215, 1967.
12. Cowen, M.A., and Cassell, W.: Some aspects of the baseline transcephalic dc potential in psychiatric patients. *J Psychiat Res, 6:*13-20, 1968.

13. Cowen, M.A., and Grant, F.: Studies of the TCDC circuit: Chlorpromazine and schizophrenia. *J Schizophrenia, 2:*81-87, 1968.
14. Cowen, M.A., and Ross, J.: On the relationships of serum electrolytes and the blood brain barrier to the TCDC circuit. *Schizophrenia, 1:* 100-112, 1969.
15. Downing, D.F.: In *Tranquilizing and Antidepressant Drugs,* edited by Wilbur M. Benson and Burtrum C. Schiele. Springfield, Charles C Thomas, 1962, p. 555.
16. Fabing, H.D., and Hawkins, J.R.: Intravenous bufotenine injection in the human being. *Science, 123:*886-887, 1956.
17. Feldstein, A.: On the relationship of adrenaline and its oxidation products to schizophrenia. *Amer J Psychiat, 116:*454-456, 1959.
18. Friedman, H., and Taub, H.: Personal communication.
19. Gessner, P.K., McIsaac, W.M., and Page, I.H.: Pharmacological actions of some methoxy indolealkylamines. *Nature, 190:*179-180, 1961.
20. Hoffer, A., Osmond, H., and Smythies, J.R.: Schizophrenia: A new approach, II. Results of a year's research. *J Ment Sci, 100:*29-45, 1954.
21. Saavedra, J.M. and Udabe, U.: A report on hallucinogen effects. *Front of Hospit Psychiat, 7:*1, 1970.
22. Smythies, J.R.: Recent advances in the biochemistry of psychosis. *Lancet, 1:*1287-1289, 1960.
23. Szara, S.: Dimethyl tryptamin: Its metabolism in man. *Experientia. 12:* 441-442, 1956.
24. Szara, S.: Hallucinogenic effects and metabolism of tryptamine derivatives in man. *Fed Proc, 20:*885-888, 1961.
25. Szara, S.: In *Drugs in Research,* edited by Paul DeHaen. New York, 1964.
26. Szara, S., and Hearst, E.: The 6-Hydroxylation of tryptamine derivatives: A way of producing psychoactive metabolites. *Ann NY Acad Sci. 96:* 134-141, 1962.

Chapter 32

Mini-Delusions

A. N. Browne-Mayers, Edward E. Seelye,
David Brown and Maria Fleetwood

THIS CHAPTER will deal with the following questions: (a) Do mini-delusions occur in the drug-dependent patient? (b) Does drug dependence *increase* a susceptibility towards mini-delusions? and, incidentally, can mini-delusions occur in normal people?

Most contributors to the literature have concerned themselves with the type of delusions seen in the psychotic disorders. However, little has been written about this recently; yet research into delusional formation at one time occupied an important segment of psychiatry.[1]

Bleuler points out that delusions are incorrect ideas created not by an accredited insufficiency of logic but out of inner need. There are no other needs than the affective. Delusion is egocentric but may be attached to a particular idea, to a complex. (This shows the Jungian influence.) Other delusions are said to originate in hallucinations, deceptions of memory and in dreams.

This explanation is generally followed by many psychiatrists. The Heidelberg School, led by Jaspers[11] with contributions by Gruhle,[9] Schneider,[21] Chapman,[5] Mayer-Gross[17] has attempted to show how in schizophrenics the primary delusions are different. In their definition a delusion is not a disturbance of sensory perception, not a disturbance of apperception, not of intelligent grasp, but the disturbance is of symbolic meaning—that is, the world is, the world is twisted like its leg (meaning the legs of a table) .

Freud[8] and his followers saw delusions as a function of childhood and interplay of particular defense mechanisms, repression and projection, with homosexuality playing a large role in the evolution of the delusion.

H. Jackson,[10] followed by H. Ey,[7] considered delusion a product of some known or as yet unspecified illness which inhibits the function of the higher centers. This is not unlike the shattering of the ego by id impulses.

Not too far removed from this theory is that of the Pavlovians,[19,20] who see some type of inhibition working on the cerebral functions. More recently, delusion formation has been analyzed from the cultural aspects.[13,25,26,28]

Finally, Strauss[24] sees the conceptualization of hallucinations and delusions as points on a continuum of functions. The suggested parameters of this continuum are the degree of a patient's conviction of the objective reality of a bizarre experience, the degree of direct cultural or stimulus determined of an experience, the amount of time spent preoccupied with the experience, the degree of plausibility of an experience.

Solomon and Patch[22] point out in their *Handbook of Psychiatry* that delusional ideation occurs in (a) infections; (b) drug intoxications, amphetamines, LSD, alcohol, bromides, barbiturates, corticosteroids; (c) physiologically altered states, sleep deprivation, sensory deprivation, electrolyte imbalance; and (d) metabolic disorders: vitamin deficiencies and endocrinopathies.

Another comment is that we have studiously avoided bringing into this discussion the problem of delirium and twilight states.

However, the Heidelberg School, led by Jaspers and his followers, has delineated areas which are different from the overwhelming delusion of the psychotic. The notions of overvalued ideas or overrated ideas or dominant ideas are very close to what we have called mini-delusions.

The following are the characteristics of mini-delusions:

1. Mini-delusions are generally plausible and not bizarre. (They could have happened, they could be factual.)

2. The emotion or the affect accompanying the belief is generally within normal range (and acceptable) .

3. These mini-delusions do not occupy the whole spectrum of the patient's mental life.

4. The conviction in the mini-delusion is puzzling because it shows, clinically speaking, many forms. It disappears completely at times, reappears in other cases, is denied in still others, and is frequently rationalized.

5. Frequently the professional therapist does not realize he is listening to a mini-delusion because, as just stated, mini-delusions are usually plausible and reasonable when they appear.*

To sum up, the definition of a mini-delusion may be given as a circumscribed false belief rooted in the emotions, and this false belief alters behavior and often self and body image. It is the plausibility of the mini-delusion and the alteration of behavior which makes these little delusions hazardous for the individual and disruptive for those around him.

To further clarify the definition, a few clinical cases will now be given. First, some mini-delusions in the abusers of marijuana are relevant.

Case 1

A 15-year-old girl—a smoker of marijuana—came for psychotherapy after a second suicidal gesture by taking some barbiturates. She complained that whenever she smoked marijuana she had a peculiar reaction. She felt that there was a naked man in the bathtub beside her as she got ready for bed. She never looked to see whether the man was there, but was quite certain that he was (Compare Parkon-Stefanescu.[18]) The experience was accompanied by excitement and overpowering anxiety. The anxiety was so severe that the patient voluntarily gave up smoking marijuana. In this instance, the marijuana exacerbated the formation of a delusion which was the result of strong oedipal feelings toward her father which were stimulated by his rather seductive behavior towards her.

Case 2

A 30-year-old man came to analysis for problems of impotence. He had smoked marijuana twice. The patient reported that when he smoked marijuana, he experienced chest pain. The drug had apparently intensified his unconscious fantasy that he was having sex with a woman, but, at the same time, he was having a heart attack as a punishment for these desires. This case illustrates the alteration of body image as mentioned in the definition of mini-delusions.

The next examples are taken from the recently reorganized

*This formulation largely derived from Strauss.[24]

alcoholism unit at The New York Hospital (Westchester Division) where the authors of this chapter are the team psychiatrists.

Case 3

A 50-year-old professional man was hospitalized for alcoholism at The New York Hospital. He told his Board of Trustees that he and his wife had visited the campuses of several colleges where he was being considered as a candidate for the presidency of that college. The wife found out about this statement casually when she was asked how she liked the campuses they had visited. When the patient was confronted with the fact that his wife had denied going to these campuses, he maintained that she was inaccurate. The patient had a desire, and possibly a fantasy, that he was being groomed for a college presidency. He then mistook the fantasy for reality.

Case 4

This 40-year-old traveling salesman was also hospitalized for alcoholism. He told of a recurrent experience. When he was on a business trip and at times cast an eye at some attractive woman whom he encountered, he would dream at night that his wife was unfaithful to him. When he awoke in the morning, he would attempt to drown his feeling about his wife's infidelity by taking a drink. One drink led to another, and the more the patient drank, the more severe his worry about his wife's fidelity became. In this patient, alcoholism intensified his mini-delusion. In addition, his guilt feelings towards his wife's fidelity were projected. This case again demonstrates how drug dependence, and in this case the drug is alcohol, intensified the susceptibility to mini-delusions.

Case 5

A married woman in her late forties had the idea that a male patient was interested in her and in love with her. After leaving the hospital, this idea disappeared. However, when she was under the influence of alcohol she called the male patient and reiterated her delusion. This patient demonstrates how alcohol agitated the recurrence of the mini-delusion.

Case 6

This patient whose symptomatology has led us to the study and formulation of "mini-delusions" was a female alcoholic, on our wards for over one year. Her intermittent complaints, "when they took me off the Debutante Committee," proved in the course of investigations to be unfounded, since she had never been elected to said committee. When confronted with the truth, she rationalized her beliefs and seemed to abandon them. However, her complaints reappeared several weeks, and even months, later. As before, they were accompanied by a mild depression. Similarly, the patient tried to deny the danger of an impending divorce sought by her husband although her husband, her family and her psychiatrist had explicitly forewarned her.

We then became alerted and began to see whether this type of thinking was present in some of our other patients. Within a short period of time, we found two other patients suffering from the same type of false belief. They were not connected with any drug abuse. We called these psychopathological findings "mini-delusions."

DISCUSSION

The relation between mini-delusion and pathological lying is close. Schneider,[21] from the Heidelberg School, in speaking about pathological lying hints at one of our findings which is as follows: The patient, like some of the examples given, creates a conscious lie and then something strange happens—he unconsciously convinces himself that his lie is a fact. In this context, the lie is only one feature of a very complicated psychic event. Actually, in such instances we have a mini-delusion.

Now, the whole question of the difference between denial mechanisms, lying and delusions is not so easily answered. For instance, the amputee in the hospital bed who tells us that he can walk about easily is someone we doctors feel sorry for and acknowledge professionally that the amputee has a denial mechanism.

On the other hand, the alcoholism patient, at a different time, in the same bed, with all sorts of withdrawal symptoms from alcohol, tells us he has had nothing to drink. His friend might call him a liar—a damn liar.

Now, who is suffering from delusion—the amputee, the alcoholic or the friend? The amputee deludes himself that he can walk, and doctors understand the problem professionally; the alcoholic deludes himself by maintaining that he did not have anything to drink; but the friend, without professional knowledge, has deluded himself by giving a moral judgment about the alcoholic.

If delusions of the psychotic border on one side with mini-delusions, are there any other borders? Another border to the mini-delusions are the delusions of everyday life. Most psychiatrists up to this time have not particularly concerned themselves with this phenomenon, except possibly Masserman,[15,16] because they have apparently not considered these everyday delusions as sick or pathological. Like death and taxes, or the common cold, they have to be lived with, and we feel little can be done about them. Whether this acceptance of these delusions will persist forever remains to be seen but, before leaving the subject of everyday delusions, a few examples will help clarify what is being mentioned.

For instance, what hospitals have a thirteenth floor? The basis for this delusion is superstition. In terms of ethnic groups, an old saying about the American Indian is, "The only good Indian is a dead Indian." This delusional thinking is based on prejudice.

Children are brought up with the ending to many fairy tales—"And they lived happily ever after." This same theme is echoed frequently in movies and the adult TV screen. In this situation, optimism also gives rise to delusional thinking, and this can blind an individual to ordinary cues and signals of danger. In reverse, pessimism can do the same thing.

Now, about Santa Claus? In this charade for their children, the adults act out their hopes that they are kind and generous adults. This ties in rather well with a child's own hope that his parents are kind and generous.

From a different direction, we see and hear about toothpastes which give your mouth sex appeal. In this instance, the delusion arises out of body image concern.

Perhaps the unrest and revolt on the campus is partly an expression of fatigue and impatience with these reassuring delusions of adults. Even some children are no longer entranced by the delusions they have been taught.

Now back to the main theme of mini-delusions and drug abuse. If a part of our everyday life is spent in the midst of false belief, what happens when a chemical substance which is toxic is added to this mixture—to this "soup"? The results can be disastrous. This has been pointed out by Andrew Malcolm[14] in Canada, Dementev,[6] and I. Atkin[2] in England. The addition of chemical toxin—whether it be alcohol, mild or hard drugs—*increases* the susceptibility to the creation of false beliefs. This appears to be especially true of the adolescent whose emotional equilibrium is easily upset.

Because mini-delusions are plausible, numerous and easily passed over, even by the psychiatrists, they may be or may become a canker worm at the root of civilized man. Unnoticed, these delusions eat away the source of man's vitality for growth and achievement. Therefore, we have concluded that mini-delusions must have our attention.

SUMMARY

The concept of mini-delusions has been defined, and clinical examples of this disorder have been given. Generally speaking, the addition of a toxic substance nourishes the underlying psychopathology so that wishful thinking, fantasies, dreams and deceptions of memory overtake and cast aside the reality testing mechanisms. Projection, rationalization and denial are significant factors in this type of psychopathology.

REFERENCES

1. Arthur, A.Z.: Theories and explanations of delusions. A review. *Amer J Psychiat, 121:*105-115, 1964.
2. Atkin, I.: Difficult delusions. *Lancet,* p. 213-14, Jan. 31, 1953.
3. Baruk, H.: *Traitéde Psychiatrie*. Paris, Masson & Cie, 1959.
4. Bleuler, E.: *Textbook of Psychiatry* (4th German ed.) New York, Macmillan 1930.
5. Chapman, J.: The early symptoms of schizophrenia, *Brit J Psychiat, 112:* 225-279, 1966.
6. Dementev, A.P. *et al.:* Forensic psychiatric aspects of delusion of jealousy and its compulsory treatment, *Zh Nevropat Psikhiat Korsakov,* 63/100 (1544-1562) , 1963; in *Excerpta Medica (Neur. & Psych.), 17:*909, 1964.
7. Ey, H.: *Psychiatrie,* Paris, Encyclopedie Medico-Chirurgicale, 1955.
8. Freud, S.: Psychoanalytic notes upon an autobiographical account of a case of paranoia (dementia paranoids) . In *Collected Papers* (Vol. III) . London, Hogarth, 1950.
9. Gruhle, H.W.: Self-description empathy. *Z Ges Neurol Psychiat, 28:*148-272, 1915.
10. Jackson, J. Hughlings: *Neurological Fragments with Biographical Memoir by James Taylor.* London, Oxford University Press, 1925.

11. Jaspers, K.: *General Psychopathology.* Translated from 7th ed. by J. Hoenig and M.W. Hamilton, 1963. London, Manchester University Press, 1913a.

12. Kraepelin, Emil: *Lectures on Clinical Psychiatry.* New York, Hafner Publishing Co., 1968.

13. Lucas, C.J.: A social and clinical study of delusions in schizophrenia. *J Ment Sci, 108:*747-758, 1962.

14. Malcolm, A.: Illusionogens: What dangers. *Medical World News,* p. 34. April 17, 1970.

15. Masserman, J.H.: Say id isn't so with music. *Science & Psychoanalysis* (Vol. I). New York, Grune & Stratton, 1958, pp. 176-187.

16. Masserman, J.H.: The UR—defenses of man, pp. 465-485. The practice of dynamic psychiatry, pp. 465-485. In *Reorientations in Psychotherapy* Philadelphia, W.B. Saunders, 1955.

17. Mayer-Gross, Slater, E., and Roth, M.: *Clinical Psychiatry,* 3rd ed. Baltimore, Williams & Wilkins, 1969.

18. Parkon-Stefanescu, C., and Procupiu, Constantinescu, T.: *Ann Med Psychol* (Bucharest) *125* II/2 (253-259), 1967; *Excerpta Medica (Psychiatry), 21:*178, 1968.

19. Pawlov, I.P.: *J Ment Sci, 80:*187, 1934.

20. Pawlov, I.P.: *Psychopathology and Psychiatry.* Moscow, Foreign Languages, Publishing House, 1961.

21. Schneider, Kurt: *Clinical Psychopathology.* Translated by M.W. Hamilton. New York, Grune & Stratton, 1959.

22. Solomon, P., and Patcher, V.D.: *Handbook of Psychiatry.* Los Altos, Lange Medical Publications, 1969.

23. Sonneman, Ulrich: *Existence & Therapy.* New York, Grune & Stratton, 1954.

24. Strauss, J.S.: Hallucinations and delusions as points on continua of function. *Arch Gen Psychiat, 21:*581-586, 1969.

25. Weinstein, E.A.: Symbolic neurology and psychoanalysis, In *Modern Psychoanalysis,* edited by J. Marmor. New York, Basic Books, 1968.

26. Weinstein, E.A.: *Cultural Aspects of Delusion; A Psychiatric Study of the Virgin Islands.* Glencoe (N.Y.), Free Press 1962.

Chapter 33

Toxic Effects Following Ingestion of C-4 Plastic Explosive

James H. Knepshield and William J. Stone

COMPOSITION C-4 is the most common plastic explosive in use by field units in the Republic of Vietnam. It is a mixture of four potentially toxic substances: RDX, 91%; polyisobutylene, 2.1%; motor oil, 1.6%; and di-(2 ethylhexyl) sebacate, 5.3%. The chemical structure for the major component, RDX, is shown in Figure 33-1. RDX is a colorless crystal which is highly insolu-

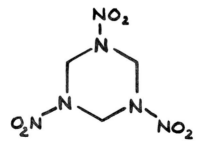

Figure 33-1.

ble in water (0.0076 gm/100 gm solvent at 25°C) [1] Because C-4 is a malleable solid, burns without explosion, and is relatively insensitive to impact or friction, C-4 can be easily transported and stored without undue precautions. A blasting cap is employed as a detonator. C-4 may even be used as a field cooking fuel when other sources of heat are unavailable. However, when ingested or inhaled in significant quantities, either by accident or intention, a dramatic clinical picture develops within a few hours. Generalized seizures, gross hematuria, severe nausea and vomiting, muscle twitching, and mentation changes are frequent presenting signs and symptoms.

It has become common knowledge among the field troops in Vietnam that the ingestion of a small quantity of this substance will produce a "high" similar to ethanol. The exact frequency of ingestion of this material is not known; however, several serious intoxications from this agent have been seen in every major military hospital in Vietnam. Toxic effects of C-4 have also involved the civilian community in the United States. Convulsions have occurred in factory workers who handle and pack this explosive.[2] Inhalation of the dust was incriminated. C-4 is a potential health hazard in the United States because of its availability on many military installations, although rigid control of its use makes this unlikely.

The six male patients summarized here had toxic effects from C-4 severe enough to warrant hospitalization (Table 33-I, 33-II).[3] Data for two patients are from a report by Merrill.[2] All patients were admitted to the hospital for the management of generalized seizures. When initially seen most patients were conscious but stared into space in a confused fashion. They were restless, un-

TABLE 33-I
PATIENTS WITH C-4 INTOXICATION

	Range	Average
Age	20–35 years	24 years
Estimated quantity ingested (3 patients)	25–180 gm	77 gm

TABLE 33-II
PATIENTS WITH C-4 INTOXICATION

Symptoms and Signs	#Positive/#Patients	%
Generalized seizures	6/6	100
Hematuria	5/6	83
Coma	4/6	67
Fever	4/6	67
Headaches	3/6	50
Lethargy	2/6	33
Nausea and vomiting	2/6	33
Oliguria	2/6	33

predictable and required restraints. At frequent intervals generalized seizures lasting one to two minutes occurred. Between seizures the state of consciousness varied from coma to lethargy. Other prominent symptoms and signs were severe neuromuscular irritability with muscular twitching and hyperactive reflexes, myalgias, bifrontal headaches, nausea, vomiting, gross hematuria and low-grade fever. Within forty-eight hours the patients were able to respond to their environment by answering simple questions and following directions. Orientation, concentration, recall and memory for recent and remote events were impaired. After one week the sensorium had cleared, however, remote memory continued to be deficient with spotty recall for both personal experiences and well-known general facts. Follow-up indicates that mental capacity had returned to normal in about one to two months. Neuromuscular irritability, gastrointestinal symptoms, hematuria and fever abated within forty-eight hours. Headaches persisted for one to three weeks.

The abnormal laboratory findings (Table 33-III—values cited are furthest deviations from normal) were a neutrophilic leukocytosis (12,000 to 41,000/cu mm), mild to moderate azotemia (20 to 69 mg/100 ml), an elevated serum glutamic oxaloacetic transaminase (170 to 1030 units), proteinuria, and hematuria. The following studies were generally normal: bromsulphalein retention, alkaline phosphatase, bilirubin, arterial pH, arterial pO_2 and pCO_2, hematocrit, serum electrolytes, methemoglobin concentration, chest roentgenogram and electrocardiogram. Within two

TABLE 33-III
PATIENTS WITH C-4 INTOXICATION

Laboratory	#Positive/#Patients	%
Anemia (HCT range 26%–36%)	4/6	67
Leukocytosis (WBC range 12,000–41,000 cell/cu mm)	6/6	100
Azotemia (BUN range 20–69 mg%)	5/6	83
Hyperbilirubinemia	0/6	0
Elevated SGOT (range 170–1,030 units)	5/6	83
Elevated alkaline phosphatase (range 48–89 units)	2/4	50
Elevated BSP retention (16.5%)	1/5	20
Normal liver biopsy	3/3	100

weeks all the abnormal tests returned to normal except for the hematocrit in one patient and urinary protein excretion in one patient.

During the first week following the ingestion of C-4, muscle, liver and renal biopsies were performed on a patient with an elevated serum glutamic oxaloacetic transaminase (354 units) and moderate azotemia with gross hematuria. The muscle biopsy was normal, however, muscle injury was still considered most likely because the patient complained of myalgias and muscle tenderness. Only a small portion of the latissimus dorsi was examined. The lack of hepatomegaly, absence of other abnormal liver function studies and a normal liver biopsy effectively excluded liver involvement. Renal biopsy showed minimal changes consisting of mild vacuolization of the proximal tubules most likely due to mannitol. In view of these findings a mild acute tubular necrosis would best explain the transient hematuria and azotemia. Although a glomerulitis could also account for these abnormalities, the absence of glomerular changes by light and electron microscopy in the renal biopsy obtained five days after the insult made this diagnosis improbable. The early administration of mannitol may have modified the course of acute tubular necrosis in this patient. Prerenal azotemia was excluded because congestive heart failure and volume depletion were not present in any of these patients. Additionally, a bone marrow aspiration was performed on the same patient because of a persistent normochromic, normocytic anemia. The findings of erythroid hypoplasia and a normal marrow iron content were consistent with toxic depression of the erythroid series. Mild anemia was found in three other patients.

Two abnormalities persisted in the patient who ingested the largest quantity of C-4. At the time of evacuation on the thirtieth hospital day, anemia (hematocrit 33%) and loss of memory for recent events were still present. The clinical course of this patient suggests that larger quantities may cause serious complications that persist for an extended period. The ingestion of a small quantity of C-4 (few grams) is unlikely to produce any serious long-term adverse effects.

The management of C-4 intoxication consists of (a) early gastric lavage; (b) maintenance of an airway and prevention of aspiration of gastric contents; (c) control of seizures with anticonvulsants; (d) monitoring of hourly urine volume to detect acute renal insufficiency at its onset; and (e) maintenance of normal fluid and electrolyte balance. If oliguria (< 25 ml urine/hour) develops in a normal state of hydration, a test dose of 25 gm of mannitol or 200 mg of furosemide should be administered intravenously. If a diuresis does not ensue, an organic acute renal failure regimen should be instituted. From its chemical structure and solubility characteristics, aqueous hemodialysis or peritoneal dialysis would not remove significant quantities of RDX, which we presume to be the cause of the toxic effects of C-4. The other constituents of composition C-4 are large molecules in low concentrations and are probably nontoxic in the quantities ingested. We were able to dissolve C-4 in cottonseed oil indicating RDX is lipid soluble. Therefore RDX is probably selectively accumulated in the central nervous system and body fat similarly to thiopental and glutethimide. This suggests that hemodialysis utilizing soybean oil or cottonseed oil in the bath may be beneficial in the critically ill patient. No patient with C-4 intoxication has required dialysis to date. To our knowledge no deaths have occurred due to C-4 intoxication.

The clinical picture of C-4 intoxication is unique. The sudden onset of multiple generalized seizures and hematuria in a previously healthy individual in a military environment should strongly suggest this diagnosis. Army physicians now recognize C-4 intoxications as by far the most common cause of recurring generalized seizures in Vietnam. Physicians newly assigned to Vietnam should be particularly aware of this intoxication and its treatment.

SUMMARY

Composition C-4 is the most common plastic explosive employed by the military in Vietnam. Ingestion is followed in a few hours by multiple generalized seizures, hematuria, severe nausea and vomiting, muscle twitching and mentation changes. Six cases are presented and therapeutic recommendations are made.

REFERENCES

1. Department of the Army: *Military Explosives.* TM 9-1910, para. 55 and 66, 1955.
2. Merrill, S. L.: Ingestion of an explosive material, composition C-4: A report of two cases. *USARV Med Bull, 3:*5-11, (March-April), 1968.
3. Stone, W. J., Paletta, T. L., Heiman, E. M., Bruce, J. I., and Knepshield, J. H.: Toxic effects following ingestion of C-4 plastic explosive. *Arch Int Med, 124:*726-730, 1969.

Chapter 34

Amphetamine Psychosis: Systems and Subjects

Everett H. Ellinwood, Jr.

IN A SERIES OF STUDIES several years ago, we found that psychopathic and borderline schizophrenic individuals are more prone to abuse amphetamines than any other specific diagnostic group. Also, schizoid and borderline schizophrenics tend to be more susceptible to developing the psychosis.[1] The predilection of these individuals to the use of amphetamines and secondarily to develop the amphetamine psychosis does not, however, explain the fairly constant form of the psychosis, usually a paranoid schizophrenic-like psychosis with certain rather constricted symptom clusters. From observations of the nature of these stereotyped behavioral patterns in humans as well as in lower animals chronically intoxicated with amphetamine, it appears that central nervous system arousal and attention mechanisms are being stimulated and are, in part, responsible for the form of the psychosis. The main thesis of this chapter is that there is a need for further phenomenological examination of the specific behaviors associated with amphetamine-induced CNS arousal. With further delineation of these behaviors both in humans as well as in lower animals, the psychotic state itself can better be understood.

The symptoms most intimately related to the evolving paranoid psychosis, because of their cognitive-perceptual nature, are difficult to directly correlate with behavioral manifestations in lower animals. There are, however, several remarkable behavioral similarities. Fear and suspicion-associated looking movements in humans with chronic amphetamine intoxication are often described even by the user himself. One individual related his own furtive, side-to-side looking, as an attempt to see who was beside and behind him without their noticing that he was looking. He described in somewhat elaborate detail his ability to look in store windows while walking and see both beside as well as behind himself. Other individuals described spending many long hours spying on people from hidden positions. One individual even went so far as to construct an elaborate system of mirrors that he might spy on people walking in the street below his window without his being seen. Evolving episodes of suspicousness appear directly related to this type of enhanced looking behavior in humans, some of whom proceed to develop the amphetamine paranoid psychosis. In lower animals such as the cat, monkey and chimpanzee, one also frequently notes side-to-side looking movements with chronic amphetamine intoxication. These behaviors evolve into intricate stereotyped patterns. In addition, certain monkeys develop repetitious ad-mixtures of eye avoidance and sideward glancing and peeking. One rhesus monkey intoxicated with methamphetamine for over five months developed a repetitious pattern of head-turning and sideward glancing. Several animals developed pronounced fearful side-to-side looking movements which would continue for two to three hours at a time.

Perhaps a more easily reconcilable common denominator of amphetamine-induced behavior across several species are the stereotyped patterns of searching and examining. At least the stereotyped motor components of these attending processes are present in all species intoxicated with amphetamine. In macronosmatic animals the primary stereotyped mode is that of sniffing. In higher mammals, one begins to note stereotyped looking-examining behaviors. In primates, a new dimension is added with the advent of eye-hand examination patterns. These eye-hand coordinated movements are quite specific and consist primarily of picking or forefinger probing, hand clasping and hand examination. Similar eye-hand coordinated movements are involved in examination of both external objects as well as in self-grooming. For example, the picking-examining component was often applied alternately to minute external objects and then to the animals' body. Often the monkey was observed in prolonged examination of his legs, arms and other parts of his body as if in search of parasites. The *abnormal feature* of this grooming response was its continuous repeti-

tous nature. Often grooming stereotypes were noted up to two
to three hours in duration; many monkeys induced rather extensive dermal excoriations. In all of these examining behaviors, the
rhesus monkey appeared to have its perceptual acuity primarily
directed towards small bits or minute objects (Fig. 34-1).

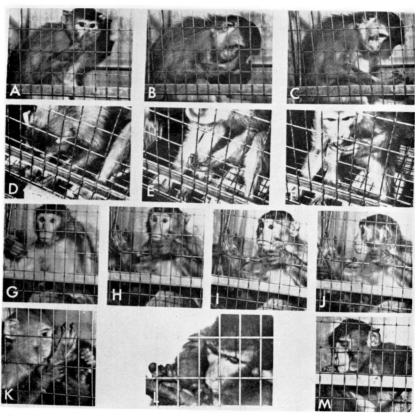

Figure 34-1. Stereotype examining and looking patterns. A-C and D-F clasp-
hand examination. G-I avoidance looking. J-K bimanual grooming. L-M
hand-mouth examination.

In humans, amphetamine-induced "grooming behavior" is not
unlike that noted in rhesus monkeys and is usually manifest as an
excessive examining, rubbing and picking which results in raw

blemishes and scars. Quite often, there is a compulsive pattern of unconsciously rubbing or probing an area with the forefinger, locating a "follicular plug" or repairative crust of a previous injury, and digging with the fingernail until an excoriation is effected. At other times, the individual may spend up to an hour examining various parts of the body as well as probing and looking at visually accessible parts (one-way screen observations by the author). Often the individual develops very stereotyped delusions of parasitosis. Many of these believe that they have minute parasites encysted under the skin or that small mites or lice have dug into the surface of the skin. As with the "cocaine bug" described in the early German literature, often the individual will not only attempt to dig these parasites out with fingernails but subsequently will use knives, needles or other instruments to extract these imaginative parasites.

In amphetamine-intoxicated individuals, there is often a rather intense curiosity and the individual may find himself engaged in repetitious examining, dismantling or rearranging tasks. There is a marked perceptual acuity associated with small bits or minute objects as with monkeys. At times there are perceptuomotor compulsions manifested as repetitious stringing of beads, acts of arranging, sorting and lining up pebbles, rocks or other small objects, and indeed most of the so-called "speed art" is replete with complicated syntheses of a multitude of minute details often depicting universal themes or mandalas. More paranoid patients tend to search intensely for minute signs and meanings. One patient stated, "I looked everywhere for clues, under rugs, behind pictures, and I took things apart; I read magazines looking at the periods with a magnifying glass for codes . . . . They were to help me solve the mystery." Another patient followed an hallucinated trail of small buttons down the street. One individual tiled his entire apartment including the walls with Armstrong vinyl pebble tiling and painted the individual small pebbles in various arrays of red, gold and black. There are frequent descriptions of taking objects apart to analyze, sort and, on rare occasions, to put the objects back together; this includes TV sets, watches, radios and phonographs. Subsequently, the various parts might be arranged, sorted, filed and catalogued. This reported repetitious behavior has been variously called pundning by Rylander,[3] obsessive compulsive tendencies,[1,2] and knick-knacking by the Haight-Ashbury inhabitants. Quite often repetitious behavior was associated with an intense "pleasurable" sense of curiosity. Other patients report simply a sense of satisfaction just from repetitiously repeating the same act. For example, some patients literally spend days cleaning various objects or polishing a car.

Currently, we are quantitatively documenting our findings in monkeys and cats by means of television recordings and subsequent analysis of behavior on rating scales. The period of amphetamine intoxication extends from two weeks to eight months; thus allowing for considerable documentation of evolving patterns of perceptuomotor responses. Thus far, the data confirms that there are several forms of behavior that are enhanced by amphetamines and that certain of these behavioral patterns interact in a potentiating manner. Emotional enhancement or central nervous system stimulation of certain perceptuomotor behaviors would have considerable relevance to the question of how psychosis is engendered in humans. Our operating hypotheses, in humans, is that amphetamines enhance certain forms of thinking, examining and attention to detail, as well as enhancing certain forms of hyperactive peripheral attention, suspiciousness and fear. These behavioral patterns interacting together within the context of a given individual's personality and his environment then leads to the evolution of paranoid delusion systems.

REFERENCES

1. Ellinwood, E. H.: Amphetamine psychosis. A description of the individuals and process. *J Nerv Ment Dis, 144*:273-283, 1967.
2. Kramer, J. C., Fischman, V. S., and Littlefield, D. C.: Amphetamine abuse. Pattern and effects of high doses taken intravenously. *JAMA, 201*:305-309, 1967.
3. Rylander, G.: Preludin-narkomaner fran klinish och medicinskkriminologisk synpundt. *Svensk Tandlak T, 63*:4973-4979, 1966.

Chapter 35

Oxymorphone Abuse Among Narcotic Addicts

Torrington D. Watkins and Carl D. Chambers

~~~~~~

NUMORPHAN® (oxymorphone), a narcotic analgesic developed and first marketed by Endo Laboratories in 1966, has become a drug of abuse among a sizeable segment of the narcotic addict population. Numorphan is one of the newer semisynthetic narcotics with a rapid onset of action and a prolonged duration of effect. When administered parenterally, Numorphan is about ten times more potent than morphine and is twice as potent as morphine when administered orally.[6,7] These action characteristics of the drug make it an obvious choice for abuse by narcotic addicts.

BACKGROUND

Our information indicates the abuse of Numorphan among street addicts began as early as 1968. Since that time, Numorphan has become a preference drug among a small number of addicts and a supplementary drug among a large number of addicts.

On the "street," Numorphan can be identified by its various subcultural names—numorphine, blue morphine, blue morphan or blues. These slang names are derived from the light blue color of the Numorphan tablet and from its identification with morphine.

Although Numorphan is manufactured in injectable form, the street addict does not normally have access to this form of the drug. The street addict typically will obtain the drug in 10-mg tablets which are then prepared for injection by crushing, diluting with water, "cooking" and straining. The normal route for administering the preparation is intravenous. Subcutaneous injections reportedly result in immediate localized irritation and abscesses appear at the site of the injection. When prepared and injected in this manner, a 10-mg tablet of Numorphan reportedly has the same intensity of immediate effect—rush—as a $10 bag of heroin, but with twice the duration. The extended effects—high— from a 10-mg Numorphan injection can be expected to last for about six hours while the effects of a heroin injection will dissipate and drug craving will return in about four hours.

Our current investigators indicate the price of Numorphan in the illicit subcultures is comparable to and directly related to the cost of heroin in the specific subculture. For example, if the price for one bag of heroin is $10, the price of a 10-mg Numorphan tablet is usually $10. If for some reason the price of heroin decreases to $7 or $5 a bag, the price of Numorphan correspondingly drops.

Although some Numorphan is diverted into the illicit subculture through theft of drug supplies or forged prescriptions, the typical source is the unsuspecting or misguided physician who is "hustled" into prescribing large supplies of the drug. We have encountered addicts who prefer Numorphan over all other narcotics and who build tolerances in excess of 400 mg per day which they support by "hustling" several physicians. More typically, however, the enterprising addict will "make" a physician for one hundred 10-mg tablets which he purchases for around $20. He then sells fifty tablets at $10 per tablet and buys heroin with the $500. The remaining fifty tablets he uses to supplement or increase the potency of his heroin or as a substitute when his heroin supply has become exhausted, his heroin supplier is not available, et cetera. A contemporary ruse is to admit ones addiction to a sympathetic physician and to convince him that Numorphan "works" like methadone. It does not appear to be overly difficult to secure ones stated "stabilized" daily dose—50 to 100 mg—in this manner. If the physician prescribes methadone instead, the methadone can be diverted with the same ease but without the profit. Ten milligrams of methadone can be marketed for only about $1 or one tenth of the price of illicit Numorphan. At least a portion of this diversion can be attributed to some physicians' mistaken belief that the Numorphan tablets are not soluble.

THE PREVALENCE OF NUMORPHAN ABUSE

The abuse of Numorphan appears to be rather widespread geographically. Without any systematic attempt to gather case histories, we have discovered Numorphan addicts in Florida, Kentucky, Pennsylvania and New York. In addition to these areas, Numorphan supplementers have been encountered in as diverse places as Tennessee, Illinois, New Jersey, Texas and California. Our most complete prevalency data were obtained among narcotic addicts in Philadelphia, Pennsylvania and our report focusses upon this study population.

During January of 1970, the 309 addict-patients undergoing detoxification or who were methadone maintenance patients at the Narcotic Addict Rehabilitation Program outpatient clinics of the Philadelphia General Hospital were interviewed relevant to Numorphan abuse. Of the 309 addict-patients, sixty-two—20.1 percent —reported they had abused Numorphan one or more times. The majority of these sixty-two Numorphan abusers had been supplementing abusers—95.2 percent—with only three reporting they had abused Numorphan exclusively for one or more weeks. A number of others indicated a preference for the drug over heroin but heroin had been more readily available and carried less risk; one did not have to confront suspicious physicians, present forged prescriptions or break into pharmacies to obtain heroin. Possibly related to the low incidence of total substitution of Numorphan for heroin is the subcultural belief that tolerance to Numorphan builds very quickly thereby increasing the cost of ones habit.

A COMPARISON BETWEEN ABUSERS AND NONABUSERS

Statistical comparisons between the sixty-two narcotic addicts who had histories of Numorphan abuse and the 247 who did not revealed a number of significant differences.

If one combines race, sex and age to form various cohorts, the following is evident:

1. White males, regardless of age, had been Numorphan abusers at approximately the same rate—40 percent.

2. Only white females age 25 or less had been Numorphan abusers.

TABLE 35-I

HE ASSOCIATION OF RACE, SEX AND AGE WITH NUMORPHAN ABUSE

Race—Sex—Age Cohorts	*Abusers*		*Nonabusers*		*Total*	
	N	%	N	%	N	%
White Males						
Aged 25—	23	40.4	34	59.6	57	100.0
26+	23	42.6	31	57.4	54	100.0
White Females						
Aged 25—	7	53.8	6	46.2	13	100.0
26+	0	—	7	100.0	7	100.0
Black Males						
Aged 25—	2	10.5	17	89.5	19	100.0
26+	7	6.3	104	93.7	111	100.0
Black Females						
Aged 25—	0	—	7	100.0	7	100.0
26+	0	—	27	100.0	27	100.0
Total						
Aged 25—	32	33.3	64	66.7	96	100.0
26+	30	15.1	169	84.9	199	100.0
Median Ages	24.8 Years		31.2 Years		29.7 Years	

These combinations suggest the overwhelming importance of race in the abuse of Numorphan, the minor association of sex in this type of abuse and the artifact association with age.

3. Black males, regardless of age, had been Numorphan abusers at approximately the same rate—10 percent—but this rate was only one fourth of the rate among white males.

4. No black females were found to have been Numorphan abusers.

GEOGRAPHICAL DIFFERENCES IN NUMORPHAN ABUSE

We have just begun to document the prevalence of Numorphan abuse within various narcotic addict populations. There would appear to be considerable variance in this form of drug abuse.

A precursory analysis of recent admissions to the Narcotic Addict Rehabilitation Act (NARA) program at the Lexington, Kentucky Clinical Research Center indicated only 5.6 percent of these addicts, drawn from throughout the United States, had ever abused Numorphan. This type of abuse appeared to be most fre-

quently associated with white addicts from southern areas who abused a number of legally manufactured and distributed narcotics.

In an attempt to assess prevalency among New York City addicts, all of the residents (N=175) at one of the Narcotic Addiction Control Commission's residential facilities were interviewed concerning any abuse of this drug. Only 2.9 percent reported they had abused Numorphan. All of the abusers were white males within this all-male institution.

COMMENTS AND DISCUSSION

We have demonstrated the rather widespread abuse of one of the newer semisynthetic narcotics—Numorphan. Numorphan is currently being abused both as a preference drug and as a drug to supplement other narcotic "habits." Although the prevalence of Numorphan abuse was found to vary from a low of 2.9 percent to a high of 20.1 percent within various narcotic addict populations, the abuse of Numorphan was found to be primarily a white pattern of abuse.

The wide variance of prevalency and the concentration of the abuse within the white addicts suggests we are seeing the first stages in the evolution of this drug abuse pattern. White addicts with their more ready access to legitimate drugs from physicians and pharmacists have traditionally been the initiators of the abuse of new drugs.[1-5,8] Physicians should be especially alert to this form of abuse. We are beginning to accumulate case histories of Numorphan addicts. In profile, these Numorphan addicts seem to be either young (21 to 25) white males who purchase all of their Numorphan from "pushers" with an occasional supplementation from pharmacy burglaries, et cetera, or older (40 to 50) white males who obtain prescriptions from a network of physicians and rarely if ever obtain any Numorphan from "pushers." Daily doses among the older abusers are more reminiscent of the morphine addicts of the 1940's—200 to 600 mg daily. These high doses would, of course, produce significantly greater withdrawal distress and require withdrawal regimens commensurate with the dose level.

REFERENCES

1. Ball, J.C.: Two patterns of narcotic drug addiction in the United States. *J Crim Law, Criminol Pol Sci, 56:*203-211, 1965.
2. Chambers, C.D.: Barbiturate-sedative abuse: A study of prevalence among narcotic abusers. *Int J Addict, 4:*45-57, 1969.
3. Chambers, C.D., and Moldestad, M.: The evolution of concurrent opiate and sedative addictions. In *The Epidemiology of Opiate Addiction in the United States,* edited by J.C. Ball, and C.D. Chambers. Springfield, Charles C Thomas, 1970.
4. Chambers, C.D., Hinesley, R.K., and Moldestad, M.: Narcotic addiction in females: A race comparison. *Int J Addict, 5:*257-278, 1970.
5. Chambers, C.D., Moffett, A.D., and Cuskey, W.R.: Five patterns of Darvon abuse. *Int J Addict, 5,* 1971.
6. Endo Laboratories: Numorphan—an advance in analgesia, Garden City (N.Y.) , Endo Laboratories, Dec. 1966.
7. Medical Economics, Inc.: *Physicians' Desk Reference,* 24th ed. Oradell (N.J.) , Litton Publishing Co., 1969, p. 703.
8. Moffett, A.D., and Chambers, C.D.: The hidden addiction. *Social Work, 15:*54-59, 1970.

Chapter 36

Cocaine Abuse Among Methadone Maintenance Patients

W. J. Russell Taylor, Carl D. Chambers and Richard Dembo

T HE EFFICACY of methadone maintenance treatment for chronic narcotic addiction has been well documented in the literature (see references at the end of the chapter). However, while methadone offers an effective cross-tolerance or blockade to the euphoric effects of opiate use, it does not prevent intrapsychic reaction to other abuse-prone substances. For this reason adequate laboratory surveilance to detect the use or abuse of nonopiate dependence-producing drugs has been accepted as a necessary adjunct to the proper management of any methadone substitution program.

The abuse of cocaine among maintenance patients has become a matter of concern to professionals administering substitution programs. Increasing evidence of widespread cocaine abuse prompted the development of a simple and reliable urine-screening method to separate cocaine from methadone during the thin-layer chromatographic process using cation exchange paper (see chapter appendix for a detailed description of the detection process). The development of this testing procedure was accomplished at the Clinical Pharmacology-Toxicology Center at the Philadelphia General Hospital. This procedure permitted the documenting of rather widespread abuse of cocaine among 173 known heroin addicts participating in the Philadelphia General Hospital outpatient methadone maintenance program; urines for 18.5 percent (N = 32) of all the patients were found to contain cocaine.

The present chapter presents the results of our analyses comparing cocaine "cheaters" and "noncheaters" on selected social, deviant behavior, adjustment and total substance abuse paramet-

Drug Abuse

ers. The detected cheating patterns of both groups were also studied. The data evaluated were derived for all clients participating in the outpatient maintenance program during the month of December, 1969.

RESULTS

The statistical comparison between the thirty-two methadone maintenance patients who were cocaine cheaters and the 141 who were not abusing cocaine produced a number of significant differences.

TABLE 36-I
COMPARISONS OF BASIC DEMOGRAPHIC CHARACTERISTICS

Characteristics	Cocaine Abusers (N=32) N	%	Nonabusers (N=141) N	%	Total (N=173) N	%	Chi-square Test For Difference
1. *Age*							
A. <35	12	37.5	85	60.3	97	56.1	$X^2=5.50$
B. 35/Above	20	62.5	56	39.7	76	43.9	P=<.05
2. *Race*							
A. White	11	34.4	90	63.8	101	58.4	$X^2=9.31$;
B. Black	21	65.6	51	36.2	72	41.6	P=<.01
3. *Sex*							
A. Male	30	93.8	123	87.2	153	88.4	No difference
B. Female	2	6.2	18	12.8	20	11.6	
4. *Education*							
A. 12	25	78.1	88	62.4	113	65.3	No difference
B. 12/Above	7	21.9	53	37.6	60	34.7	
5. *Marital Status*							
A. Single	4	12.5	33	23.4	37	21.4	$X^2=6.17$;
B. Married	15	46.9	79	56.0	94	54.3	P=<.05
C. Divorced/Widowed	13	40.6	29	20.6	42	24.3	(2 degrees freedom)
6. *Working At Admission*							
A. Yes	6	18.8	63	44.7	69	39.9	$X^2=7.31$;
B. No	26	81.2	78	55.3	104	60.1	P=<.01
7. *Legal Status*							
A. Probation/Parole	13	40.6	50	35.5	63	36.4	No difference
B. Cases Pending	3	9.4	19	13.5	22	12.7	
C. Both of Above	2	6.2	1	.7	3	1.7	
D. None of Above	14	43.8	71	50.4	85	49.1	

Note: Some percentages do not total 100 due to rounding.

Basic Demographic Characteristics

1. A majority of the 173 maintained addict-patients were under the age of 35 (N = 97 or 56.1 percent). Cocaine cheating was significantly related to the older addict-patients. Among the cocaine abusers, 62.5 percent were *over* 35 while 60.3 percent of the noncheaters were *under* age 35 ($X^2 = 5.50$; P = < .05). The mean age of the total study group was 32.9 years, the mean age of the cocaine cheaters was 36.4 years and that of the noncheaters was 32.1 years. The strength of this age relationship was further demonstrated by ascertaining that only 12.4 percent of those addict-patients under age 25 were cocaine cheaters while 26.3 percent of those age 35 or older were detected as cheaters.

2. Cocaine cheating was found to be significantly related to the race of the addict-patients. While the total maintained population was 58.4 percent white and 41.6 percent black, the cocaine-cheating subpopulation was only 34.4 percent white and 65.6 percent black ($X^2 = 9.31$; P = < .01), while only 10.9 percent of the white addict-patients were found to be cheating with cocaine, 29.2 percent of the black patients were. The finding that cocaine cheaters tended to be black is consistent with data "from the street" that cocaine is generally more available in the black communities than in the white communities.

3. Cocaine abuse is most frequently a male phenomenon. Within this study population, 19.6 percent of all the male addict-patients were cheating with cocaine while only 10.0 percent of the females were found to be doing so. There was, however, no significant sex distribution differences between the cocaine abusers and nonabusers—93.8 percent of the cocaine abusers were male as were 87.2 percent of the nonabusers.

4. Our analysis indicated that the cocaine abusers were less likely to be single or married and more likely to be divorced or widowed than the nonabusers ($X^2 = 6.17$; 2 df; P = < .05). Over 40 percent of the cocaine abusers were found to be divorced or widowed—occurring twice as often as among nonabusers. Almost one third of all divorced or widowed patients were abusing cocaine as compared to 10.8 percent of the single patients and 16.0 percent of the married patients. We do not know, however, how

much of this status is attributable to the significantly higher ages among the cocaine abusers.

5. It was apparent that within our study population, those addicts who were maintaining a legal work role at the time they were admitted into treatment are significantly less often cocaine cheaters. Only 18.8 percent of the cocaine cheaters were working at the time of admission compared to 44.7 percent of the non-cheaters ($X^2 = 7.31$; $P = < .01$). The strength of this association can be seen when stated somewhat differently. Of all the addicts working at time of admission, only 8.7 percent found to be cheating with cocaine while 25.0 percent of those who had not been working were detected as cocaine cheaters.

Related Deviancy Characteristics

1. Cocaine abuse was found to be significantly related to length of the addict-patients' drug-taking career. Over 80 percent —81.3 percent to be precise—of the cocaine cheaters had been abusing drugs, primarily heroin, for a minimum of ten years as compared to 53.2 percent of the noncheaters ($X^2 = 8.45$; $P = <$

TABLE 36-II

COMPARISONS OF SELECTED RELATED DEVIANCY CHARACTERISTICS

Characteristics	Cocaine Abusers (N=32) N	%	Nonabusers (N=141) N	%	Total (N=173) N	%	Chi-square Test For Difference
1. *Heroin Addict*							
A. Yes	31	96.8	138	97.9	169	97.7	No difference
B. No	1	3.2	3	2.1	4	2.3	
2. *Years of Drug Use*							
A. <10	6	18.7	66	46.8	72	41.6	X^2=8.45;
B. 10/Above	26	81.3	75	53.2	101	58.4	P=<.01
3. *Previous Treatment*							
A. Yes	25	78.1	92	65.2	117	67.6	No difference
B. No	7	21.9	49	34.8	56	32.4	
4. *Arrests (Total)*							
A. None	2	6.2	18	12.8	20	11.6	No difference
B. 1–4	11	34.4	46	32.6	57	32.9	
C. 5–14	12	37.5	59	41.8	71	41.0	
D. 15/Above	7	21.9	18	12.8	25	14.5	

.01). Stated differently, only 8.3 percent of those with abuse histories of less than ten years were cocaine cheaters but 25.7 percent of those with more than ten years were cocaine cheaters.

2. Cocaine cheaters were more frequently found to have previously undergone treatments for their addictions—78.1 percent of the cheaters versus 65.2 percent of the noncheaters. Although the differences are not statistically significant, only 12.5 percent of those addicts with no treatment experience became cocaine cheaters during this current treatment attempt, while among the more experienced, 21.4 percent violated their treatment by cheating with cocaine.

3. Cocaine cheaters were found more frequently among those who had extensive arrest histories. Although the differences are not statistically significant, only 10.0 percent of the addicts with no arrests were detected cocaine cheaters while 19.6 percent of those with arrest histories were found to be cocaine abusers. Again, this may be an age factor difference.

Treatment and Adjustment Characteristics

1. The majority of cocaine cheaters—84.3 percent—had been stabilized at daily methadone doses of at least 100 mg. Although high-dose addict-patients were more likely to be cocaine cheaters than noncheaters—84.3 percent versus 75.2 percent—the distributions were not statistically different. It should be noted, however, that while 20.3 percent of all the patients stabilized at 100 mg or more, were found to be cheating with cocaine, only 12.5 percent of those stabilized at lower doses were doing so.

2. At least in this Philadelphia General Hospital Clinic, the number of required clinic visits is related to how one's counselors perceive the treatment progress. For example, the "better" one is doing, the fewer the number of visits. Most addict-patients, regardless of their cocaine-cheating status, were reporting to the clinic five days per week with everyone taking home a weekend supply of methadone. Although the differences were not statistically significant, the more frequently one was required to report to the clinic, the more often he was likely to be one of the cocaine cheaters—19.6 percent of those who reported five times per week

TABLE 36-III

COMPARISONS OF TREATMENT AND ADJUSTMENT CHARACTERISTICS
(All distributions are for the 30-day study period)

Characteristics	Cocaine Abusers (N=32) N	%	Nonabusers (N=141) N	%	Total (N=173) N	%	Chi-square Test For Difference
I. *Treatment*							
1. *Daily methadone dose*							
A. <100 mg	5	15.6	35	24.3	40	23.1	No difference
B. 100 mg/Above	27	84.3	106	75.2	133	76.9	
2. *Weekly clinic visits*							
A. Once	–	–	2	1.5	2	1.2	No difference
B. One	3	9.4	3	2.2	6	3.5	
C. Two	1	3.1	15	11.3	16	9.2	
D. Three	8	25.0	34	22.6	42	24.3	
E. Four	–	–	–	–	–	–	
F. Five	20	62.5	87	62.4	107	61.8	
3. *Other chemotherapy*							
A. Yes	5	15.6	36	25.5	41	23.7	No difference
B. No	27	84.4	105	74.5	132	76.3	
II. *Adjustment Indices*							
1. *Any criminal behavior*							
A. Yes	9	28.1	14	9.9	23	13.3	X^2=7.49;
B. No	23	71.9	127	90.1	150	86.7	P=<.01
2. *Any arrests*							
A. Yes	1	3.1	1	.7	2	1.2	No difference
B. No	31	96.9	140	99.3	171	98.8	
3. *Working*							
A. Yes	13	40.6	56	39.7	69	39.9	No difference
B. No	19	59.4	85	60.3	104	60.1	
A. White Collar	2	6.3	6	4.2	8	4.6	No difference
B. Skilled/Semiskilled	5	15.6	18	12.8	23	13.3	
C. Unskilled	6	18.8	32	22.7	38	22.0	
D. Not Working	19	59.3	85	60.3	104	60.1	
4. *Receiving welfare*							
A. Yes	10	31.3	52	36.9	62	35.8	No difference
B. No	22	68.7	89	63.1	111	64.2	

were cocaine cheaters as compared to 6.3 percent of those reporting only twice a week.

3. The incidence of concurrent chemotherapy, for example, sedatives, tranquilizers, et cetera, is also an index of how well one is doing in the maintenance program. A substantial number of the addict-patients—23.7 percent—were receiving psychotropic medication. Nonabusers of cocaine were more frequently receiving the concurrent chemotherapy than were the cocaine cheaters— 25.5 percent versus 15.6 percent. This difference is not, however, statistically significant. While we are unsure of the interpretation, we did find that only 12.2 percent of those who were receiving a psychotropic medication were among the cocaine cheaters, while 20.5 percent of those not receiving the medication were cocaine cheaters.

4. One of the most potent associations discovered in this study was between a continuation of criminal involvement while undergoing treatment and cheating with cocaine. We found 39.1 percent of those who continued their criminal activities were also cocaine cheaters. Only 9.9 percent of the noncheaters were criminally involved but 28.1 percent of the cocaine cheaters had remained involved. This difference is statistically different ($X^2 = 7.49; P = < .01$).

Other Cheating

The urine surveillance program includes routine tests for the presence of methadone, opiates other than methadone, amphetamines and barbiturates. Substantial abuse with all of these drugs was detected in our study population.

All of the addict-patients had methadone in their urines indicating they were taking at least a portion of their medicine. However, 15.0 percent reportedly were supplementing their daily doses with methadone purchased from other patients, purchased from patients from other programs or from physicians who could be "hustled" into prescribing the drug illegally. In addition to this supplementation, 84.2 percent were found to have cheated with heroin, 60.8 percent with amphetamines and 32.2 percent with the barbiturates.

TABLE 36-IV
COMPARISONS OF THE ABUSE OF DRUGS BESIDES COCAINE

Other "Cheating"	Cocaine Abusers (N=32)		Nonabusers*** (N=141)		Total (N=173)		Chi-square Test For Difference
	N	%	N	%	N	%	
1. *Extra Methadone**							
A. Yes	3	9.4	23	16.3	26	15.0	No difference
B. No	29	90.6	118	83.7	147	85.0	
2. *Heroin***							
A. Yes	30	93.8	114	82.0	144	84.2	No difference
B. No	2	6.2	25	18.0	27	15.8	
3. *Other Opiates***							
A. Yes	8	25.0	46	33.1	54	31.6	No difference
B. No	24	75.0	93	66.9	117	68.4	
4. *Amphetamines***							
A. Yes	20	62.5	84	60.4	104	60.8	No difference
B. No	12	37.5	55	39.6	67	39.2	
5. *Barbiturates***							
A. Yes	15	46.9	40	28.8	55	32.2	$X^2=3.90$;
B. No	17	53.1	99	71.2	116	67.8	$P=<.05$
6. *No Cheating Except With* Cocaine/No Cheating	1	3.1	14	10.1	15	8.8	No difference

*Admitted abuse on interview

**Detected with urinalysis

***Urines were not available for 2 subjects who were not required to come to the clinic to receive their medication. The N for items 2-5 is 139 and the total N for the same items is 171.

A comparison between the cocaine abusers and nonabusers with respect to their concurrent abuse of the other drugs indicated: cocaine abusers less frequently supplemented their methadone dose but cocaine abusers more frequently cheated with heroin, amphetamines and barbiturates. Only the difference between the two groups on barbiturate cheating, however, was statistically significant—46.9 percent versus 28.8 percent were barbiturate cheaters $(X^2 = 3.90; P = < .05)$.

SUMMARY

Our results indicate a rather high incidence of cocaine abuse among methadone maintenance patients—18.5 percent. The high-

est incidence of this form of abuse was among the black male patients over age 35 who had been heroin addicts for more than
ten years. These cocaine cheaters were also abusing drugs other
than cocaine and had continued to engage in illegal activities
even though they no longer could rationalize this behavior on the
basis of their addiction.

One should not assume that this pattern of cheating is unique
to the clinics at the Philadelphia General Hospital or to Philadelphia. Cocaine abuse undoubtedly occurs in all methadone
substitution programs. Our earlier reports documented an even
higher incidence of cocaine abuse—23.1 percent—among ambulatory detoxification patients.

In New York City, liquid methadone is readily available on
the illicit market. This methadone reportedly is available as the
result of maintenance patients selling a portion of their "take-
home" medicine, in order to purchase cocaine. They retain
enough to keep from becoming "sick" and yet sell enough so they
can experience "some kind of rush." The methadone they divert
into the illicit market is in much demand by addicts who want to
reduce their "habits" or "kick" without going into a hospital.

Significantly, none of the addict-patients or their counselors
were aware that urines were being analyzed for the detection of
cocaine. Only at the end of the test period did this information
become known. Most of the treatment personnel were unaware
of the extent of cocaine abuse until confronted with the urinaly-
sis-derived data.

During the subsequent 30-day period, the incidence of detected cocaine in the urines of the addict-patients decreased to 10.4
percent. This incidence decrease from 18.5 to 10.4 percent is a
statistically significant decrease $(X^2 = 4.58; P = < .05)$. Clinicians and researchers involved in the surveillance process attributed the decline in cocaine cheating to the addict-patients being
confronted with their urine test results.

Our results have shown the necessity of having an adequate
surveillance procedure to detect the abuse of cocaine as well as
the abuse of sedatives, amphetamines and opiates.

APPENDIX

Procedure for the Detection of Abuse-Potential Drugs in Urine Used in the Clinical Pharmacology-Toxicology Center Philadelphia General Hospital

1. 30 to 50 ml of urine is diluted in a 175 ml Erlenmeyer-type plastic container with an equal aliquot of distilled water.

2. pH is adjusted to between 5 and 6 using either 2N hydrochloric acid or 2N sodium hydroxide as indicated.

3. A 6 cm x 6 cm square of cation exchange paper (Reeve Angel, grade SA-2) is placed in each container of urine and allowed to shake for 60 minutes.

4. Urine is discarded and the cation exchange paper that remains is rinsed with distilled water in the plastic container.

5. To the plastic container with the cation exchange paper remaining is added 25 ml of pH 2.2 citrate buffer and 25 ml of chloroform.

6. This mixture is allowed to shake for 15 minutes.

7. The mixture in the plastic container is then poured into a standard 40 ml extraction chamber and allowed to separate.

8. 10 ml of the lower solvent phase is delivered into a 15 ml conical glass centrifuge tube and evaporated to dryness in a 63°C water bath under a constant stream of dry nitrogen.

9. To the plastic container with the cation exchange paper still remaining is added 25 ml of pH 9.3 borate buffer and 25 ml of a 3:1 chloroform: isopropyl alcohol mixture.

10. Steps 6, 7 and 8 are repeated.

11. To the plastic container with the cation exchange paper still remaining is added 25 ml of pH 11.0 carbonate buffer and 25 ml of chloroform.

12. Repeat steps 6, 7 and 8 with the following exceptions:
    a. the plastic container with the cation exchange paper and solution mentioned in step 11 is left on the shaker for 25 minutes instead of 15 minutes and
    b. 25μl of glacial acetic acid is added to the 10 ml extract before drying.
13. Residues at the bottom of each set of 3 conical glass centrifuge tubes are carefully redissolved in 50μl of methyl alcohol.
14. 30μl is removed in a 100μl Hamilton syringe and spotted on a 10 cm x 20 cm thin-layer chromatographic plate (Silica Gel G for pH 2.2 and pH 11.0, Silica Gel F-254 for pH 9.3) using a hairdryer to dry the spots between applications.
15. 16 specimens are spotted on each plate in 4 groups of 4 specimens each. 5μl of standard is spotted on each side of each group of 4 specimens, i.e. 5 standards on each plate.
16. pH 2.2 and 11.0 TLC plates are placed in a standard glass developing tank containing a mixture of ethyl acetate, methyl alcohol and ammonium hydroxide (85:10:5 respectively) and pH 9.3 plates are placed in a tank containing ethyl acetate, methyl alcohol, water and ammonium hydroxide (85:10:3.75:1.25 respectively).
17. Solvent fronts are allowed to run to $\frac{1}{4}''$ below the top of the TLC plates.
18. TLC plates are removed and dried under a stream of cold air from the hairdryer. Then they are sprayed with various chromogenic reagents and/or examined in a Chromato-Vue box (Model CC-20) under long and short ultraviolet light.
19. pH 2.2 TLC plates are sprayed with 0.1N sodium hyroxide, allowed to dry and then are sprayed with 1% silver acetate. Urine specimens positive for barbiturates will yield a white spot at the same Rf locations as the barbiturate standards.
20. pH 9.3 TLC plates are viewed and sprayed as follows:

a. When viewed under ultraviolet light:

Morphine   —a blue spot seen at Rf 0.31 under short waves cannot be seen under long waves

Quinine   —a blue spot seen at Rf 0.53 under both long and short waves

Meperidine   —a purple spot seen at Rf 0.64 under short waves cannot be seen under long waves

Chlordiazepoxide —a yellow spot seen at Rf 0.68 under long waves cannot be seen under short waves

Chlorpromazine —a purple spot seen at 0.74 under both long and short waves

Methadone   —not visible under long or short waves

Cocaine   —not visible under long or short waves

b. When sprayed with Iodoplatinate (K_2PtI_6) :

Morphine   —the blue spot seen at Rf 0.31 under short waves remains

Quinine   —the blue spot seen at Rf 0.53 under both long and short waves turns purple

Meperidine   —the purple spot seen at Rf 0.64 under short waves turns pink

Chlordiazepoxide —the yellow spot seen at Rf 0.68 under long waves turns pink

Chlorpromazine —the purple spot seen at Rf 0.74 under both long and short waves remains

Methadone   —a heavy reddish-brown cobbled spot appears at Rf 0.84

Cocaine   —a dark brown spot appears at Rf 0.94

c. When sprayed with ammoniacal silver nitrate ($AgNO3$) and heated to 100°C on a hot plate:

Morphine	—the blue spot at Rf 0.31 turns black
Quinine	—the purple spot at Rf 0.53 disappears
Meperidine	—the pink spot at Rf 0.64 disappears
Chlordiazepoxide	—the yellow spot at Rf 0.68 disappears
Chlorpromazine	—the purple spot at Rf 0.74 turns lilac
Methadone	—the brown spot at Rf 0.84 disappears
Cocaine	—the brown spot at Rf 0.94 disappears

d. When a second pH 9.3 TLC plate is sprayed with potassium permanganate (KMn04) :

Morphine	—a yellow spot appears at Rf 0.31
Quinine	—a yellow spot appears at Rf 0.53
Meperidine	—a delayed yellow spot appears at Rf 0.64
Chlordiazepoxide	—a delayed yellow spot appears at Rf 0.68
Chlorpromazine	—a yellow spot appears at Rf 0.74
Methadone	—a yellow spot appears at Rf 0.84
Cocaine	—not visible at Rf 0.94 with this stain

e. When a third pH 9.3 TLC plate is sprayed with 0.5% sulfuric acid and viewed under ultraviolet light:

Morphine	—not visible under long or short waves
Quinine	—a blue spot seen at Rf 0.53 under both long and short waves
Meperidine	—not visible under long or short waves
Chlordiazepoxide	—a purple spot seen at Rf 0.68 under short waves and a delayed blue spot appears under long waves

Chlorpromazine   —a blue spot seen at Rf 0.74 under long waves which appears purple under short waves

Methadone   —not visible under long or short waves

Cocaine   —not visible under long or short waves

21. pH 11.0 TLC plates are sprayed with 0.2% ninhydrin polychromatic detection reagent (Gelman), placed on a hot plate and heated to 100°C. A positive amphetamine will appear as a deep pink spot.

REFERENCES

1. AMA Committee on Alcoholism and Drug Dependence: Management of narcotic-drug dependence by high-dosage methadone—HCL technique: Dole-Nyswander Program. *JAMA, 201:*956, 1967.
2. Ausubel, D.P.: The Dole-Nyswander treatment of heroin addicts. *JAMA, 195:*949, 1966.
3. Brill, L., Jaffe, J.H., and Laskowitz, D.: Pharmacological approaches to the treatment of narcotic addiction: Patterns of response. In *National Academy of Sciences, National Research Council Committee on Problems of Drug Dependence,* 1967, p. 5145.
4. Dole, V.P.: Drug maintenance as a treatment approach. *J Hillside Hospital, 16:*157, 1967.
5. Dole, V.P., and Nyswander, Marie: The use of methadone for narcotic blockade. *Brit J Addiction, 63,* 1968, p. 55.
6. Dole, V.P., and Nyswander, Marie: A medical treatment for diacetylmorphine (heroin) addiction. *JAMA, 193(8):*80, 1965.
7. Dole, V.P., and Nyswander, M.: Rehabilitation of the street addict. *Arch Environ Health, 14:*477-480, 1967.
8. Dole, V.P., Orraca, J., Robinson, J.W., Towns, E., Searcy, P., and Caine, E.: Methadone treatment of randomly selected criminal addicts. *New Eng J Med, 280:*1372, 1969.
9. Dole, V.P., Nyswander, M., and Warner, A.: Successful treatment of 750 criminal addicts. *JAMA, 206:*2708, 1968.
10. Fink, M., Saks, A., Roubicek, J., and Freedman, A.: Methadone induced cross-tolerance to heroin. In *National Academy of Sciences, National Research Council, Committee on Problems of Drug Dependence,* 1969, p. 5733.
11. Gewirtz, Paul D.: Methadone maintenance for heroin addicts. *The Yale Law Journal, 78(7):*1175, 1969.

12. Jaffe, J., Zaks, M.S., and Washington, E.N.: Experience with the use of methadone in a multi-modality program for the treatment of narcotics users. *Int J Addictions, 4:*481, 1969.
13. Jaffe, J. *et al.:* Comparison of Acetylmethadol and methadone in the treatment of long-term heroin users. *JAMA, 211(11):*1834, 1970.
14. Nix, J.Y.: Methadone for narcotic addicts. *JAMA, 207:*2439, 1969.
15. Nyswander, M.: Methadone treatment of heroin addicts. *Bull NY State District Branches of Amer Psychiat Ass,* 1967.
16. Nyswander, M., and Dole, V.P.: The present status of methadone blockade treatment. *Amer J Psychol, 123:*1141, 1967.
17. Wieland, W.F., and Chambers, C.D.: Two methods of utilizing methadone in the outpatient treatment of heroin addicts. Paper presented at the Second Annual Methadone Conference, New York City, 1969.
18. Wieland, W., and Chambers, C.D.: Methadone maintenance—A comparison of two stabilization techniques. *Int J Addictions, 5:*4,645-659, 1970.
19. Wikler, A.: Methadone maintenance treatment of chronic addiction. *New Physician, 18:*210, 1969.
20. Wikler, A.: The methadone treatment of heroin addiction. *Hospital Practice, 2:*4, 1967.
21. Wikler, A.: Rehabilitation of the street addiction, *Arch Environ Health, 14:*477, 1967.
22. Wikler, A.: Rehabilitation of heroin addicts after blockade with methadone, *N Y State J Med, 66:*2011, 1966.
23. Wikler, A.: Study of methadone as an adjunct in rehabilitation of heroin addicts. *Illinois Med J, 130:*487, 1966.

Chapter 37

Patterns of "Cheating" Among Methadone Maintenance Patients

Carl D. Chambers and W. J. Russell Taylor

METHADONE maintenance as a treatment modality can be traced to the original efforts of Dr. Dole and Dr. Nyswander during the early 1960's. From the very onset, clinicians and researchers have expressed concern with the possibility of the patient's cheating with drugs while being maintained with the methadone. Our clinical judgments and indeed the professional literature would suggest that once the addict becomes stabilized on the methadone, a narcotic blockade occurs and drug craving is extinguished or reduced to a level where cheating will cease. Unfortunately, our clinical judgments and assumptions have not been exposed to an empirical test. We hope this current report will stimulate such empirical tests. In brief, we have looked at the incidence and patterns of cheating among this type of patient and herein report the results of this inquiry.

THE DESIGN

During May, 1969, the researchers and clinicians of the Narcotic Addict Rehabilitation Program—a NARA Title IV program —decided to conduct an extensive analysis of the incidence and patterns of cheating among the methadone maintenance patients being serviced through an ambulatory clinic at the Philadelphia General Hospital. In order to restrict the analysis to those patients who were stabilized, only those patients who had been on the program at least six months were to be included in the study group. Forty patients met this single selection criterion.

Data were collected from four sources: each patient was interviewed by his counselor/therapist relative to his behavior, including any cheating during the month; each counselor/therapist was interviewed by a researcher relative to his clinical judgment of the patient's cheating; each patient's urine sample, which were deposited during each clinic visit, were analyzed for the presence of heroin, barbiturates and amphetamines, and finally, data were extracted from the clinical records maintained on each patient.

The process was to be replicated for the month of January, 1970, to determine what changes had occurred.

THE INCIDENCE AND PATTERNS OF CHEATING

Utilizing a cation exchange, fractional extraction and thin-layer chromatography procedure, we were able to detect the following abuses:

1. During May, 1969, 82.5 percent of the patients had abused at least one of the detectable drugs. Specifically, 77.5 percent had abused *heroin*, 30.0 percent had abused the *barbiturates* and 25.0 percent had abused *amphetamines*. Sixty percent had abused at least two different classes of drugs and 22.5 percent had abused all three. Although no corroborative urinalyses were available, 5.0 percent admitted to some psychedelic abuse, 7.5 percent reported they had smoked marijuana and 25.0 percent had been intoxicated at least once (Table 37-I) .

2. Eight months later, during January, 1970, 39 of the 40 patients were still in the program. Among these 39 patients, we found the incidence of cheating had *increased* from 82.5 to 97.4 percent. In fact, all forms of cheating which could be detected through our analyses of the urines had increased. Heroin cheating had increased from 77.5 to 92.3 percent; barbiturate cheating had increased from 30.0 to 43.6 percent; and amphetamine cheating had increased from 25.0 to 69.2 percent. Only the increase in amphetamine cheating, however, is significant statistically ($X^2 = 15.51$; $P = <.001$) .

During the interim period, urine surveillance techniques were expanded to include the detection of cocaine. The incidence of cocaine abuse among these patients was 43.6 percent.

Multiple cheating was also found to have increased. Cheating with at least two drugs increased from 60.0 to 76.9 percent; cheat-

TABLE 37-I

THE TYPES AND INCIDENCE OF CHEATING AMONG METHADONE MAINTENANCE PATIENTS

Cheating Pattern	Maintenance Patients May, 1969 N	%	Maintenance Patients January, 1970 N	%	Statistical Test For Significant Differences
I. Results from Urinalysis					
1. Heroin	31	77.5	36	92.3	None
2. Barbiturates	12	30.0	17	43.6	None
3. Amphetamines	10	25.0	27	69.2	$X^2=15.51$; $P=<.001$
4. Cocaine	Test Not Available		17	43.6	No Test
a. Total with any cheating	33	82.5	38	97.4	None
b. Cheating at least 2 drugs	24	60.0	30	76.9	None
c. Cheating at least 3 drugs	9	22.5	20	51.3	$X^2=7.04$; $P=<.01$
d. Cheating all 4 drugs	Not Applicable		8	20.5	No Test
II. Results from Interview					
1. Extra methadone	0	0.0	3	7.7	No tests were
2. Psychedelics	2	5.0	3	7.7	attempted on
3. Marijuana	3	7.5	7	17.9	interview
4. Excessive alcohol	10	25.0	2	5.1	data

ing with at least three drugs increased from 22.5 to 51.3 percent; and 20.5 percent were found to have cheated with all four of the drugs.

In addition to the above detected cheating, 7.7 percent admitted to self-administered supplementation of their methadone dose, 7.7 percent reported some psychedelic abuse, 17.9 percent reported smoking marijuana but only 5.1 percent reported they had been intoxicated during the 30-day reporting period.

RELIABILITY OF CHEATING DATA OBTAINED FROM INTERVIEW

Our experiences clearly demonstrate the futility of attempting to elicit information from addict-patients concerning their cheating. The data are highly unreliable even when the interviews are conducted by professionally trained counselor/therapists or by trained ex-addicts. In all of the forms of cheating where urinalyses could be used to assess the validity of the answers, gross discrepancies were found (Table 37-II).

TABLE 37-II

A COMPARISON OF CHEATING DATA OBTAINED FROM INTERVIEW AND FROM URINALYSIS

Type of Cheating	May, 1969		January, 1970	
	Interview % of 40	*Urinalysis* % of 40	*Interview* % of 39	*Urinalysis* % of 39
Any cheating	45.0	82.5	33.3	97.4
Heroin	40.0	77.5	23.1	92.3
Barbiturates	7.5	30.0	5.1	43.6
Amphetamines	5.0	25.0	10.3	69.2
Cocaine	0.0	No test	0.0	43.6

1. During the initial analysis (May, 1969), only 45.0 percent ($N = 18$) of the 40 patients admitted to abusing a drug which would be detectable by urinalysis. The urinalyses, however, indicated at least 82.5 percent ($N = 33$) had abused at least one of the detectable drugs. During the second analysis (January, 1970), only 33.3 percent ($N = 13$) admitted to any cheating but we detected cheating for 97.4 percent ($N = 38$) of the patients.

2. During the initial analysis, 31 of the 40 patients (77.5 percent) were found to have been *heroin* cheaters but only 16 or 51.6 percent of them had admitted this abuse. Eight months later, 36 of these same patients (92.3 percent) were again detected as *heroin* cheaters and an even smaller minority—25.0 percent (N = 9) —had admitted the abuse when confronted.

3. During the initial analysis, 12 of the 40 patients (30.0 percent) were detected as *barbiturate* cheaters but only 3 or 25.0 percent of them had admitted this abuse. Eight months later, the incidence of detected *barbiturate* cheating had risen to 17 or 43.6 percent of the total study group and only 2 or 11.8 percent of them had admitted the abuse when confronted.

4. During the initial analysis, 10 of the 40 patients (25.0 percent) were detected as *amphetamine* cheaters and only 2 or 20.0 percent of them had admitted this abuse. Eight months later, we found a marked increase in this form of abuse. During this second analysis, 17 or 43.6 percent of those patients still in treatment (N = 39 of 40) were found to be abusing *amphetamines* and only 4 or 23.5 percent of them had admitted the abuse when confronted.

In summary, the admission or volunteering of cheating information by these maintenance patients was very low. During the second analysis only a third of those cheating had actually admitted it. The probability of admitting the cheating was lowest for barbiturate abusers (Table 37-III).

TABLE 37-III
THE RELIABILITY OF CHEATING DATA OBTAINED FROM INTERVIEWS

Type of Cheating	40 Patients–May, 1969		39 Patients–January, 1970	
	Cheaters (% of Total)	Cheaters Who Admitted It	Cheaters (% of Total)	Cheaters Who Admitted It
Heroin	77.5	51.6	92.3	25.0
Barbiturates	30.0	25.0	43.6	11.8
Amphetamines	25.0	20.0	43.6	23.5
Cocaine	No Test	No Test	43.6	0.0
Any cheating	82.5	54.5	97.4	34.2

At least within this nonselected study population, the incidence of detected heroin, barbiturate and amphetamine cheating increased during the eight-month study period but the admission of the cheating had generally decreased.

During the initial analysis, the counselor/therapist for each of the 40 addict-patients were asked to indicate which of their clients had ceased to use heroin. Seventeen or 42.5 percent were clinically judged to be totally abstinent from heroin. The urinalyses, however, indicated that at least 70.6 percent (N = 12) of these clinical judgments were inaccurate. There was no significant difference between professionals and ex-addicts on their ability to predict heroin abstinence. It was impossible to retest the clinicians' judgments. Once it was known that the first set of judgments had been compared with the urinalysis results, the counselor/therapists tended to not want to make any decision or to label every patient a cheater.

FREQUENCY OF CHEATING

A precise determination of the frequency with which a patient cheats is, of course, not possible. One possible index of the frequency of cheating is the proportion of "dirty" to "clean" urine samples deposited by each patient. The proportion must be ascertained for each patient rather than for the total since the number of specimens collected and analyzed varies. For example, the range of specimens analyzed per patient was from 2 to 25 with a median of 10.

During the second analysis period (January, 1970) :
1. 2.6 percent (N = 1) had all clean urine samples
2. 12.8 percent (N = 5) had dirty urine samples 1 to 25 percent of the time
3. 25.6 percent (N = 10) had dirty urine samples 26 to 50 percent of the time
4. 15.4 percent (N = 6) had dirty urine samples 51 to 75 percent of the time
5. 43.6 percent (N = 17) had dirty urine samples 76 to 100 percent of the time

Almost one third (30.8 percent) of all of these long-term methadone maintenance patients submitted urines which were dirty 100 percent of the time. The range of specimens analyzed for these continuous cheaters was from 2 to 15 with a median of 8 specimens.

THE CHEATERS

Who then are these methadone maintenance patients who after at least a full year of treatment continued to regularly cheat with a variety of drugs?

1. They were *not* new patients.

   The median length of maintenance treatment was 22 months with a range from 14 to 40 months.

2. They were *not* low-dose patients.

   The median daily dose was 120 mg with a range from 60 to 190 mg.

3. They were *not* neglected patients.

   The median number of clinic visits was 3 per week with a range from 1 to 5 visits. In addition, 15.4 percent were receiving concurrent phenothiazine chemotherapy.

4. They were *not* novice patients.

   The median number of prior treatments was 2 with a range from 0 to 11 "cures."

5. They were *not* young addicts.

   The median age was 35 years with a range from 18 to 50 years.

6. They were *not* inexperienced addicts.

   The median years of opiate use was 15 with a range from 1 to 28 years. In addition, the median number of arrests was 7 with a range from 0 to 25.

7. In spite of the extensive addiction careers and the current extensive cheating on the maintenance program, 51.3 percent were maintaining an intact marriage, 53.8 percent were legally employed on a full-time basis (92.3 percent were males) and only 28.2 percent were receiving welfare (Table 37-IV).

TABLE 37-IV
CHARACTERISTICS OF THE STUDY POPULATION

I. *Clinical Characteristics*	II. *Personal Characteristics*
1. Total years of opiate use (N=37) Range —1–28 years Median— 15 years	1. Current age Range —18–50 years Median— 35 years
2. Total prior detoxification (N=37) Range —0–11 Median— 2	2. Race/Sex cohorts White Males—51.3% Black Males—41.1% White Females—None Black Females—7.7%
3. Months of methadone maintenance Range —14–40 Median— 22	3. Current marital status Never Married—12.8% Married—51.3% Divorced/Separated—35.9%
4. Daily methadone dose Range —60–190 mg Median— 120 mg	4. Total number of arrests (N=36) Range —0–25 Median— 7
5. Weekly clinic visits Range —1–5 Median— 3	5. Current full-time employment Yes—53.8%
6. Concurrent phenothiazine chemotherapy Yes—15.4%	6. Current welfare recipient Yes—28.2%

COMMENTS

We are not totally sure what our findings mean. It does appear that the degree and variety of cheating among methadone maintenance patients are both greater than we had anticipated. It would also appear that even after a year on relatively high doses of methadone, neither a narcotic blockade had occurred nor had drug craving significantly diminished. These findings must also be viewed within the context that neither the patients themselves nor the program within which they were being treated are significantly different from most other methadone programs or patients.

We are sure that our findings define a specific problem area which clinicians must very carefully consider. Adequate laboratory surveillance of urine to detect the possible self-administration of such abuse-potential drugs as the amphetamines, the barbiturates, cocaine and heroin is a necessary adjunct to the appropriate and effective management of any addict rehabilitation program.

The extent to which the various patterns of cheating are detrimental to the therapeutic process has yet to be documented. We should begin now to document the effects and this documentation will require the data inputs from all types of treatment programs.

Chapter 38

Patterns of Pentazocine Abuse

James A. Inciardi and Carl D. Chambers

~~~~~~

SINCE THE first reports of the synthesis and testing of pentazocine almost a decade ago,[1,2] there has been a polarization among the drug companies, clinicians and researchers regarding the abuse liability of the drug. Praised in the popular media as a nonaddicting substitute for morphine,[3-5] pentazocine is an effective analgesic which appears to have a more rapid onset than does morphine,[6] and as an antagonist, it will not substitute for morphine in a morphine-dependent individual. The World Health Organization Expert Committee on Dependence-Producing Drugs, during their 1965 session in Geneva, concluded that there was little likelihood of pentazocine being abused, that it presented no significant risk to public health and that there was no need at that time for narcotics control of pentazocine either internationally or nationally.[7] In July, 1967, the Food and Drug Administration granted permission to Sterling-Winthrop Laboratories to market the drug under the trade name of Talwin.

A major thrust of the advertising for Talwin has been that it is an analgesic which may be effectively used in place of other narcotic analgesics without being subject to narcotic controls, and indicative of the widespread use of the drug, Talwin was recently reported as being one of the one hundred most prescribed drugs in the United States.[8] While clinical findings of psychic craving, euphoria, tolerance and dependence have been reported,[9-11] those who would oppose controls for pentazocine insist that the addiction liability is minimal or that the potential for abuse is centered only among those persons who are "addiction-prone" and have misused other drugs.[12-15]

Much of the confusion and multiple contradictions which are apparent in the medical literature can be traced to the fact that the majority of the reports are based on limited and anecdotal experiences or upon a vested interest on the part of the writers. Furthermore, since no attempts have been made to undertake a large-scale assessment of the abuse liability of pentazocine, the major questions still to be answered are centered upon whether this analgesic can produce a "true" addiction and in what ways and to what extent the drug is being misused.

With respect to the former question, a recent report of a series of controlled experiments conducted at the NIMH Clinical Research Center, Lexington, Kentucky, is suggestive of pentazocine's ability to produce dependence and addiction.[16] The results indicated not only that pentazocine in single doses will produce an euphoric effect, but the notion was also supported that the drug produces physical dependence and its abstinence syndrome is associated with drug-seeking behavior.

In an effort to gain further insight as to the structure and process of pentazocine abuse, the nature and extent of such abuse within three divergent populations of narcotic addicts was determined. Specific questions relative to the misuse of pentazocine were addressed to (a) all 1,096 narcotic addicts consecutively admitted to the NIMH Clinical Research Center in Lexington, Kentucky as part of the Narcotic Addict Rehabilitation Act (NARA) program during the period May 1967–July 1969; (b) all 273 narcotic addicts undergoing detoxification or methadone maintenance treatment during December 1969 in the Narcotic Addict Rehabilitation Program (NARP) outpatient clinics at the Philadelphia General Hospital; and (c) 125 narcotic addicts undergoing treatment during June and July 1970 in two New York State Narcotic Addiction Control Commission (NACC) facilities.

The incidence of pentazocine among these populations of narcotic abusers (Table 38-I) was found to be relatively infrequent. Less than 6 percent of the combined patient populations had ever abused pentazocine, and slightly less than 1 percent had become addicted as the result of this abuse. On the basis of the abuse histories of these pentazocine users however, combined with the numerous case reports which have appeared in the medical

TABLE 38-I

THE INCIDENCE OF PENTAZOCINE ABUSE AND ADDICTION WITHIN
THREE NARCOTIC ADDICT POPULATIONS

| *Addict Populations* | *Total Narcotic Addicts* | *Pentazocine Abusers* | | | | *Users and Addicts* | |
| | | *Addicted* | | *Use Only* | | | |
		No.	%	No.	%	No.	%
TOTAL	*1494*	*11*	*.7*	*69*	*4.6*	*80*	*5.4*
NARA (USA)	1096	11	1.0	61	5.6	72	6.6
NARP (Philadelphia)	273	—	—	7	2.6	7	2.6
NACC (New York)	125	—	—	1	.8	1	.8

literature, several divergent patterns of pentazocine abuse and addiction can be isolated.

PENTAZOCINE AS A DRUG OF ADDICTION

Within the patient populations described, eleven pentazocine abusers had become physically dependent on the drug. Such addiction was overwhelmingly associated with white abusers, especially males. Furthermore (Table 38-II) these cases were predominantly from southern residences with intact marriages, had above average educations, and a median age of 29 years.

The ages of onset of drug abuse for the eleven cases (Table 38-III) ranged from 13 to 50 years with a mean of 22.5, and the mean duration of abuse was 10.5 years. While a legitimate medical onset was reported for only three (27 percent) of the eleven, *a legally manufactured and distributed drug was the onset drug for 9 (82 percent) cases.* Furthermore, such legally manufactured drugs were also the primary drugs of abuse for eight (73 percent) cases, with heroin being the primary drug for only one individual. Injectable pentazocine was both a drug and narcotic of perference in several cases (Table 38-IV) and was reported by some as a drug and narcotic most frequently abused.

An additional twelve cases of pentazocine addiction were found within the medical literature,[9,11,17-19] and among these several divergent patterns of addiction were apparent.

Addiction to pentazocine through medical onset was characteristic of eight cases. The patients were predominantly females ranging in age from 27 to 58 (Table 38-V). Dependence and

TABLE 38-II

BASIC DEMOGRAPHIC CHARACTERISTICS OF ELEVEN PENTAZOCINE ADDICTS

Pentazocine Addicts			General Characteristics		
Age–Race–Sex	Residence	Marital Status	Education	Any Illegal Activity	Arrest History
1. 19—White Male	Miami, Florida	Single	12	Yes	Yes
2. 21—Black Male	Knoxville, Tennessee	Married	10	Yes	Yes
3. 25—White Male	Norfolk, Virginia	Married (addict spouse)	14	Yes	Yes
4. 27—White Male	Baltimore, Maryland	Separated	8	Yes	No Data
5. 29—White Female	Louisville, Kentucky	Single	15		
6. 29—White Male	St. Petersburg, Florida	Single	8	Yes	Yes
7. 35—White Female	Richardson, Texas	Married	10	Yes	Yes
8. 37—White Male	Baltimore, Maryland	Married	14		
9. 40—White Male	Indianapolis, Indiana	Married	14		
10. 46—White Male	Tuscaloosa, Alabama	Married	10	Yes	Yes
11. 56—White Female	Tulsa, Oklahoma	Separated	15		

TABLE 38-IIIA
PATTERNS OF DRUG ABUSE OF ELEVEN PENTAZOCINE ADDICTS

Pentazocine Addicts	Age First Abuse	First Drug of Abuse	Medical Onset	Years of Abuse	Primary Drug of Abuse
1. 19—White Male	15	Codeine Cough Syrup		4	LSD (Oral)
2. 21—Black Male	13	Methedrine		8	Heroin (IM–SQ)
3. 25—White Male	16	Marijuana		9	Morphine (IV)
4. 27—White Male	13	Marijuana Phenmetrazine		14	Cocaine (IV)
5. 29—White Male	19	(Preludin®) Atropine®	Yes	10	Codeine (Oral)
6. 29—White Male	16			13	Ritalin® (IV)
7. 35—White Female	18	Codeine		17	Talwin® (IM–SQ)
8. 37—White Male	22	Propoxyphene (Darvon®)		15	Seconal® (Oral)
9. 40—White Male	32	Codeine	Yes	8	Placidyl® (Oral)
10. 46—White Male	34	Meperidine (Demerol®)	Yes	12	Dolophine® (IM–SQ)
11. 56—White Famle	50	Chloropromazine (Thorazine®)		6	Thorazine® (Oral)

Darvon®—Lilly
Demerol®—Winthrop
Dilaudid®—Knoll
Dolophine®—Lilly
Seconal®—Lilly
Numorphan®—Endo
Placidyl®—Abbott
Ritalin®—Ciba
Talwin®—Winthrop
Thorazine®—S.K. & F.
Atropine®—B.W. & Co.

TABLE 38-IIIB

				Drugs Abused Other Than Pentazocine								
Pentazocine Addicts	*Opiates (not heroin)*	*Sedatives or Hypnotics*	*Tranq.*	*Anti-dep.*	*Anti-hist.*	*Heroin*	*Mari-juana*	*Methe-drine*	*Other Stimu-lants*	*LSD*	*Other Psycho-togens*	*Glue*
1. 19—White Male	Yes	Yes	Yes	Yes		Yes	Yes	Yes	Yes	Yes	Yes	Yes
2. 21—Black Male	Yes	Yes	Yes		Yes	Yes	Yes	Yes	Yes	Yes	Yes	Yes
3. 25—White Male	Yes	Yes	Yes	Yes		Yes	Yes	Yes	Yes	Yes	Yes	Yes
4. 27—White Male	Yes	Yes	Yes			Yes	Yes	Yes	Yes	Yes	Yes	
5. 29—White Male	Yes	Yes							Yes		Yes	
6. 29—White Male	Yes	Yes	Yes			Yes	Yes				Yes	
7. 35—White Female	Yes	Yes	Yes		Yes						Yes	
8. 37—White Male	Yes	Yes	Yes			Yes						
9. 40—White Male	Yes	Yes	Yes									
10. 46—White Male	Yes	Yes	Yes								Yes	
11. 56—White Female	Yes	Yes	Yes	Yes								

TABLE 38-IV

DRUG HISTORIES OF ELEVEN PENTAZOCINE ADDICTS

Pentazocine Addicts (Age-Race-Sex)	Onset Drugs		Most Preferred Drugs		Most Frequently Abused Drugs	
	First Drug	First Narcotic	Of All Drugs	Of the Narcotic	Of All Drugs	Of the Narcotic
1. 19—White Male	Codeine Cough Syrup	Codeine Cough Syrup	LSD (Oral)	Opium (Smoke)	LSD (Oral)	Talwin® (IM—SQ)
2. 21—Black Male	Methedrine	Codeine Cough Syrup	Numorphan® (IM—SQ)	Numorphan® (IM—SQ)	Heroin (IM—SQ)	Heroin (IM—SQ)
3. 25—White Male	Marijuana	Heroin	Morphine (IV)	Morphine (IV)	Morphine (IV)	Morphine (IV)
4. 27—White Male	Marijuana	Codeine Cough Syrup	Cocaine (IV)	Heroin (IV)	Cocaine (IV)	Heroin (IV)
5. 29—White Female	Preludin®	Demerol®	Codeine (Oral)	Codeine (Oral)	Codeine (Oral)	Codeine (Oral)
6. 29—White Male	Atropine®	Codeine	Demerol® (Oral)	Demerol® (Oral)	Ritalin® (IV)	Demerol® (Oral)
7. 35—White Female	Codeine	Codeine	Talwin® (IM—SQ)	Talwin®* (IM—SQ)	Talwin® (IM—SQ)	Talwin®* (IM—SQ)
8. 37—White Male	Darvon®*	Darvon*	No Data	No Data	Seconal® (Oral)	Demerol® (IM—SQ)
9. 40—White Male	Codeine	Codeine	No Data	No Data	Placidyl® (Oral)	Demerol® (Oral)
10. 46—White Male	Demerol®	Demerol®	Dilaudid® (IM—SQ)	Dilaudid® (IM—SQ)	Dolophine® (IM—SQ)	Dolophine® (Oral)
11. 56—White Female	Thorazine®	Demerol®	Thorazine® (Oral)	Talwin®* (IM—SQ)	Thorazine® (Oral)	Talwin®* (IM—SQ)

Darvon® — Lilly Numorphan® — Endo Talwin® — Winthrop
Demerol® — Winthrop Placidyl® — Abbott Thorazine® — S. K. & F.
Dilaudid® — Knoll Ritalin® — Ciba Atropine® — B.W. & Co.
Dolophine® — Lilly Seconal® — Lilly

*Darvon and Talwin have been classed as "narcotic" on the basis of existing evidence which is suggestive of their ability to produce physical dependence and tolerance.

TABLE 38-V

ABUSE CHARACTERISTICS OF EIGHT PENTAZOCINE ADDICTS INITIATED THROUGH MEDICAL ONSET

Age-Sex	Abuse Dose	Length of Abuse	Euphoric	Tolerance	Dependence	Route	Previous Drug History
59—Male	600 mg/day	4½ months	Yes	Yes	Yes	SQ, IV, Oral	Narcotic Analgesics
24—Female	120–720 mg/day	No Data	Yes	Yes	Yes	IM, IV	No Data
27—Female	135–960 mg/day	12 months	No Data	Yes	Yes	No Data	Medicine Misuse
30—Female	135–960 mg/day	12 months	No Data	Yes	Yes	No Data	Medicine Misuse
48—Female	135–960 mg/day	12 months	No Data	Yes	Yes	No Data	Medicine Misuse
58—Female	135–960 mg/day	12 months	No Data	Yes	Yes	No Data	Medicine Misuse
39—Female	1500 mg/day	several months	No Data	Yes	Yes	IM	Marijuana
Young Female	60-270 mg/day	2 months	Yes	Yes	Yes	SQ	None

tolerance had been observed in all cases, and abuse dosages were as high as 1500 mg/day. These patients had been introduced to pentazocine in a hospital setting and for analgesic purposes; yet due to the ready availability of the drug, they increased their dosages subsequent to discharge.

Of the remaining four cases extracted from the literature, three had been introduced to pentazocine while in the hospital and became addicted subsequent to discharge when the dosage was increased in pursuit of the drug's euphoric effects. Pentazocine was perceived as *a drug of preference* in one of these cases. One 21-year-old female college student abused pentazocine for a period of four months. She had a previous history of drug misuse involving the use of narcotic analgesics, sedative-hypnotics, LSD and organic solvents and inhalants, and in spite of her ready access to all the drugs of abuse, pentazocine was selected as her drug of choice. Pentazocine represented the *drug of substitution* for the final case extracted from the literature, a heroin addict with an abuse history of two years. This patient, a 27-year-old male, substituted pentazocine for heroin during a "panic" when the latter drug was in short supply in New York City, and he reported the drug's effect to be similar to that of codeine.

The potential for the abuse of pentazocine can be more readily perceived when one considers that in some cases, *pentazocine was the only drug ever abused by the addicted individual.* The following case history encountered at an ambulatory drug treatment clinic at the Philadelphia General Hospital exemplifies how in some cases the abuse of pentazocine can be attributed to its ready availability and to the insufficient controls placed upon its sale and distribution.

The 22-year-old white male first encountered pentazocine in 1967 in the Philadelphia Naval Hospital where he was recovering from a severe leg wound received in Vietnam. This subject had received an estimated fifty injections of morphine and/or meperidine per week during the initial four months of surgical procedures to repair his leg. The narcotics were abruptly stopped after four months and while he reportedly "wanted a shot" he was in no discernible physical distress. After being transferred to a less intensive care ward for recuperation, the subject was approached by the hospital corpsmen to purchase a "shot" of pentazocine to reduce any residual pain and to get a "tremendous high" which would alleviate the boredom on the ward. The subject rationalized the illicit purchase and use of the drug at three levels: (a) the physicians were no longer prescribing medication for him even though his leg still "bothered" him; (b) he had not experienced any withdrawal from the morphine and meperidine, and he knew both to be addicting drugs while the pentazocine was not addicting; and (c) most of the patients sharing his ward were amputees who had been there for extended periods of time, had been using pentazocine for several months and reported no ill effects. With this rationale, the subject began purchasing 1 cc injections of pentazocine from the corpsmen who would administer the drug intramuscularly. There was reportedly no internal control of the drug at this hospital, so the drug was always available for purchase at $5 per 1 cc.

After four months of regular abuse of the pentazocine, the subject was injecting 1 cc every three or four hours during the day but none during the night. While he was still paying only $5 per day for the increased dosage, the corpsmen were not always available to administer the injections and had taught him to prepare for and complete the intramuscular injections into his thighs and arm. At approximately this time the subject was discharged from the hospital for further recuperation at his home in a suburban community of Philadelphia.

Within three months after discharge from the hospital, the subject had increased his daily dose to 10 cc in 1 cc injections. At this level, he was no longer receiving any euphoric effects and was taking the drug solely to prevent the onset of withdrawal. He was able to secure the drug from pharmacists who did not question his forged prescriptions. He was even able to find a "sympathetic" pharmacist in his local community who would refill his prescriptions thirty to forty times. In fact, this pharmacist was providing the subject and two other pentazocine addicts with a total of fifty 10 cc vials of pentazocine every week. The subject maintained a stabilized dose of 10 cc per day for approximately six months. At this time the pharmacist supplier questioned the legitimacy of his continuing to use such high doses.

In order to prevent any further embarrassment by approaching the local pharmacist, the subject began shopping for drugs in all pharmacies within a thirty to forty mile radius of his home. After approximately three months of this "hassling" for the drug, the subject finally admitted to himself he was an addict and sought admission to a private hospital which specialized in the therapeutic community approach to the treatment of alcoholism and all drug addictions. After nine days of treatment, he illegally secured a supply of pentazocine from a neighboring pharmacist who had him arrested. Although he was released on bail, the hospital refused to take him back into treatment. He became re-addicted, and accepting the fact he was an addict, sought treatment at a Veteran's Administration Hospital where he was referred to an outpatient clinic rehabilitating narcotic addicts at the Philadelphia General Hospital.

While this subject was able to report "several" of the wounded veterans on his hospital ward had used pentazocine as much or more than he and that he also knew "several" "pentazocine only" addicts on the streets, we did not have the means of ascertaining the prevalence of this type of pentazocine abuse. As demonstrated in this case example, the drug has an euphorogenic effect, there exists a mistaken belief that it is nonaddicting, there is a high degree of accessibility and there are inadequate regulatory controls on its distribution—all of these factors can combine with the strong potential of creating a population of addicted persons who could be highly visible in the near future.

PENTAZOCINE AS A DRUG OF SIMULTANEOUS ABUSE

Within the three study populations described earlier, there were sixty-nine pentazocine abusers (4.6 percent) who used the drug, but with insufficient extent and duration to become addicted. Such abuse was not necessarily on a regular basis but rather simultaneously with and incidental to the dominant patterns of abuse.

Examination of these sixty-nine cases suggests that the abuse of pentazocine is not necessarily a localized phenomenon, in that twenty-four different states and the District of Columbia were represented. Furthermore, as with the first cohort of pentazocine addicts described, the simultaneous abuse of pentazocine was more often an activity of white males (Table 38-VI).

TABLE 38-VI

PATTERNS OF DRUG USE AMONG NARCOTIC ADDICTS WHO SIMULTANEOUSLY ABUSED PENTAZOCINE (NARA, NARP, NACC)

	Drugs	First Drug		First Narcotic		Most Frequent Narcotic	
		N	%	N	%	N	%
	Total	69	100.0	69	100.0	69	100.0
I.	Narcotic Analgesics						
	a. Heroin	2	2.9	17	24.6	38	55.1
	b. Morphine	3	4.3	4	5.8	5	7.2
	c. Meperidine	5	7.2	6	8.7	10	14.5
	d. Dilaudid	--	—	1	1.4	3	4.3
	e. Dihydrocodeinone	—	—	—	—	1	1.4
	f. Dihydrocodeine	1	1.4	1	1.4	—	—
	g. Codeine*	13	18.8	24	34.8	4	5.8
	h. Dolophine	—	—	--	—	1	1.4
	i. Paregoric	2	2.9	3	4.3	1	1.4
	j. Oxymorphon	1	1.4	2	2.9	3	4.3
	k. Pentazocine**	—	—	3	4.3	1	1.4
	l. Propoxyphene**	3	4.3	8	11.6	—	—
II.	Sedative–Hypnotics	2	2.9	—	—	—	—
III.	Relaxants–Tranquilizers	2	2.9	—	—	—	—
IV.	Stimulants	4	5.8	—	—	—	—
V.	Marijuana	27	39.1	—	—	—	—
VI.	Psychotogens	—	—	—	—	—	—
VII.	Inhalants	4	5.8	—	—	—	—
	No Data	—	—	--	—	2	2.9

Codeine category includes those cough syrups which contain codeine.

**Pentazocine and propoxyphene have been classed as "narcotic analgesics" on the basis of existing evidence which is suggestive of their ability to produce physical dependence and tolerance.

Analysis of the first narcotic drugs ever abused by the simultaneous pentazocine abusers suggests a rather unique onset pattern in that 75.4 percent began their careers in narcotics use with one of the legally manufactured and distributed drugs. Of these, as many as 34.8 percent began with codeine or codeine base cough syrups, while only 24.6 percent were initially exposed to narcotics with heroin. Three subjects (4.3 percent) were initiated into their careers of narcotic addiction with pentazocine. Although the legally manufactured and distributed drugs were most often the narcotics of onset, heroin subsequently became the most frequently abused narcotic (55.1 percent) (Table 38-VII).

TABLE 38-VII

RACE-SEX DISTRIBUTION OF 69 NARCOTIC ADDICTS WHO
SIMULTANEOUS ABUSED PENTAZOCINE (NARA, NARP, NACC) *

Race-Sex Cohort	Distribution	
	No.	%
Total	69	100.0
White Males	33	47.8
White Females	14	20.3
Black Males	18	26.1
Black Females	4	5.8
All White Abusers	47	68.1
All Black Abusers	22	31.9
All Male Abusers	51	73.9
All Female Abusers	18	26.1

*Distributions are not fully representative since NACC population was all males.

PENTAZOCINE AS A DRUG OF TEMPORARY EXPERIMENTATION

The previous discussion of simultaneous abusers suggests that knowledge of pentazocine as a drug of abuse might be widespread, and as with any new drug of abuse, a certain degree of experimentation with pentazocine is to be expected. This notion is somewhat substantiated in that experimental use was detected during the course of field investigations incidental to this study. Six heroin addicts were encountered in New York City's Greenwich Village who had experimented with pentazocine. In this instance, Talwin tablets had been brought from Chicago by a 24-year-old white male. Only one addict preferred the drug to heroin, and the duration of abuse was extremely short.

COMMENT

The patterns of abuse described in this study suggest that the greatest potential for abuse falls within the medical-medicine context. A lack of interest in pentazocine seems to be shared by the heroin street addict, and few instances of pentazocine being offered for sale on the illegal market have been isolated.

A somewhat greater interest in pentazocine is indicated by narcotic "medicine" abusers. Pentazocine being diverted for abuse was obtained as a result of physician overprescription, pharmacists overfilling prescriptions and inadequate control of institutional drug supplies. Furthermore, the professional and lay confusion concerning the addiction liability of the drug, combined with its ready availability in a legal market, seem to have contributed to the increasing incidence of abuse and addiction.

REFERENCES

1. Archer, S., Albertson, N.F., Harris, L.S., Pierson, A.K., Bird, J.G., Keats, A.S., Telford, J., and Papadopoulos, C.N.: Narcotic antagonists as analgesics. *Science, 137*:541, 1962.
2. Archer, S., Albertson, N.F., Harris, L.S., Pierson, A.K., and Bird, J.G.: Pentazocine: Strong analgesics and analgesic antagonists in the benzomorphan series. *J Med Chem, 7*:123, 1964.
3. Boehm, G.A.W.: At last—a nonaddicting substitute for morphine? *Today's Health, 48*:69-72, 1968.
4. *US News and World Report,* July 31, 1967, p. 11.
5. *Time,* July 7, 1967, p. 67.
6. Bellville, J.W.: Pentazocine—a nonaddicting analgesic. *Ann Intern Med, 67*:1114-1115, 1967.
7. WHO Expert Committee on Dependence-Producing Drugs, World Health Org, 1966, p. 6.
8. Times-Union: *Pain Drug Use May Be Curbed as Addictive.* Albany (N.Y.), June 18, 1970.
9. Schoolar, J. C., Idanaan-Heikkila, P., and Keats, A.S.: Pentazocine addiction? *Lancet, 1*:1263, 1969.
10. Smith, J.W.: Drug abuse with pentazocine. *Northwest Med,* Dec. 1969, p. 1128.
11. Keup, W.: Abuse-liability and narcotic antagonism of pentazocine. *Dis Nerv Syst, 29*:599-602, 1968.
12. A.M.A. Council on Drugs: The misuse of pentazocine, its dependence-producing potential. *JAMA, 209*:1518-1519, 1969.

13. Fraser, H.F., and Rosenberg, D.E.: Studies on the human addiction liability of 2-hyroxy-5,9-dimethyl-2 (3,3-dimethylallyl) 6,7-benzomorphan (WIN 20, 228) : A weak narcotic antagonist. *J Pharmacol Exp Ther, 143:*149-156, 1964.

14. Winthrop Laboratories: *Talwin Brand of Pentazocine (as Lactate).* New York, Sept. 1969 (7026D), pp. 1-8 (Product Information Advertisement) .

15. Mungavin, J.M.: Pentazocine addiction. *Lancet, 2:*56-57, 1969.

16. Jasinski, D.R., Martin, W.R., and Hoeldtke, R.D.: Effects of short and long-term administration of pentazocine in man. *Clin Pharmacol Ther, 11:*385-403, 1970.

17. Gibson, R.D., and Nebe, F.M.: Physical dependence to pentazocine (Talwin: A case history.) *Nebraska State Med J, 54:*689-690, 1969.

18. Hart, R.H.: Pentazocine addiction. *Lancet, 2:*690, 1969.

19. Sandoval, R.G., and Wang, R.I.J.: Tolerance and dependence on pentazocine. *New Eng J Med, 280:*1391-1392, 1969.

SECTION V

CLINICAL AND TREATMENT ASPECTS

Chapter 39

New Treatment Concepts at the NIMH Clinical Research Center, Lexington, Kentucky

Louis A. Cancellaro

D
URING THE pre-NIMH era, a repressive penal atmosphere per-
vaded the institution, and rigid custodial practices prevailed.
So effective was the pall which covered the place that it maintained
its position of isolation almost like an island regarded by most
townspeople as inaccessible. Little information about it was released, few visited it, and those who did were discouraged from
meeting and knowing patients. As a consequence, there were tales
of imagined dangers in an institution where it was supposed that
employment automatically entailed serious physical risks. Neither
the hospital nor its patients were understood. Not understood,
they tended to be distrusted and feared. Through publications,
emmissaries going out to give talks and to present papers at professional meetings, and visitors coming to the Center even from
other countries, its sphere of influence continued. Ironically, however, even today the Center is locally known by the cognomen of
either NARCO or the Narcotic Farm.

Pessimism and defeatism were common among patients and
staff. Staff caught these attitudes from patients, and patients
caught them from staff, so that they were continually reinforced.
It seems that there were employees who resented hearing about
the successes of ex-patients because success stories were at variance
with the conviction that addicts could not get well. The old saying
"Once an addict, always an addict" also gave patients an excuse
for returning to drugs. Since drugs were capable of satisfying
psychological needs and since it was easier to relapse than to remain drug-free, some patients resented it when they learned that
certain ex-patients were doing well.

Short stays in the hospital were the mode for voluntary patients. Though they were inclined to leave against medical advice, the majority sought readmission. By and large, the focus was on failure. Because they were expected to fail, patients themselves anticipated failure and partly as a consequence, the relapse rate was higher than it would have been if there had been more optimistic expectations all around. Lay and professional skeptics often remarked to employees how discouraging their work must be. Moreover, they promoted further discouragement by inquiring about the failure rate.

Relapse rates reported in the literature were widely variable because of sampling biases and other weaknesses of research methodology. Three follow-up studies were qualitatively superior to and more exhaustive than the others. These are conveniently spoken of as the New York City, the Kentucky, and the Puerto Rico studies.

Each of these three follow-up studies reveals an abstinence rate that is roughly proportional to the passage of time since discharge. Collectively they indicated that some 20 to 40 percent of ex-patients who had been hospitalized for addiction were by age 40 permanently abstinent from narcotics. However, when the lives of ex-patients are viewed longitudinally, abstinence is seen as a relative phenomenon. From this vantage point, data are more encouraging than when considered cross-sectionally at different time intervals. What is revealed is that ex-patients who were products of the old hospital regime were periodically drug-free and productive before their middle years. When George Vaillant conducted psychiatric interviews with Lexington ex-patients twelve years after release, he found that "almost half were drug-free" and currently living productive lives, even though most had at some time relapsed since their hospital discharge.

Vaillant's study provided a basis for new hope. Many addicts were at least intermittently leading responsible lives and were successful in adjusting to complex environments.

It should be pointed out that ex-patients were succeeding to this extent in spite of the absence of after-care programs in the communities where they were living. After-care programs subsequently provided for under the Narcotic Addict Rehabilitation Act of 1966 afford emotional support and demonstrate continuing concern through services such as counseling, job placement, training and schooling, and selective kinds of physical care. It is hoped that these variables will be found to increase substantially the success rate of addicts who seek help. The liaison which is currently being maintained between the Clinical Research Center and the receiving communities enables us to continually obtain data which are being processed by our Social Science Research Section and are being evaluated by research specialists to learn how patients who have been released from the Center are now faring. The total program, including institutional stay and aftercare, is of a minimum duration of forty-two months. We hypothesize that the success rate will improve under the new program, for we have faith that it is superior to that of the past.

The new era began with the enactment of the Narcotic Addict Rehabilitation Act of 1966, familiarly called NARA for the sake of convenience. Since July 1967, the Center has accepted only patients committed under NARA. Prisoner patients and voluntary patients have not been eligible for admission since that date. Concomitant with unprecedented developments under National Institute of Mental Health management, a renaissance has occurred with respect to staff attitudes toward patients and patient attitudes toward staff. Emphasis on self-help, cooperative decision-making involving patients and staff, and the gearing of treatment modalities to the differences and needs of individual patients have emerged from a revised and revitalized philosophy. A smaller population and decentralization of various services have made possible individualization of treatment to an extent that was formerly impossible. From admission through after-care, a humanization process has been taking place at an accelerating pace where once within the rigid confines of a monolithic penal structure there was much dehumanization. It seems appropriate at this time to turn to the provisions of NARA, the vehicle which has made these things possible.

Title I authorizes federal courts to commit for treatment certain eligible narcotic addicts who are charged with a federal offense and who desire to be treated for their addiction instead of being prosecuted for the criminal charge. If the patient successfully completes the regimen of treatment, the legal charge is dismissed. If, on the other hand, the consensus is reached that the patient is not amenable to treatment, he may be dropped from the program and legal prosecution may be resumed.

Title II provides that addicts who have already been convicted of a crime and who qualify for treatment may be committed to special treatment facilities in the Federal Bureau of Prisons. Following release, follow-up services are extended to them in home communities.

Title III provides civil commitment for addicts who are not charged with any legal offense. The majority of our patients at the Center come under this title.

Commitment is initiated by petition to the United States Attorney in the district where the addict lives. The petition may be made either by the addict himself or by a relative. The U.S. District Court then sends the candidate to the Center for a period of examination lasting up to thirty days. During this period two physicians, one of them a psychiatrist, determine whether the patient is truly an addict and, if so, whether the prognosis is favorable with respect to treatability. If both questions are answered in the affirmative, the U.S. District Court may then judicially commit him for treatment leading toward ultimate rehabilitation. At present, about 40 percent of the patients examined are accepted for treatment.

Treatment entails an additional period of hospital care not to exceed six months, followed by a 36-month period of supervised after-care within the patient's home community. Should he again become addicted to a narcotic drug while in after-care, the patient may be recommitted for additional in-hospital treatment. Up to this time, about 27 percent of after-care patients have been recommitted to inpatient care, having relapsed to narcotics.

Services that may be provided along the continuum of inpatient and outpatient care include vocational training, continuing education, job placement, social case work, individual psychotherapy and group or family therapy. All patients are subjected to routine urine testing to determine whether they have returned to the use of narcotic drugs.

At the Clinical Research Center in Lexington, we believe that in order to overcome the crippling effects of narcotic addiction our patients need to search within themselves to discover their own identities, to develop a feeling of personal worth, to acquire satisfying and sustained work experience, to relate to others in mutually beneficial ways, to become creative along at least one dimension, to embrace new values, to practice behavior that is socially acceptable and constructive, and to have reciprocal learning experiences involving concern and trust. It is our observation that to remain drug-free, former addicts must pursue some consuming interest to replace the addictive way of life which was theirs in the past. The activities generated by this interest, it would seem, necessarily have a generous component of unselfishness and even altruism if the neoteric drug-free life style is to continue indefinitely. Probably every addict who can be considered rehabilitated has found along the route of recovery a kind of love involving mutual respect that he has never before known.

The Center itself is continually developing with respect to organizational philosophy or *raison d'être,* treatment programs, administrative and management methods, reevaluation of goals and improvement within the physical plant.

Our approaches are multiple and eclectic. It follows that we have borrowed from many sources, though we feel that what may be observed while visiting and considering our Center in depth does bear the stamp of individuality. In passing, acknowledgment should be given to the Synanon program which originated in California. We have admittedly learned much from Synanon both by example and by avoiding exploratory mistakes which otherwise might have been made. It was provided guidelines, utilized with modifications, for various living units within our Center. For Synanon has demonstrated quite convincingly the effectiveness of original group methods in reducing behavioral symptoms associated with the acquisition of drugs and their abuse. The chief of one of our living units is currently concluding a stay of three months as a nonaddict member of that organization.

In accordance with conceptual precedents advanced by Synanon, patient residents at Lexington are active agents of change. Standing committees and task forces include residents among the members. These groups were created some fifteen months ago by the then newly inaugurated chief of the Center—a practical realist with vision—with diversified assigned missions to revamp the entire organizational and operational structure of our facility. Patient residents with a genuine commitment to rehabilitation are eagerly and unselfishly showing their willingness to work cooperatively with staff in developing innovative approaches. Residents and staff located together in the various living units have been simultaneously developing relatively different kinds of therapeutic communities.

The formerly centralized and authoritarian program of the Clinical Research Center, then officially named the U.S. Public Health Service Hospital, has given way to a decentralized therapeutic program. An array of separate treatment units are by design allowed and encouraged to function autonomously. Efforts are made to maintain communication between these units, to provide those decentralized services which are efficacious, to share in-service training opportunities, to exchange ideas and to do collective planning. Individuals with outstanding leadership qualities, the ability to work effectively in multidisciplinary teams and to draw out the best that others have to offer have been selected to serve as chiefs of the resident units. Interestingly enough, the chiefs themselves represent several professional disciplines. One holds a doctorate in clinical psychology, the second is a graduate social worker, the third holds a master's degree in nursing administration and the fourth is a doctoral candidate in correctional administration. Each has had a variety of work experience since completing his graduate training. Thus it is seen that ability is capitalized upon wherever it is found among the professions. This is in contrast to the past, when only physicians were awarded leadership positions, and then typically with extremely limited professional experience.

Chiefs are delegated the authority to plan and conduct their own unit programs, utilizing the talents and resourcefulness of others as they see fit. They are also given control over sufficient funds to bring about periodic physical improvements that are deemed desirable. Unit staffs have been allocated, organized and trained to function smoothly as a coordinated team in offering a comprehensive program to the residents whom they serve.

A schedule for each day of the week provides the structure for positive activities. General expectations are clearly expressed, yet there is sufficient flexibility within the structure for individual obligations to be met and for individual preferences to be pursued. Each daily schedule begins with wakeup at 7:30 AM and ends at 9:00 PM. Activities that are regarded as conductive to the socialization process are distributed throughout the day and evening. Citizenship skills developed at the Center should be directly applicable to citizenship requirements in outside communities. The criteria of an individual's adjustment are ultimately and unequivocally social ones.

The schedule provides cleanup periods, regular meal times, community morning meetings, work on job assignments, appointments with staff, religious observance, recreation, encounter sessions for the discussion of the daily behavior of individual community residents, and coeducational socializing in lounge areas.

No community within the Center is characterized either by regimentation or by complete noninterference. Neither extreme would help individuals to prepare for democratic living back home. It is our hope that each resident will learn and accept the precept that with privileges there should go responsibilities for the welfare of others.

Center staff are cognizant that attitudes toward patient residents are communicated to them nonverbally as well as verbally. One study indicates that when two people communicate, the preponderance of total impact is transmitted in a nonverbal way—through what has been called "body talk"—rather than by the words that are used. When we accept the resident as a person of basic worth with potential for improvement and when we anticipate that he will benefit from his stay at the Center, he in turn may be expected to sense these feelings and expectations. Such messages from the initial contact on should help him along the road to recovery. We think that today optimistic messages are transmitted and received. Formerly residents picked up clear suggestions of rejection and pessimism. Those whom they regarded by training, position and experience to be experts commonly expected them to fail and not uncommonly told them as much. As a consequence, residents usually adopted the same expectations. Lack of success then became a self-fulfilling prophecy. We now hope that expectations of success will make for success and that each increment in the curve of positive change will beget further change.

In an effort to maintain a drug-free environment without recourse to harsh security measures, the Center employs random urine testing to detect the presence of any drugs illicitly obtained and abused. This provision for urinalyses affords a reasonably accurate appraisal of whether, and to what extent, a contraband drug problem may exist at any given time.

In addition, urine testing obviates the need for other kinds of security measures and acquaints each resident with the routine procedure that will be required of him during his three years of after-care. Judging from urine tests conducted at the Center during the course of a recent month, unannounced urine tests presumably serve to discourage drug abuse, suggest that we are interested in what our residents do and provide a kind of support to residents in their efforts to remain off drugs during a phase of personal adjustment when most are experiencing considerable internal struggle. Of 265 urine samples randomly selected and tested, during a recent month, only five were found to contain drugs of abuse. This indicated 1.13 percent of illicit drug use within our population.

To generate individual and group motivation, systems of positive incentives and rewards are in continuous operation. These are given for mature behavior, productivity and progress in therapeutic and rehabilitative activity. Incentives include increased freedom, social and recreational functions, choice of rooms and special vocational opportunities. Such practices are predicated on the tacit assumption that positive reinforcement results in greater gains than does negative reinforcement. This hypothesis has been well supported by research studies conducted in a variety of settings with a variety of subjects. By contrast, the erstwhile observer might have inferred during the bygone era that negative reinforcement was the method of choice by the staff during those beleaguered times.

Grounds privileges, escorted and unescorted visits to town for individuals who demonstrate readiness for this amount of self-control, and selected field trips for small groups are examples of graduated freedom for self-expression and personal fulfillment. Opportunities for enriching work and educational experiences outside the institution have been developed, and it is hoped that proliferation will occur.

Specific illustrations could be given, but I wish to avoid becoming prolix.

During the course of renovation, tons of massive iron grilles and bars have been removed by the use of cutting torches and have been salvaged as scrap metal later adapted to more useful purposes. This action is symbolic of the openness and pleasant atmosphere that have replaced the dismal and oppressive prison air. A dank, pervasive miasma no longer exists. Recent visitors, who at some time in the past had occasion to enter the forbidding institution that once was, are quick to notice contrasts between the old and the new.

Telephones exist in dormitories for the first time in a history of thirty-five years. Dayrooms are furnished with drapes and carpeting. Residents may decorate their own rooms in accordance with personal tastes. Together they may decide how they would like to improve dayrooms, hallways and activity areas. Men and women regularly enjoy together meals, social hours, dances, religious services and seasonal picnics. Many are now exercising the restraint and dignity and the regard for the rights and feelings of others that typify the manners and morals of ladies and gentlemen.

The conditions just described are a far cry from former days when male patients were sometimes required by security officers to turn and face the nearest wall during the passage of escorted groups of female patients.

Dehumanizing and depersonalizing procedures were once instituted to maintain environmental security. They were perpetuated to keep patients contrite and penitent and to mete out retributive punishment proportional in severity to the magnitude of the sin of drug abuse.

The previous security force has diminished through attrition, and it no longer has any direct responsibility for patient care. The nursing service has been correspondingly increased in size and has assumed full responsibility for patient care units. The fundamental objective of our total program is effectual and humane treatment of drug-habituated persons. The corresponding objective is the conducting of research, both inductive or empirical, and deductive or experimental, with a view to understanding and breaking the habituation pattern. Built into and integral to the program are means for studying and evaluating progress along a multiplicity of dimensions. Rather than assuming that we have most of the solutions to the problems related to drug dependency, we frankly admit that we do not have. Implicit in research is the admission and identification of problems. Without these considerations and consequent exploratory activity, a program must remain static. When there is immobility, there is resistance to change. It is therefore with pride I point out the fact that a movement involving carefully controlled research in the treatment of drug-prone subjects is increasing and is expanding withal.

In October 1969, we began to develop a self-help program styled after Synanon. The program, known as Matrix House, though stylistically similar to Synanon, possesses basic differences that render it unique. Several other therapeutic communities have become well established in the Center, but I should like to tell you something of Matrix House because it serves as a prototype for the others. Its members are required by the total citizenry of Matrix to demonstrate willingness to abide by basic rules adopted for the betterment of all, and they are expected to emulate the behavior of senior members who serve as role models.

Matrix House is a self-help residential community located in a building which is geographically separate from the complex of interconnected buildings that together comprise the NIMH Clinical Research Center and the Addiction Research Center.

This domiciliary organization was created for the avowed purpose of the residents helping one another to live effectively in the present as a prelude to effective living in the future.

Viewing themselves as individuals who in a broad sense have been addicted most of their lives to stupid behavior, the culmination of which was addiction to narcotics and probably dependence on additional drugs, they are in accord that they require confrontation with evidence of immature and self-defeating behavior whenever it is so recognized by their peers. Essential to the confrontations are personal concern, brotherhood or sisterhood, and love. All are in agreement regarding the two inescapable rules of abstinence from drugs and sex and absence from violence and threats of violence.

Confrontation sessions serve as an instrument to persuade each member of the family within the home to perceive himself realistically as others perceive him, to recognize his weaknesses as evidence of the need for change and to aspire to the assumption of progressive responsibility for self and others.

Group members have developed a peculiar vernacular which includes terms such as "games," "pullups" and "haircuts." For the sake of simplicity, I shall say at this time that techniques include encounter sessions, educational seminars, assigned readings, pointing out inappropriate behavior during the course of everyday activity, emphatic verbal reprimands, planning and decision-making meetings, and extended marathon sessions.

The so-called street code and underworld value system are rejected. Negative behavior is immediately dealt with by brothers and sisters of the community. It may be accurately stated, in fact, that any adverse behavior that is recognized as such inevitably results in concerted group pressure directed toward the individual guilty of that behavior.

Professional staff have no official function within Matrix House, though they are welcome as visitors and equals. In short, the staff of Matrix consists of fellow residents. They are specifically the Director, the Deputy Director and various department heads. Headquarters has approved the Director, the Deputy Director and two department heads as the first ex-addict employees in federal service.

The credo of Matrix House is a kind of gospel and its way of life is a kind of religion. In keeping with these concepts are efforts made by the membership to serve humanity in various ways. They present programs in different communities, provide leadership for encounter meetings engaged in by interested people from outside their community, and welcome visitors. It is their contention that all of us engage in immature, self-defeating be-havior and so can benefit from confrontation within the context (Matrix) of constructive living.

The psychology research sections consist of separate investiga-tive units. For example, a physiological psychology laboratory utilizes a variety of measures including a promising approach, namely gauging pupillary size as indicative of anxiety and other emotionally aroused states in patients experiencing simulated and hypothetical drug conditions.

The social psychology laboratory uses games of chance—the prisoners' dilemma to start—to furnish social situations within which the addict's and ex-addict's social behavior can be examined.

The social science section consists of sociologists, anthropol-ogists and supporting staff engaged in research endeavors dealing with the addiction subculture and with the Center itself as a distinct culture. One investigator has been working on the history of the institution from a sociological point of view. Another study involves ex-patients in five widely separated cities. Its purpose is to determine ways in which being labeled an addict may affect behavior subsequent to release.

All of the research sections have for a larger purpose the evaluation of the effectiveness of the NARA program. It is hoped sets of psychological and sociological data will be accumulated that will yield predictors of outcome in and after treatment. It is also sincerely hoped that we shall one day locate variables that can be controlled for the purpose of determining the relative effectiveness of optional kinds of treatment. Local data are con-tinually being evaluated in relation to data furnished by after-care agencies numbering in excess of one hundred.

In addition to the treatment and research sections that have been sketchily described, there is a third major category. This goes by the designation of the Education and Training Sections. Though the last named is the most recently established, it is perhaps the most dynamic and energetic. Within the umbrella of these sections, we have initiated many educational functions for staff, patient residents and outside groups who are interested in learning about drug dependence and what may be done about it.

The Education and Training Sections are responding to a plethora of requests from many groups and organizations throughout the United States. One of the most successful techniques seems to be utilizing the services of a patient or patients as ancillary team members in speaking engagements. Resident participation is very successful in making a gut-level impact of what it is like to be an addict. As team members of a panel, well-chosen patients and staff together provide a gestalt whose effects are recognizably more than additive.

The Education and Training Sections are pleased to announce approval by headquarters of a wide-range video tape and closed circuit television studio on the premises. The facilities are to be used to conduct a broad spectrum of training functions, including the production of films relevant to our mission.

In balance, we at the refurbished and rejuvenated NIMH Clinical Research Center in Lexington aver that drug addiction can be effectively treated through concerted efforts. We feel strongly that through the NARA program, involving the coordinated efforts of the Lexington and Fort Worth Centers and aftercare agencies, this will be demonstrated beyond doubt. If over the years we can help to establish to a satisfactory degree the ability to effect behavioral changes in addicts, we shall then make a substantial contribution to the alleviation of serious social symptoms in the field of public health.

Chapter 40

Drug Addiction Programs Sponsored by New York State

S. Seymour Joseph

O NE CANNOT SPEAK of drug addiction programs sponsored by the State of New York since 1967 in a knowledgeable manner without some substantial understanding of the New York State Narcotic Addiction Control Commission. This newest of state agencies was created as a result of the legislature's passage of the Narcotic Control Act of 1966, an amendment to Article 9 of the Mental Hygiene Law.

The Commission has broad powers encompassing the entire field of narcotic addiction. It has established and operates rehabilitation centers and other facilities for the care, custody, treatment and after-care of narcotic-dependent individuals certified to its supervision. It has the right to approve and accredit private and local facilities for the treatment of addicts. The Commission also may assign and transfer addicts to facilities which it has established or to other state, local, federal and private agencies. It may conduct experimental programs involving the administration of drugs with substantial abuse liability and can give grants to and accept grants from private and governmental units. As one of its mandates, it is also to conduct broad programs of public education and to devise long-range programs for the prevention and control of drug abuse.

A chairman, vice chairman and three commissioners were appointed. Mr. Milton Luger, formerly of the Division for Youth, now heads the Commission. The organizational structure includes the following divisions:

1. *Treatment and Rehabilitation: Intramural Services and*

Community-based Services (T & R, IMS, CBS). These resources are only available to those addicts judicially certified to the supervision of the NACC for periods of three or five years with only one exception. If a certificand participates in the NACC Methadone Program and his certification expires, he may continue voluntarily by signing a release but may withdraw at any time.

2. *Research* (including a testing and research laboratory)

3. *Prevention and Education*

4. *Contractual Agencies (Public and Private)*. These resources treat both those addicts not certified and those who have been certified to the NACC. In the case of the latter, periodic progress reports are submitted to the NACC.

5. *Administrative*

On the basis of the experience of most individuals who have long-term clinical involvement in the field of narcotic addiction, there would appear to be a general recognition of the need for multimodality treatment approaches. One could postulate that this is probably due to the varying degrees of motivation in addicts as well as their rather diverse presenting psychopathology. There is little doubt that they seem to cover a wide range of psychiatric diagnostic categories. A body of information does exist about the narcotic-dependent individual. Yet, the effectiveness of treatment approaches has been difficult, if not impossible, to *ascertain* partly because of the emotional involvement of the treaters together with their defensive reactions to such frustrating involvement. (I am sure that readers of this book are all too aware of the "conning" expertise of these patients.)

As a result of this, enthusiasts of each program assert that they have the only remedy, a panacea if you will, and derogate all others as well as all who are associated with other treatment programs. As our former Director of Research has stated, "In this setting of vociferous claim and counterclaim, research is needed to provide a rational basis for public policy." Moreover, this is an essential need if any valid appraisal of treatment modalities, treatment inputs or meaningful educational thrusts may be made.

Some individuals, including professionals, feel that the closed ward treatment setting is a construct based on a moralistic puni-

tive approach to the addicts rather than a realistic pragmatic response to a scientifically indicated need or, in other terms, an appropriate extrapolation of public health measures to an illness
vitally concerned with public health. In short, if open ward treatment settings cannot keep addicts involved, should they—the addicts—be abandoned or should further attempts be made to retain
them so they can be exposed to treatment modalities. One question would appear to be posed: Is it probable or even possible
that substitutive appropriate adaptive mechanisms can be learned
and incorporated in various kinds of settings, from open to closed,
with different kinds of staffs—from a medical model psychiatric to
ex-addict self-help with professional inputs to a nonmedical
model interdisciplinary framework—that would permit an individual to field test the newly learned skills?

It would follow, with respect to treatment and rehabilitation,
that all efforts be made to collect and accumulate data that should
speak to providing valid appraisals and evaluations of the various
programs. In order to do so, the NACC proceeded to sponsor the
following treatment thrusts:

1. Psychiatric Department of Mental Hygiene (D.M.H.)
2. Interdisciplinary (NACC)
3. Self-Help (Daytop Village, Samaritan, Exodus, etc.)
4. Community (Greenwich House, etc.)
5. Drug Maintenance (Beth Israel, Einstein Medical, NACC)
6. Drug Antagonist (New York Medical College)
7. Correctional and Division for Youth
8. Dept. of Social Services (D.S.S.)

Over and above these that have been sponsored and supported
by the Commission through its regular budgetary allocation, the
State of New York has approved the following proposals presented by Governor Rockefeller to the legislature during the early
part of this year:

1. A total of $65 million was allocated for state aid to local
government agencies for operating drug-abuse treatment programs.

2. Local government agencies would be authorized to provide

such services directly or by contract with qualified voluntary agencies.

3. The Health & Mental Hygiene Facilities Improvement Corp. was authorized to construct, acquire or rehabilitate facilities for use by local agencies in the conduct of drug-abuse treatment programs.

4. The State Housing Finance Agency was authorized to issue additional $200 million in notes and bonds to finance the construction, acquisition or rehabilitation of such facilities.

5. The Division for Youth was authorized to establish and operate residential youth development programs in which any youthful addict or drug abuser under 18 could be admitted.

The implementation of these would encourage local governments, either acting directly or through qualified voluntary agencies, to call upon and utilize the NACC, the State Health and Mental Hygiene Facilities Improvement Corporation and the State Housing Finance Agency for developing new and improved programs to provide inpatient and outpatient care. The state would provide up to 50 percent of full operating costs.

Moreover, in an effort to provide them with the greatest possible financial assistance, marked liberalization of the standards of eligibility for the $65 million in matching funds was accomplished. (Labor and value of volunteer personnel included as local contribution.)

Also, $200 million in state loans was segregated to build more treatment facilities.

Another $15 million were allocated for an expanded methadone maintenance program at Beth Israel, Einstein Medical and others.

Arrangements were finalized for the special training for upwards of 10,000 teachers of public and private schools to help in preventing drug experimentation.

Organization and support of local narcotic guidance councils were accelerated.

Plans were set in motion for the training of youth workers ("Helping Services") in the counseling of the young and their parents.

With respect to research, the NACC Research Division was mandated to direct or conduct surveys and analyses of the state's needs, to engage in basic clinical, social and behavioral science studies, and to gather and maintain statistical records and data relevant to addicts and addiction. In an effort to accomplish this expeditiously, the Division of Research expanded its potentia by awarding contracts to private research groups. (Columbia University School of Public Health and Administrative Medicine, Columbia University Bureau of Applied Social Research, the New York Medical College, Rockefeller University and Audits and Surveys, Inc., of New York).

With respect to Prevention and Education, the NACC has conceived and developed one of the most comprehensive engagements in an effort to disseminate legitimate information about this ubiquitous drug abuse problem. Here, too, research is pursuing various strategies in an effort to evaluate the validity of such antinarcotic or anti–drug-abuse activities.

Because of the unpredictable epidemic-like increase in the enormity of the problem and the further realization that to meet such an overwhelming situation, engagement has to take place in a total sense both qualitatively and quantitatively throughout the entire gamut from a parental one-to-one interaction, through local community and local governmental intervention, to that of the state intervention. In an effort to initiate this total thrust, local governmental agencies and/or communities were actively encouraged to present comprehensive abuse programs by November 1, 1970. They were to undertake the following:

1. Outline the extent of drug problem in the community; review of existing programs, progress and needs still to be met.

2. Formulate supplemental program plans and state aid payment requests to fund new, broadened or reoriented programs highest priority for an integrated approach.

3. Examine the existing resources now utilized in program areas of lesser priority which can be shifted (drug emergency).

4. Present evidence of a reasonable degree that new or existing drug abuse programs will be sufficiently flexible to insure continuing adaptability to changing needs.

The essential need for a total response to a total need cannot be overemphasized. Yet, it should be recognized that one of the unfortunate responses to a problem of this kind can very well be an overreaction to the need, regardless of the severity of the problem. We have seen all too frequently the rather inappropriate responses of a community, well-meaning as it is, to the manipulative energies of the very individuals against whom it is attempting to protect other members of the very same community.

SUMMARY

The Narcotic Addiction Control Commission has broad powers encompassing the entire field of narcotic addiction in the State of New York. It is the specific agency through which the state acts in evaluating and funding programs: Upon application to the NACC, a program may be (a) accredited, (b) provisionally accredited or (c) disapproved.

Only those programs of the first two categories are eligible for state monies. Provisional accreditation may be granted when a determination is made that an agency is in substantial compliance with the standards established by the Commission but is unable to immediately meet all such standards yet gives evidence of being able to meet them within a reasonable period of time.

As mentioned previously, there is a plethora of claims and counterclaims. This, in itself, should make the scientifically oriented quite wary indeed. When medical or psychiatric problems blend into philosophical frameworks or conceptualizations, then it should be all too obvious that verbosity could very well be substituted for rationality; enthusiasm and aggressivity for therapeutic efficacy.

Despite some indications of results that could generate optimism, I would strongly recommend caution. We are fielding and funding a diversity of programs both public and private; we are collecting and accumulating what appears to be meaningful data. It would be well to postpone so-called conclusions until our Division of Research or others under contract can present to all of us the "way it is" rather than the way we would like it to be. They may very well coincide, but then again they may not!

Yet, we must always keep in mind the complexity of the addict and not succumb to the siren songs of those who would reduce the matter to simplistics. After all, we are dealing with patients who are adaptational cripples who, in all too many instances, have utilized heroin as a maladaptive reparative device. Consequently, it would appear to be decidedly unrealistic for one to proceed on the basis of standardized and generalized goals.

Rather, there must be an individuation of expectations with the realization that each rehabilitant should be considered as having immedate, intermediate and long-range goals. Abstinence and self-reliant functioning in all behavioral spheres are much to be desired and, in fact, possible for some. But the vast majority have progressed even if they evidence minimal improvement in personal and environmental functioning, for them, a positive point of departure for even future treatment reengagement.

This is the reality—not to recognize it is to negate the chronicity and the very nature of the problem itself.

REFERENCES

1. Lang, Irving: Narcotics legislation—total approach. *The Catholic Lawyer*. Spring 1966.
2. Glaser, Daniel: Research for rationality in narcotics policy. *The Analyst, Vol. 2,* April 1969.
3. Rockefeller, Nelson A.: Proposals—Drug Abuse. Press Release: March 20, 1970.
4. Rockefeller, Nelson A.: Letter to Heads of Municipalities. Press Release: August 27, 1970.
5. Rockefeller, Nelson A.: Grants for Program (Abstinence and Drug Maintenances) . Press Release: September 8, 1970.
6. Chambers, Carl D.: *Research Objectives and Priorities.* NACC Publication, April 1970.
7. Rado, Sandor: *Psychoanalysis of Behavior.* New York, Grune & Stratton, 1956.

Chapter 41

Phoenix Houses: Therapeutic Communities
for Drug Addicts
A Comparative Study of Residents in Treatment

D. Vincent Biase

P HOENIX HOUSE is the popular name for a drug-free rehabilitation system and for the fifteen individual therapeutic communities. It began with five detoxified ex-addicts in May 1967 and by
1970, less than three and one half years later, it has flourished to
more than one thousand residents. The term "resident" desig-
nates a former drug abuser in the full-time treatment program
within a Phoenix House therapeutic community. The program is
the country's largest drug rehabilitation program of its kind. During the past three years, 148 residents have completed the program. Phoenix House carries a major share of New York City's
attack on the problems of drug abuse. It operates within the Addiction Services Agency part of the city's Human Resources Administration and is supported by city and state funds and private
donations as well as the welfare payments contributed by residents. The foci of the program are the residential therapeutic
communities—Phoenix Houses—where residents work and take
part in a variety of rehabilitative activities designed to modify
drug abuse behavior and its frequently negative social concom-
mitants. The therapeutic communities are run mostly by former
addicts. Nine such houses are located in renovated buildings in
high drug-abuse areas in Manhattan, the Bronx, Brooklyn and
Queens. Another five houses are on Hart Island, while a special

Note: The author wishes to express his appreciation for the helpful assistance
given to this study by Sherry Holland, Sandy Newman and Gwen Cavanaugh.

residence for young people is located in Putnam Valley, New York.

Most of the approximately two hundred Phoenix House staff members are trained former addicts and drug abusers, supported by fifteen medical doctors, seven nurses, four research psychologists, fifteen licensed teachers, four social workers and numerous ancillary professionals. A more complete description of the program specifics can be found in an article by Rosenthal and Biase.[4]

The Phoenix House group encounter is the major therapeutic tool; it is designed to facilitate emotional catharsis and increased self-understanding of the participants. Recently published research has demonstrated that Phoenix House residents report decreases in states of anxiety, depression and hostility after participation in encounters.[2] Further investigation of the physiological parameter as related to encounter participation is being conducted by the Research Unit at Phoenix House.

Since Phoenix House is a drug-free program, urinanalysis was the technique used to detect resident drug violaters while in treatment. Presently this technique has been terminated. The results of 2,874 urine tests of residents were tabulated monthly from July 1, 1969, through January 31, 1970. The number of positives (excluding those from prescribed medication) was 115 or 4 percent for all types of drugs, less than 1 percent were positive for heroin or other opiates.

Although a complete follow-up of Phoenix House graduates is in progress, a recent summary indicates that of thirty-five graduates of the program all but one have been found to be drug-free and have made adjustments to drug abstinence.

METHODOLOGY AND RESULTS

In the present study, the author surveyed 173 Phoenix House residents in October 1968. This randomly selected group represented 37 percent of the total population. The sample comprised 147 males representing 35 percent of the overall male population and 26 females representing 55 percent of the female population. Data was collected by self-report and included demographic information, time in program, criminal and drug history and academic history. Scores on the Adult Basic Learning Examination (ABLE) [3] and Interest and Preference Test Form II [5] were also obtained. The progress of this sample was reevaluated in March 1970, seventeen months later. Because of a system of data decentralization, information was obtained on 158 residents or 91 percent of the original sample. A portion of the results of that survey will be reported here today.

In our efforts to define the characteristics of resident success within the program, statistical comparisons were made between reentry and non–reentry residents. The reevaluation data in March 1970 permitted an analysis of variables which had particular program relevance. Included in this analysis were total time in program as of March 1970, number of splits or abscondences between entry into the program and the reevaluation period, time between entry and splits, the number of residents who achieved reentry status and the number of reentry candidates who were gainfully employed.

Reentry or eldership status is achieved after a resident has been a member of a Phoenix House therapeutic community for a minimum of eighteen months. A resident is recommended for this status on the basis of a drug-free history during these eighteen months and satisfactory interpersonal, attitudinal and performance criteria. Presently, a resident is recommended for this status by a regional board which is comprised of ex-addict addiction specialists. The reentry phase is that specific period of time prior to graduation from the program wherein a resident confronts the issues of transition from the closed microcosm of the therapeutic community to the open society. Since his past experiences with society have tended to be negative and corrosive, emphasis is placed on offering the candidate opportunities for more positive experiences and new options for dealing with the new challenge. During this period he continues to attend encounters with older staff members including those members without addiction histories. He receives social assignments, receives private consultation with his house director and is expected to generate a social network of family, friends, employers or teachers. Continued academic and or vocational training is included in this period.

Reentry status data was available for 158 residents out of the initial 173 surveyed. Seventy or 44 percent of this group had achieved reentry status. Twenty-six of these reentry candidates had graduated from the program and were gainfully employed in a variety of jobs both within and outside of the agency.

TABLE 41-I
SIGNIFICANT DIFFERENCES BETWEEN REENTRY AND RESIDENT GROUP

Variables	Reentry N	Resident N	X^2	df	p
Volunteer-NACC					
(967,968)	70	88	6.437	1	<.02
Time in program					
as of 3/70	53	78	35.458	2	<.001
No. of splits	66	85	35.137	2	<.001
Time between entry					
and splits	70	88	49.823	2	<.001
Opiates	45	40	6.675	1	<.05
Stimulants	45	44	3.899	1	<.05

Fifty-one percent of the reentry group had been in the program six to ten months at the time of the initial survey as compared to 39 percent of the resident group. An analysis of the mean time in program was not significant. The mean time in program for both groups was greater than eighteen months. Although Phoenix House is a voluntary program, residents are discouraged from splitting until they have completed the program. Seventy-three percent of those who achieved reentry as compared to 27 percent of the resident group (p < .001) had never split from the program. These splits included both temporary abscondences and terminal splits from the program. The majority of the resident group who split did so only once. There was also a significantly different pattern when splits occurred; 57 percent of the resident group split within the first twelve months of treatment, while 56 percent of the reentry group split after ninteen or more months (p < .001).

Analysis of past drug abuse patterns of forty-five reentry candidates and forty-four residents indicated no differences in the abuse of heroin as the chief drug abused. Further analysis of the multi–drug-abuse patterns indicated that a greater number of the resident group, 46 percent used other opiates while only 18 percent of the reentry group reported abusing the same drug (p < .05). This difference between the two groups also existed with respect to past abuse of stimulants, 87 percent of the resident group had abused them in contrast to 69 percent of the reentry group (p < .05). No significant differences were found in the mean number of drugs in addition to their chief drug compared to 3.3 additional drugs reported by the reentry group. It should be noted that these means reflect the average number of drugs abused at any time in the subject's past history and do not necessarily reflect active addiction to these drugs in the same manner as do the chief addicted drugs.

A comparative analysis indicated that a significantly greater proportion of persons who volunteered off the street for the rehabilitation program achieved reentry status when compared to a group of penitentiary convicts (NACC 967,968) who chose to enter the program while incarcerated (p < .02). A comparative report of these two groups is presently in preparation.[1]

Analyses of these following variables did not yield any differences between the reentry and non-reentry groups: ethnic group; sex; age (less than 34 years—35 years or more); highest school grade completed; holder of high school diploma; type of secondary school course; age of first abuse; chief drug abused; use of marijuana, barbituates, inhalants, psychedelics, tranquilizers or antidepressants; number of arrests; number of convictions; grade score in Vocabulary, Spelling, Arithmetic, Problem Solving from the Adult Basic Learning Examination; and scores on the Interest and Preference Test Form II, an early measure of stimulus-seeking behavior.

The present data provides information on some of the differences between more successful and less successful residents within the Phoenix House treatment program. The present criteria for success is considered with respect to the internal program criteria. At this time researchers, and particularly those in the addiction field, must admit that our definitions of success criteria are at an elemental stage. We must remember that many of the therapeutic programs were and are still being born from an incubator of social crises and need. Thus they will influence how and what phenomena we study about them. At the same time, how can we hope to measure with confidence the specific effectiveness of treatment programs particularly when the norm for drug taking in the general population is anything but stable. I think we must consider that the criteria of abstinence is certainly more appropriate for another period in history. Of course, some major demographic variables—that is, status of criminal activity, gainful employment and marital stability—may be useful, but they are obviously limited to the parlance of legislators and program evaluators. This is the pivotal point—we must maintain a differentiation between research and program evaluation. Each has its specific demands and goals, and while they may fertilize each other, their issues and level of inquiry should be different. The challenge that both the researcher and program evaluator face, if met, will yield pertinent information for personality theory and for the issues of adult resocialization to help determine the extent and limits of group influence and, moreover, to help formulate a concept of change in human behavior.

REFERENCES

1. Biase, D.V.: A Comparative Study of Addicted Community and Penetentiary Volunteers NACC (967, 968) for Treatment at Phoenix House. Unpublished manuscript 1970.
2. Biase, D.V., and De Leon, G.: The encounter group—measurement of some affect changes. In *Proceedings of the 77th Annual Convention of the American Psychological Association*. Washington D.C., American Psychological Association, 1969.
3. Karlsen, B., Madden, R., and Gardner, E.I.: *Adult Basic Learning Examination*. New York, Harcourt, Brace & World, 1967.
4. Rosenthal, M.S., and Biase, D.V.: Phoenix Houses: Therapeutic communities for drug addicts. *Hosp Community Psychiat, 20*:26-30, 1969.
5. Zuckerman, M., Kolin, E.A., Price, L., and Zoob, I.: Development of a sensation seeking scale. *J Consult Psychol, 28*:477-482, 1964.

Chapter 42

Reality House, A Self-help Day-Care Center for Narcotic Addicts

Edward Kaufman

R EALITY HOUSE is a day-care center for the treatment of narcotic addicts which was established in the midst of New York City's drug-ridden Harlem in September 1967. It was originally staffed by a group which had worked closely together for almost three years at another day-care center for the treatment of addiction (Exodus House). Reality House differs from other self-help programs in several ways: there is no residential treatment, many professionals including psychiatrists are used to augment the predominantly ex-addict staff, "love and concern" are more basic than confrontation, and group therapy and vocational training are gradually stratified at five distinct levels. The five levels of the program are orientation, pretherapy, preshop, workshop or "B" and vocational training or "A." Urine specimens are analyzed three times weekly at all levels as a check against drug use.

Orientation is open to everyone who applies. This group varies greatly in size (6 to 40) and meets six days a week for two hours daily. The average stay is two weeks. The addict is asked to withdraw on his own and if he cannot he is referred for detoxification (through the Reality House Community Orientation Center) and then returned to orientation. The two co-therapists are both ex-addicts at this level and are therefore able to confront the addict with all of his "games" and with his problems other than those directly related to drugs. These confrontations are generally less brutal and denigrating than the techniques used in other programs.[1,4] The therapist begins to instill in the individual a sense of responsibility for his own self-destructiveness. Being on time is emphasized as an example of a personal responsibilty which can (and must) be fulfilled, even at this first level. The therapist uses a type of identification which can only be utilized by the ex-addict. He may be the first to verbalize feelings in order to draw the addicts out. He may offer a confessional catharsis of his own drug experience and cure, particularly of his difficulties during his own orientation period. He is particularly adept at recognizing the addict's underlying anxieties and at utilizing these as motivation for treatment. As one ex-addict states, "If you have any experiences within your life that are similar, you let him know how you have dealt with them. First you may help him recognize his fear by saying, "Yeh, I can remember how afraid I was to be able to do that" and then he begins to feel his own fear. Once you can get to the fear, the other problems come pretty easily."

Relationships begin through the ex-addict's firm responses to the endless testing which occurs and his development of a genuine concern for the program member. Despite the concern and involvement of the therapist, those members who will remain in the program readily realize that not using heroin is helpful to themselves, not to their therapist, and that lying about themselves or their drug use is only self-defeating. The member's efforts at being drug-free, truthfulness and coming on time are readily recognized and reinforced by the therapist and group.

At the pretherapy level groups of six to ten are led by a pair of therapists, one an ex-addict and one a professional; usually one of the pair is a woman. Here the emphasis is on the member's relationships in the reality world and the practical difficulties involved in living in that world as a nonaddict. Rationalizations for drug use such as race, social problems and environment are rapidly confronted by the ex-addict. The addict is made to see that he has chosen this "subhuman" existence for reasons within him which he must begin to explore. Even before he has fully understood his behavior, he is asked to behave *as if* he did; this is particularly true with regard to alcohol, drug abuse and grossly inappropriate and antisocial behavior. There is emphasis on replacing intellectualizations with feelings. The group is taught that there is only one way to look good and that is by looking "bad" reveal-

ing one's deepest and ugliest feelings. The therapist utilizes identification at a deeper level at this phase. An example of this is
with homosexual problems, where the ex-addict has a unique
ability to recognize and tap the homosexual problems of the program member. He may have developed this ability from an inte-
gration of the homosexual fears and experiences which were an
inevitable part of his own prison experiences. The expression of
"love and concern" is crucial at this level. These feelings are con-
veyed by recognition, identification, physical touching and support in crises at any place and hour, including dealings with social
agencies. These supportive measures are gradually withdrawn as
the member develops more ego strength and obtains his own
reality gratifications.

The next level is preshop which lasts about six weeks. This
level consists of pretherapy, plus four hours of workshop experience daily. Here the member's tolerance for a work situation is
evaluated and a vocational plan is formulated. His difficulties in
obtaining gratification from ordinary work are explored and the
value of obtaining meaning from work is developed. To help
achieve these goals vocational group meetings are held three
times a week. Here there are three shops: carpentry, pottery and
jewelry. The shops are not directly involved with career training
at this phase, but focus instead on the individual's ability to turn
his verbal insights into behavior and productivity. Here too his
relationships with his peers and supervisors are closely examined.
At this level the member begins to relate to and identify with the
professional therapist as his defenses against that relationship are
removed. An individual is returned to lower levels if there is an
inability to function at work or psychotherapy and, of course, for
any drug use. These "setbacks" are utilized as valuable learning
experiences for handling frustration and defeat.

The "B" (workshop) level usually lasts for five to seven
months. Here there is greater emphasis on the end products of
the craft and their relevance to career choice. Intensive vocational
groups continue in addition to group psychotherapy four times
weekly. Here the co-therapists are a psychiatrist and an ex-addict.
At this phase it is felt that the individual is prepared for the

type of group reconstructive techniques employed by the psychiatrist.

The final phase of the program is "A" level where the individual is involved in a vocational placement. He may attend college, study cabinet making, computer programming or train as a paraprofessional therapist. He stays in group therapy throughout the training period, although the time is diminished to two-hour sessions twice a week. Here the therapist is mainly a psychiatrist, although occasionally ex-addicts are used as co-therpists. The average total stay for a successfully treated addict in this program is eighteen months.

RESULTS

As of May 1, 1970, approximately 1300 individuals attended orientation at Reality House. Of this total, 80 percent progressed to pretherapy, 18 percent to preshop, and 6 percent to "B" level. A description of the "B" level population at Reality House is as follows. The percentage of blacks is 85 percent with the remainder evenly split between whites and Puerto Ricans. Eighty percent are males. The average age is 28.6 years. The average length of drug use is ten years. The average number of years spent in an institutional environment is 6.8 years. The average educational level is 11th grade and the average full-scale IQ on the WAIS is 110.7.[2]

An eighteen month follow-up was performed on a group of forty-seven randomly selected from orientation. The results were as follows:[2]

Category	No.	%
Not using narcotics (includes three referred to other programs)	12	25.5
Using narcotics	20	42.6
In prison	6	12.7
Deceased (overdose)	2	4.3
No accurate information	7	14.9
	47	100.0

A random sample of twenty-six members who reached at least "B" level in the first $2\frac{1}{2}$ years of the program revealed:

Category	No.	%
Not using narcotics	17	66
Using narcotics	4	15
In prison	3	11
Referred to other programs	1	4
No accurate information	1	4
	—	—
	26	100

At the time of the above evaluation, nineteen members were still in the program. An estimate of each member's present status was ascertained by either urinalysis or home visits or discussion with the parole or after-care worker. As of November 1, 1970, twenty-one individuals have completed the full program at Reality House. All of them have returned to society and are drug-free. Sixteen are employed in some capacity in self-help movements, three being currently employed at Reality House.

DISCUSSION

The high (82 percent) dropout rate in the first two stages of the program warrants discussion. This period can be looked upon as a screening process which eliminates those addicts who are not motivated or suitable for this type of program. This method of screening is in some ways less selective than those utilized by other treatment centers of addiction.[3,4] That 25.5 percent of those who have entered the doors of Reality House are drug-free eighteen months later is in itself quite impressive. The 66 percent drug-free rate of those who stayed the few months in the program to achieve "B" level status is also quite high. However, the success of Reality House cannot be measured by statistics alone. It offers a treatment opportunity to many individuals who could not be reached by other types of programs. These include those who resist the dependency of methadone maintenance or residential treatment, individuals with close family ties who are not willing to interrrupt these ties for one to two years, or those who require immediate gratification and cannot tolerate waiting lists or denigrating confrontation. The most important difference between Reality House and other programs is that it is a nonresidential center. Therefore, the individual is dealing with the anxieties of existing in the real world and there is no need to mobilize anxieties by overemphasizing minor incidents. There is much less use of harsh, devastating confrontations and the individual is not stripped rapidly to the level of a helpless three-year-old. There is more emphasis on an ego reconstruction, utilizing the past when necessary. This is done through the use of psychiatrists at advanced levels of the program, after the member has been prepared by the ex-addict for this type of approach.

Although the current number of graduates of Reality House is relatively small, the program is worth examining because it is without the protection of a closed treatment center or a drug such as Methadone. Because the emphasis is placed on reconstructive change, the graduates of Reality House have acquired strengths which have enabled them to become leaders in the fields of ex-addict psychotherapy, as well as other self-help movements. The ghetto-bred addict can best be reached by the ex-addict who can speak his language, tap his anxieties and provide a figure with whom he can identify. The experience of Reality House in utilizing these specialized techniques indicates that the ex-addict therapist is able to treat a group of hard-core addicts in a nonresidential setting with some degree of success.

REFERENCES

1. Casriel, D.: *So Fair a House: The Story of Synanon.* Englewood Cliffs, Prentice Hall, 1964.
2. Lentchner, L.: *Annual Report of Reality House,* April, 1970.
3. Perkins, M.E., and Bloch, H.I.: Survey of a methadone maintenance treatment program. *Amer J Psychiat, 126(10):*1389-1396, 1970.
4. Shelly, J.A., and Bassin, A.: A new treatment approach for drug addicts, *Corr Psychiat & J. Soc Ther, 11(4):*186-195, 1965.

Chapter 43

Schizophrenics Anonymous and the Drug Abuser

Ralph S. Ryback

Schizophrenics Anonymous (SA) is a self-supporting, self-help organization.[1] SA was begun less than ten years ago in Saskatoon, Saskatchewan, Canada, by twelve patients of Dr. Abram Hoffer. The group has grown rapidly so that there are now thirty-eight active groups in the United States alone.[1] SA was modeled along lines similar to Alcoholics Anonymous (AA) and has adopted and adapted the twelve traditions, twelve steps and mutual member support outside of meetings of AA.

In most groups there are usually two simultaneous meetings, a beginners and regular member meeting, held once a week. Nevertheless, both meetings start with the traditional serenity prayer, which has also been adopted from AA. The meetings last $1\frac{1}{2}$ hours with a 15-minute coffee break. The beginner's meeting is run by one of the regular members who acts as a chairman. The chairman describes the history of the group and attempts to define schizophrenia in terms of its symptoms.

Schizophrenia is seen as primarily an inherited biochemical disorder which produces (a) changes in perception such as seeing, hearing, tasting, et cetra and (b) difficulty in judging whether these changes are real or not. Other symptoms may be "trouble concentrating, difficulty with talking to others, and withdrawal." The chairman also usually defines, with the group, depression and paranoia. The biochemical explanation offered for these misperceptions is one developed by Hoffer and Osmond.[2-5,10,11]

The newcomers are encouraged to talk about their personal or interpersonal difficulties (misperceptions) and this is supported by several older members who relate how the program (Table 43-I) has helped them. The chairman stresses that there are no musts

TABLE 43-I
THE SA PROGRAM

1. *The Vitamins*
   A. Niacin—at least 3 gm a day
   B. Vitamin C—at least 1 gm a day
   C. Vitamin E—at least 400 IU a day
   D. Vitamin B-6—at least 50 mg a day
   E. Vitamin B-1—use if you are extremely nervous or cannot sleep well.

2. *The Diet*
   A. Main portion of the meal should be protein: meat, fish, poultry, eggs and milk.
   B. Moderate fats.
   C. Eliminate sugars: no tonics or soft drinks, pastries or pies.
   D. Eat equally proportioned meals at REGULAR hours.

3. *Group Therapy*
   A. This is extremely important—attend at least one meeting a week.

4. *Exercise*
   A. Walking, swimming, bicycling
   B. Adequate rest

5. *The 12 Steps*—with particular emphasis on the following steps:
   A. Second half of the first step, "We admitted that our lives had become unmanageable."
   B. The third step where "We turned our lives (problems) over to the care of God as we understand Him."

   To quote from another source: "Half measures avail us nothting." It takes an honest attempt at working these five parts of the program in order for us to obtain any worthwhile results.

in the program except a desire to get well. He suggests that the newcomers attend at least three beginner's meetings to see if the group is useful for them or if they can identify with other peoples' problems. If so, they take the Hoffer-Osmond Diagnostic Test (HOD) [6-9] which gives them a total score and also paranoid, perceptual and depression scores. If they obtain a total score of over 30 and/or high scores on the paranoid, perceptual or depression sections, they are strongly encouraged to contact a doctor before beginning the complete program to determine whether additional treatments or other drugs such as tranquilizers, antidepressants, sleeping pills or even a series of ECT are indicated. Finally, the chairman often suggests that "schizophrenics already have a very low self-image and many doubts. Accordingly an analysis (psychoanalysis) of their problems just makes them look at upsetting things which only makes them feel worse. You should do what works since if you have a problem it doesn't matter what the label is, it's still a problem with living. One day at a time, work on your good points, and believe in and use the whole program."

The regular meetings are chaired on a weekly rotating basis by one of the regular members. After talking to the group about how SA has helped him, the chairman systematically goes around the room addressing each person individually, by first name, and asking how they are and how their week went. In this manner, each member present has an opportunity to speak and share his success or failure with both the chairman and the group. Members may pass without speaking or they may comment on another member's statement which seems especially helpful if it is relevant to their own difficulties. The chairman acts as a moderator, supporting person, advice giver and clarifier in terms of his own experiences. He may ask a member questions such as: Can you recognize a depression coming, and how can you get out of it?

The 150 members in the Boston group vary in age from 15 to 70 years with the majority being 25 to 55 years of age. Thirty to forty percent of the members also belong to AA. About 40 percent are married, 40 percent single and the other 20 percent divorced or separated. One third can be considered clinically to be ambulatory schizophrenics and another 20 percent psychoneurotics. About 50 percent are self-confessed alcoholics or multiple drug abusers. The latter group lends itself easily to division into neurotic, character disorder and psychotic diagnosis with the majority being in the latter category. One such member related to the group, "if you're an alcoholic and a schizophrenic, you've got to take care of both problems. If you don't take care of your schizophrenia, you'll end up drinking. There's no substitute for AA, but SA is a supplement. AA doesn't have all the answers as there are other physical or mental problems. AA may get you off the booze, but you still can be miserable and unhappy." Another member added, "I was in AA for 10 years and I've been drinking since age 10. I used a hallucinate, saw statues moving, had nightmares and a HOD score of 137. Yet since I started with SA, I'm a new man." At a recent group meeting a member related, "I'm an alcoholic and a schizophrenic. I don't know what came first, probably schizophrenia. I think I became an alcoholic to feel normal. I didn't like to go to the doctors because they gave me pills. I'm afraid of pills because I was on them too when I was drinking." Another member added, "It's a matter of pride that I didn't want to take pills. I wasn't afraid of vitamins." At the end of the meeting a member related, "I've been drinking for years, maybe because of my severe depressions which often occurred about once a month. I've been in AA two years, and one year sober. After my first five months of sobriety, I began thinking crazy. Get this, this is off the booze! I thought I was one of the apostles. At the hospital they said I had a schizophrenic reaction. They put me on Etrafon® and it helped me with both my depressions and my thinking. So, I take the vitamins and Etrafon."

DISCUSSION

The focus of SA is learning how to function personally and interpersonally in a comfortable manner, with meetings providing an arena where members can find support and express their feelings or misperceptions without fear of being treated degradingly. But, SA is more, it is a program, a new way of living and looking at the world. It educates its members and explains what schizophrenia, paranoia and depression are. It affords them self-esteem, not only because it allows them to help themselves but because it proposes a "scientific theory" to explain their difficulties which makes their mental discomfort not only understandable but respectable. For the drug abuser, it allows him to discover that his difficulties with living are not just the drugs but his inner being and that, in many cases, he used the drugs to self-medicate himself, not be himself, or to make himself feel normal. Indeed, many AA members in the Boston area are often referred to SA when their interpersonal and intrapersonal problems are overwhelming for themselves and/or the AA chapter. It could be asked whether having a drug abuser take 3 to 20 gm of niacin a day as well as vitamin C, E and B-6 is really only switching an "addiction" as might be suggested between the minor tranquilizers and alcohol. Yet, all will agree that it is better to pop vitamins than to take alcohol or speed. The young drug abuser, age 15 to 20 years, has usually felt somewhat uncomfortable in an SA meeting because of the age differential. However, recently in Boston, the first teenage group of SA called SA-TEEN was founded and it is hoped that it will provide a program for teenagers who are finding their lives uncomfortable, including those who abuse drugs. In short, SA is a self-help group which can often help patients who abuse drugs. Yet, at the same time, SA encourages professional medical intervention.[12]

REFERENCES

1. Schizophrenics Anonymous International, P.O. Box 913, Saskatoon, Saskatchewan, Canada.
2. Hoffer, A., and Osmond, H.: *The Chemical Basis of Clinical Psychiatry.* Springfield, Charles C Thomas, 1960.
3. Osmond, H., and Hoffer, A.: A comprehensive theory of schizophrenia. *Int J Neuropsychiat, 2:*302-309, 1966.
4. Hoffer, A.: Review of nicotinic acid nicotinamide and NAD, combination of nicotinic acid with other schizophrenic chemotherapy. Read at the Amityville Conference, Brunswick Hospital, New York, Jan. 21/22, 1967.
5. Hoffer, A.: A Program of Testing Schizophrenia and Other Conditions Using Megavitamin Therapy. 1967 (Available for physicians only directly from the author: 1201 CN Towers, First Avenue South, Saskatoon, Saskatchewan, Canada) .
6. Hoffer, A., and Osmond, H.: A card sorting test helpful in making psychiatric diagnoses. *J Neuropsychiat, 2:*306-330, 1961.
7. Hoffer, A., and Osmond, H.: A card sorting test helpful in establishing prognosis. *Amer J Psychiat, 118:*840-841, 1962.
8. Kelm, H., and Hoffer, A.: A revised score for the Hoffer-Osmond Diagnostic Test. *Dis Nerv Syst, 26:*790-791, 1965.
9. Hoffer, A., and Kelm, H.: *HOD Test and Manual.* Willner Chemists Inc., 330 Lexington Ave. New York. N.Y. 10016.
10. Hoffer, A.: *Niacin Therapy in Psychiatry.* Springfield, Charles C Thomas, 1962.
11. Hoffer, A., and Osmond, H.: Treatment of schizophrenia with civotinic acid, a ten year follow-up. *Acta Psychiat Scand, 40:*171-189, 1964.
12. Hyback, R.: Schizophrenics Anonymous: A treatment adjunct. *Psychiat in Med, 2:*247-253, 1971.

Chapter 44

Some Roots of Psychotherapeutic Aspects of Treatment of Drug Dependence and Abuse

Henry Brill

IT HAS OFTEN BEEN SAID that the present state of treatment of drug dependence is one of the strongest arguments in favor of prevention. Yet in spite of all limitations, treatment programs are developing in this field, and the results reported are becoming more favorable with the passage of time.

How these results are being achieved and to what specific elements in the various programs one may attribute the favorable, or the unfavorable, outcomes remains a problem of great importance. In examining the various programs of treatment, one is impressed that they differ more in theory than they do in practice. In theory one can distinguish some program protocols that emphasize psychic causality and their treatment plan follows the psychic causality; others stress environmental causality and their treatment plan emphasizes that, and finally some techniques emphasize somatic underlying causes.

One element in the psychotherapeutic pattern appears to be relatively new, at least it has not been widely used in psychiatry, and it has assumed a very prominent role in a wide variety of drug treatment programs. This approach has, I think, jarred the sensibilities of most of the psychiatrists who have come in contact with it. I refer to an approach which features an aggressive or abrasive psychotherapy in which the group attacks the individual. When one is exposed to an actual session, it is a bit startling and seems to go completely contrary to the theory and practice of psychiatry as it has been traditionally understood and to all the aims of psychiatry as it has been built up for at least a hundred years. I have been interested in this radical and new approach; how it came about, how it entered this field. This chapter will deal with this question.

My first lead as to origins came from a purely political direction in a book on Communist China which described the so-called brainwashing techniques as they were developed and widely used in that country after World War II. The volume quotes a 1957 article in which these were analyzed and described by Lifton, a Yale Psychiatrist, who was familiar with the Chinese scene. From this article and from others in the book, it appears that after the Communist Revolution there remained large intellectual groups who had to be converted from their Mandarin class type of philosophy to a people's anti-intellectual egalitarian view. All over China the government created mind-changing or thought-changing colleges where such people were gathered together and put through a purely verbal training experience. The physical tortures described at that time as part of the brainwashing of American prisoners were not a feature of "thought reform." The old orientation of the intellectual Mandarin groups was actually classified as "sick thinking." Those gathered for "retraining" were encouraged to expose their feelings and their ideas and to describe their backgrounds in a completely soul-baring experience in groups of eight to ten, all under suitable leadership by staff and by "converted" students. After this had gone on for a period of time, pressure gradually began to be put on them to confess their errors of thought and deed and to trace these errors to their culture, to their experiences and to their own psychological weaknesses. Those who did so were welcomed into the group while those who were not capable of being "converted" in this fashion were subjected to bitter recriminations by their associates. In these group criticisms, they were subjected to the full pressure of the group, and it is said that with this compulsory type of group psychotherapy the Chinese were able without violence actually to change the orientation of great numbers of their intellectuals and to reclaim them for the revolution. In some cases, of course, they failed, but Lifton[1] pointed out that this technique actually represented a type of compulsory psychotherapy that might well be examined for what we would consider more legitimate purposes.

A further examination of recent history indicates that the Chinese procedure was by no means without its predecessors even though the Chinese story is thought to go back to the early 1920's. In other words this technique has been used in one or another form for some time. The story is a much older one if one wishes to follow history further. Homer Lane,[2] for example, carried out work somewhat of this type with delinquents between about 1900 and 1918. He began as an occupational therapist (a Sloyd specialist, in the terminology of that day) and used the group as a therapeutic agent to change deviant behavior patterns by use of social pressure guided from above. If one wishes to go further he can trace the idea much further back; the Protestant sects used similar techniques under the name of "mutual criticism."[3] I think the Quakers are said to have used mutual criticism for correction even in Colonial times, and I have been told that this has a place among the Amish practices.

Now, where most of us first came into contact with this technique was as applied to addicts in connection with Synanon,[4] a name under which Charles Dederich, in 1958 began a type of group therapy characterized by direct "confrontation"—an abrasive attack to force the addict to confront his own hypocrisy— and by other social pressure of the group on the individual. He is punished by group disapproval for deviating and rewarded by approval for conforming. I do not know whether Dederich had any immediate knowledge of what happened in China, and I do not know whether he was influenced by what was going on, but the idea must have been in process of diffusion because it was tried elsewhere at about this time. Maxwell Jones used this same technique with a group of returning prisoners of war starting in 1945.[5] He emphasized the free and democratic social structure of the group and felt that as a result of exposure to others in this social structure, the individual suffering from character disorder could be changed in his orientation, and I know from descriptions by witnesses of the actual procedure in the groups of this therapeutic community that there was a rather vigorous group pressure, a type again of verbal assault if you like, on any deviant behavior pattern, a process which most of us would have found quite contrary to our underlying orientation toward psychiatric patients.

Another historical strand which indicates that this was in the air at the time goes back to about 1946.[6] We know it now as the T-group, the sensitivity group and many other names. It began after World War II when a group of experts was called together to work out a way of increasing the effectiveness of community workers in dealing with racial tensions. In the process they evolved the T-group type of procedure from which has come a training laboratory movement that has developed in many directions under various names. Disregarding the controversy which they have aroused,[7] we may for our purpose here recognize that an essential element is the use of the group as a therapeutic instrument for changing the individual by group pressure, not necessarily supported by any kind of professional help and the technique can be highly abrasive.

The contrast between the basic philosophy of this procedure and the basic philosophy that has tended to guide orthodox psychiatry is rather sharp. To begin with it is judgmental, whereas normal psychiatric procedure is likely to look at this as potentially harmful and to favor a nonjudgmental attitude. It is active, a talking operation in which the group talks to the individual; it is direct and uses group pressure often of the sharpest type although physical aggression is forbidden to all. The terminology of existential psychiatry has been brought into this aspect of the drug treatment field,[8] learning theory has also been used as has terminology derived from operant conditioning, and all this has now given this procedure a theoretical background, but I think that this came secondarily after the special group techniques were developed empirically and after they diffused from various foci such as those that I have just described. I think it was in the air, a sort of Zeitgeist perhaps a historical turnabout from the very nondirective and accepting type of psychiatry that had prevailed in the past and had been designed for neurotics and psychotics rather than for treatment of character disorder.

It has been said very often that in the treatment of these drug-dependent persons we need more new methods, but after attempting to review the methods that are now being used for the treatment of drug dependence, I come away with a very strong feeling that we need also to analyze and to understand better what we are doing and, particularly, to try to understand the group dynamics which promotes recovery, because it seems to me that the therapeutic process is a manifestation of the same group dynamics which brings a very large number of people into drug dependence, only the direction is reversed. Drug dependence is predominantly the product of group pressures toward taking drugs; abstinence can be achieved by group pressures in the opposite direction. The group members are the same in both instances, and the quality of pressure may have points of similarity; the aim is different.

In closing, I am reminded that Dr. Joyce said that he might very well be misunderstood, and I, too, am worried about being misunderstood. My use of the term "brainwashing" in connection with the psychiatric treatment is open to misunderstanding. I do not mean it in any demeaning way, my purpose is to call attention to an area of study which may very well give us interesting and useful approaches to prevention as well as to treatment.

REFERENCES

1. Lifton, R.: Peking's "Thought Reform"—Group psychotherapy to save your soul. In *The China Reader Communist China,* edited by F. Schurman and O. Schell. New York, Random House, 1967, pp. 137-147.
2. Willis, D.W.: *Homer Lane, a Biography*. London, Allen & Unwin, 1964.
3. Halloway, M.: *Heavens on Earth; Utopian Communities in America (1680-1880)*. New York, Dover, 1966.
4. Yablonsky, L.: *Synanon: The Tunnel Back*. Baltimore, Pelican, 1965.
5. Jones, M.: *The Therapeutic Community: A New Treatment Method in Psychiatry*. New York, Basic Books, 1953.
6. Gottschalk, L.A., and Pattison, E.M.: Psychiatric perspectives on T-groups and the laboratory movement—an overview. *Amer J Psychiat, 126:*823-839, 1969.
7. Rakstis, T.J.: Sensitivity training: Fad, fraud or new frontier? *Today's* Health, Jan. 1970, pp. 21-25, 86-87.
8. Miller, M.H., Whitaker, C.A., and Fellner, C.H.: Existentialism in American psychiatry—ten years later. *Amer J Psychiat, 124:*1112-1115, 1969.

Chapter 45

Differences in Therapy for Drug Users According to Their Motive for Abuse

Wolfram Keup

~~~~~~~~~~~~~~~~~~~~~~~~~~~~~~~~~~~~

P ATIENTS WITH A HISTORY of both drug abuse and psychotic symptoms are admitted to mental hospitals in still increasing numbers. The hospital physician is faced with the dual task of treating both conditions—if he can. But too often, he resigns to the treatment of the psychotic symptomatology only. Here, tranquilizing and/or antidepressant agents might be indicated. However, one may be reluctant to preach "abstinence from all drugs" and, at the same time, prescribe drugs, strengthening oral needs. Experience shows that only some patients of this group benefit from psychotropic medication. Since there seems to be characteristic differences between those improved by such medication and the ones not improved, we set out to investigate diagnostic criteria of responders and nonresponders, a total of 160 such patients (Table 45-I).

We used five groups for classification. The first group holds those patients in whom drug dependence or abuse was the leading symptom; there were no signs of an endogenous psychosis. The most frequent diagnoses within this group were character disorder, juvenile reaction, maladaptation syndrome, psychopathy and drug addiction. Some of these were complicated by drug-induced toxic psychoses, "bad trips," et cetera (group 1B). The following three groups show gradually increasing involvement of an endogenous psychosis besides drug abuse which, in turn, gradually decreases in importance. In the center group, group 3, both drug abuse and psychosis are present and do require treatment.

Note: This presentation won the 1970 EPRA Award.

TABLE 45-I

Group	Condition of Patient as to Drug Abuse and Psychosis	Male Patients	Female Patients	Both Sexes	Therapeutic Approach Indicated
1	Drug abuse leading syndrome:				
	(A) Drug addiction, charact. disorder, etc. No endogenous psychosis.	31.1 ⎱ 44.3	35.0 ⎱ 50.0	31.7 ⎱ 45.2	Treat Drug abuse. Group-, milieu-, and/or individual therapy.
	(B) Possible toxic psychosis.	13.2 ⎰	15.0 ⎰	13.5 ⎰	
2	Drug abuse in foreground. Psychosis present but of negligible symptomatic.	8.5	10.0	8.7	Suited for specific treatment against drug abuse.
3	Drug abuse & psychosis: Both present and both requiring treatment. Understood as independent syndromes, occurring simultaneously.	33.0	20.0	31.0	Drug abuse and antipsychotic therapy indicated
4	Drug abuse understood to be "symptomatic" of underlying endogenous psychosis (not always in foreground).	8.5	10.0	8.7	Primarily antipsychotic therapy (gradual introduction into drug program).
5	Psychosis, florid, in pats. with history of drug abuse:				
	(A) Schizophrenic episode.	3.8 ⎱ 5.7	— ⎱ 10.0	3.2 ⎱ 6.4	Not (or not yet) fit for drug abuse program—treat psychosis first!
	(B) Drug-induced psychosis.	1.9 ⎰	10.1 ⎰	3.2 ⎰	
	Expressed in % of sex group:	100	100	100	

Relative distribution of patients, newly admitted to **BSH**, in five groups of graded coexistence of psychotic symptoms and history of drug abuse causally linked as well as coincidental; expressed in percent of sex group.

Group 5 contains patients in whom a florid endogenous psychosis was in the foreground; drug abuse was negligible or had existed in the past only. This group, however, does contain a subgroup, group 5B, analog to group 1B, in which drug abuse seemingly had precipitated a psychotic episode or had aggravated a preexisting schizophrenia through different mechanisms; some of these patients we have discussed elsewhere.[3,4] As can be seen from the table, those patients with endogenous psychoses as leading syndrome (groups 4 and 5) constituted a minority, approximately 15 percent of the sample. At the other end of the scale, the groups with slighter involvement of endogenous psychopathology or without endogenous psychosis (groups 1 and 2) were more frequent, constituting about half of the total sample. Those patients with both an endogenous psychosis and a history of drug abuse (groups 2, 3 and 4) total slightly less than 50 percent.

There were only minor differences between the sexes, except, perhaps, for a higher incidence of drug-induced psychoses among the female patients.

In general, patients with more serious psychotic involvement more readily accepted the use of tranquilizers. But among them, and even more so among the group of patients with less serious psychotic symptoms, substantial numbers of patients felt tranquilizers to be "backwards," describing them as dysphoriant. We found that patients of this latter type often were rather experienced multiple-drug takers. Among those patients with experience with few drugs, on the other hand, there were fewer patients rejecting tranquilizers.

Because of this relation, we tentatively classified our patients by number of drugs experienced. There were patients with long-term single-drug use in the past, later switching to multiple-drug usage and vice versa. Table 45-II shows the corresponding groups progressing from single-drug use to extensive multiple-drug use. It should be mentioned that the number of heroin addicts within our patient group was insignificant although past heroin use, be it occasionally or for trial purposes only, was reported by a fair number of patients.

Those patients with extended single-drug use only and those

TABLE 45-II

Group			Classification of Drug Abuse		Frequency of Abuse in percent of all patients		
			Single Drug Use	Multiple Drug Use	In Past	At Admission	Per Group
Single Use {		1	Exclusive	—		5.6	5.6
						9.5	
Mixed Use {		2	yes	in past			4.0
		3	yes	continued or added	29.4	12.7	12.7
		4	in past	yes			7.1
						94.4	
Multiple Use {		5	—	mild, "Searcher"			14.3
						77.8	
		6	—	pronounced, "Experimenter"	70.6		30.9
		7	—	omnivorous user			25.4
			Total:			100%	

Classification of drug abuse patients in a mental hospital by single and/or multiple drug use.

who had settled on a single drug after some multiple-drug use, represented as little as 5.6 and 4 percent of the total group respectively. The remaining 90.4 percent were multiple-drug users (group 3 through 7). A total of 12.7 percent favored one drug but continued to use other drugs, whereas a total of 77.8 percent strictly adhered to multiple-drug usage. We concentrated on those patients who never had shown a fixation to a single drug for any length of time, the groups 5, 6 and 7—a total of 70.6 percent of the sample.

The complex relations between number of drugs used and time are again shown in the semiquantitative schema of Figure 45-1. Here, the different groups are represented in the context of a flow chart, showing the mutations from single to multiple drug use and back to single drugs, together with the relative frequencies of such moves.

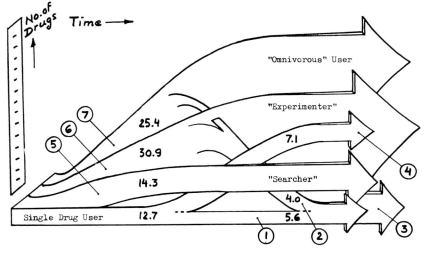

Figure 45-1.

Among the class of multiple-drug users, we distinguish three main groups. These groups are being tentatively described; we are aware that not all multiple-drug users fall into one of the types delineated below and that there might be other types besides the ones described in this chapter. We still continue our efforts of classification.

The *types of multiple drug users* can be described as follows:

A. *"The Searcher"* is a rather withdrawn individual, often a loner, lacking contact with others, usually not belonging to a peer group, not a leader if he does belong to a group, an observer and not a doer, often taciturn and unproductive, at times shy and hesitant. He usually suffers from his lack of contact and his lack of achievement and usually knows that "there is something wrong with me." He goes methodically from one drug to the next, mostly practicing single drug use at any given time. He looks for alleviation of his psychological problems, his anxiety and depression and his difficulties to concentrate. He rejects a drug if it does not "help" him and goes on to the next. What he practices is a kind of self-treatment attempt. He may share his experiences with others of the same type but rarely spreads the habit to others. Psychopathology and outright psychotic behavior, in particular, is frequent in this group.

B. *"The Experimenter"*, psychologically, constitutes probably the most diversified group of the three described here. He is the most intelligent of the three types and often is a college student. He has an open-minded, sophisticated approach to life, thinks lowly of those who get drunk either on alcohol or on drugs, is an ardent discusser, talks the specific "drug language," and is the all-round specialist in questions of drug use, consulted by others. He often becomes the leader of a peer group, functions as babysitter for newcomers. He might spend his evening in a medical library and read up on the pharmacology of antidotes against the drugs he uses or intends to use next. He is in revolt against the Establishment, has no contact difficulties, except with elders; he is very self-assured and often scholarly. Around him, one not rarely finds a cluster of pseudo-intellectuals, bluffers in drug knowledge, and power-hungry "fakes." These might or might not themselves belong to the group of experimenters. Members of this group often are rather skilled in avoiding overdose conditions, "bad trips" and side effects of drugs. They are the ones who find out that nausea experienced during the initial phase of mescaline usage can effectively be counteracted by antiemetics and who apply other such refinements. From a psychiatric point of view, the group is mixed. Diagnoses range from normality to psychopathy and endogenous psychosis, but the diagnosis of schizophrenia is not as frequent as in the group of the searchers.

C. *"The Glutton"* and/or *"Dionysian"* ("Omnivorous" user) is often a sociable, outgoing person. Typically, he is jovial, pyknic, somewhat superficial, easily contented, at times euphoric but he has depressive episodes. He is rather self-assured, not always on good grounds. The gluttons and dionysians are not exactly the same type, but differences are often slight, and we have seen transitions from one to the other type. The dionysian's motive is the drunkenness, the elation and the euphoria, but also the social experience under drug influence. Heroin users, then, are rare in this group. The dionysian enjoys "being in orbit," uses drugs as sexual stimulants and often is "addicted" to being the center of attention. The glutton on the other hand does not discriminate much between different drugs; he takes what he gets, and if somebody walks up to him and tells him "take this, this is good for you," he will "drop" it on the spot. His drug taking is haphazard, without plan, periodic, at times excessive, "living it up." His exposure to serious side effects and overdoses naturally is high. Both subtypes are unrestrained, do not like to control their drug taking, contrary to the habits of the experimenter. Psychopathology in this group is frequent but different from that of group A: Among the glutton/dionysian group, we find many psychopaths, character anomalies and rejects of society, and the rate of endogenous psychoses is smaller than in the other groups.

If clinical psychiatric diagnoses are assigned to these groups of multiple drug users, certain differences become evident (Table 45-III). The table lists the diagnostic groups of Table 45-I once

TABLE 45-III

		\multicolumn{8}{c}{*Psychotic Multiple Drug Users*}	
No. of Drugs Used:		\multicolumn{2}{c}{*1–2*}	\multicolumn{2}{c}{*3–5*}	\multicolumn{2}{c}{*6–10*}	\multicolumn{2}{c}{*more*}	*Total*
\multicolumn{2}{c}{*Group*}	\multicolumn{2}{c}{"Single" Drug Users}	\multicolumn{2}{c}{"Search- ers"}	\multicolumn{2}{c}{"Experi- men- ters"}	\multicolumn{2}{c}{"Omni- vorous Users"}	
		No.	%	No.	%	No.	%	No.	%	
1A—	*No* endogenous	4	16	6	27	26	47	8	61	44
1B—	psychosis	2		2		7		6		17
2—	*With* endogen.	1		3		6		4		14
3—	psychosis	3	54	10	73	23	53	5	39	41
4—	(increasing importance	3		5		4		—		12
5A—	of psycho-	—		3		1		—		4
5B—	sis ↓)	—		1		3		—		4
	Total	13	100	30	100	70	100	23	100	136

Involvement of *endogenous psychosis* in groups of "multiple drug users".

more, at the left; the columns show the diagnostic distribution within the group of single drug users as well as of the three described subgroups of multiple drug users; all had been admitted to Brooklyn State Hospital because of their need of psychiatric treatment. The group of single drug users is too small in size to allow final conclusions. Among the multiple drug users, endogenous psychoses are prevalent in the searcher group with 73 percent, whereas 61 percent of the omnivorous users (glutton/dionysian) showed no symptoms of endogenous psychosis. Among the experimenters, absence and presence of endogenous psychoses were about equally frequent. Toxic psychoses appeared more often in experimenters and omnivorous users while precipitated or aggravated endogenous psychoses occurred in searchers and experimenters as well.

A preliminary count of all our patients with psychiatric symptomatology and multiple drug use shows the group of experimenters to be the largest, followed by the one of omnivorous users, and the group of searchers to be the smallest. Our latest figures on their frequency, obtained from a sample of 160 patients, are shown in Table 45-IV. About one fifth of the total falls into the

TABLE 45-.IV

Group Type of Drug User	% of Total Population	
	Psychiatric Patients (N=160)	College Student Volunt. (N=39)
A "Searcher"	24.0	39.5
B "Experimenter"	56.9	21.0
C "Glutton/Dionysian"	19.1	39.5
Total	100.0	100.0

Percentage frequency per type of drug user among psychiatric patients and volunteering (sic) college students.

groups of searchers and gluttons/dionysians, and three fifths into the group of experimenters. In a recent, not yet fully evaluated, study conducted on a college campus, we found a somewhat different distribution when asking student volunteers with drug abuse to come forth and discuss their drug problem with us. The figures, then, certainly entail an expression of willingness on the part of the user to discuss drug taking in the open which will not be constant among the different types; thus, the distribution shown might not be entirely factual. Unfortunately, anonymous techniques are not suited for determining more realistic frequencies of the drug-user types on college campuses.

The *treatment* approaches for the different types are distinctly different from each other in some respects.

The *searchers* often respond well to the treatment with psychotropic drugs, tranquilizers or antidepressants and anxiolytics. Often, they readily accept such medication and are well motivated for the therapeutic situation. Once psychiatric improvement is achieved, they are rather open to anti–drug-taking therapy, since one of the mainsprings of their drug abuse, self-treatment, has now been channeled properly. It is indicated to discuss this situation with the patient and to draw his attention to the fact that self-treatment was the main cause of his drug abuse prior to psychiatric interference and can now be abandoned.

In the treatment of the *experimenter,* psychotropic drugs are often contraindicated. These patients are eager to learn about the drugs themselves and have a tendency to abuse them. In the case of experimenters, an entirely intellectual approach seems to be best. An attempt to "promote them through" the storehouse of knowledge on psychotropic drugs often is more reasonable than withholding information. Once they "know it all," they are likely to lose interest and to go on to the next, hopefully more rewarding, challenge instead. They are useful members of a drug-treatment staff once they have graduated from such a program and easily become AA-type converts using their knowledge for the teaching against drug addiction and abuse. This, in turn, helps them stay away from drug taking for reasons of self-respect.

The *omnivorous users (gluttons/dionysians)* are the most difficult group to treat. The intellectual approach often is entirely fruitless, and psychotropic drugs frequently are not indicated either, as is the case in the group of experimenters. Still the best seems to be a group approach with simultaneous but separate group sessions for users and their families. It would seem to us that this type of drug users has the poorest prognosis of all. Time might do for them more than the therapist.

Surprisingly few attempts have been made to group drug users by their motives for abuse or even by general psychological, structural characteristics. It has been tried, touched upon by Glaser, Inciardi and Babst,[2] to describe groups on the basis of particular settings, slum delinquency area, Bohemian neighborhood and college and high school campus. Torda[5] has worked out certain characteristics of users of particular drugs—LSD, heroin and alcohol. Biener[1] has reported trends similar to those which we have used to formulate our types.

I have presented our types of multiple drug users here not as final entities but as a working hypothesis in order to enable us and other workers to differentiate further among different entities with different motivations and subsequent different approaches of therapy. It is particularly obvious to us that the group of experimenters needs further subclassification. We have also seen a number of patients not fitting into any of the groups described above without violating their characteristics. Thus, we might have to reappraise these particular patients. Yet, we felt that we should present our preliminary data here in order to make them available to others working in a similar direction.

Before the clinical physician decides on a therapy plan for a given patient with psychiatric symptomatology and a history of drug abuse, he should, we believe, try to classify the patient and then apply the treatment appropriate for the group into which this patient seems to belong. A thorough psychiatric interview, supported by projective tests, seems to be the most helpful procedure for the differentiation of the different types of drugs users.

REFERENCES

1. Biener, K.: Jugend und Rauschgift. *Fortschr Med, 87:*1449-1452, 1969.
2. Glaser, D., Inciardi, J.T., and Babst, D.V.: Later heroin use by marijuana-using, heroin-using, and non–drug-using adolescent offenders in New York City. *Int J Addict, 4:*145-155, 1969.
3. Keup, W.: Psychotic symptoms due to cannabis abuse. *Dis Nerv Syst, 31:* 119-126, 1970.
4. Keup, W.: Psychoses connected with cannabis abuse as compared to amphetamine psychoses. *Proc VIIth Int Meeting of CINP,* Prague, Aug. 11-15, 1970.
5. Torda, C.: LSD users. Character structure and psychodynamic processes. *NY State J Med, 69:*2243-2247, 1969.

Chapter 46

Cyclazocine in the Treatment of Narcotics Addiction—Another Look

Leon Brill and David Laskowitz

~~~~~~

IN 1966, DR. JEROME JAFFE and the senior author instituted one of the first field tests of cyclazocine in the context of a multimodality approach to treating narcotic addicts at the Albert Einstein College of Medicine. This approach was based on the concept that there are different kinds of addicts who require different kinds of treatment intervention. Martin and co-workers[12] had proposed earlier in 1965 that the regular administration of cyclazocine, a long-acting narcotics antagonist, might be useful in the treatment of ambulatory patients who were highly motivated to avoid relapse to the compulsive use of narcotics.

Cyclazocine, a long-acting, orally-effective narcotic antagonist in the benzomorphan series, when given in appropriate doses, was found to reduce the subjective and physiological effects of any morphine-like drug. When given to subjects physically dependent on opiates, it, like nalorphine, precipitated a severe abstinence syndrome. However, when 60 mg of morphine was given four times daily for several weeks to "post addicts" already stabilized on 4 mg of cyclazocine per day, the withdrawal symptoms that appeared when morphine was stopped were much less intense than those usually seen when the same amount of morphine was withdrawn from control subjects. In other words, the regular use of cyclazocine reduced or prevented the development of physical dependence in morphine-like drugs. Presumably, once present, cyclazocine blocked morphine from reaching the usual receptor sites in the nervous system.

A patient maintained on 4 to 6 mg of cyclazocine per day would probably be unable to feel any of the effects of 60 mg of morphine or 20 mg of heroin within the first eighteen to twenty hours after the cyclazocine was taken. In common with other narcotic antagonists, cyclazocine has pharmacological actions other than blockade and antagonism of opiate-like drugs. In moderate doses, it produced a demonstrable analgesic effect (equivalent to 10 mg of morphine) . In some subjects, cyclazocine like nalorphine induces mental clouding, sensory distortions, illusions, weird thoughts and frank hallucinations and, at times, amphetamine-like or barbiturate-like effects. Tolerance develops to all these pharmacological effects, however, though not to the blocking effect.

In common with other narcotic antagonists, cyclazocine produces its own particular variety of physical dependence. For patients stabilized on cyclazocine, withdrawal symptoms appeared about thirty-six hours after the last dose. The signs of withdrawal were not severe. They included lacrimation, runny nose, dilated pupils, perspiration, fatigue, inability to sleep, headache, nausea, loose bowels and sudden brief episodes of weakness, back pains and loss of environmental contact described by patients as "electric shocks." There was little or no craving for cyclazocine in the sense of opiates once it was discontinued.

RATIONALE BASED ON CONDITIONING THEORY

In 1965, Wikler[14] proposed that, in addition to the underlying personality problems which predisposed an individual to the initial use of narcotics, the compulsive user had acquired a complex set of instrumentally and classically conditioned responses which perpetuated use and impelled him to relapse following detoxification. In effect, this constituted a two-factor learning theory of relapsing behavior: the relief of tension" (or anxiety, depression, guilt or anger) produced a progressively stronger tendency to seek out the drug as each reduction in tension reinforced the previous drug-seeking behavior. Physical dependence then developed, and this gave rise to new tensions—fear of withdrawal distress. The second factor was based on the more classical linkage involving repeated temporal contiguity between abstinence phenomena and the environmental cues of the "drug scene." Within

this conditioning framework, extinction of the drug-seeking behavior could best be accomplished by having the addict use his
illicit narcotics in his old haunts, but experience no effects whether
of tension-reduction or high from the drug. This could be accomplished if the narcotic antagonist occupied the receptor sites
and prevented the opiates from reaching these sites.

CYCLAZOCINE AND AVERSIVE THERAPY (ANTABUSE®)

Although there are certain similarities, the use of cyclazocine
in narcotics abusers should be distinguished from the chemical
aversion therapy model represented by Antabuse with alcoholics.
The patient taking Antabuse must carefully avoid all contact
with alcohol to avoid serious toxic effects. The patient on cyclazocine, however, is in no way hurt if he uses a narcotic. There is
merely no effect or else a very attenuated effect. This aversive
effect would come if the patient first used opiates, then took
cyclazocine. Thus, cyclazocine serves as a negative reinforcer,
rather than an aversive stimulus—that is, it blocks the incentive
value of heroin. This gives the therapist time to change his life
style by encouraging alternate patterns of response.

In the initial program with Dr. Jaffe at the Albert Einstein
College of Medicine, an attempt was made to answer three questions: Would addicts voluntarily take cyclazocine; how would
these addicts differ from other addicts seen; and would their progress on cyclazocine support the conditioning hypothesis?

COMPARISON OF CYCLAZOCINE AND METHADONE

Cyclazocine is a more difficult drug to work with than methadone. Methadone is itself a narcotic which relieves the drug craving and substitutes for the opiates, while cyclazocine does not
satisfy the craving, though it interferes with the effects of the
opiates like methadone.[15]

There is much frustration inherent in taking cyclazocine, since
it is not a pleasurable drug in itself and serves to block the effects of other pleasurable drugs—the opiates—which the addict has
been using. Selection, therefore, entails finding addicts who can
withstand frustration, have at least moderate ego strength and

motivation as well as indications of "community embeddedness" —for example, a history of social competence as with job, family ties, "square" associations and conventional areas of functioning —that is, they are not completely caught up in the drug culture. For others lacking some of these characteristics, it was felt that the use of probation or parole controls might serve as a reinforcement. Further, it was felt that cyclazocine might be useful in the area of secondary prevention for users who were becoming compulsively involved with opiates. Finally, there were addicts who were not interested in being admitted to a methadone program and were geared to an abstinence program. A serious deficiency was the lack of trial with lower-class or "street" addicts. Though a few came into the program early, they were not helped—except, perhaps, in a screening sense—since they were later referred to a methadone program.

The following exclusions were observed:

1. Persons with a history of florid psychosis, especially when there was indication that opiate use had been a form of pharmacologic self-help for poorly-contained aggressive or sexual impulses or stress. In a few cases, cyclazocine had stripped psychotics of their defenses and unmasked the underlying psychopathology; and they appeared worse because of the cyclazocine.

2. History of major medical complications, such as liver disease.

3. If the patient's spouse was also an addict, she was expected to participate in the program.

METHOD OF INDUCTION IN LINCOLN HOSPITAL PROGRAM IN THE SOUTH BRONX AREA OF NEW YORK

At first, this was entirely inpatient, approximately two weeks; but, in later phases, it needed to be ambulatory because we lost our hospital base. This was possible for candidates who had stable family and work ties. After the initial screening, patients were admitted to a medical ward and were stabilized on methadone (20 to 40 mg/day). The methadone was withdrawn in decrements of 5 to 10 mg daily over a period of three to six days.

At least forty-eight hours after the last dose of methadone, the

patients were tested with nalorphine (Nalline), 3 mg subcutane-
ously. If the first dose produced no discomfort for the patient, it
was followed after a twenty-minute interval by 4 mg. The test
was considered negative if there were no marked pupillary
changes, sweating, gooseflesh or discomfort. Administration of
cyclazocine was begun about eight hours later with an initial dose
of 0.25 mg. Patients were specifically told that methadone withdrawal was not yet completed forty-eight hours after the last dose,
that restlessness and insomnia sometimes persisted for an additional seven to ten days and that the negative nalorphine test merely
indicated that cyclazocine, at this time, would not make them feel
worse.

Some patients found the mild hallucinogenic effects quite distressing, while others seemed to enjoy it. For the former, it was
necessary to raise the dose very slowly in order to permit them to
develop tolerance for these side effects. Patients were permitted to
leave the hospital on pass when the daily dose reached 1.5 mg, and
they could be discharged when it reached 2.0 mg. However, they
were specifically instructed that they were not yet on full blocking
doses. This minimized the possibility that experimentation would
lead to either toxicity—that is, by overestimation of the effectiveness of the dosage—or disappointment with the efficacy of cyclazocine. Most patients stayed in the hospital less than two weeks. During this time, we attempted to establish sufficient rapport to ensure
that they would continue their contact after discharge.

The treatment philosophy of the cyclazocine program differed
from that of the Dole-Nyswander methadone-maintenance program, in that it is believed that a susained involvement in
psychotherapy is important for the rehabilitation of patients
stabilized on cyclazocine. Consequently, a commitment to a group
therapy experience was made a condition for acceptance into the
program. There are presently six patients who have requested and
are receiving individual therapy.

SHORTCOMINGS OF CYCLAZOCINE AS A
MAINTENANCE SUBSTANCE

It was originally thought that because cyclazocine has low
abuse potential, the patient could be given a single daily dose and,

by virtue of the same logic, could be seen twice or at most three times a week. Patients soon learned that the duration of the shielding action of cyclazocine ranged from eighteen to twenty-four hours, with peak effectiveness reached approximately eight hours after the last dose. Efforts to circumvent cyclazocine's blocking action took two forms: (a) occasional premature experimentation with opiates before a blocking dose was reached despite attempted indoctrination to avoid this and (b) use of heroin when the shielding effect of cyclazocine was at its low point. Indeed, several patients reported on the effectiveness of heroin in suppressing the cyclazocine withdrawal syndrome.

SUMMARY OF EARLIER CYCLAZOCINE STUDIES

Jaffe and Brill[10,11] conducted an early study of twenty-seven patients at the Albert Einstein College of Medicine, essentially middle class with evidence of conventional ties and modes of living, who came into treatment voluntarily. At the time of first publication of results, of the twenty-seven patients, 33 percent (nine cases) had remained on cyclazocine for over nine months; two patients had remained totally abstinent (a physician and a student) ; and several converted to weekend or spree use of continuing cyclazocine between sprees. A total of eleven patients or 40 percent had withdrawn from the project at the time of the evaluation. The authors concluded, however, that the majority of the patients "did well," in that they were abstinent or had reduced drug intake to a weekend basis.

Freedman *et al.*[7] also used cyclazocine in three studies. In the first, fifty-one patients who were also part of a therapeutic community volunteered for cyclazocine treatment. The structure and processes of the therapeutic community clearly operated in antithesis to the chemotherapy. The long residential stay provided little opportunity for field "drug testing," and hence, many discontinued the use of the antagonist. In the second study,[8] sixty patients from 17 to 64 years of age with addiction histories of two to fifteen years were hospitalized for treatment. Of these sixty cases, fifty-eight completed the cyclazocine induction period.

Varying induction periods, ranging from ten to thirty days

were also studied. The twenty- and thirty-day induction periods were well tolerated. Following stabilization and opiate challenge, patients were discharged and instructed to return to the clinic three times weekly for medication. Findings suggested that among the patients studied, anxiety was relieved, criminality declined and interest in vocational activity was increased. It was felt that the high dropout rate could have been obviated by more intensive treatment efforts.

More recently, cyclazocine was administered to thirty-one chronic male addicts, ages 19 to 43 years who sought treatment at the Metropolitan Hospital in New York City.[13] Criteria for treatment included New York City residence, two or more unsuccessful hospital treatments for addiction, absence of any psychosis and physical illness, no current addiction to a non-narcotic substance or pending court cases. Patients seemed to fall into two groups: those for whom heroin acted as a "normalizer" and increased their capacity to function and those for whom drug-seeking behavior was related to environmental factors and in whom the feeling of an inability to function did not predominate.

The follow-up study revealed that the program retained 50 percent of the patients in treatment (as of January 1969). Length of outpatient treatment was from four to thirty-three months, with a mean of twenty months; and the mean age of this group was 31.6 years with a range of 22 to 44 years. Staff felt that marital status most clearly distinguished the two groups in that married patients less often discontinued treatment. Neither age, duration of addiction nor length of time abstinent from drug use were differentiating factors. In the two addict categories outlined by the staff, the comparative success of one group as against the other did not appear significant.

STUDY RESULTS AND GENERAL IMPRESSIONS AT LINCOLN HOSPITAL

In the course of the past three years, thirty-five patients participated in this pilot study. The number was small because of the very meager resources available to the program. The median age of this group was 32, ranging from 22 to 49. Ten patients of this group (29 percent) are listed as failures. It is noteworthy that most of these were recruited early in the program's development when screening and follow-up procedures were rudimentary. Of this subgroup, half did not respond because of the existence of craving which they sought to gratify by not taking their blocking dose of cyclazocine or by overcoming its blockade by using heroin when the cyclazocine shield was at its weakest. The other five members either complained of distressing side effects, including loss of appetite and nausea, loss of libido, skin hypersensitivity and allergic reaction, or were confronted with emotional decompensation when the adaptational value of the opiates was not available. Of this group of ten, eight patients were administratively discharged and two left against medical advice.

A total of eight patients (22 percent) were transferred to other programs; seven of this group were transferred to the Methadone Maintenance Program and one sent to Daytop Village, a non-chemical therapeutic community.

Three patients (9 percent) died. One patient was dropped from the program and died one year later in a narcotics-related accident.

There are seven patients (20 percent) who are presently off cyclazocine and remain opiate-free. In this group, however, two of the patients were involved in intermittent experimentation with amphetamines.

Finally, there are seven patients (20 percent) currently taking cyclazocine who are opiate-free. The median length of stay of this group is two and a half years.

One is impressed with the polarity of the findings. Patients either succeeded or failed with this modality. The fact that 40 percent are opiate-free, many without the need of cyclazocine for chemical support, makes this a promising approach for a limited sector of the addict population. The failures were largely with ghetto addicts who were left with inadequate program supervision and chemical protection and were returned to survive in their narcotics-infected habitats. Given the relatively short-acting blockade provided by cyclazocine, under conditions of high environmental drug exposure, it is mandatory that the ghetto addict be seen on a daily basis for at least the first several months.

CONCLUSIONS

The question is no longer whether the opiate-antagonist model has rehabilitative value since experience has demonstrated its utility for a special segment of the addict population. A priority research task centers on the identification of those who will profit from this type of modality and under what circumstances. Clearly, the efficacy of the narcotics antagonist model would be immensely strengthened if we could find a longer-acting substance with fewer side effects which would extend its usefulness, also, to other groups.

Interest has moved from the use of cyclazocine as a form of tertiary intervention for a select group of addicts to its use as a vehicle for secondary prevention. In the latter case, cyclazocine would be given the novice opiate user to short-circuit his drift to addiction. Though cyclazocine offers promise as a modality for secondary prevention, its effectiveness needs to be tested. In contrast, methadone is clearly counterindicated for at least most neophyte users, since it may prematurely consolidate them in chemical-dependency patterns. Dr. Herbert Kleber, in New Haven, has found naloxone a useful reinforcement in his Day Center program for younger heroin users, most still in their teens or early twenties.

There needs to be further testing also of the use of rational authority—that is, use of probationary or court controls, as an adjunct to cyclazocine intervention. Another critical issue involves the concept of "modality strain." At what point is it prudent to transfer a patient to another modality, despite his pleading for another chance? In some cases, the cyclazocine served as a screening device for sifting out those patients who could not "make it" on cyclazocine; and these were then transferred to methadone maintenance. With the majority of patients, it was found that they continued to work and support their families, even though some continued to "chip"—that is, use chemicals intermittently— and that these patients did maintain contact with the program. It was felt that cyclazocine kept their narcotics use from becoming an overwhelming preoccupation and thereby permitted them to remain in the program. The continuing interest in cyclazocine by persons of all socioeconomic groups suggests that it will become a permanent addition to the treatment modalities in this field. Cyclazocine thus has a definite role within a multimodality approach and "armamentarium" of services for selected addicts, including those who do not wish to enter a methadone program. This role should be augmented as we develop better antagonists— longer acting and with fewer side effects than cyclazocine.

Cyclazocine is at present difficult to work with, for the reasons mentioned, and appears to require far greater investments in terms of staff, time and services than methadone. Further research is required therefore to (a) find ways to extend its effectiveness to other segments of the addict population—to neophyte users and hard-core addicts—and as a reinforcement for probation and parole, and (b) develop innovative uses as in support of other treatment modalities—such as Dr. Kleber's Day Center in New Haven or with therapeutic communities, for residents who are having difficulty making their "reentry" back to the community.

REFERENCES

1. Banay, R.S.: Progress in "cyclazocine plus." *Corr Psychiat & J Soc Ther,* Winter 1968 Edition, pp. 187-195.
2. Brill, L.: Three approaches to the casework treatment of narcotic addiction. *Soc Work, 13*:25-35, 1968.
3. Brill, L., and Jaffe, J.H.: The relevancy of some newer American treatment approaches for England. *Brit J Addict, 62*:375-386, 1967.
4. Brill, L., and Lieberman, L.: *Authority and Addiction.* Boston, Little Brown, 1969.
5. Fink, M., Zaks, A., Sharoff, R., Mora, A., Bruner, A., Levit, A., Levit, S., and Feldman, A.M.: Naloxone in heroin dependence. *Clin Pharmacol Ther, 9(5)*:568-577, 1968.
6. Fraser, H.F., and Rosenberg, D.E.: Comparative effects of I. Chronic administration of cyclazocine. II. Substitution of nalorphine for cyclazocine. III. Chronic Administration of morphine. *Int. J Addict, 1*:86-98, 1966.
7. Freedman, A.M., Fink, M., and Sharoff, R.: Clinical evaluation of cyclazocine in the therapy of narcotics addiction. Read at the Ann. Mtg. Am. Psychiat. Assoc., Detroit, May 1967.
8. Freedman, A.M., Fink, M., Sharoff, R., and Zaks, A.: Clinical studies of cyclazocine in the treatment of narcotic addiction. *Amer J Psychiat, 124*:11, 1968.

9. Inciardi, J.A.: Methadone and the antagonists. In *Methadone Mainten-ance,* edited by A.C. Chambers and L. Brill. 1971.

10. Jaffee, J.H., and Brill, L.: Cyclazocine, a long-acting narcotic antagonist: Its voluntary acceptance as a treatment modality by narcotics abusers. *Int J Addict, 1*:99-123, 1966.

11. Jaffe, J.H., Brill, L., and Laskowitz, D.: Pharmacological approaches to the treatment of narcotics addiction: Patterns of response. Presented at 29th Mtg. Natl. Acad. Sci., Natl. Res. Council, Comm. on Problems of Drug Dependence, Lexington, Ky., Feb. 1967.

12. Martin, W.R., Fraser, H.F., Gorodetzky, C.W., and Rosenberg, D.E.: Studies of the dependence-producing potential of the narcotic an-tagonist cyclazocine. *J Pharmacol, 150*:426-436, 1965.

13. Resnick, R.B., Fink, M., and Freedman, A.M.: A cyclazocine typology in opiate dependence. *Amer J Psychiat, 126*:9, 1970.

14. Wikler, A.: Conditioning factors in opiate addiction and relapse. In *Narcotics,* edited by D.M. Wilner and G.G. Kassebaum. New York, McGraw-Hill, 1965, pp. 85-100.

15. Brill, L., and Lieberman, L.: Major modalities in the treatment of drug abuse. Behavioral Publications, New York, in press.

Chapter 47

Methadone Maintenance Treatment: An Overview

Edward Gordon

NOW THAT MOST OF US are accustomed to the once radical idea of maintenance therapy for narcotic addicts, it is worthwhile to review the course of development of methadone treatment, summarize its current status, discuss some problems regarding the theoretical understanding of addiction as a chemical and psychological process and point toward future developments.

The history of opiate addiction in this country has been essentially biphasic. During the nineteenth century, addiction was rather widespread, with popular nostrums commonly containing various opiate drugs as their major active ingredient. The passage of the Harrison Narcotic Act in 1914 in the United States has led to both a decrease in the number of addicts and the emergence of a different addict population, differing from the previous in ethnic and cultural characteristics and in life style. For many years, the Bureau of Narcotics interpreted the Harrison Act as forbidding physicians from prescribing narcotics to addicts "for the purpose of providing the abuser with narcotics sufficient to keep him comfortable by maintaining his customary use". It is not the purpose of this chapter to discuss the history of federal regulations regarding the treatment of heroin addicts; this was reviewed in the *Yale Law Journal*.[1] The most recent applicable federal regulation is dated March 25, 1971.[2] The overall effect of these regulations and their implementation has been to limit addiction treatment to abstinence methods. A relative therapeutic vacuum existed for many years with most physicians dissuaded by either the regulations or the patients from attempting treatment. Most treatment efforts were poorly controlled and evaluated, but it was generally considered that results of treatment attempts had been poor.[3,4]

Treatment failures were generally blamed on the patient: poor motivation or defective personality structure were blamed and not the treatment modalities involved.

Beginning in the middle 1950's, as the heroin addiction prevalence rose, there was renewed interest in understanding and treating narcotics addicts. It was generally concluded that addiction was produced by a complex of social and psychological factors which included (a) a specific premorbid personality, (b) a primitive, often narcissistic and orally-driven personality structure, and (c) the use of narcotics for anxiety-reduction and the conditioning and reinforcement which result from this.[5-8]

In 1957, thirty analysts cooperated in a study designed to evaluate the effectiveness of ambulatory outpatient psychotherapy on the treatment of drug addicts. Seventy addicts voluntarily contacted the project but only thirty-five effected initial contact with the therapist. At the end of one year, thirteen were still in treatment. Ten were drug-free.[9] No follow-up data has been presented on this group, but it must be noted that the 14 percent remission rate approximates the rate of remission observed in other studies and, in this remitting disease, approaches chance expectations.

The evaluation of the Riverside Hospital Treatment Program was even more discouraging.[10] Of 250 adolescent addicts admitted, no documented remissions were found on follow-up.

THE DEVELOPMENT OF THE METHADONE PROGRAM

As a member of New York City's Health Research Council, Dr. Vincent Dole had become interested in the problem of the treatment of heroin addiction. Starting with a small group of patients at Rockefeller University, he and Dr. Marie Nyswander experimented first in maintenance with various narcotics, then with methadone as a maintenance drug. They discovered that where maintenance with short-acting narcotics led to demands for larger and larger doses, methadone given orally had a stabilizing effect, decreased narcotic drug hunger and permitted improvement in social functioning. Large dose maintenance was found to "blockade" against the effects of intravenous heroin or morphine.[11,12] Attempts to apply methadone maintenance to larger populations led to the opening of an inpatient unit at the Beth Israel Hospital which has since expanded to a combination of inpatient and outpatient facilities currently treating 3,800 patients.

The program, as originally developed, consisted of an inpatient phase lasting six weeks (phase I) during which tolerance was developed to methadone in the dose range of 80 to 120 mg. During this time, the individual's health needs were met and planning for employment and postdischarge life began. Phase II, beginning on discharge from the inpatient phase, is the period of clinic attendance to the point of vocational and personal stability. Patients attend daily at first but by the end of phase II attend clinic only weekly, requiring a minimum of the many supportive services which are offered in phase I and II. Within the last two years, phase I, the induction phase, has been carried out quite successfully in outpatient clinics. There seems to be little need for inpatient induction for most patients.[13] An inpatient stay still is useful for selected individuals whose physical and mental state requires inpatient stabilization and for readmission at times of crisis.

Methadone maintenance has been almost uniformly acceptable to patients. Few voluntarily withdraw from the program at any stage and regular attendance has been the rule. Results have been dramatic in permitting stabilization, with most patients discontinuing regular heroin use. From its inception, there has been an independent evaluation by the Columbia University School of Public Health. Eighty percent of patients admitted have remained in treatment. Of these, a similar percentage are currently either working or living socially acceptable lives. There has been a dramatic (94 percent) decrease in criminal activity reported.[14] Experience of other researchers with modifications of this modality has been similar.[15,16]

Because of the demonstrated effectiveness of this treatment program in improving social, vocational and personal functioning, there has been a recent major influx of funds supporting its expansion. Credibility of such dramatic and impressive research results would most certainly have been impaired if not for the presence from the start of an independent evaluation committee separately funded and separately reporting.

The safety of high dose maintenance with methadone appears to be generally accepted. There have been no deaths reported due to methadone use in the patient group nor organ toxicity. Pregnancy and menstrual function has been observed to return to normal in methadone stabilized patients.[17] Of twenty-four patient deaths in 1968, none were reported to be related to the treatment program.[18]

Experiments continue into ways of improving the effectiveness of treatment. Currently nearly one fifth of all patients admitted fail, generally because of other drug activity, continued criminal activity, and behavioral or personality reasons.

In a trial with acetylmethadol and methadone, Jaffe found that the long-acting congener taken three times weekly was equally effective in stabilization as methadone.[19]

In a pioneering experiment at the New York City Correctional Institution for Men, methadone maintenance was demonstrated to prevent reincarceration in nine of twelve randomly selected patients at the end of a year of treatment, compared to the reincarceration of fifteen of sixteen untreated controls.

To summarize, methadone treatment has been demonstrated by independent evaluation and by multiple investigators to be effective in reducing heroin use and in permitting rehabilitation. Although much "research" into methadone maintenance treatment involves simply the manipulation of variables such as dose level, frequency of visits, presence or absence of counseling or psychotherapy, the prospect of large numbers of patients continuing to attend relatively expensive outpatient clinics well beyond the period when significant clinic services other than medication are required suggests the need for the development of alternative phase III methods. In addition, techniques to reduce current treatment failures are required.

ETIOLOGY OF ADDICTION

Few investigators today consider opiate addiction to be wholly psychological in origin. Stabilized patients represent no specific personality types or groups, and there seem to be no specific psychodynamics represented. Dole and Nyswander have proposed a metabolic theory to account for heroin addiction, feeling that "the new evidence provided by the results of maintenance treatment strongly suggests that the 'addict traits' are a consequence, not a cause of addiction."[20] In a review of the biochemistry of addiction,[21] Dole remarks on the inability of pharmacologists to separate the analgetic effects of narcotic drugs from addictive capacity and suggests that analgesia, tolerance, physical dependence and drug-seeking behavior are various "expressions of the same biochemical events." He concludes that future research should direct itself to an investigation of the biochemical events involved in the narcotic drug-cell interactions. The experience in methadone treatment programs has been that of dramatic decrease in drug-seeking behavior during treatment with resumption of heroin use after detoxification, even after long periods of heroin abstinence. With the example of continued failures of abstinence-type programs, either with or without added therapy, supervision and group support to produce a significant body of heroin-abstinent individuals,[22] it seems quite plausible to assume that regardless of the social and personality factors involved at the onset of heroin use and regardless of the personality traits which result from adaptation to a heroin subculture, certain primary biochemical events take place as a result of the experience of heroin addiction which account for both failure on the one hand and successes on the other.

SUMMARY

Starting as a radical departure, the success of maintenance therapy has caused a reexamination of theoretical assumptions concerning addiction. Problems which need to be solved include ways of increasing the efficiency of delivering services, developing means of rehabilitation of those who are currently unable to benefit from this treatment and clarification of the biochemical mechanisms underlying addiction, with an ultimate goal of undoing the addictive state.

REFERENCES

1. Editorial: Methadone maintenance for heroin addicts, *Yale Law J, 78.* 1175-1211, 1969.
2. *Federal Register,* Vol. 36, F.R.6075 Part 130; Vol. 36 F.R.6081 Part 151.

3. O'Donnell, J.A.: In *Narcotics,* edited by D.M. Wilner and G.G. Kassebaum. New York McGraw-Hill, 1965.

4. Vaillant, G.E.: Drug dependence and alcohol problems; a twelve year follow-up of New York narcotic addicts. (1) Relation of treatment-outcome. *Amer J Psychiat, 122:*727-737, 1967.

5. Nyswander, M.: *The Drug Addict as a Patient.* New York, Grune & Stratton, 1956.

6. Chein, I., and Rosenfeld, E.: In *Law and Contemporary Problems, 22:*52-68, 1967.

7. Nyswander, M.: Drug addictions. In *American Handbook of Psychiatry, 1:*614-622.

8. Chein I., Gerard, L., and Rosenfeld, E.: *The Road to H.* New York, Basic Books, 1964.

9. Nyswander, M., Winick, C., Bernstein, A., Brill, L., and Kaufer, G.: Treatment of the narcotic addict, Workshop, 1957; I. The treatment of drug addicts as voluntary outpatients; a progress report. *Amer J Orthopsychiat, 28(4):*714-727, 1958.

10. Greater New York Hospital Association: Conference on Methadone Maintenance—How It Works in Hospitals, January 21, 1970.

11. Dole, V.P., and Nyswander, M.: A medical treatment for diacetylmorphine. *JAMA, 193:*646-650, 1965.

12. Dole, V.P., Nyswander, M., and Kreek, M.J.: Narcotic blockade. *Arch Int Med, 118:*304-309, 1966.

13. Report of the Methadone Evaluation Unit. Columbia University School of Public Health, May 8, 1970.

14. Dole, V.P., Nyswander, M., and Warner, A: Successful treatment of 750 criminal addicts. *JAMA, 206(12):*2708-2711, 1968.

15. Jaffe, J.H., Zacks, M.S., and Washington, E.N.: Experience with the use of methadone in multi-modality programs for the treatment of narcotic users. *Int J Addict, 4(3):*481-490, 1969.

16. Williams, H.R.: Using methadone to treat the heroin addict. *Canada's Ment Health,* March-April, 1970, pp. 4-9.

17. Wallach, R.C., Jerez, E., and Blinick, G.: Pregnancy and menstrual function in narcotic addicts treated with methadone. *Amer J Obstet Gynec, 105(8):*1226-1229, 1969.

18. Baden, M.: Report at Second National Conference on Methadone Treatment, New York City, October 27, 1969.

19. Jaffe, J.H., Schuster, C.R., Smith, B.B., and Blachley, P.H.: Comparison of acetylmethadol and methadone in the treatment of long term heroin users. *JAMA, 211(11):*1834-1836, 1970.

20. Dole, V.P. and Nyswander, M.: Heroin addiction—a metabolic disease. *Arch Intern Med (Chicago), 120:*19-24, 1967.

21. Dole, V.P.: Biochemistry of addiction. *Ann Rev Biochem, 39:*821-840, 1970.

22. Kramer, J.C., and Bass, R.A.: Institutionalization among civilly committed addicts. *JAMA, 208(12):*2297-2301, 1969.

Chapter 48

Withdrawal and Detoxification in New York City Heroin Users

Alex Richman, Marcus A. Feinstein and Harold L. Trigg

> . . . Most people who come into contact with addicts will have to deal with this phenomenon (withdrawal) and will gain their knowledge of addiction rather from the effects of the absence of drugs than from their direct effect on people.
>
> *Maurer and Vogel*

THIS CHAPTER DESCRIBES the procedures used for detoxification of heroin users seen at the Morris J. Bernstein Institute of the Beth Israel Medical Center. The Bernstein Institute (formerly the Manhattan General Hospital) has cared for over 30,000 individual narcotics addicts since the initiation of a detoxification service in 1961. During 1970 there were 7,843 admissions for detoxification, half of whom were first admissions. In addition, there were over two thousand applicants for detoxification who were accepted for admission but did not appear on their Guaranteed Admission Date. Currently we have 305 beds: 229 for men and 76 for women. In addition to a medical inpatient service for 31 patients and a methadone maintenance inpatient induction unit of 15 beds, extension clinics of the Bernstein Institute care for 1,779 patients in the Methadone Maintenance Program (June 1971).

Since the detoxification service began in 1961, patients have been hospitalized on a voluntary basis. Applicants are not screened on the basis of subjective estimates of motivation or "suitability." Patients are given a medical discharge fourteen days after their last dose of methadone. Readmission is possible after seven

Note: The assistance of Miss E. V. Bowles, Mr. C. La Porte and Mrs. J. Riegel is acknowledged.

days of discharge for those who achieved a medical discharge or who gave twenty-four hours notice of their desire to leave earlier. Unless there are exceptional circumstances patients with other types of discharge must wait at least three months before applying for readmission.

Patients apply from all parts of New York City for detoxification. Although the Bernstein Institute is located in the Lower East Side of Manhattan, the geographic distribution of first admissions is similar to that of addicts first reported from all community sources to the Narcotics Register of the New York City Department of Health. The detoxification or Drug Addiction Service is funded by New York City with the state sharing the cost.

During 1970, there were from 800 to 1,200 patients on our waiting list with guaranteed admission dates extending from six to eight weeks in advance for men and about two weeks for women. From 60 to 70 percent of the applicants on the waiting list will show up for admission.

The objectives of the Drug Addiction Service are detoxification, to have the patient spend fourteen drug-free days in hospital following detoxification, and to involve the patient in a community program for long-term rehabilitation after discharge. This chapter will focus on detoxification; other essential aspects of in-patient care involve individual and group treatment by counselors, nurses, social service workers, occupational and recreational therapists.[3-5]

EXPERIENCE OF WITHDRAWAL

Applicants for detoxification were interviewed about symptoms experienced when they were "sick from not having drugs." Most of the 156 patients interviewed reported having had the withdrawal symptoms shown in Table 48-I. There was considerable variation among patients as to which were the *worst* symptoms they had experienced. It is evident that some patients have not experienced Grade III or IV withdrawal symptoms.

Some patients gave more than one symptom as being worst so these percentages add up to more than 100 percent.

TABLE 48-I
WORST WITHDRAWAL SYMPTOMS REPORTED BY 156 APPLICANTS FOR
DETOXIFICATION MORRIS J. BERNSTEIN INSTITUTE

Withdrawal Symptom	Percentage of 156 patients who considered this symptom was the worst.
Cramps or stomach pains	33
Nausea	14
Restlessness	11
Pains in back or legs	10
Chills	8
Running nose	8
Anxiety	7
Twitches	7
Yawning	7
Vomiting	6
Sweating	5
Sleeplessness	4
Weakness or tiredness	3

DETOXIFICATION SCHEDULE FOR HEROIN USERS

The detoxification schedule used at the Bernstein Institute
was initiated in 1961 by Dr. Harold L. Trigg. In the early years
up to 20 mg of methadone was given intramuscularly four times a
day in addition to chloral hydrate for nighttime sedation. Medical
and nursing attention was focused upon the avoidance of withdrawal symptoms during the course of detoxification. Methadone
dosage was reduced by 5 mg a day following the first two full days
of hospitalization, so that the duration of methadone administration could be up to eighteen days.

Currently, methadone is given orally in two divided doses at
8:30 a.m. and 8:30 p.m. The maximum dosage is 20 mg orally,
twice per day. The dosage of methadone given on the first day of
hospitalization is repeated on the second full day of hospitalization
and then decreased by 5 mg a day subsequently (see Table 48-II).

The dosage of methadone prescribed for detoxification is based on the history of drug usage obtained by the physician from
the patient at the time of admission. Although it is difficult to
assess the validity of patients' statements regarding their drug intake, it is uncommon to have to modify the schedule initially prescribed.

TABLE 48-II

CONVERSION TABLE FOR PRESCRIBING METHADONE SCHEDULE ON
BASIS OF SIZE OF PATIENT'S DAILY HABIT

(Initiated and developed by H. L. Trigg, M.D. at the Morris J. Berstein Institute,
Beth Israel Medical Center, New York)

Size of Heroin Habit Per Day	Methadone Schedule for First Full Day of Hospitalization	
($5.00 bags in New York City are estimated to contain up to 8–10 mg of heroin.)	9 a.m.	9 p.m.
9 bags or more	20 mg	20 mg
8 bags	20 mg	15 mg
5–7 bags	15 mg	15 mg
4 bags	15 mg	10 mg
3 bags	10 mg	10 mg
2 bags	10 mg	5 mg
1 bag	5 mg	5 mg

Notes

1. This methadone schedule is intended to deal with the "average" habit of a heroin user who is getting heroin from a "street" source. The content of heroin varies considerably from place-to-place and from time-to-time.

2. For bags costing less than $5.00 each, give one-half the calculated dose.

3. On admission to the ward the patient (if not nodding) gets 5 mg orally in order to allay withdrawal symptoms. The next dose will be at 9:00 p.m.

4. The first full day's dose is repeated on the second full day. For example: a patient with six $5.00 bags per day habit who is admitted in the afternoon would get 5 mg stat, 15 mg at 9:00 p.m. and the following:

Day 2	15 mg	15 mg
Day 3	15 mg	15 mg
Day 4	15 mg	10 mg
And then decreasing by 5 mg/day to		
Day 8	5 mg	0 mg
Day 9	0	0

A methadone schedule is prescribed on the day of admission for heroin addicts (or users of other opiates) who have taken their last dose within the three days before admission. If the addicting opiate had not been taken in the three days before admission, methadone is not given since moderate symptoms of withdrawal are not expected. Patients who have not had any opiates in the three days preceding admission may complain of muscle spasm in the lower part of the legs (or lumbosacral region), insomnia and loss of appetite. Thorazine® is prescribed for these patients:

Thorazine 30 mg t.i.d. p.o. × 3 days
60 mg t.i.d. p.o. × 3 days
90 mg t.i.d. p.o. × 3 days

This Thorazine schedule can be discontinued earlier if the patent feels better and can do without medication. (It should be noted that Thorazine in this dosage is prepared by our pharmacy from a hospital concentrate.)

Admissions usually arrive on the ward between 9:30 A.M. and 4:30 P.M. Five milligrams of methadone is given upon admission except when the patient is drowsy or nodding. Methadone is administered in liquid rather than tablet form.

Barbiturates or Doriden® are given only to patients addicted to these drugs. The schedule for withdrawal from barbiturate uses Seconal® (see Table 48-III) Doriden is also frequently used by heroin addicts and the schedule for Doriden withdrawal is in Table 48-IV.

For nighttime sedation chloral hydrate is used. One gram of chloral hydrate is given to adults and 500 mg to adolescents. In *verified* insomnia up to 2 gm of chloral hydrate may be given to adults, and up to one gm to adolescents, *after* the patient has been hospitalized for one week. In patients with hepatitis, Benadryl® 50 mg capsules is used instead of choral hydrate at bedtime. Paraldehyde is used for addicts who are also alcoholic.

Thorazine is not used routinely for insomnia nor when chloral hydrate or paraldehyde are effective. Thorazine is avoided when there is any past or present history of liver disease. Patients are asked about any sensitivity to Thorazine. Thorazine is used for agitated, hyperkinetic or apprehensive patients, usually 30 mg t.i.d. and as described above; Thorazine is not continued for longer than nine days. It is never given orally after 6 P.M. because of the 8:30 P.M. dose of methadone and h.s. sedation. Intramuscular Thorazine is used on an emergency basis for patients who are unusually apprehensive or hyperkinetic. It is noted that the larger

TABLE 48-III
SCHEDULE OF SECONAL GIVEN TO BARBITURATE ADDICTS FOR PREVENTION OF WITHDRAWAL SYMPTOMS

This schedule is based on the number of barbiturate capsules taken daily for at least one month before admission.

Careful history taking is necessary to assess this usage. Serious withdrawal symptoms (including convulsions) can appear as late as 12 days after the last ingestion of barbiturates; the 3rd and 4th days are particularly critical.

For convulsive seizures judged to be due to barbiturates withdrawal give 2 grains of sodium phenobarbital IM as soon as possible.

Patients may name the barbiturate or describe them by color—red (Seconal®) yellow (Nembutal®) red and blue (Tuinal®) blue (Amytal®). Each capsule is considered to be 100 mg even though Amytal may be a 200 mg capsule.

If the patient has convulsive seizures start with the first day of the schedule.

If the patient has been taking daily *20* or more capsules and has *no* convulsions, start with 4th day of schedule. The day of admission does not count.

Daily Barbiturate Ingestion During Previous Month	*Dosage Begins at Level Shown on Schedule for Day*
20 or more capsules	4
16–18	6
12–14	8
8–10	10
4–6	12

Day	*Elixir Seconal (Teaspoons per dose)*	*Seconal® Per Dose (grains)*	*Doses Per Day*
1–3	5	1¼	q.i.d.
4–5	4	1	q.i.d.
6–7	3	¾	q.i.d.
8–9	2	½	q.i.d.
10–11	1	¼	q.i.d.
12–13	1	¼	t.i.d.
14–15	1	¼	b.i.d.
16–17	1	¼	daily
18	0	0	

the methadone dose, the lower the dose of Thorazine and that Thorazine potentiates barbiturates and narcotics.

During 1969, about one third of our patients were given methadone schedules beginning with a total of 40 mg daily: 20 percent started with 30 or 35 mg per day: 10 percent, started with 20 or 25 mg per day: and one third began with 15 mg or less a day.

For analgesia, Zactirin® or aspirin are usually prescribed. Tigan® is usually used for antiemesis, orally (250 mg) or rectally (100 mg suppositories) rather than intramuscularly.

TABLE 48-IV

SCHEDULE OF GLUTEHTHIMIDE (DORIDEN) GIVEN TO PREVENT
WITHDRAWAL SYMPTOMS IN PERSONS DEPENDENT ON DORIDEN

Daily Intake Prior to Admission	Withdrawal Schedule
4–6 Tablets (for 3 or more months)	250 mg t.i.d. x 3 days 250 mg b.i.d. x 2 days 250 mg o.d. x 2 days
8–10 Tablets per day	250 mg q.i.d. x 3 days and then continue as for 4–6 tablets
12–14 Tablets per day	250 mg t.i.d. 500 mg at 10 p.m. } x 3 days and then continue as for 4–6 tablets
16–18 Tablets per day	500 mg t.i.d. x 3 days 250 mg t.i.d. 500 mg at 10 p.m. } x 3 days and then continue as for 4–6 tablets
20–24 Tablets per day	500 mg q.i.d. x 3 days 250 mg t.i.d. 500 mg at 10 p.m. } x 3 days and then continue as for 4–6 tablets

Note: If there is any history of previous seizures during withdrawal, maximum
schedule is given even if patient is taking less than 20–24 tablets per day.

Detoxification with methadone usually occurs over a period of
from three to eight days and averages about five days. Sometimes
detoxification takes longer. It is important to note that *apparent*
withdrawal symptoms may be expressed in patients who have not
had opiates for some time. This topic deserves further investigation. On the other hand, patients with exceptionally large habits
or with above-average concentrations of heroin may take longer
for detoxification than is shown in our schedule.

Pharmacological detoxification is achieved for over 95 percent
of our patients currently. That is, 95 percent of our patients remain in hospital and either complete the schedule of methadone
initially assigned by the physician or after prematurely discon-

tinuing the prescribed schedule have two drug-free days prior to discharge.

TWICE-DAILY USE OF METHADONE

In 1969, administration of methadone was changed from three times a day to twice a day. This resulted in decreasing nursing activities in methadone administration by one third. Little change was noted in symptoms or behavior of patients. Our overall use of methadone for detoxification (based on data from our pharmacy) changed from 10.08 mg per patient-day during January-June, 1969, to 10.04 mg per patient-day in January-June, 1970. (The mean stay of patients during this time was about twelve days so total methadone consumption averaged 120 mg for a patient during the course of his stay.) While there was a major reduction in the nursing procedures for administering methadone, total daily methadone consumption for the 276 patients on the Drug Addiction Service changed a total of 11 mg.

VOLUNTARY TERMINATION OF METHADONE SCHEDULE

Although the dosages of methadone shown in the above schedule are not large, many patients volunteer to stop their medication before the end of the schedule originally prescribed.

A patient can refuse a dose of methadone. This happens through social pressure or when a patient may no longer feel the need for medication, or when a patient wishes to achieve an earlier medical discharge. Patient may receive 10 mg of methadone within forty-eight hours of his last methadone dosage.

The following data are based on the detoxification schedules prescribed for 259 consecutive patients admitted in July of 1969. The initially prescribed schedule was adequate for at least 92 percent of the 259 patients; there was no increase of dosage or prolongation of schedule for 238 patients who stayed in hospital for at least forty-eight hours following their last dose of methadone, whether they had terminated the schedule prematurely or as prescribed. Seven patients had prolonged detoxification because of intercurrent physical disorder or major concomitant anxiety. Another fourteen patients left against medical advice *during* the course of their detoxification.

Sixty-nine of the patients were given the maximum schedule of methadone, 40 mg daily — nearly one half of these patients had terminated their schedule by the time it had been reduced to 10 mg a day. Termination of a schedule means that they refused four consecutive doses of methadone over a 48-hour period and had not expressed or shown symptoms of withdrawal which would cause the resumption of methadone. Among patients given initial schedules of 20 to 35 mg of methadone, from 43 to 65 percent were able to terminate their schedule by the time a level of 15 mg per day had been reached. These data can be shown in the form of "dose-reaction" curves.

These graphic representations of withdrawal can be drawn for patients of various social characteristics or in different treatment settings. Patients with small habits should complete detoxification at faster rates than patients with higher habits. These dose-reaction curves will be plotted for larger groups of patients and for groups classified by demographic and drug factors.

DISCUSSION

This chapter has considered some aspects of withdrawal and detoxification for the patient population of our particular institution. It is recognized that our findings may not apply to patient groups seen at other facilities in New York City or other cities.

Grades III and IV[1] of withdrawal syndrome are rarely seen. Among the 900 to 1,200 heroin users seen in our intake unit each month, most applicants for detoxification had heroin within the previous three hours and very few have not had heroin within the previous twenty-four hours.

Although most patients have had withdrawal symptoms in the past, their severity varies although some patients report having had some severe symptoms of withdrawal. More frequently the worst symptoms described by patients are of milder grades of withdrawal.

During inpatient detoxification in our setting, few withdrawal signs or symptoms are evident. Withdrawal, based on the methadone schedule described, is smooth and comfortable. Although a few patients, with concomitant physical illness or major anxiety require extended schedules, the majority of patients seen at Bernstein Institute voluntarily stop their schedule before the prescribed time. On the average withdrawal is accomplished with a total of 120 mg of methadone per patient.

The biometrics of considering the duration of detoxification as a dose-response curve promises to provide new information on the way detoxification is used at our institution and to give another index of the rate of detoxification among our patient population.

REFERENCES

1. Himmelsbach, C.K.: The morphine abstinence syndrome, its nature and treatment. *Ann Intern Med, 15:*829-839, 1941.
2. Maurer, D.W., and Vogel, V.H.: *Narcotics and Narcotics Addiction,* 3rd ed. Springfield, Charles C Thomas, 1967.
3. Richman, A., Amiel, M., and Perkins, M.E.: From Pre-admission to Follow-up of Adolescent Heroin Users. Presented at 98th Annual Mtg. American Public Health Association, Houston, Texas, October 28, 1970.
4. Richman, A., Richman, E.L., and Riordan, C.E.: Staff Decentralization and Psychosocial Function on an In-patient Ward. Presented at 46th Annual Mtg. American Orthopsychiatric Assoc., April 2, 1969.
5. Richman, A., Richman, E.L., and Riordan, C.E.: Psychosocial Criteria for Evaluating a Detoxification Program for Heroin Addicts, Presented at 47th Annual Mtg. American Orthopsychiatric Assoc., San Francisco, March 25, 1970.

Chapter 49

Treatment of Heroin Addiction with Behavioral Therapy

John S. O'Brien and A. E. Raynes

Behavior therapists have thus far only published five preliminary studies dealing with the problem of drug addiction.[15-17,21,27] The first four of these studies dealt with aversion therapy as the primary behavior therapy technique and all met with limited success. The last study used systematic desensitization alone and was not successful.

Rachman[19] and Rachman and Teasdale[20] have discussed the relatively successful history of aversion therapy and evaluated its present use in the areas of alcoholism, compulsive eating and sexual disorders. In the past ten years there has been an increase in the application of aversion therapy in these areas which has met with success.

Briefly what aversion therapy consists of is taking an object or an activity that is pleasure associated (drug-induced state or relaxation) and pairing it repeatedly with an aversive experience. The result is that the original activity (conditioned stimuli for drug usage) acquires some of the negative properties of the aversive stimulus. As long as all the activities and all the objects associated with a particular self-destructive but pleasurable behavior are associated with the aversive stimulus and they retain their negatively conditioned state (conditioned response), the individual will be inclined to avoid them.[5] However, there appear to be several problems concerned with the application of aversion therapy in extinguishing a maladaptive behavior. These problems include failure of the aversive conditioned response to generalize outside the therapy area, failure to deal with anxiety which may

434

be cuing or driving the occurrence of the maladaptive behavior, and failure to establish permanency of the strength of the aversive conditioned response.

In the current investigation, a behavioral treatment approach has been used to develop an effective treatment of heroin addiction. Aversion therapy designed to develop aversive conditioned responses which were resistant to extinction and which would generalize to the real life settings of an addict was used as a rapid means of extinguishing the use of heroin. Both electric shock,[18,19] and verbal aversive imagery[1,8] were used as noxious stimuli in the aversion therapy. Combined with this, an alternate behavior[4] was developed by using a modified form of Jacobson's 1938 relaxation technique.[14] This was used both to overcome tension and as a substitute for drug-induced relaxation. Finally systematic desensitization was used to treat the anxiety which cued or was associated with the use of heroin.[28] Further a rating scale was developed to evaluate the development and generalization of the aversive conditioned response.

PROCEDURE

The first session was used to acquaint the patient with the procedures that would be used in therapy and their consent was gained. The next two sessions were used in acquiring a complete history of all the intrinsic and extrinsic stimuli that the patients associated with heroin use. A maximum level of electric shock bearable to the patient was also determined. These stimuli were arranged in three categories: first, intrinsic stimuli associated with physiological or psychological craving responses; second, the intrinsic and extrinsic stimuli associated with preparing to inject; and third, stimuli associated with the effect of heroin injection. Stories which contained all the stimuli grouped above were written. This pattern of stimuli was considered the complex behavioral chain in which each response is essential to the next response and the response itself being reinforced.

The next three sessions were used to teach the patients the relaxation technique. The patient was given a copy of the relaxation procedures and told to practice frequently between sessions.

The successful state of relaxation was paired with a key word, "alpha," by repeating the word frequently after a deep state of relaxation had been reached. The patients were told that after learning to relax skillfully, they could counteract tension by concentrating on the word "alpha."

The next ten to twenty sessions consisted of both aversion therapy and relaxation training in that order. Stories or imaginal stimuli which represented the complete behavioral chain of heroin use were presented to the patient. Whenever possible, items used in preparing and injecting heroin were shown to the patient. Initially all three groups of stimuli or the complete behavior chain were presented and paired with the aversive stimuli (electric shock). The intensity and duration of the shock was gradually increased in these sessions until a level 25 percent above the original estimated pain threshold was reached. These stories and the electric shock were directed at all areas where injection had occurred, so that each area would gain aversive properties. Eventually the electric shock was paired with progressively smaller segments of the behavioral chain until individual events in the categories were actually paired with the shock. After initial presentation of the complete behavioral chain, which was always paired with the aversive stimulus (reinforcement), a partial reinforcement schedule was used so that the patient would not know which stimuli presentation would be paired with shock. An example of a story including the complete behavior chain and the verbal aversive stimulus is as follows:

> You're taking the subway to Charles Street. You sit, you wait, your breath is heavy, your back aches. You're tense, hypertense. Sweat rolls down your forehead. You need a fix. Just a chance to cool your head out. Your mind races on. As the train pulls out of Park Street you nearly forget about the leg cramps. God, if I can't cop a bag at Jack's, God! The train rolls on to Charles Street. Sore track marks, but that doesn't matter now, just a rush. Just to cool out your brain. The train stops at Charles. Beacon Hill, Jack's apartment. You need some works, a drugstore, an eyedropper, a pacifier, and a spike. Then suddenly you're in Jack's basement apartment. You stick the works together. It's a new spike. The point hurts your finger as much as the pounding inside your brain hurts. Now it's time to fix. The thought enters your mind that you might get burned or ripped off. You grab your cigarette

lighter and hold your cooker with the skag in it over the flame. A bobby pin, a match and a bottle cap and I'm ready for a bag, a bundle. That vein! Then the spike hits home. As you get off, you feel the rush going to your head. Those track marks don't hurt, your head floats and heat rises in your body as the spike goes home—and a pain flashes from your arm to your heart. As the fluid goes in, the pain becomes more intense. You start to sweat, to feel nauseous. Your head nods and you start to vomit, to puke. Vomit and snot come out of your mouth and nose. You can't breathe and the pain becomes more intense. Pull out the spike—get away! Push the thoughts of shooting out of your mind and notice the quick relief of the pain and tension.

A self-rating scale was devised to evaluate the strength of the aversive conditioned response. This incorporated all the stimuli originally used in the three groups of stimuli and each stimulus was scored from 1 to 5 for its aversive conditioned response evoking strength. The following criteria were explained to the patients so that a numerical value could be assigned to each of the stimuli:

(1) Evoking a strong and uncontrollable desire to use heroin
(2) Evoking a strong but controllable desire to use heroin
(3) Evoking a desire to take heroin that could easily be changed
(4) Evoking no desire to use heroin
(5) Evoking an aversive or avoidance response to the stimuli and the use of heroin

This scale was administered before the first therapy session and often during therapy. Each of the items of the scale were presented twice to the patient to attain a greater degree of reliability. If any discrepancy occurred between the scores, the lower numerical value was adopted. The reliability between the two ratings was high, 97 percent.

The last block of sessions included aversion, relaxation and systematic desensitization. Systematic desensitization was employed for about one to ten sessions to help the patient deal with anxiety that was paired with heroin use and physiological cravings. This involved pairing the events or activities associated with anxiety which cued the use of heroin with a response incompatible with anxiety (relaxation) until the objects or activities acquired the properties of the pleasurable conditioned response (relaxation) .

After the therapy sessions were completed, the patients were assisted in planning for employment and a place to live. They were asked to return for follow-up and booster sessions after discharge and were instructed to practice the relaxation training frequently.

DISCUSSION AND RESULTS

The treatment procedure described has thus far been used to treat three patients who had all been addicted for more than ten years and were taking at least ten bags of heroin a day. Two of the three have remained free of injecting heroin for nine and six months respectively while the third, who did not complete the aversion therapy procedure, has reported to have injected several times in the two months since treatment while under acute stress. He has, however, only been using half the original quantity of drugs and has recently returned to complete the treatment.

In summary, these investigators realize that results cannot be generalized to all addicts from these few treatments but suggest the combination of aversion therapy, relaxation training and systematic desensitization, as a useful and rapid therapeutic resource in the treatment of heroin addiction. With detoxification and the combined use of these three techniques this treatment offers a total hospitalization treatment time of three weeks. In any treatment of drug addiction, readjustment to the new drug-free life requires a great deal of attention. There is need for a multi-dimensional approach to treatment in which behavioral therapy can play an important role.

REFERENCES

1. Anant, S.S.: A note on the treatment of alcoholics by a verbal aversion technique. *Canad Psychol, 80*:19-22, 1967.
2. Anant, S.S.: Treatment of alcoholics and drug addicts by verbal aversion technique. *Int J Addict, 3*:2, 1968.
3. Ashem, B., and Donner, L.: Covert sensitization with alcoholics: A controlled replication. *Behav Res Ther, 6*:7-12, 1968.
4. Azrin, N.H., and Holz. W.C.: Punishment. In *Operant Behavior,* edited by W.K. Honig. New York, Appleton-Century-Croft, 1966.
5. Bandura, A.: *Principles of Behavior Modification.* New York, Holt, Rinehart & Winston, 1969.

6. Blake, B.G.: The application of behavior therapy to the treatment of alcoholism. *Behav Res Ther, 3:*75-85, 1965.

7. Blake, B.G.: A follow-up of alcoholics treated by behavior therapy. *Behav Res Ther, 5:*89-94, 1967.

8. Cautela, J.: Treatment of compulsive behavior by covert sensitization. *Psychol Rec, 16:*33-42, 1966.

9. Cautela, J.: Covert sensitization. *Psychol Rep, 20:*459-468, 1967.

10. Church, R.M., Raymond, G.A., and Beauchamp, R.: Response suppression as a function of intensity and duration of a punishment. *J Comp Physiol Psychol, 39-*44, 1967.

11. Eysenck, H.S.: Summary and conclusion, In *Behavior Therapy and the Neuroses,* edited by H.S. Eysenck. Oxford, Pergamon Press, 1960.

12. Eysenck, H.S.: A theory of the incubation of anxiety/fear responses. *Behav Res Ther, 6:*309-322, 1968.

13. Isbell, H.: Perspectives in research on opiate addiction, In *Narcotics,* edited by D.M. Wilner and G.G. Kassebaum. New York, McGraw-Hill, 1965, pp. 36-50.

14. Jacobson, E.: *Progressive Relaxation.* Chicago, University of Chicago Press, 1938.

15. Kraft, T.: A short note on 40 patients treated by systematic desensitization. *Behav Res Ther, 8:*219-220, 1970.

16. Lesser, E.: Behavior therapy with a narcotics user: a case report. *Behav Res Ther, 5:*251-252, 1967.

17. Liberman, R.: Aversive conditioning of drug addicts: a pilot study. *Behav Res Ther, 6:*229-231, 1968.

18. McGuire, R.J., and Vallance, M.: Aversion therapy by electro shock: A simple technique. *Brit Med J, 1:*151-153, 1964.

19. Rachman, S.: Aversion therapy: chemical or electrical. *Behav Res Ther, 2:*289-300, 1965.

20. Rachman, S., and Teasdale, J.: *Aversion Therapy and Behaviour Disorders: An Analysis.* Coral Gables, University of Miami Press, 1969.

21. Raymond, M.: The treatment of addiction by aversion conditioning with apomorphine. *Behav Res Ther, 1:*287-291, 1964.

22. Razran, G.: Studies in configural conditioning. VI. Comparative extinction and forgetting of pattern and of single stimulus conditioning. *J Exp Psychol, 24:*432-438, 1939.

23. Razran, G.: Conditioning and perception. *Psychol Rev, 62:*83-95, 1955.

24. Voegtlin, W.L., Lemere, F., and Borz, W.R.: Conditioned reflex therapy of alcoholic addiction: III. An evaluation of present results in the light of previous experiences with this method. *Quart J Stud Alcohol, 1:*501-516, 1940.

25. Walton, D., and Mather, M.D.: The application of learning principles to the treatment of obsessive-compulsive states in the acute and

chronic phases of illness, In *Experiments in Behaviour Therapy,* edited by H.J. Eysenck. Oxford, Pergamon Press, 1964.

26. Wiler, A.: Conditioning factors in opiate addiction and relapse. In *Narcotics,* edited by D.M. Wilner and G.G. Kassebaum. New York, McGraw-Hill, 1965, pp. 85-100.

27. Wolpe, J.: Conditioned inhibition of craving in drug addiction. *Behav Res Ther, 2:*285-287, 1965.

28. Wolpe, J.: *Psychotherapy by Reciprocal Inhibition.* Stanford, Stanford University Press, 1958.

29. Yates, A.J.: *Behavior Therapy.* New York, John Wiley & Sons, 1970.

30. Yates, A.J.: Symptoms and symptom substitutions, In *Behavior Therapy and the Neuroses,* edited by H.J. Eysenck. Oxford, Pergamon Press, 1960.

Chapter 50

Treating the Drug Abuser: Relevant and Irrelevant Factors

Stanley Einstein, Mark A. Quinones and Marvin A. Lavenhar

TRADITIONALLY THE TREATMENT of drug abuse has focused upon the various characteristics of the drug abuser, the physical, psychological and sociolegal consequences of drug abuse, the drugs used and the pattern of their use. Although many therapeutic modalities have been used, and in recent years new techniques have arisen, the goal of treatment has almost invariably been abstinence.

It has been the feeling of many that there continues to be a rather set, if not rigid, way of looking at drug abuse and its treatment. So much so that one of the rationales for employing ex-addicts in rehabilitation programs is that they have a different and more effective rapport with drug abusers.

The major purpose of this pilot study, which has been done with various disciplines in various countries, was to determine (through a questionnaire) empirically what positions treatment agents are committed to when they intervene in effecting changes in a drug abuser's life.

CHARACTERISTICS OF THE SAMPLE

The sample consisted of twenty psychiatrists, fourteen from the United States and six from Australia. All but one were male, ranging in age from 27 to 68 with a median age of 40.

The sample had been involved in treating patients for approximately $10\frac{1}{2}$ years (4 years to 45 years) and had been treating drug abusers for a median of 7 years (2.5 years to 20 years). During 1969 these psychiatrists treated approximately 5,000 drug abusers, with a median of 50 drug abusers on an inpatient basis. As a group they felt that they successfully treated half of their drug abuse patients.

Abstinence as a criteria for successful treatment was the major concern of this sample, it being noted 50 percent of the time. Other criteria mentioned were improvement in functioning (35 percent), work (30 percent), changing one's life style (30 percent), decreased involvement with the law (10 percent), reduction in drug use (15 percent), and good health (10 percent) (Table 50-I).

TABLE 50-I

CATEGORIZED CRITERIA FOR THE SUCCESSFUL TREATMENT OF DRUG ABUSERS

	N	%
Drug-related Criteria		
Drug abstinence	10	50
Drug reduction	3	15
Law-related Criteria		
Decreased legal involvement	2	10
Conventional Life-Style–Related Criteria		
Improved psychological and/or social status	7	35
Life style changes	6	30
Vocational status	6	30
School status	2	10
General rehabilitation	1	5
Improved health	1	5
Total*	20	100

*The 20 participants in this pilot study often noted more than one criteria in their treatment plans.

Forty percent (8) noted that they had never received any specialized training in the field of drug abuse, and only four of the respondents actually noted that they had received some type of formal education in this area. Four of the psychiatrists noted that they had been trained on the job. This is interesting in that although 88 percent of the sample felt that receiving training was important and although one psychiatrist noted it was unimportant and one that it was irrelevant, 40 per cent of the sample felt they did not have a need to be given special education and/or training concerning drug abuse.

The psychiatrists relied on the following publications for information about drug abuse: professional journals (100 percent), *International Journal of the Addictions* (45 percent), *British Journal of Addiction* (20 percent) and books (5 percent).

THE PATIENT'S PATTERN OF DRUG ABUSE

The respondents were asked to assess the importance and relevance of four patterns of drug use in their treatment of drug abusers. The *length of time* of drug abuse, the *frequency* and the *types of drugs* used were felt to be most important factors (95 percent, 90 percent, 90 percent), with the *amount* of drugs being less important (75 percent). Only 5 percent of this sample, one psychiatrist, felt that these factors were not relevant in treatment (Table 50-II).

TABLE 50-II

THE PATIENTS' PATTERN OF DRUG ABUSE AS AN IMPORTANT
AND RELEVANT TREATMENT FACTOR

Drug-related Factors	Very Important		Important		Unimportant		Not Relevant	
	N	%	N	%	N	%	N	%
Length of drug abuse	12	60	7	35	0		1	5
Frequency of drug abuse	9	45	9	45	1	5	1	5
Type of drug abused	10	50	8	40	1	5	1	5
Amount of drug abused	5	25	10	50	4	20	1	5

It is interesting to note when one considers that the psychiatric consequences of drug abuse is most often a function of amounts of drugs used, that what appears to be of concern to the psychiatrist is that the patient is using some drug over time and not *how much* is being used.

BEHAVIOR OF THE DRUG ABUSE PATIENT

Traditionally the drug abuser has been experienced as a person with a poor prognosis for change. This is generally related to viewing the drug abuser as being unable to abstain or to maintain abstinence for any appreciable length of time. Abstinence is a useful goal if it is related to the person being able to function fairly well in day-to-day living, and thus it should follow that areas of daily functioning should have top priority in the treatment of the drug abuser.

Of twelve non–drug-related behavioral areas that were surveyed, the respondents all agreed that the areas of family, friends, work and leisure time were important and relevant to treatment, and 95 percent of the sample noted that school- and community-related behavior, as well as motivation and the patients' health (65 percent), and religious (50 percent) functioning were of lesser concern for the psychiatrist (Table 50-III).

TABLE 50-III

NON–DRUG-RELATED BEHAVIORAL AREAS AS IMPORTANT AND RELEVANT TREATMENT FACTORS

Areas of Functioning	Very Important		Important		Unimportant		Not Relevant	
	N	%	N	%	N	%	N	%
Family-related behavior	12	60	8	40	0		0	
Friends and acquaintances	10	50	10	50	0		0	
Work-related behavior	10	50	10	50	0		0	
Leisure time activity	7	35	13	65	0		0	
Motivation of patient	12	60	7	35	1	5	0	
Sexual-related behavior*	4	21	11	58	4	21	0	
Mental-health–related behavior*	8	40	11	55	1	5	0	
Community involvement	6	30	13	65	1	5	0	
School-related behavior	4	20	15	75	1	5	0	
Physical health	2	10	11	55	5	25	2	10
Religious-related behavior**	2	11	7	39	8	44	1	5

*One psychiatrist noted no "opinion" to this factor.

**Two psychiatrists noted "no opinion" to this factor.

That the therapist is not concerned about his patient's physical health as a factor influencing psychotherapy, let alone the person's sexual functioning, raises the issue as to whether a person or a stereotype is being treated.

The drug-related behavior which was felt to be of importance in the patient's treatment was abstinence (95 percent), social functioning (95 percent), drug user relationships (95 percent) and the patient's mental condition (95 percent). One's physical condition as a result of drug use was of lesser importance (80 percent) as was support of one's drug habit (80 percent) (Table 50-IV).

TABLE 50-IV
DRUG-RELATED BEHAVIOR AS IMPORTANT AND RELEVANT
TREATMENT FACTORS

Drug-Related Factors	Very Important		Important		Unimportant		Not Relevant	
	N	%	N	%	N	%	N	%
Abstinence	10	50	9	45	1	5	0	
Relationships with drug users	9	45	10	50	1	5	0	
Social functioning	13	65	6	30	1	5	0	
Mental condition	9	45	10	50	1	5	0	
Drug-related behavior*	10	53	7	37	1	5	1	5
Physical condition	4	20	12	60	4	20	0	
Support of drug habit	5	25	11	55	2	10	1	5

*One psychiatrist noted "no opinion" to this factor.

One tentative interpretation that can be made at this point is that the psychiatrist treating the drug abuser feels that if the patient could only stop his drug use and drug-oriented life, psychosocial functioning would improve.

TREATMENT-RELATED FACTORS

Obviously treatment is more than the use of a particular technique. It must include the training of the treatment agent, the evaluation techniques used to determine if treatment is necessary and/or possible, what modalities to use, the choice of appropriate goals and whether the necessary inpatient and outpatient services are available and accessible (Table 50-V).

All of the sample agreed that the availability of outpatient resources was a most important and relevant factor in doing treatment. Current treatment goals (95 percent), professional training (95 percent), treatment modalities (90 percent) and available in-

TABLE 50-V

TREATMENT FACTORS AFFECTING TREATMENT OF THE
DRUG ABUSER

Treatment Factors	Very Important		Important		Unimportant		Not Relevant	
	N	%	N	%	N	%	N	%
Availability of necessary outpatient treatment resources	16	80	4	20	0		0	
Treatment goals	9	45	10	50	0		1	5
Professional training of psychiatrist	6	30	13	65	1	5	0	
Treatment modalities being utlized*	8	42	10	53	0	5	0	
Availability of necessary inpatient treatment resources	13	65	5	25	1	5	0	
Current evaluation techniques	4	20	12	60	2	10	2	10

*One psychiatrist noted "no opinion" to this factor.

patient treatment resources were also considered important. What is surprising is that 20 percent of the sample felt that current evaluation techniques were either unimportant or not relevant to the treatment procedure. How one goes about effectively treating someone without knowing his strengths and weaknesses is a mystery unless, of course, the patient comes preevaluated as an "addict." This potential source of confusion is further added to by the fact that while a series of evaluations are used the importance and relevance are questioned. For example, physical examinations are used by 100 percent of the psychiatrists responding but is felt to be an important technique by only 77 percent. Psychological testing and neurological evaluations are each used by 75 percent but are felt to be important by only 60 percent and 51 percent of the sample respectively (Table 50-VI).

Since evaluation of any problem will determine to a very large degree what will be done about the problem, the existing differences between the use of certain standard evaluation techniques and their imputed unimportance and/or irrelevance to treatment is really a significant issue that must be considered in the treatment of drug abuse.

TABLE 50-VI

EVALUATION TECHNIQUES AND GOALS AS TREATMENT FACTORS

Evaluation Techniques	Use		Don't Use		*	Very Important		Important		Unimportant		Not Relevant		*
	N	%	N	%		N	%	N	%	N	%	N	%	N
Physical Examination	16	100			3	6	33	8	44	3	17	1	5	1
Psychiatric examination	16	100			3	10	55	8	45	0		0		1
Urine testing	14	88	2	12	3	8	47	5	29	3	18	1	6	2
Psychological testing	12	75	4	25	3	3	16	8	44	7	39	0		1
Neurological examination	12	75	4	25	3	5	32	3	19	8	50	0		3
Treatment Goals														
Abstinence	14	100			5	6	37	7	44	3	18	0		3

*Number of psychiatrists not answering this part of the questionnaire.

Current Treatment Goals

All of the responding psychiatrists used abstinence as a treatment goal, but three of them noted that it was an unimportant treatment factor. While one can debate the merits of abstinence, it is confusing yet important to know why one should use a goal which one feels is not important. Perhaps the psychiatrist "knows" beforehand that abstinence is difficult to achieve, but having other goals in mind, some which were previously mentioned (changes in life style, work, decreased involvement with the law, and drug use reduction), he continues to treat with a hope of the achievement of abstinence. Perhaps the psychiatrist has some difficulty with the concept of abstinence. How long does one have to abstain before we professionals consider him *abstinent,* as well as abstinent for what.

Treatment Modalities

If the evaluation of a patient has been accurate and his problem areas, strengths and weaknesses have been accurately assessed, and the appropriate treatment goals selected, the next step is the choice and use of those treatment modalities best suited to the patient's needs.

The modalities of psychological therapy used in order of actual use and importance were individual and group therapy, couple and family therapy, confrontation therapy, counseling, psychodrama, behavior therapy and hypnotherapy.

The order of *acutal use* and *importance* of medical therapies were not as consistent. Modalities of medical therapies were not as consistent. Modalities used were conventional chemotherapy, methadone maintenance, vitamin therapy and cyclazocine. The order of importance was methadone maintenance, conventional chemotherapy, cyclazocine and vitamin therapy.

It would appear that once the psychiatrist involves himself in what he is ostensibly best suited and trained to do, psychiatric verbal treatment, there are little if any inconsistencies between what he is doing and how important he may feel it is.

Theoretical Factors Affecting Treatment of Drug Abusers

The training that the psychiatrict receives not only serves to develop and improve his technical skills but should in some way introduce him to and/or reinforce his theoretical position. It has already been noted that 40 percent of the sample received no formal training in drug abuse. The following theoretical issues were explored in this pilot study: *the present state of theoretical knowledge* and *drug abuser typologies* and *the use of drug abuser typologies*. These issues were chosen because it was felt that the way the therapist perceives the problem and the person with the problem will greatly determine his response to that person.

It is interesting to note that although 80 percent responded that the present state of theoretical knowledge was important and relevant in treating the drug abuser, and 60 percent indicated that drug abuser typologies were important and relevant, only 25 percent of the sample used a particular typology in their treatment.

It would appear that theoretical considerations are for reading and talking about, but when it comes to treatment it is "the addict" that we treat and obviously everyone knows who and what an addict is. At present, the trend is to view drug abuse as being related to sociological and environmental factors (85 percent, 80 percent), which, through learning and specifically conditioning (80 percent, 75 percent), introduces the drug abuser to the drug scene and results in a psychopathological condition (65 percent).

Attitudinal Factors Affecting Treatment of Drug Abusers

The way in which the drug abuser is stereotyped and treated is no doubt mainly a function of attitudinal factors. Some of these attitudes are derived from the community at large, others have been developed during training and still others are derived from actually treating drug abusers.

The results of this part of the study leaves little doubt as to the tremendous effect that attitudes of the therapist play in treating the drug abuser.

Ninety percent of the psychiatrists responded that their own attitudes regarding *drugs, drug use* and *drug abusers* were important and relevant in treating drug abusers. The same percentage noted that attitudes of *other professionals,* the *patients' general attitudes* and those of *significant others* in the patient's life were important. Attitudes of the *general public* (85 percent) and those derived from the *mass media* (80 percent) were quite important in affecting treatment.

Perhaps what all of this may mean is that the traditionally conceived "poor prognosis" of the addict does not relate to the addict's strengths and/or weakness, or the therapist's skills but rather to the acceptance of "facts" that everyone knows, which are rarely if ever critically evaluated and which become part of a polarization of attitudes that can only serve to interfere with effective treatment.

A cogent example of this is that of the various legal factors affecting the treatment of drug abusers, such as the laws regarding *possession, sale, use of illicit drugs, drug abusers* and those legal factors affecting the *psychiatrist's acceptance of drug abusers for treatment.* It was this latter factor, which was most often noted (70 percent) .

The reality is that the licensed psychiatrist can see whoever he decides to and he knows fully well that the APA diagnosis of drug addiction is a meaningless classification which neither illuminates etiology, process or prognosis. It is his own set of attitudes which determine the acceptance and/or rejection of a potential patient whose behavior and life style may include drug abuse among other behavioral manifestations and not the laws on the books.

SUMMARY AND CONCLUSIONS

A questionnaire was developed to determine empirically what factors various treatment agents felt affected their treatment of the drug abuser. The twenty psychiatrists who responded to this pilot study during 1970 and who have been treating drug abusers for approximately seven years (over 5000 during 1969) with a 50 percent success rate, essentially verified what many of us have known for a long time: the treatment of the drug-abusing patient generally becomes transformed into treating a drug abuser or addict, which is a stereotype and not a person with specific problems who may benefit from therapeutic intervention.

What was important and relevant in treatment, to the respondents, was (a) the use of drugs over time, rather than the amount of drugs used; (b) abstinence as a goal which somehow could result in improved psychosocial functioning; (c) the use of specific verbal therapies without the use of evaluating techniques that might match the patient, goal and specific treatment modality; (d) the use of specific treatment modalities, without the use of a classification system of drug abusers; (e) the use of specific modalities to treat patients with the therapist being commited to theoretical frameworks which remain unverified to date; and (f) the forceful influence of attitudinal factors regarding drugs, drug users and their treatment derived from a variety of sources.

The major conclusion to be drawn from this pilot study is that a variety of drug abusers are generally perceived as being a homogeneous group not so different from one another and are treated by professionals who may or may not be trained in the various facets of drug abuse, but who want to treat motivated drug abusers who will abstain in a community which at best manifests ambivalent attitudes about them and their behavior.

Somehow, somewhere, the psychiatrist treating the drug abuser has lost sight of the fact that successful treatment cannot emerge from stereotypes, lip service and/or abstinence alone as a goal.

Chapter 51

Psychiatric Management and the Future System of Care in Drug Abuse

Marvin E. Perkins

A LITTLE OVER ten years ago, I was invited to present a paper to the annual meeting of the Public Health Association of New York City,[1] attempting to look ahead in mental health. One perhaps may be excused on the grounds of inexperience, an intrepid willingness to attempt to foretell the future in 1960. If so, what is the basis for forgiveness to be extended to the same person ten years later who undertakes a similar assignment? Perhaps I can put some hope in your more generous human qualities. I trust you will view my kind of foolishness as a response to temptation which, by grace, you may have been spared from publicly demonstrating. So, I appeal to your charity, as I attempt to redeem my promise to the President of the Eastern Psychiatric Research Association.

Possibly the following description[2] most aptly expresses the vague discomfort which some of you may be feeling about the term "psychiatric management" which I have put into the title of this address.

> The art of management consists of issuing orders based on inaccurate, incomplete and archaic data, to meet a situation which is dimly understood, and which will not be what the issuer visualizes, orders which will be frequently misinterpreted and often ignored, to accomplish a purpose about which many of the personnel are not enthusiastic.

Although the foregoing is not from the literature on drug abuse —in fact, is not from medical or public health literature—many may share with me the impression that this describes the nature of much that has been experienced in attempting to deal therapeutically with the addictive patient.

We can no longer afford to wring our hands in despair at the problem. Nor can we turn our backs in sorrow or anger at the patient to whom we ascribe wilfulness, intransigence or opposition when thwarting our therapeutic aims and our clinical skills. We can no longer afford to behave in this way because we now know through demonstrable evidence that persons with serious addictions can be greatly helped.

The common denominator, as I see it among various styles of help, is that all bring a combination of efforts to bear upon the addict in a variety of settings. Most programs which have reported recent successes make use of nonprofessional as well as professional personnel in different arrangements of group and individual activities. In my view, the style of this help suggests a modern adaptation of the old child guidance model, transformed by over five decades of experience into what has become lately known as community mental health or community psychiatry.[3] These expressions really embody a combination of historical interests in the development of contemporary psychiatry, which collectively emphasizes the approach to individual problems through groups. The approach does not obviate the need for individualization of therapy, including the prescription of medicine. In fact, the sharing of responsibility with nonpsychiatric and nonmedical personnel may be the way that individual help becomes acceptable and effective. This observation scarcely needs elaboration.

The psychiatric management issue, in this context, now becomes clear. We are not talking here about psychiatrically managing the life of a patient. As clinicians we should know the folly of such a pursuit. No, we can visualize the management issue as a requirement because groups of workers—including patients—are involved in the helping process at the very threshold of the helping agency. Moreover, participatory management would appear to be the coming mode, with addict-patients, ex-addicts, nonprofessionals, allied professionals and the medical professionals all engaged in the transmuting of a style of living disastrous to the individual, to his family and to his society.

Patient care of the addict is a complex management task. Among the medical specialties, this task is probably most compatible with the eclectic psychiatry of hospital practice which has developed in the past two decades. Practice has moved toward a multidisciplinary and multiple-therapeutic service, with increasingly effective interfaces adjoining other specialized services of the hospital. The addict may not want, and in fact, may not be able to use, psychotherapy initially. Yet, there is some evidence to suggest that a psychotherapeutically oriented staff, with limited formal training and limited objectives, may provide a most effective form of help early in the course of treatment of the addict. My opinion is that this may best be done under the guidance and direction of a professional staff which in the organization of hospital services becomes clinically departmentalized in psychiatry. When the more formal methods of psychotherapy are indicated, the transition should be made with ease.

The hospital setting also affords the addict access to other, often vitally needed services, available through the other departments of the hospital. This, of necessity, calls for a major commitment to the treatment of the addict by the entire medical complex —as an obligation and opportunity. In accepting this service responsibility, the training mission of the hospital becomes enlarged and in fact responsive to the expressions of young professional trainees for knowledge in the medical, social and psychiatric aspects of this major problem for the seventies.

Now I want to share with you some misgivings. We have been hearing addiction and drug abuse described in such terms as "communicable," "epidemic" or "endemic." These terms are from the lexicon of public health. Yet, I am not impressed that schools of public health or even many of the official departments of health have begun to cope with either the training or the service requirements related to this modern plague. The same criticism may be leveled at medical schools and departments of psychiatry of most major hospitals. Could any hospital, medical school or health institution in this or any major city be thought to be alive to our times without a solid commitment to service, education and training in drug abuse and addiction? The future is today for such a reorganization of curricula and services of these institutions. Innovation of programs in training and services for drug abuse and the addictions is an imperative.

As a psychiatrist addressing a conference organized by a group of psychiatrists, I might expect to have dismissed this emphasis upon psychiatry as the preferred medical specialty for developing service. On the one hand, this might be taken as an expression of narrow "professionality" by some outside of my field; on the other, as one of grandiose territoriality by some of my own specialist colleagues. Let me register a modest defense against both criticisms. I do not intend to convey that the old psychiatry with obsolete training and anachronistic methods could do the task asked. I do envision a new psychiatry which refines the legacies of the past—insights, treatments and missions—into a psychiatry for the seventies. I believe the new psychiatry must better encompass the range of the ages of man from early developmental problems, including the deficiencies, to the problems of the aging. Included also must be the challenges of the schizophrenias,[4] the reactive and behavioral disorders and the addictions. These are really not new territories for psychiatry at all, but areas which may have suffered some neglect. Renewed effort is what is required in these relatively neglected areas, creating a new order and balance in training and service.

Of course, a renewal of psychiatry could emerge without including the addictions, so a few words of explanation on this point seem to be in order. To illustrate my point, I should like to refer to the influence of methadone maintenance treatment upon my thinking. As you all should know, methadone maintenance was conceived at Rockefeller University. The systematic regime of Dole and Nyswander was cradled and further developed at Morris J. Bernstein Institute of the Beth Israel Medical Center. While certain aspects of the treatment may be controversial still, no other program has been so well evaluated; none other can demonstrate such impressive rehabilitation rates. That the methadone maintenance treatment program has enjoyed a phenomenal success rate seems to me to be almost beyond dispute.[5,6]

The rationale of the approach calls for the use of methadone as a substitute for heroin, satisfying a drug hunger and eventually creating a narcotic blockade for opiates. In defending this substitution method, proponents often have drawn upon analogy: a diabetic's need for insulin is not to be denied on the basis that he may need the substitute indefinitely; nor should the methadone-maintained patient be denied what he requires for treatment.

To me, another analogy may be as pertinent as the diabetic-insulin one. Methadone may provide the same clinical opportunity in opiate addiction as Thorazine has in some schizophrenics. In both, the heavy burden of symptoms is so lightened by the medication that other interventional techniques from counseling to therapy may be employed as needed. In fact, the group activities and the supporting services which methadone patients receive are more nearly psychiatric in style than otherwise, at least on our service. Great variation exists, of course, among patients in the need for, or interest in, counseling or psychotherapy. Hence, individualized treatment is a factor to be dealt with.

Advocates of methadone maintenance may be of the view that methadone without any supporting services would suffice. For some individuals this may be the case; for others probably not. If use of methadone has demonstrated anything, it is that addicts are not of a type. The one common characteristic of heroin addicts seems to be only that all use heroin.

Methadone maintenance has opened our eyes and our minds to new prospects for viewing addiction as a research problem. For instance, one may speculate that heroin use creates a direct metabolic deficiency—by interference with a specific receptor in a complex enzyme or other biological exchange system. Of course, this has yet to be demonstrated. To ponder the matter further, methadone conceivably could patch up the bodily processes in such a way that, over time, a normal restoration of the system becomes possible. For this mechanism to be operative, one has to postulate that heroin not only replaces some normal radical and enters the usual receptor for that radical but also works to inhibit the normal production of the radical. Perhaps methadone works in two ways: (a) by not inhibiting production of the normal radical and (b) by permitting the system to use methadone temporarily as a substitute for the heroin replacement of the normal radical. The importance of methadone maintenance is that speculations of this sort may be made by more accomplished scientists hopefully leading us nearer to an understanding of opiate addiction.

This leads me to my final point. We need a phased program of care for the recovering addict in a systematic arrangement of outpatient services flanking the hospital. I would be apprehensive should we, in our zeal to demonstrate the medical efficacy of methadone, ignore the life experience of the patient in having been an addict, and as such, a part of the addict subculture of the street society. Here, it seems to me is the point at which a real difference begins to emerge. I would be troubled if we were to develop simple dispensaries for the purpose of easily serving flavored drinks of methadone, without sufficient ancillary support to give the recipient the opportunity to work for his own personal and social salvation. The sciences of medicine and public health should not deprive the individual of this important choice.

If counseling and psychotherapy are not made available to those in need, the system of treatment portends ominously like Anthony Burgess'[7] *A Clockwork Orange*—that is, something mechanical that looks organic. In the instance of methadone maintenance, the offer of methadone without support services might be so mechanistic as to be nontherapeutic while having the appearance of being therapeutic simply because a medication is involved. For this reason, I look for the scientific discoveries in medicine concerning addiction to be implemented in large measure through the new psychiatry, which ought to bring the humanistic qualities to the treatment situation.

REFERENCES

1. Perkins, M.E.: Some antecedents of mental health with a look forward. *Med Ann D C, 30*:13-19, 1961.
2. Quoted in Cleveland, H.: A philosophy for the public executive. In *The Influences of Social, Scientific and Economic Trends on Government*

Administration, edited by E.W. Fulker. US Dept. of Agriculture Graduate School, Washington, D.C., 1960.

3. Perkins, M.E.: The concept of community psychiatry. *J Hillside Hosp, 14*:211-226, 1965.

4. Perkins, M.E., and Bluestone, H.: Hospital and community psychiatric approaches. Chapter 16 in *The Schizophrenic Syndrome,* edited by L. Bellak and L. Loeb. New York, Grune & Stratton, 1969. pp. 667-713.

5. Perkins, M.E., and Bloch, H.I.: Survey of a methadone maintenance program. *Amer J Psychiat, 126*:1389-1396, 1970.

6. Perkins, M.E., and Bloch, H.I.: A study of some failures in methadone treatment. *Amer J Psychiat* (in press).

7. Burgess, A.: *A Clockwork Orange.* New York, W.W. Norton (Ballantine Books), 1963.

Index

459